"This wonderfully engaging volume author introduces us to a chorus of media. David Gowler's immense lear making interpretations of the parables across two millennia accessible to all. Highly recommended."

—**Christine Joynes**, Centre for Reception History of the Bible, University of Oxford

"For most of its history, parable research has, perhaps rightly, focused on the composition history of Jesus's parables from the oral period in which they were spoken to their placement in the Christian Gospels. David Gowler has studied, taught, and written about the parables for many years, and in this fascinating study he has trained his eagle eye on the latter part of the parables' 'career'—the impact of their afterlife on the literature, music, and art that stand as heirs to this remarkable corpus of stories. Arranged chronologically, Gowler's study spans two thousand years of reception. This treasure trove belongs in the library of anyone interested in the ways Jesus's parables have challenged our hearts, minds, and imaginations, and it confirms that the world the parables has produced is no less interesting and complex than the world that produced the parables."

—**Mikeal C. Parsons**, Baylor University

"David Gowler invites us to participate in a two-thousand-year-old dialogue with those seeking to understand and implement the simple, yet often perplexing, parables of Jesus. Gowler has assembled fifty conversation partners from literature, poetry, hymns, the visual arts, and theater that span the Christian era. These voices hail from a broad and diverse range of historically, theologically, and culturally significant contexts. By entering into this dialogue, Gowler hopes that rather than find what we expect to find in the parables, we can take off our own interpretive blinders and come to a fuller understanding of the meanings and applications of the parables to our lives. He succeeds! The conversation in which he engages us here is truly an eye-opening and enriching experience."

—**Duane F. Watson**, Malone University

"If the parables stimulate your mind, feed your soul, upset your values, and occasionally confuse you, you're in good company. Exegetes, poets, hymn writers, allegorists, social reformers, novelists, and painters feature in this brisk tour through two thousand years of parable interpretation, often urging readers to see more in the parables or to view them through a different set of eyes. As a knowledgeable guide through a lively history, David Gowler highlights the evocative interpretations that emerge when a parable encounters a fertile imagination."

—**Matthew L. Skinner**, Luther Seminary

The Parables
after Jesus

Their Imaginative Receptions across Two Millennia

David B. Gowler

B
Baker Academic
a division of Baker Publishing Group
Grand Rapids, Michigan

Published by Baker Academic
a division of Baker Publishing Group
P.O. Box 6287, Grand Rapids, MI 49516-6287
www.bakeracademic.com

Printed in the United States of America

Library of Congress Cataloging-in-Publication Data
Names: Gowler, David B., 1958– author.
Title: The parables after Jesus : their imaginative receptions across two millennia / David B. Gowler.
Description: Grand Rapids, MI : Baker Academic, 2016. | Includes bibliographical references and index.
Identifiers: LCCN 2016033234 | ISBN 9780801049996 (pbk.)
Subjects: LCSH: Jesus Christ—Parables.
Classification: LCC BT375.3 .G69 2016 | DDC 226.8/0609—dc23
LC record available at https://lccn.loc.gov/2016033234

Unless otherwise indicated, Scripture quotations appearing in the expositions of the church fathers are in the form in which those quotations appear in the ANF and NPNF translations of those works under discussion.

17   18   19   20   21   22   23   7   6   5   4   3   2   1

In memory of

Robert Warren Runnels
(March 3, 1934–June 13, 1991)

and

Gary Warren Gowler
(December 30, 1953–April 8, 2013)

Then the king will say to those at his right hand, "Come, you that are blessed by my Father, inherit the kingdom prepared for you from the foundation of the world; for I was hungry and you gave me food, I was thirsty and you gave me something to drink, I was a stranger and you welcomed me, I was naked and you gave me clothing, I was sick and you took care of me, I was in prison and you visited me."

—Matthew 25:34–36

Contents

List of Illustrations   ix

Preface   xi

Abbreviations   xv

Introduction   1

1. The Afterlives of Jesus's Parables in Antiquity (to ca. 550 CE)   15

Irenaeus   16
The Gospel of Philip   20
Clement of Alexandria   21
Tertullian   25
Origen   30
John Chrysostom   35
Augustine   40
Macrina the Younger   44
Ephrem the Syrian   47

The Good Shepherd in Early
   Christian Art   50
   Oil Lamp   51
   Roman Catacombs   51
   Dura-Europos House Church   53
Illuminations from the Rossano
   Gospels   54
Byzantine Mosaics, *Christ
   Separating Sheep from Goats*,
   Sant'Apollinare Nuovo
   (Ravenna, Italy)   58
Romanos the Melodist   60

2. The Afterlives of Jesus's Parables in the Middle Ages (ca. 550–
   1500 CE)   65

Gregory the Great   66
Sahih al-Bukhari   71
Wazo of Liège   74
The Golden Gospels of
   Echternach   76
   The Laborers in the Vineyard   77
   The Wicked Tenants   78

The Great Dinner   79
   The Rich Man and Lazarus   81
Theophylact   82
Hildegard of Bingen   85
Chartres Cathedral   89
Bonaventure   95
Thomas Aquinas   98

John Gower   102   Albrecht Dürer   110
Antonia Pulci   105

3. The Afterlives of Jesus's Parables in the Sixteenth
   and Seventeenth Centuries   115
   Martin Luther   116   Domenico Fetti   137
   Anna Jansz of Rotterdam   120   George Herbert   142
   John Calvin   124   Roger Williams   147
   John Maldonatus   128   Rembrandt Harmenszoon
   William Shakespeare   132   van Rijn   151
                                    John Bunyan   158

4. The Afterlives of Jesus's Parables in the Eighteenth
   and Nineteenth Centuries   163
   William Blake   164   John Everett Millais   187
   Søren Kierkegaard   168   Emily Dickinson   193
   Frederick Douglass   173   Charles Haddon Spurgeon   197
   Fanny Crosby   178   Adolf Jülicher   201
   Leo Tolstoy   183

5. The Afterlives of Jesus's Parables in the Twentieth
   and Twenty-First Centuries   207
   Thomas Hart Benton   209   Two Latin American
   Parables and the Blues: Rev. Robert   Receptions   233
     Wilkins   213   The Peasants of Solentiname   233
   Flannery O'Connor   218   Elsa Tamez   237
   Martin Luther King Jr.   223   David Flusser   240
   Godspell   228   Octavia Butler   243
                                    Thich Nhat Hanh   249

   Conclusion: What Do Parables Want?   255

   Appendix: Descriptions of the Parables
     Cited in the Interpretations   259

   Works Cited   275

   Scripture Index   289

   Subject Index   293

Illustrations

Figure 1.1   Domitilla catacomb, Good Shepherd   52

Figure 1.2   Dura-Europos house church, Good Shepherd   53

Figure 1.3   Rossano Gospels, Good Samaritan   55

Figure 1.4   Rossano Gospels, Wise and Foolish Bridesmaids   56

Figure 1.5   Sant'Apollinare Nuovo (Ravenna, Italy), Fifth-century mosaic, Sheep and Goats   59

Figure 2.1   Golden Gospels of Echternach, Laborers in the Vineyard   78

Figure 2.2   Golden Gospels of Echternach, Wicked Tenants   79

Figure 2.3   Golden Gospels of Echternach, Great Dinner   80

Figure 2.4   Golden Gospels of Echternach, Rich Man and Lazarus   81

Figure 2.5   Albrecht Dürer, *The Prodigal Son amongst the Pigs*   112

Figure 3.1   Domenico Fetti, *The Mote and the Beam*   138

Figure 3.2   Domenico Fetti, *The Parable of the Lost Coin*   140

Figure 3.3   Domenico Fetti, *The Unmerciful Servant*   141

Figure 3.4   Rembrandt, *The Return of the Prodigal Son*   153

Figure 3.5   Rembrandt, *The Return of the Prodigal Son* (detail)   154

Figure 3.6   Rembrandt, *The Good Samaritan Bringing the Wounded Man to the Inn*   155

Figure 4.1   William Blake, *The Parable of the Wise and Foolish Virgins* (ca. 1825)   166

Figure 4.2   John Everett Millais, *The Pharisee and the Publican*   189

Figure 4.3   John Everett Millais, *The Importunate Widow*   191

Figure 5.1   Thomas Hart Benton, *Prodigal Son* (1939)   211

Figure 5.2   José Arana, *The Rich Epicure and Poor Lazarus*   236

Preface

My father loved parables—stories that taught, stories that presented ideas and morals in ways that made pictures in people's minds. He used the ones he found in the Bible, the ones he plucked from history, or from folk tales, and, of course, he used those he saw in his life and the lives of the people he knew. He wove stories into his Sunday sermons, his Bible classes, and his computer-delivered history lectures. Because he believed stories were so important as teaching tools.

—Octavia E. Butler, *Parable of the Talents: A Novel*
(New York: Seven Stories Press, 1998), 19

I also love parables; they are stories, like Butler notes, that create vivid pictures in one's mind, stories that enable us to experience profound truths in often deceptively simple ways, stories that challenge us to respond and act—not only to do better, but also to be better. I especially love the parables of Jesus and have spent much of my career studying, teaching, and writing about them.

Some parables are relatively simple and straightforward. "Go and do likewise," says Jesus after he tells the parable of the good Samaritan in the Gospel of Luke (10:25–37): the command makes the parable easier to understand, perhaps, but more difficult to put into practice. Other parables are more challenging even to comprehend. How can Jesus apparently praise, for example, a steward who acts dishonestly (Luke 16:1–8)? Still other parables offer even more complexity; they permit and even sometimes encourage a range of responses and interpretations. As I read Jesus's parables and the divergent ways in which various people have responded to them, I am reminded of the August 23, 1799, letter of William Blake to Rev. Dr. Trusler after Trusler had complained about one of Blake's works of art that Blake had sent to him (see the introduction for details). Blake compares his own *Visions of Eternity* to, for example, the parables and fables of Aesop and argues: "The wisest of the Ancients considerd what is not too Explicit as the fittest for Instruction because it rouzes the faculties to act. I name Moses Solomon Esop Homer Plato." The parables are "not too Explicit": in the famous words of C. H. Dodd, a parable leaves "the mind in sufficient doubt about its precise application to tease it into active thought" (1961, 16). That aspect of parables can give them tremendous power to affect their hearers and readers in numerous ways.

Parables, then, like other great works of art, challenge our hearts, minds, and imaginations. As Richard Pevear writes about the works of Fyodor Dostoevsky: "They leap out of their historical situation and confront us as if they had not yet spoken their final word" (Dostoevsky 1993, viii). But the parables of Jesus go further than just "rouz[ing] the faculties to act": they also challenge us to act in other ways, to change our priorities, not just our perspectives; to change our behaviors, not just our attitudes.

This book seeks to explore some of the more important, interesting, and/ or compelling interpretations and applications of the parables of Jesus, what scholars call the "receptions" or "afterlives" of parables. Yet such interactions are never solitary or unique endeavors, for all of us stand on the shoulders of interpreters who preceded us; all of us are continually in dialogue with fellow interpreters past and present. Part of the essential elements of reception history, therefore, is listening to and interacting with a wide range of voices, including those not usually heard. These interpretations are often as interesting as the parables themselves, and I hope that you find the explorations in this book as significant, exciting, and fascinating as I did as I was researching and writing about them.

For those readers who wish to learn about the process of writing this book and to explore additional receptions of the parables, you may find such discussions on my blog, *A Chorus of Voices* (http://www.parablesreception.blogspot .com). More details about sections of the book may be found there, as well as many additional discussions of various receptions of the parables of Jesus.

I am grateful to many members of Baker Publishing Group for their work in producing this volume, but four people deserve special mention. The idea for the book stemmed from conversations with James Ernest, and he provided many helpful insights as the work began to take shape. Bryan Dyer, who inherited the project when the manuscript neared its final form, was also exceedingly helpful, especially as I worked to revise my (lengthy) drafts into a finished manuscript. Rachel Klompmaker proved invaluable as a partner in acquiring permissions for images and other copyrighted materials, and Eric Salo and his team worked diligently to shepherd the manuscript into its published form. I am grateful to have had this opportunity to work with them.

Most of the people about whom I write in this book are outside my primary area of expertise as a New Testament scholar. I am grateful, therefore, to three of the Emory University libraries—Oxford, Woodruff, and Pitts—for their outstanding resources upon which I greatly depended for my research. In addition, the Prints and Drawings Rooms of the Tate Gallery in London granted me access to prints by John Everett Millais that are not on display, and the Ackland Art Museum of the University of North Carolina gave me access to its Print Study Room to examine prints by Rembrandt and Thomas Hart Benton.

Some sections of the book were written for my 2014 Hussey Seminar Lecture at The Centre for Reception History of the Bible at the University of Oxford. I am grateful to Christine Joynes (Trinity College, Oxford) both for the invitation and for her hospitality during my visit. I am also grateful to Chris and Catherine Rowland for their gracious hospitality at Cambridge, which included the opportunity to explore Ely Cathedral and the stained-glass windows depicting parables of Jesus. A few insights from this book appear in condensed form in a chapter titled "The Characterization of the Two Brothers in the Parable of the Prodigal Son (Luke 15.11–32): Their Function and Afterlives," in *Characters and Characterization in Luke-Acts*, edited by Frank Dicken and Julia Snyder (London: Bloomsbury, 2016).

I owe a debt of gratitude to Emory University colleagues who read sections of the book within their own areas of expertise and lent their wise counsel about those sections: Maria Archetto, Lucas Carpenter, Sheila Cavanagh, Clark Lemons, Eve Mullen, and Florian Pohl. As I was writing this book, I also had the good fortune to teach an honors seminar, A Chorus of Voices: The "Afterlives" of Parables, at Oxford College of Emory University, and I am grateful to those students who read through sections of the manuscript in that class and offered their helpful insights: Rema Elmostafa, Robert Howell, Alicia Johnson, and Garrett Shuler. I am especially grateful for how they all became excellent dialogue partners as we presented and discussed our own explorations of the receptions of Jesus's parables in literature, music, visual art, and other media.

Most of all, I am grateful to my family—Rita, Camden, and Jacob—for their boundless patience for a spouse and father whose head is often buried in books and who sometimes seems permanently (and physically) attached to his laptop.

Finally, this book is dedicated as a memorial to my uncle, Robert Warren Runnels, and my brother, Gary Warren Gowler. Uncle Bob and Gary, who both left this earth far too soon, share a middle name because our mother named her second son in honor of her beloved brother.

Uncle Bob died in 1991 at the age of fifty-seven, and he is survived by his wonderful family: his wife Laures, his son Loren, and his daughter Melissa (and now two grandchildren). Uncle Bob was an extremely talented professional artist, and three of his works of visual art adorn the walls of our home. One of those prized works he created just a few months before his death: a pencil drawing (dated January 4, 1991) of our then newborn son, Camden. The art in this book is especially dedicated to Uncle Bob's memory.

I wish I had known my uncle better. He and his family moved to Denver when I was young, and we rarely saw each other. I remember well, however, his joy of life, his sense of humor, and his infectious laugh. I also remember the last serious conversation I had with him. That discussion served as a memorable coda to our relationship, one I will always cherish.

My older brother, Gary, died from non-Hodgkin's lymphoma in 2013 at the age of fifty-nine, and he is survived by his wonderful family: his wife Lori, his son James, and his daughter Anna (and now six grandchildren). One daughter, Bethany, was killed in a tragic automobile accident in 2002.

Among many other things, Gary was a brilliant teacher and a talented musician, so I especially wrote the sections of the book about music for him, most notably the one on Robert Wilkins. Although I have little of Gary's musical talent, we shared a love for the blues. The last time we saw each other, Gary, Lori, Rita, and I spent a couple hours listening to blues at Buddy Guy's Legends in Chicago, before walking down the street to get Gary's favorite pizza, Lou Malnati's deep dish (the sausage pizza was mandatory for Gary). That evening we spent together served as a memorable coda to our relationship, one I will always cherish.

I know it is a cliché to say this about those who have left us, but Uncle Bob's and Gary's influence live on—through their wonderful families, their extended families, and through all the friends, students, and others whose lives they touched so deeply.

Abbreviations

ANF   *The Ante-Nicene Fathers.* Edited by Alexander Roberts and James Donaldson. 1885–1887. 10 vols. Repr., Peabody, MA: Hendrickson, 1994.

NPNF[1]   *The Nicene and Post-Nicene Fathers*, Series 1. Edited by Philip Schaff. 1886–1889. 14 vols. Repr., Peabody, MA: Hendrickson, 1994.

NPNF[2]   *The Nicene and Post-Nicene Fathers*, Series 2. Edited by Philip Schaff and Henry Wace. 1886–1900. 14 vols. Repr., Peabody, MA: Hendrickson, 1994.

Introduction

So the parable should not be lightly esteemed in your eyes, since by means of
the parable a man arrives at the true meaning of the words of the Torah.

Midrash Song of Songs Rabbah 1.8

Parables, at first glance, often seem to be relatively simple stories; their complexity and power can be overlooked. Hence John Bunyan, in the prologue
of *The Pilgrim's Progress*, somewhat apologetically asks a key question of
his readers: "Would'st thou see a truth within a fable?" (Bunyan, n.d., 20).
Bunyan hopes that they will, of course, because seeing truth is usually the
point of using fables and parables.

Some parables are indeed relatively simple and straightforward; others,
however, can create unforeseen depths of insight and meaning. Parables usually involve some sort of implied analogy, but since the parallels between the
things being compared are often not made explicitly, they actively engage
their audiences to understand and apply their messages. Parables, by their
analogical nature, therefore, encourage hearers/readers to imagine new possibilities as they explore the hermeneutical potential of these brief narratives
(cf. Kermode 1979, 44).

So many parables, as the parables of Jesus illustrate, are not innocuous, simple stories; they can be deceptively complex, enigmatic, and dialogic—drawing
listeners and readers into continuing conversations. Jesus told these often
challenging stories with one ear already listening for his hearers' responses.
These dialogues developed in ever-expanding circles as these stories have been
told and retold, read and reread, over the centuries, dialogues that, I argue,
deepen and enrich our understandings of what Jesus's parables denote and

1

connote. To make the dialogues even richer, the responses to Jesus's parables are not limited to texts or speech; they include music, visual art, poetry, and other modes of interpretation in new contexts. Thus interpreters, ancient and modern, participate in the formation of meaning, and any interpretation of Jesus's parables is incomplete if it does not incorporate the responses of those interpreters who have preceded us; we stand, whether we recognize it or not, on their shoulders (see Gowler 2000, 38–39, 101–3; cf. 2014, 4–5).

This book discusses more than fifty modes of "reception" of Jesus's parables that span the first century to the twenty-first. The primary goal is to introduce and discuss a number of diverse voices from a variety of eras, perspectives, media, and contexts. Since one of the primary goals is to introduce readers to the ways in which Jesus's parables have been received over the centuries, the book is primarily arranged chronologically, not thematically, by genre, or by any other categorization. There are, of course, advantages and disadvantages to this structure, but not only is a basic chronological understanding of the receptions of the parables a necessary first step; the structure is also intended to encourage readers to follow other fruitful modes of reception history. The numerous excerpts from primary sources also facilitate further dialogue, and, as an additional catalyst, individual sections often include connections or comparisons between interpreters. Chapter 1, for example, compares the more allegorical interpretations of the "Alexandrian school" (e.g., Origen) with the more "restrained" exegesis of the "Antiochene" school (e.g., John Chrysostom), with the caveat that the contrasts between them are sometimes overdrawn. Such observations, once again, serve as starting points for further explorations.

Which interpretations to include was as difficult a decision as how to structure the volume. The historical and theological importance of the selections was key, but so was including a diversity of media, approaches, voices, and perspectives. The book does not dwell on academic debates in modern scholarship (rarely are biblical scholars included): those conversations are adequately covered elsewhere (e.g., Gowler 2000). The goal is to include a number of diverse responses to the parables—some of which have dominated discussions and others of which have been marginalized—to allow a wide variety of responses to be heard while attempting to balance depth and breadth.

I include not just biblical commentaries and other theological works such as sermons, but also plays, music, literature, poetry, visual art, and social and political materials, ranging from Augustine to Kierkegaard, from Romanos the Melodist to Fanny Crosby to Robert Wilkins, from Wazo of Liège to Thomas Aquinas to Roger Williams, from Ephrem the Syrian to George Herbert to Emily Dickinson, from Byzantine mosaics to illuminated Gospels to Rembrandt to William Blake to Thomas Hart Benton, from Antonia Pulci to William Shakespeare to *Godspell*, from Islamic *hadith* to David Flusser to Thich Nhat Hanh, from John Chrysostom to Martin Luther King Jr., and so on.

The options for what to include are almost endless; breadth has sometimes been sacrificed for depth, and sometimes depth has been sacrificed for breadth. How to do justice to these more than fifty voices, for example, in approximately two thousand words each? Yet even in these relatively short sections, the profundity of the interpreters and the profundity of the parables with which they interact shine through.

The Invisible Gorilla, Parables, and Reception History

> Truth is not born nor is it to be found inside the head of an individual person, it is born between people collectively searching for truth, in the process of their dialogic interaction. (Bakhtin 1984, 110)

This quote, perhaps better than any other, helps to illustrate the philosophical foundation of my approach to reception history—and why I do reception history in the first place. No one person or interpreter holds a monopoly on truth, and an essential element of reception history—and the search for meaning in these biblical texts—is listening to and interacting with a wide range of voices, including those usually not heard.

One basic truth concerning the interpretation of any narrative is that interpreters tend to find what they expect to find. What interpreters expect to see influences what they see. This selective attention places blinders on interpreters, blinders that can be removed only when they join in dialogue with other interpreters who have different perspectives, presuppositions, and modes of analysis.

The famous "invisible gorilla" experiment (http://www.theinvisiblegorilla .com) by Christopher Chabris and Daniel Simons illustrates how our perceptions of what we think is "reality" are skewed by our preconceptions. Participants in the experiment were asked to watch a brief video in which three people in white shirts pass a basketball back and forth to each other and three people in black shirts also pass a basketball back and forth to each other. Viewers of the video were instructed to count the number of passes the people in white shirts made. In the middle of the brief video, a person dressed in a gorilla suit walks slowly from the right side of the screen into the middle of the six people passing basketballs, stops, faces the camera, and beats his chest before slowly walking off to the viewers' left. The person in the gorilla suit spends a total of nine seconds on the screen.

Surprisingly, almost half of the video's viewers did not see the gorilla; because they were focused on counting the number of passes made between the players in white shirts, the gorilla became invisible to them. I have shown students this video in some of my classes over the past few years, and a similar percentage do not see the gorilla. Since what we look for influences what we see, interpreters can miss a significant number of elements in a narrative simply because of their own contexts and presuppositions. Interpreters may believe that they interpret the text "as it is" as objectively and completely as possible but actually overlook a number of significant elements; metaphorical gorillas stroll through the narrative sight unseen. Reception history helps to overcome these shortcomings and to remove exegetical blinders from interpreters, especially when diverse voices from various perspectives are included in the conversations.

The Dialogic Nature of Parables

The riddle-like nature of parables inherently includes some ambiguity, which makes it even more critical for interpreters to gain insight, wisdom, and greater clarity through dialogues with other interpreters. I do not mean to suggest that all interpretations are of equal value or importance—even dialogic narratives like parables provide buoys in the channel of interpretation that encourage interpreters to navigate within certain boundaries of readings—but engagement with other interpretations can make one's own interpretations more cogent and more comprehensive.

We do not know and cannot recover the specific historical circumstances in which Jesus of Nazareth first uttered his parables. The New Testament Gospels of Matthew, Mark, and Luke provide the earliest extant written receptions/interpretations of them; where they are found in the Gospel narratives and how they are used necessarily influence readers' interpretations of those parables. Sometimes embedding a parable into a larger narrative can change its meaning dramatically, because the author uses that parable from a certain authorial point of view to make a particular point in the attempt to elicit a preferred response from readers. Tensions can arise between a parable and its literary context in the Gospels, and a larger narrative framework in which a parable is embedded cannot control or contain or complete the parable's ability to create or communicate meaning. The Gospel authors implicitly or explicitly offer their own interpretations of the parables, and the dialogues between the voice of Jesus and the voices of the Gospel authors continue, develop, and expand as hearers and readers over the centuries add their own responses and voices to the ongoing dialogues (see Gowler 2000, 38–39).

As this book demonstrates, interpretations of Jesus's parables are extremely diverse; they vary from era to era, context to context, person to person, and sometimes depend upon the medium in which the parables are (re)presented. Yet one aspect of the parables remains constant: their sometimes-untamable dialogic power. These often-enigmatic stories continue to engage and indeed challenge our hearts, minds, and imaginations.

The Impulse to Control or Restrain Parables

Modern interpretations of Jesus's parables stand on the shoulders of centuries of interpretations, and all those interpretations have necessarily wrestled with the enigmatic nature of parables and responded in different ways. One impulse within the history of interpretations is to attempt to control or tame those readings—what Bakhtin would call trying to impose a monologic discourse on a dialogic parable—an impulse that arises especially in situations of controversy, where some interpretations are seen as harmful, dangerous, or even heretical.

Irenaeus of Lyons, for example, writes in the context of combating the esoteric wisdom of the heretics called gnostics and their speculative interpretations of Scripture (see chap. 1). He seeks to protect what he sees as the authentic traditions that the church received from the apostles of Jesus and cautions his readers not to adapt parables "to ambiguous expressions." If interpreters follow this guidance, Irenaeus claims, then "parables will receive a like interpretation from all" (*Against Heresies* 2.27.1, in *ANF* 1:398–99).

Irenaeus does admit, however, that "parables admit of many interpretations" (*Against Heresies* 2.27.3, in *ANF* 1:399), so he advises that hard-to-understand parables must be harmonized with biblical passages that are easier to understand, advice that many early Christian interpreters followed.

The Impulse to Engage the Enigmas and Challenges in the Parables

Other interpreters explore more fully why Jesus used these powerful and sometimes hard-to-understand stories. Clement of Alexandria, for example, compares the parables of Jesus to the enigmatic symbolism used by other people who seek the truth, including poets and philosophers (*Miscellanies*

5.8). Symbolism conceals the truth of holy secrets from those who are not worthy to understand them (cf. Matt. 13:10–17, 34); it contains more power than simple, direct statements, and it enables multiple layers of meaning. In addition, parables stimulate the hearts and minds of their hearers to be even more active in their search for words of salvation. It is through such parables and metaphors, Clement argues, that we can discern spiritual realities revealed in Scripture (chap. 1).

John Chrysostom also approaches the enigmatic nature of parables from the perspective that, like Hebrew Bible prophets, Jesus uses vivid parables such as the parable of the sower to make hearers more attentive, to "rouse" their minds, to stimulate his audience to inquire further, and to make his teaching memorable. Parables do perplex some in Jesus's audience, but they also bring clarity in the minds of those with "ears to hear" (chap. 1).

In a manner reminiscent of Chrysostom, John Calvin discusses the increased rhetorical effect parables can have on their hearers/readers. Parables have more energy and force than do simple, direct expressions, produce greater impact on the minds of their hearers/readers, and also can make truths more clear. Calvin warns, however, that although the use of parables could allow God's truth to shine forth more brilliantly, their obscurity can lead to that light being hidden by the darkness of human beings and becoming more confusing and unclear (chap. 3).

In a much different way, the poetry of Emily Dickinson can illustrate this two-edged sword of how parables can both illuminate and conceal meaning, since Dickinson's poetry can both use Jesus's parables and also operate in a "parabolic" way. Dickinson's "riddle poems" use many biblical literary forms, including rhythm, parallelism, and sometimes baffling paradox, as she seeks to "tell all the truth but tell it slant." Truth, in other words, must be told in a circuitous fashion; otherwise, its brilliance will blind its viewers. Truth must arise slowly like the dawn (chap. 4).

Søren Kierkegaard approaches the enigmatic power of parables by stressing that truth must be presented through indirect communication, such as parables, which necessarily involves a "double reflection" on the alternative possibilities that such indirect communication presents. Parables thus challenge their hearers/readers to "untie a knot," to make a decision, an "appropriation" that must be done by every individual. Not only do you interpret a parable; the parable also "interprets" you, and you are called to respond. Thus the parables uttered by Jesus—or even the parables constructed by Kierkegaard— challenge their hearers/readers to become participants, examine themselves, and reach greater spiritual and moral heights, and therefore the parables affect the fundamental choices their hearers/readers make (chap. 4).

The Impulse to Embrace the Dialogic Nature of Parables

Some interpreters are even more receptive of the dialogic nature of parables, such as Ephrem the Syrian in his mystical poetry. For Ephrem, symbols are dialogic or polyvalent in that one meaning does not exhaust their potential, and one meaning does not exclude another meaning. In Ephrem's *Hymns on the Pearl*, for example, the pearl can serve as a door that opens and reveals many facets of the "Truth"; it can symbolize the kingdom of heaven, Christ, faith, the virgin birth, Jesus's crucifixion, and many other realities. This symbol also serves as the invitation and beginning point for spiritual meditation (chap. 1).

As someone who speaks of the "doors of perception" (in *The Marriage of Heaven and Hell*), William Blake is one of the best examples of an interpreter who creatively embraces the dialogic nature of Jesus's parables and their ability to engage their hearers/readers in "perceiving" infinite reality. Blake's poetry and images stem from his visionary, supernatural impulse (i.e., his "Genius" or "angel"). As noted in the preface, Blake's blunt reply to a complaint about one of his works from Reverend Trusler—who demanded an explanation of the work sent to him—demonstrates Blake's view of what true art (like good parables) should do. Trusler, a wealthy cleric, writer, and publisher, had commissioned Blake to create a watercolor illustrating the topic "Malevolence." As was often the case, Blake's vision took precedence; he created the watercolor *Malevolence: A Husband Parting from His Wife and Child; Two Assassins Lurking in Ambush* (currently in the Philadelphia Museum of Art). The "malevolence" in the work was that the assassins would murder the mother and child once the father left them unprotected. Trusler, who ultimately rejected the work, wrote Blake to complain that the work did not fulfill the commission and that the fantasy contained within it was "unnatural." Blake responded that he was "compell'd by [his] Genius or Angel to follow where he led." As Blake's letter of August 23, 1799 (postmarked August 28), states:

> I really am sorry that you are falln out with the Spiritual World Especially if I should have to answer for it I feel very sorry that your Ideas & Mine on Moral Painting differ so much as to have made you angry with my method of Study. If I am wrong I am wrong in good company. I had hoped your plan comprehended All Species of this Art & Especially that you would not reject that Species which gives Existence to Every other. namely Visions of Eternity You say that I want somebody to Elucidate my Ideas. But you ought to know that What is Grand is necessarily obscure to Weak men. That which can be made Explicit to the Idiot is not worth my care. The wisest of the Ancients considerd what is not

too Explicit as the fittest for Instruction because it rouzes the faculties to act.
I name Moses Solomon Esop Homer Plato. (Blake 1969, 793)

For Blake, there is no one "correct" meaning attributed to a biblical text. Instead, Jesus's parables in particular and the Bible in general are doors to perception and stimuli to the prophet's imagination (chap. 4).

The play *Godspell* illustrates the dialogic nature of parables in a very different way, but it also emphasizes the challenging nature of parables and the ultimate responsibility of hearers/listeners to engage, respond, and take action. The following dialogue takes place between Jesus and Judas about a saying that Luke 6:39–42 designates as a "parable":

Jesus: Now, how can you take a speck of sawdust out of your brother's eye when all the time there's this great plank in your own?

Judas: I don't know. How can you take the speck of sawdust in your brother's eye when all the time there's this great plank in your own?

Jesus: You hypocrite! First you take the plank out of your own eye so you can see clearly to take the speck of sawdust out of your brother's.

Judas: Wait a moment! That's no answer to the question.

Jesus: Did I promise you an answer to the question?

Judas: No.

Godspell, more than any other play or film, uses the parables of Jesus (and the Sermon on the Mount) as the primary foundation for its portrayal of Jesus and his message, a message in which Jesus's followers are challenged to listen, understand, and believe in a message of love, forgiveness, humility, and service that often contravenes human expectations and cultural conventions (chap. 5). This approach aptly illustrates the dialogic nature of Jesus's parables: all are called to respond.

This Book as a Stimulus to Further Discussions

This book is a basic introduction to the different ways Jesus's parables have been interpreted over the millennia, so it is closer to an anthology than to a diachronic analysis over time, although readers will find some diachronic discussions in numerous sections of the book. The number of receptions in the book limits the number of such reflections, but the breadth of receptions will illuminate many aspects for readers. The book also can serve as a resource, a starting place for readers' further explorations in investigating the reception history of Jesus's parables (see the appendix for a description of each parable cited and for lists of each parable's interpretations included in the book).

One of the goals of this book is to help readers better understand the importance of context for interpreters' responses to Jesus's parables. The different ways interpreters respond to the wheat and weeds parable, for instance, are influenced by their historical contexts. Wazo of Liège, for example, lived in the mid-eleventh century in (what is now) Belgium during a time in which a number of Christian heresies arose, and Wazo uses the wheat and weeds parable to argue that the church should not execute such "heretics" or turn them over to the state to be executed. Circumstances changed, however, as the church began to respond more vigorously to various heresies. Pope Gregory IX started a papal inquisition in 1231 to suppress such groups as the Cathars, Christian heretics who flourished in southern France and northern Italy in the twelfth through the fourteenth centuries (Fichtenau 1998, 27). By the thirteenth century, heresy was a capital offense in most of Europe, a context in which Thomas Aquinas interprets the wheat and weeds parable in a much different fashion than did Wazo: he argues that the state is responsible for executing heretics that the church deems worthy of death. The historical context is also entirely different for Roger Williams's interpretation of the wheat and weeds parable four centuries later, in a post-Reformation context in the New World. Williams famously advocates for religious liberty and that neither the church nor the state should use any coercive force against perceived heretics.

Several examples in this book also demonstrate that even the same person can interpret the same parable in different ways, depending on the context. Note in chapter 4, for instance, how Frederick Douglass interprets the parable of the rich man and Lazarus during the Civil War to depict slaves (Lazarus), slave owners (the rich man), and Abraham Lincoln (Father Abraham). More than two decades after the war (and slavery) ended, however, Douglass uses the same parable to argue for the liberation, or emancipation, of a different oppressed group: women.

A Test Case for Further Explorations: The Prodigal Son

The parable of the prodigal son, since it arguably has been referenced and interpreted more than any other parable of Jesus, provides almost countless examples of the directions further explorations could take. Receptions of this parable are so numerous that even book-long analyses are not able comprehensively to explore the majority of receptions (see Fenske 2003). Since the materials are so vast, one approach is to focus on receptions during specific eras, such as the time period covered in chapter 1 (most of the era that is often called the "patristic age"). Once the overview of the receptions during the period covered by chapter 1 is completed, it will be clear that early Christian interpretations fall within four categories (see Tissot 1978), most of which use allegory. In brief, during this era the father symbolizes God, but interpretations vary according to how the two brothers are received:

- *Ethical interpretations* view the elder brother as symbolizing the righteous and the younger brother as symbolizing sinners (e.g., Jerome and Cyril of Alexandria).
- *Ethnic interpretations* equate the elder brother with Israel and the younger brother with gentiles (e.g., Tertullian and Augustine). Sometimes ethnic interpretations incorporate aspects of ethical interpretations, such as that gentiles are sinners because they are idolaters.
- *Penitential interpretations* see the elder brother as rigid Christians who oppose reconciliation with baptized Christians who afterward fall into sin and then repent (e.g., Clement of Alexandria and John Chrysostom).
- *Gnosticizing interpretations* envision the elder brother as symbolizing the angels and the younger brother as symbolizing humanity (e.g., Pseudo-Jerome, Epistle 35).

Likewise, an analysis of the receptions of the parable in the medieval period reveals that interpretations during that era also focused on allegorical understandings in the ethical, ethnic, and penitential modes.

Innumerable other attempts have been made to explore the impact of the prodigal son parable in a more manageable selection of materials, such as narrowing the focus to a specified corpus of materials (e.g., English literature: Siebald and Ryken 1992; European literature: Brettschneider 1978), a particular perspective or methodology (e.g., feminist readings: Beavis 2002; social-scientific readings: Rohrbaugh 1997), the work of an individual (e.g., William Shakespeare: Tippens 1988), or an individual work (e.g., Rembrandt's *The Return of the Prodigal Son*: Nouwen 1994, 6).

This volume, even though it discusses receptions of the vast majority of Jesus's parables, provides enough examples of the reception of the prodigal son parable that trends in the reception history of the parable are evident. Insights may be gleaned in all five chapters of this book concerning interpretations of the prodigal son parable in a variety of media, such as visual art

(Albrecht Dürer, Rembrandt, John Everett Millais, Thomas Hart Benton), plays/film (Antonia Pulci, William Shakespeare, *Godspell*), sermons (Hildegard of Bingen), music (Romanos the Melodist, Robert Wilkins), poetry (George Herbert), and other literature.

Receptions of the parable during the succeeding centuries almost always followed the trend in the earliest interpretations that equated the father in the parable with God. There are, however, interesting variations in the "afterlives" of the two brothers—their impacts on audiences and interpreters—from the earliest to the most recent interpretations. As the opening lines of James Weldon Johnson's poem "The Prodigal Son" note:

> But Jesus spake in a parable, and he said:
> A certain man had two sons.
> Jesus didn't give this man a name,
> But his name is God Almighty.
> And Jesus didn't call these sons by name,
> But ev'ry young man,
> Ev'rywhere,
> Is one of these two sons. (Johnson 1990, 21)

The afterlife of the elder brother almost always fits into one of three categories. More often than not he is marginalized, ignored, or minimized. A second trend, following the readings of some early interpreters, is to identify him with those unrepentant Jews who are indignant at the emergence of Christianity. A third mode of reading, following other early interpreters, is to envision the elder brother as self-righteous Christians who are urged to move beyond their feelings of jealousy concerning the return of repentant sinners (Parsons 1996, 147–74).

Even within the receptions of the prodigal son documented and discussed in this book, there are fascinating impulses within the third trend above, those which identify the elder brother with self-righteous Christians and the younger brother with sinners who return: (a) reconciliation between the two brothers after the prodigal's return, and (b) self-identification with the younger son. Both impulses primarily stem from penitential interpretations of the parable, but they also include ethical interpretations, since the younger son depicts those Christians who fall away from their faith but repent and return, and the elder son symbolizes those "righteous" Christians who are being urged to celebrate the return of their repentant brothers and sisters (for more details, see Gowler 2016).

Reconciliation between the two brothers: Included in this volume are a few examples of receptions that "finish" the story and supply a joyful ending to the parable, just as the other two "lost" parables of Luke 15 (sheep, coin) conclude with joyful celebrations. In these examples, the elder brother listens to his father's pleas and joins the celebration over his errant brother's return. Reconciliation between the two brothers is portrayed or assumed in Antonia Pulci's *The Play of the Prodigal Son* (chap. 2), a stained-glass window in Chartres Cathedral (chap. 2), the blues song "The Prodigal Son," by Robert Wilkins (chap. 5), and the play/film *Godspell* (chap. 5).

Self-identification with the younger son: There are also fascinating developments in receptions of the younger son, most notably self-identification with the prodigal, whether in his debauchery, repentance, or reconciliation with his father. Important examples of such receptions are found in the selections of visual art in this volume, where the artist apparently self-identifies with the prodigal son. The first (probable) self-identification within visual art is Albrecht Dürer's engraving *The Prodigal Son amongst the Pigs* (1496), which depicts the son's moment of repentance in his desperate circumstances as he tends the pigs and longs to eat their food (chap. 2). The most famous self-identifications with the parable, however, are found in Rembrandt's works (chap. 3), such as one of his early paintings, *Self-Portrait with Saskia in the Guise of the Prodigal Son* (1634–1636), where Rembrandt portrays himself as the prodigal son celebrating extravagantly in a tavern with a prostitute— depicted by his wife, Saskia—on his lap. Roughly contemporaneous with this painting is an etching in which an emaciated prodigal kneels before his father in repentance. Perhaps the best-known example of Rembrandt's apparent self-identification with the prodigal is found in his masterpiece—and one of his last paintings—*The Return of the Prodigal Son* (1667–1679), of which Henri Nouwen writes: "I knew that Rembrandt deeply understood this spiritual homecoming. I knew that, when Rembrandt painted his *Prodigal Son*, he had lived a life that had left him with no doubt about his true and final home" (1994, 6). I also include one other probable self-identification by a visual artist with the prodigal son: Thomas Hart Benton's 1939 lithograph *Prodigal Son*, an idiosyncratic depiction of a prodigal like Benton (and others) who had waited far too long to return home. That haunting image offers no joyful reconciliation of any kind (chap. 5).

This book also includes two examples in music—one ancient and one modern—of the afterlives of the two brothers. These examples both involve some form of identification with the younger brother and the reconciliation between the two brothers.

The first example is the *kontakion* (chanted sermon) by Romanos the Melodist, the great Byzantine poet and hymn writer (chap. 1). It contains the earliest self-identification with the prodigal son included in this book. The *kontakion* begins with the speaker/singer identifying with the sinful prodigal, since all have sinned and fallen short of the glory of God. It then urges the members of the congregation not only to repent from their own sins but also to celebrate the repentant returns of other prodigal sons and daughters. Reconciliation between the two brothers thus symbolizes reconciliation between Christians, which is something to be greatly desired.

The second example involves an even more complex dynamic found in blues music: the "prodigal son" motif among some early blues artists. This motif is illustrated, in part, with Robert Wilkins's song "The Prodigal Son." The song originally was a classic blues lament in which a young man complains to his mother about the women who have treated him wrong. This secular song, however, was then "converted" into a religious song with the same tune but new lyrics based on the parable itself. This "conversion," in part, resembles the prodigal son motif found within some early blues artists, who self-identified with the prodigal son and envisioned their lives as reenactments of the parable. The debauchery of the prodigal son represented their "sinful" lives playing blues, the "devil's music," and many early blues artists underwent dramatic conversions in which they "returned home" to their heavenly Father (chap. 5).

Conclusion

These examples from the afterlives of the two brothers in the prodigal son parable give just a glimpse of the further discussions and explorations that this book is meant to encourage and enable. As you work your way through the different responses, approaches, and voices, I hope that you reflect on the different treatments, methods, and perspectives of the various interpretations. Maybe, at the very least, some "invisible gorillas" will be revealed as you read, reflect, and begin your own explorations.

1

The Afterlives of Jesus's Parables in Antiquity (to ca. 550 CE)

Developments, elaborations, and reinterpretations of Jesus's parables already are found in the New Testament Gospels, including various stages of allegorical interpretations, such as the explanation of the parable of the sower in Mark 4:13–20. Scholars still debate whether or how much the historical Jesus used allegory, but it will become clear in this chapter that, from the earliest period in the reception of his parables, allegorical interpretations dominated. Interpreters understand the Scriptures as including various symbols, parables, and riddles that require explanation for the "spiritual" sense, so allegorical readings were the most commonly held understandings of the parables and other biblical texts for hundreds of years (see Crouzel 1996, 153). As Frank Kermode puts it: "Allegory is the patristic way of dealing with inexhaustible hermeneutic potential" (1979, 44). Scripture, these early interpreters believe, is the Word of God, inspired by the Holy Spirit, and, when interpreted correctly, consistent in its message. It is also, however, filled with mysteries: "God is able to speak in riddles and metaphors and has an exceptional ability to stir the curiosity of true listeners" (Studer 1996, 357).

Interpretations during this period vary, but they have some common elements. Foundational to most interpretations is the belief that Scripture—whatever that encompassed—is divinely inspired and unified; thus one easily understood biblical text can be used to explain another hard-to-understand biblical text (e.g., some parables). In addition, God is more fully known through the revelation of Jesus and the New Testament, and, as the parable of the laborers in the vineyard demonstrates to many interpreters, God's revelation is progressive in that mysteries are revealed over time. Another common element is that the Hebrew Bible is often interpreted typologically or allegorically: interpreters believe, for example, that events or concepts found in the Jewish scriptures foreshadow, symbolize, or prophesy the life, ministry, or teaching of Jesus (Papandrea 2012, 126–30).

Most of the interpreters in this chapter illustrate these trends, and they also reflect some of the diversity within the church of this period. These interpreters are primarily "ante-Nicene"—before the important Council of Nicaea in 325 CE—and some are Nicene or post-Nicene, working during or after the Council of Nicaea. They include the more well-known "church fathers," such as some of the "Greek Fathers" (e.g., Irenaeus, Clement of Alexandria, Origen, and John Chrysostom), the "Latin Fathers" (e.g., Tertullian and Augustine), and one "Syriac Father" (Ephrem the Syrian). Also included is the significant voice of Macrina the Younger, who is often overshadowed by her three brothers, Peter of Sebaste, Basil the Great, and Gregory of Nyssa, the latter two being two of the three famous "Cappadocian Fathers." In addition, the chapter includes a divergent voice, The Gospel of Philip, a representative of Christian gnosticism that was deemed heretical by the church. Finally, the chapter concludes with important examples of parable interpretation from both art (e.g., frescoes, illuminated manuscripts, and mosaics) and music (Romanos the Melodist).

Irenaeus (ca. 140–ca. 200)

Irenaeus writes that in his "early youth" he saw Polycarp, the bishop of Smyrna (martyred ca. 156), who "always taught the things which he had learned from the apostles, and which the Church has handed down, and which alone are true" (*Against Heresies* 3.3.4, in *ANF* 1:416). Since Polycarp might have listened to John the Apostle, as the early church historian Eusebius reports (*Church History* 5.20.4–8), Irenaeus possibly was one of the last witnesses to the generation who learned at the feet of the apostles of Jesus.

According to Eusebius, Irenaeus became bishop of Lyon after a local persecution killed numerous Christians, including Pothinus, Lyon's first bishop (*Church History* 5.1.1–63). Irenaeus's major surviving work, *Against Heresies*, is a sustained polemic against the teachings and practices of the gnostics, particularly Valentinian gnostics (Norris 1965, 45) and Marcion. Gnostics like Valentinus claimed to have a special saving revelation, as the Greek word *gnōsis* (knowledge) implies, a secret tradition of esoteric wisdom that Jesus privately transmitted to select disciples who, in turn, delivered those traditions to them. This esoteric wisdom allowed gnostics, they believed, to move from the corporeal realm to the pure spiritual realm. Marcion is best known for distinguishing the "lesser" God of the Hebrew Bible, which he called the *demiurge*, from the transcendent God of Jesus. Irenaeus envisions such gnostics as a central threat to the Christian church, but, in the process of refuting them, *Against Heresies* also makes significant contributions to the development of what will become Christian orthodoxy.

The gnostics were dangerous, in Irenaeus's view, because they led Christians astray with their claims of esoteric wisdom transmitted by Jesus in secret. In contrast, Irenaeus points to the authentic tradition passed on by apostolic succession, that is, from the apostles down through the bishops to the church. A defense of Scripture as apostolic writings thus plays a key role in Irenaeus's arguments, although Irenaeus's authoritative writings include only the four Gospels, Acts, the Pauline Letters, Revelation, and possibly 1 John and 1 Peter—not all the other works that eventually made their way into the Christian canon.

Irenaeus's interpretations of the parables influenced a number of later interpreters, and he succinctly states his interpretative approach in *Against Heresies* 2.27 (ANF 1:398–99). God has made it possible for anyone who is "devoted to piety and the love of truth" to study Scripture to understand the "things which God has placed" within our power to understand, because Scripture speaks "clearly and unambiguously in express terms" about those things:

> And therefore the parables ought not to be adapted to ambiguous expressions. For, if this be not done, both he who explains them will do so without danger, and the parables will receive a like interpretation from all, and the body of truth remains entire, with a harmonious adaptation of its members, and without any collision. But to apply expressions which are not clear or evident to interpretations of the parables, such as every one discovers for himself as inclination leads him, [is absurd]. For in this way no one will possess the rule of truth; but in accordance with the number of persons who explain the parables will be found the various systems of truth, in mutual opposition to each other, and setting forth antagonistic doctrines, like the questions current among the Gentile philosophers. (*Against Heresies* 2.27.1, in ANF 1:398)

Interpreters such as the gnostics inquire but never find, according to Irenaeus, because they improperly reject the authoritative "method of discovery" (adherence to the apostolic tradition). Irenaeus points to the parable of the wise and foolish bridesmaids (Matt. 25:1–13) to explain. If a person's lamp is untrimmed and burning with an unsteady light, that person obscures the "plain announcements" of the parables and will be excluded from the "marriage-chamber." Not just the parables but also all of Scripture "can be clearly, unambiguously, and harmoniously understood by all, although all do not believe them" (*Against Heresies* 2.27.2, in *ANF* 1:398). Thus the secret knowledge allegedly passed by Jesus only to certain disciples and the resulting obscure interpretations of the parables by the gnostics actually are self-imposed chains that bind them in darkness.

Irenaeus acknowledges that "parables admit of many interpretations" (2.27.3, in *ANF* 1:399), but argues that the solution to this problem is explained by the parable of the wise and foolish builders (Matt. 7:24–27 // Luke 6:47–49): one should build one's house on the rock that is "certain, indubitable, and true"; building "upon the shifting sand," as the gnostics do, is to "act as if destitute of reason" (2.27.3, in *ANF* 1:399). The gnostics twist Scripture "from a natural to a non-natural sense" that supports "any kind of hypothesis they fancy" (1.9.4, in *ANF* 1:330). Irenaeus argues that imperfect human beings cannot have perfect knowledge in this life and that some things are beyond human understanding (2.28.2). The Scriptures, however, are perfect and "perfectly consistent." Therefore, the sometimes-hard-to-understand parables must be harmonized with other, more easily understood passages, whose meanings are clear and which can "serve to explain the parables; and through the many diversified utterances [of Scripture] there shall be heard one harmonious melody in us, praising in hymns that God who created all things" (2.28.3, in *ANF* 1:400).

Most of Irenaeus's discussions of the parables occur in book 4 of *Against Heresies*. This section seeks to demonstrate the unity of the Hebrew Bible and Christian scripture (4.36.1–41.3), and in it Irenaeus discusses nine parables (cf. Minns 2012, 56–58):

1. wicked husbandmen (Matt. 21:33–45; *Against Heresies* 4.36.1–4)
2. wedding feast (Matt. 22:1–14; *Against Heresies* 4.36.5–6)
3. prodigal son (Luke 15:11–32; *Against Heresies* 4.36.7)
4. laborers in the vineyard (Matt. 20:1–16; *Against Heresies* 4.36.7)
5. Pharisee and the tax collector (Luke 18:9–14; *Against Heresies* 4.36.8)
6. two sons (Matt. 21:28–32; *Against Heresies* 4.36.8)
7. barren fig tree (Luke 13:6–9; *Against Heresies* 4.36.8)
8. sheep and goats (Matt. 25:31–46; *Against Heresies* 4.40.2)
9. wheat and weeds (Matt. 13:24–30, 36–43; *Against Heresies* 4.40.2)

The first three parables signify that "the prophets were sent from one and the same Father" as the God of Jesus (*Against Heresies* 4.36.5, in *ANF* 1:516), an argument that strikes directly at Marcion's claim that the God of the Hebrew Bible is different from the Christian God. The parable of the wicked husband-men, for example, demonstrates the unity of the God of the "Mosaic dispensation" and the God of Jesus, because it is the same "householder" (Jesus's Father) who sends both his servants (i.e., the prophets) and his son (i.e., Jesus). God now rejects those who rejected the Son of God—those of the "former dispensation to whom the vineyard was formerly entrusted"—and has given the vineyard to the gentiles (the church), who were formerly outside the vineyard (cf. the denunciation of the "former dispensation" in Irenaeus's interpretation of the wedding feast parable, Matt. 22:11–13; *Against Heresies* 4.26.6).

Irenaeus's discussion of the parable of the laborers in the vineyard provides an excellent example of his parable interpretation: the householder is God, and the laborers called at different times of the day demonstrate the continuity between the God of the Hebrew Bible and the Christian God:

> The same God is declared as having called some in the beginning, when the world was first created; but others afterwards, and others during the intermediate period [i.e., the time between Moses and Jesus; cf. *Against Heresies* 4.25.1], others after a long lapse of time, and others again in the end of time; so that there are many workmen in their generations, but only one householder who calls them together. For there is but one vineyard, since there is also but one righteousness, and one dispensator, for there is one Spirit of God who arranges all things; and in like manner is there one hire, for they all received a penny each man, having [stamped upon it] the royal image and superscription, the knowledge of the Son of God, which is immortality. And therefore He began by giving the hire to those [who were engaged] last, because in the last times, when the Lord was revealed He presented Himself to all [as their reward]. (*Against Heresies* 4.36.7, in *ANF* 1:518)

Irenaeus's use of allegory is rather restrained in comparison to other early interpreters, such as the gnostics against whom he writes, and this example does not take interpreters much further down an allegorical path than does the author of Matthew's Gospel. Irenaeus's interpretation of the parable of the good Samaritan, however (*Against Heresies* 3.17.3), lays the foundation for later allegorical interpretations of the parable. Irenaeus implies that the Samaritan represents Jesus, who has compassion on and tends to the wounds of the injured man, who symbolizes the human race. Jesus also pays "two royal *denaria*" to the innkeeper, who represents the Holy Spirit and is our advocate against the "accuser" (i.e., the devil).

Irenaeus was a pioneer in many ways. He emphasized the harmony of the Hebrew Bible and the Christian scriptures, and he was one of the first writers who cited Christian writings as authoritative scripture on the same level as the Hebrew Bible. As Robert Grant notes, Irenaeus used the traditions of his predecessors to refute the gnostics and, in the process, "built up a body of Christian theology that resembled a French Gothic cathedral, strongly supported by columns of biblical faith and tradition, illuminated by vast expanses of exegetical and logical argument, and upheld by flying buttresses of rhetorical and philosophical considerations from the outside. In his own person he united the major traditions of Christendom from Asia Minor, Syria, Rome, and Gaul" (1997, 1). As we shall see, Irenaeus also influenced the biblical interpretation of many Christian authors who came after him, including their interpretations of the parables of Jesus.

The Gospel of Philip (Late Second–Early Third Century)

The Gospel of Philip, the only extant ancient copy of which was discovered at Nag Hammadi, Egypt, in 1945, appears to belong primarily (but not completely) to the most well-known stream of Christian gnosticism, the Valentinian tradition. Valentinus himself was active in Rome (ca. 140–160), and from the fragments of his writings that survive (mostly via Clement and Epiphanius), it seems that Valentinian Christianity blended Platonic, biblical, and gnostic elements into its version of Christianity.

The Gospel of Philip contains approximately seventeen sayings of Jesus, nine of which are found in some form in the New Testament Gospels, but it also includes additional stories, such as the account that Joseph the carpenter made the cross on which Jesus died (Gospel of Philip 73.8–15). A major theme of The Gospel of Philip is the reunification of soul and spirit in a heavenly union that culminates in the identification of the soul with the "true self." This reflects the myth of Sophia (wisdom), who is eager to rejoin her spiritual companion, the Logos (the "Word"), and their reunification is often symbolized by the allegory/metaphor of marriage, which is itself a symbol of knowledge, truth, and freedom (e.g., John 8:32; Gospel of Philip 84.8–9; Meyer 2007, 157–60). One such passage about spiritual love, for example, mentions Luke's parable of the good Samaritan (Gospel of Philip 77.35–78.12):

> Spiritual love is wine and perfume. People who anoint themselves with it enjoy it, and while these people are present, others who are around also enjoy it. If the people who are anointed leave them and go away, the others who are not anointed but are only standing around are stuck with their own bad odor.

> The Samaritan gave nothing to the wounded person except wine and oil—that
> is, only ointment. The ointment healed the wound, for "love covers a multitude
> of sins." (citing 1 Pet. 4:8; Meyer 2007, 181)

This passage alludes only to the Samaritan giving wine and oil to the wounded
person, and it is in a section of The Gospel of Philip that focuses on knowledge
(Greek: *gnōsis*) and love (Greek: *agapē*) in the context of sharing spiritual
love with others: wine and perfume symbolize spiritual love, which is then
compared to the wine and oil of the good Samaritan parable (Turner 1996,
195–96).

This allusion to the parable of the good Samaritan is almost the opposite
of allegorical interpretations offered by such people as Irenaeus or Augustine,
who seek deeper, spiritual meanings in the details of the parable. Instead,
The Gospel of Philip uses what Turner describes as "reverse" allegorization.
It begins with an abstract quality (spiritual love) that then moves to concrete
images (wine and perfume/ointment). Then it places those concrete images
into narrative contexts: (1) perfume, which both the one who wears it and
those who smell it enjoy, and (2) wine and perfume/ointment, which are used
by the good Samaritan on the wounded person. The allusion to the parable is
an integral element of the argumentation, but the point is not interpretation
of Scripture (Turner 1996, 197–98).

The main point appears to be a vital element of the gnostic message:
knowledge of the truth should inspire one to love others who are not yet
spiritually freed by truth so as to assist them in gaining this liberating truth
and attaining spiritual freedom. The Samaritan, like in the parable itself,
serves as an example of how one should act, to "go and do likewise." Yet this
message is given a gnostic slant, because the Samaritan, it seems, becomes
an example of a gnostic Christian with advanced knowledge who loves and
cares for those people who do not yet have this advanced knowledge. The
Samaritan with advanced knowledge offers such "wounded" people the perfume, wine, and oil of the spiritual love inspired by *gnōsis*. Those who lack
such knowledge are "stuck with their own bad odor," so it is necessary for
those who are enlightened to share their perfume/wine/ointment with them
(see Roukema 1999, 68).

Clement of Alexandria (ca. 150–ca. 215)

Alexander the Great founded the city of Alexandria in Egypt in 331 BCE.
During the Roman era, the city was the second largest of the empire, next

to Rome, and it housed the world's most illustrious library. It also was home to a million Jews and, in the Christian era, became one of the great centers of Christianity.

According to the church father Jerome (ca. 347–420), Clement was a presbyter in the church at Alexandria, was "the author of notable volumes, full of eloquence and learning, both in sacred Scripture and in secular literature," and succeeded Pantaenus as the head of the Christian catechetical school in Alexandria (*Lives of Illustrious Men*, chap. 38, in *NPNF*[2] 3:371).

The Christian "school" in Alexandria is known for using typology or allegory to interpret Scripture, an approach also taken by Philo of Alexandria and similar to that of many Greek interpreters of Homer and other ancient works. More than other Alexandrian interpreters, however, Clement can show much interest in the literal words of the biblical text (Cosaert 2008, 23).

An essential element of Clement's biblical interpretation is that he envisions the divine Word (Greek: *logos*) as being active in all nations to prepare the world for the coming of Christ. Thus Clement attempts to integrate faith and reason; Christianity is the fulfillment of both Greek philosophy and the Hebrew Bible. As a result, Clement alludes to a multitude of writings (e.g., Homer, Euripides, and Plato) and argues, as did Philo and Josephus before him, that the best Greek philosophers derive their ideas from Jewish scriptures (see *Miscellanies* 1.5.14, 1.29.1). Clement therefore can discern a divine message in any author, although the divine voice is heard only indirectly in pagan literature or philosophy (see *Miscellanies* 6.8, in *ANF* 2:495, where Clement says that Greek philosophy can be "a stepping-stone to the philosophy which is according to Christ"). The *logos* of God is found more directly in the Hebrew scriptures, but the epitome is, of course, Christian scripture (Cosaert 2008, 21), where Jesus is explicitly declared the Word of God (e.g., John 1:1–18). Thus, like Irenaeus, Clement argues that the Hebrew Bible and the Christian scriptures point to one and the same God.

Clement's interpretations of parables are more understandable after one has read his discussion of the "symbolic" style of poets and philosophers (*Miscellanies* 5.8). Symbolism, including "concealment" and enigma, is used by all who seek the truth—whether Hebrew, Egyptian, Greek, or even "barbarian." Similar to how the secrets of the Jewish temple were restricted to a few, Egyptians, for example, "did not entrust the mysteries they possessed to all and sundry, and did not divulge the knowledge of divine things to the profane" (5.7, in *ANF* 2:454). They instead divulged those mysteries only to royalty and the "worthiest" among the priests.

Symbolism is important, Clement argues, because truth must be concealed from those who might abuse or pollute it. Symbolism also contains more power than simple, direct statements of truth and permits more than one layer of meaning. When Scripture "hides the sense" by using parabolic, symbolic language, it stimulates one to be inquisitive: "ever on the watch for the discovery of the words of salvation" (*Miscellanies* 6.15, in *ANF* 2:509). Therefore, teachers who understand symbolism must be sought so they can discern and explain the truth within it, because God's prophetic Scriptures, which contain the plan of salvation, are filled with metaphors and parables, and Christ the incarnated logos gives us the knowledge by which we can reach the spiritual world beyond our senses. Some people will remain ignorant and unable to understand such enigmatic parables (Matt. 13:13–15, 34; cf. Mark 4:10–12, 33–34), but for those "who have ears to hear," the truth of the Scriptures will be explained (Hägg 2010, 180). So, unlike the gnostics, Clement views *gnōsis* not as a secret teaching revealed and passed on to only a select few; it is a collective truth contained in the Scriptures and the apostolic tradition.

Clement's use of allegory is amply demonstrated in an oration on Passover in which he discusses the prodigal son parable. The prodigal son designates those who have squandered their inheritance from God in a "profligacy of debauchery" (*Fragments* 11, in *ANF* 2:582). These prodigals, however, can return to God, and, in response, God is moved with compassion and bestows glory and honor upon them. The actions of the father in the parable are also symbolic: the best robe denotes the robe of immortality; the ring is a royal signet ring and divine seal of "consecration, signature of glory, pledge of testimony" (citing John 3:33); the shoes are "suited for the journey to heaven," such as the ones put on by those whose feet have been "washed by our Teacher and Lord" (an apparent allusion to John 13:13). Thus the shoes given to the repentant son "are buoyant, and ascending, and waft to heaven, and serve as such a ladder and chariot as he requires who has turned his mind towards the Father."

Clement then argues that the fatted calf killed to celebrate the son's return may be "spoken of as a lamb (not literally)" because it is "the great and greatest" (*Fragments* 11, in *ANF* 2:582). Christ, then, is the fatted calf (lamb), because he is "the Lamb of God who takes away the sin of the world" (John 1:29) and who "was led as a sheep to the slaughter" (Acts 8:32; cf. Isa. 53:7). The sacrifice of the lamb symbolized in the killing of the fatted calf is also symbolic of the Eucharist, because Christ "is both flesh and bread and has given himself as both to us to be eaten." To the "sons" who return to God as Father, God gives them the calf, "and it is slain and eaten." But those who do not return to God, God "pursues and disinherits, and is found to be a most powerful bull," whose "glory is as that of an unicorn" (Num. 23:22) and who gives this strength to those who partake in the Eucharist and are given the power to "butt [their] enemies" (Ps. 44:5).

Clement's *Who Is the Rich Man That Shall Be Saved?* gives a fascinating example of how he intertwines allegorical interpretation with a more literal understanding of a parable. The treatise includes an interpretation of the parable of the good Samaritan as an example story almost completely free from allegorization before offering an allegorical explication of the parable. Clement paraphrases the story about the rich man whom Jesus told to sell all that he had and give to the poor (Mark 10:17–31) but argues that it is not the outward act of giving away one's possessions that Jesus desires; instead, it is "the greater, more godlike, more perfect, the stripping off of the passions from the soul itself," the ridding of one's soul of the lust for money (12, in *ANF* 2:594; cf. Clement's discussions of the parables of the rich man and Lazarus and of the great dinner: possessions themselves are not condemned, but the covetous "inordinate affection" for possessions is condemned; *Miscellanies* 4.6 in *ANF* 2:414). Clement's reasoning also has a practical benefit; rich people should not become destitute—and therefore in need of assistance themselves—but they must help others with their possessions (*Who Is the Rich Man That Shall Be Saved?* 13, in *ANF* 2:594): "How could one give food to the hungry, and drink to the thirsty, clothe the naked, and shelter the houseless, for not doing which he threatens with fire and the outer darkness, if each man first divested himself of all these things?" Clement concludes that although we must "renounce those possessions that are injurious" (15), riches used to benefit our neighbors "are not to be thrown away" (14, in *ANF* 2:595).

In that context, Clement notes that Jesus declares the greatest commandment to be, "Love the Lord your God with all your soul, and with all your strength" (Clement tends to cite biblical passages imprecisely), with the second being, "Love your neighbor as yourself." When the lawyer then asks, "Who is my neighbor?," Jesus does not speak of relatives or fellow citizens or fellow Jews. Instead, Jesus tells a parable about someone who was stabbed and left half dead by robbers, neglected by the priest and Levite, but pitied by the vilified and excommunicated Samaritan. The Samaritan, unlike the others, did not travel by chance, but came with things the wounded man needed to nurse him to health—oil, bandages, a beast of burden, and money for the innkeeper. The point is that the despised Samaritan proved to be the neighbor of the man in distress, and Jesus says to go and do likewise (28, in *ANF* 2:599).

After this discussion of the moral aspects of the story, however, Clement begins to apply the parable to his contemporaries with some allegorized elements. Jesus is the good Samaritan, because he has "pitied us, who by the rulers of darkness were all but put to death with many wounds, fears, lusts, passions, pains, deceits, pleasures." Jesus is the true physician who has "poured wine on our wounded souls . . . , brought the oil which flows from the compassions of the Father, and bestowed it copiously. He it is that produced the ligatures of health and of salvation that cannot be undone" (*Who Is the Rich Man That Shall Be Saved?* 29, in *ANF* 2:599). Jesus thus proves to be the ultimate "neighbor" (Luke 10:36), who heals the wounds of sinful human beings (see Roukema 1999, 61). Clement then closes his treatise by saying that the one who loves Christ will keep his commandments to love God and neighbor (citing Matt. 7:21; 8:16–17; Luke 6:46), including caring for the needy, since Jesus identifies himself with the hungry, thirsty, naked, and sick, the stranger and the prisoner (Matt. 25:34–40).

Clement's contributions to the interpretation of the parables include his understanding of both what parables are and how they function. When Jesus uses such metaphorical descriptions, Clement says, he speaks of a subject that actually is not the main subject but is similar to it. The parable is a more "vigorous" way of presenting the principal subject, and those hearers who understand, who have "ears to hear," are therefore led by the parable to the "true and principal thing" (*Miscellanies* 6.15, in *ANF* 2:509). Through this mode of symbolism, then, the Holy Spirit can speak to Greek and "barbarian" philosophers and other enlightened ones (e.g., *Miscellanies* 1.7; Clement comments on the parable of the sower and illustrates how the preparatory knowledge of God comes through Greek philosophy).

Tertullian (ca. 155–ca. 225)

Tertullian evidently was raised as a non-Christian in Carthage in Africa and converted to Christianity after witnessing the courage of Christian martyrs. Eusebius claims that Tertullian was "well versed in the laws of the Romans" (*Church History* 2.2.4, in *NPNF*[2] 1:106), but the legal terminology in his writings may simply derive from Tertullian's rhetorical brilliance.

Because Tertullian was a rhetorician engaged in vigorous debates with his opponents, his interpretation of Scripture is sometimes contingent on the necessities of the dispute in which he finds himself (Dunn 2010, 155). Like Irenaeus, Tertullian argues from the "rule of faith" found in Scripture: the essential doctrines of authentic apostolic tradition. The church determines the rightful use of Scripture, and authority is bestowed through apostolic succession from Christ through the apostles to the bishops of the church. Tertullian also uses Scripture as testimony against the speculative doctrines of others (e.g., gnostics), and his concise, unadorned writing style exudes certitude. Although he recognizes the presence of allegory in Scripture, Tertullian's use of it is restrained; the allegorical is used only after the literal is demonstrated to be inadequate (*Against Marcion* 3.5; McKim 2007, 965), a restraint partly due to the gnostics' extensive use of allegory (see *On the Resurrection of the Flesh* 63).

Tertullian argues, however, that some biblical passages do not permit a literal reading: "Very many events are figuratively predicted by means of enigmas and allegories and parables, and . . . they must be understood in a sense different from the literal description" (*Against Marcion* 3.5, in *ANF* 3:324). Joel 3:18 ("The mountains shall drip sweet wine, the hills shall flow with milk"), for example, does not mean that the mountains actually will drip wine and that milk will flow down from the hills. Even when such metaphorical elements occur, though, the literal can still be critically important (see *On the Resurrection of the Flesh* 30).

An example of Tertullian's use of the parables (against Marcion) to demonstrate the oneness of God, the continuity between the Hebrew and Christian scriptures, and the authority of the apostolic tradition may be found in his brief discussion of the wheat and weeds parable. In *The Prescription against Heretics*, Tertullian interprets the parable in a relatively simple figurative sense: the apostolic "truth" has priority over the heretical "falseness," as evidenced by the Lord sowing "the good seed of the wheat" first. Only later is the crop "adulterated" by the "useless weed of the wild oats" that is sown by the "enemy the devil" (chap. 31, "Truth First, Falsehood Afterwards, as Its Perversion", in *ANF* 3:258). Since Tertullian, like Irenaeus, believes in the coherence and noncontradiction of Scripture, any apparently relevant passage in Scripture may be used to interpret another passage. Therefore, Tertullian can connect the seed in the parable of the sower with the wheat seed in this parable to argue that the seed designates the word of God in both:

> For herein is figuratively described the difference of doctrines, since in other passages also the word of God is likened unto seed. From the actual order, therefore, it becomes clear, that that which was first delivered is of the Lord and is true, whilst that is strange and false which was afterwards introduced. This sentence will keep its ground in opposition to all later heresies, which have no consistent quality of kindred knowledge inherent in them—to claim the truth as on their side. (*The Prescription against Heretics*, chap. 31, in *ANF* 3:258)

In contrast to Clement's more optimistic view about Greek philosophy, Tertullian often blames philosophy for the errors of the gnostics, as indicated by his famous words, "What indeed has Athens to do with Jerusalem?" (*The Prescription against Heretics*, chap. 7, in *ANF* 3:246). Christians are to be on guard against "philosophy," which corrupts the truth and includes "repugnant" heresies (chap. 7). In the same vein, Tertullian demonstrates his disdain for gnostic allegorical interpretations in his discussion of the wise and foolish bridesmaids (Tertullian uses "virgins") parable. He blames Plato for the gnostics' error of separating the corporeal aspects of existence from the spiritual in their interpretation of the parable:

> It is from this philosophy that [the gnostics and Valentinians] eagerly adopt the difference between the bodily senses and the intellectual faculties,—a distinction which they actually apply to the parable of the ten virgins: making the five foolish virgins to symbolize the five bodily senses, seeing that these are so silly and so easy to be deceived; and the wise virgin to express the meaning of the intellectual faculties, which are so wise as to attain to that mysterious and supernal truth, which is placed in the pleroma. (*A Treatise on the Soul*, chap. 18, in *ANF* 3:198)

Tertullian concludes that both the interpretation of this parable and the philosophy behind the interpretation are faulty and asks, "Why adopt such excruciating means of torturing simple knowledge and crucifying the truth?" (*A Treatise on the Soul*, chap. 18, in *ANF* 3:198).

Tertullian's approach to parable interpretation is evident in his discussion of several parables in book 4 of *Against Marcion*. He again stresses, like Irenaeus, the continuity between the God of the Hebrew Bible and Jesus despite Marcion's claims otherwise (4.19, 25, 26, 28). The parable of the great dinner (Luke 14:16–24), for example, illustrates the continuity between Jesus's parables and the teaching of the Hebrew Bible prophets (4.29), because Jesus's advice to invite the poor mirrors that of Isaiah 58:7. Yet the parable is also symbolic of God's "dispensations of mercy and grace" in salvation history: the preparation for the dinner "is no doubt a figure of the abundant provision of eternal life," and the Jewish people were the first ones invited to the dinner. Despite God's invitations in the Hebrew scriptures, though, the Jewish people refuse to respond (e.g., Jer. 7:23–24), so God invites people "from the highways and the hedges," who denote the "Gentile strangers" (*Against Marcion* 4.31, in *ANF* 3:401–2), an invitation to God's dinner that, Tertullian argues, is also reflected in the Hebrew scriptures (e.g., Deut. 32:21–22).

The three "lost" parables of Luke 15—sheep, coin, and prodigal son—are among Tertullian's favorites, and in the next chapter (*Against Marcion* 4.32), he cites the parables of the lost sheep and the lost coin (Luke 15:1–10) to argue against Marcion's view of Jesus as not sent by the same God as the one in the Hebrew Bible. Human beings cannot be the ones searching for what is lost, contra Marcion, because, in reality, the lost sheep and the lost coin both symbolize human beings who are "the property of none other than the Creator" (the God of the Hebrew Bible) (4.32, in *ANF* 3:402). God is the Creator ("owner") of human beings, so God looks for the lost, finds them, and rejoices over their recovery. Thus Tertullian's figurative interpretation of these two parables does not go beyond their meaning in the context of Luke's Gospel.

Tertullian also discusses the "lost" parables to offer guiding principles for parable interpretation in his work *On Modesty*. His treatment of the parable of the lost sheep, for example, is guided by its context in Luke: "The Pharisees were muttering in indignation at the Lord's admitting to his society heathen publicans and sinners, and communicating with them in food." Therefore, Tertullian concludes, the lost sheep designates "the lost heathen," not a Christian who was restored (chap. 7, in *ANF* 4:80). Numerous interpreters before and after Tertullian argue that the "sheep" designates a Christian, the "flock" represents the church, the "good shepherd" is Jesus, and the lost sheep is a Christian who has gone astray from the church. Tertullian disagrees with this interpretation: "In that case, you make the Lord to have given no answer to the Pharisees' muttering, but to your presumption." Also, from the context in Luke, Jesus calls the remaining flock the "righteous," and by that he means not Christians but the "Jews"; Jesus was "refuting them, because they were indignant at the hope of the heathens" (chap. 7, in *ANF* 4:80).

Likewise, Tertullian writes, most interpreters of the parable of the prodigal son incorrectly argue that the elder brother represents the Jews and the younger brother represents Christians (*On Modesty*, chap. 8). That cannot be the case, Tertullian points out, because the parable indicates that the elder brother claims to have never transgressed his father's precepts (Tertullian assumes the elder son's claim is accurate). The Jews, however, had transgressed the law of God, so the elder brother cannot represent them; he represents Christians. Instead of following the path that the parable naturally bids interpreters to follow, some interpreters have invented "allegorical gestures to their ditties, giving expression to such as are far different from the immediate plot, and scene, and character." The "heretics" do this, Tertullian charges, because their interpretations of the parables are predetermined by their theological presuppositions: "Loosed as they are from the constraints of the rule of truth, they have had leisure, of course, to search into and put together those things of which the parables seem (to be symbolical)" (chap. 8, in *ANF* 4:82).

Faced with that problem, Tertullian then offers some "general principles of parabolic interpretation" (*On Modesty*, chap. 9, in *ANF* 4:82). Interpreters should not "twist all things" in their expositions, should avoid contradictions, and should not overextend allegorical meanings into every detail of a parable, because "curious niceties of this kind . . . , by the subtlety of forced explanations, generally lead [one] away from the truth. There are, moreover, some points which are just simply introduced with a view to the structure and disposition and texture of the parable, in order that they may be worked up throughout to the end for which the typical example is being provided" (chap. 9, in *ANF* 4:82).

How does this approach apply to the parable of the prodigal son? The context demands, Tertullian says, that the three "lost " parables have the same basic meaning and speak to the same problem: the "grumbling" of the Pharisees and scribes about Jesus welcoming and eating with sinners (Luke 15:1–2). Tertullian also invokes the historical context to argue that the "publicans" signified "heathens" (non-Jews): "If any doubts that in the land of Judea, subjugated as it had been long since by the hand of Pompey and of Lucullus, the publicans were heathens, let him read Deuteronomy: 'There shall be no tribute-weigher of the sons of Israel'" (*On Modesty*, chap. 9, in *ANF* 4:82). In addition, Tertullian reasons that Jesus would not have been criticized for eating with Jews but only for eating with "heathens, from whose board the Jewish discipline excludes (its disciples)" (chap. 9, in *ANF* 4:83).

The younger brother cannot symbolize Christians who wander away from God, squandering such gifts as baptism, the Holy Spirit, and eternal hope, because then "the whole 'substance' of the sacrament is most truly wasted away." An apostate cannot recover the "garment" (the robe of the Holy Spirit) and the "ring" (the sign and seal of baptism), because then "Christ will again be slaughtered" (*On Modesty*, chap. 9, in *ANF* 4:83). If that were true, Christians would not be afraid to "squander" what they could easily recover, because such security whets an appetite for sin.

Instead of these false interpretations, Tertullian wants to recover the meaning intended by Jesus: "Our interpretation shall be simply governed with an eye to the object the Lord had in view" (*On Modesty*, chap. 9, in *ANF* 4:83). Jesus came to save the perishing, so, as noted above, the younger brother designates both unbelieving gentiles who wander in ignorance, error, and sin (although they should have known better; cf. Rom. 1:21) and Jews who grumble against those converting to Christ. Although they had received wisdom from God, the Jewish people "squandered it" through their moral failings and handed themselves over to "the prince of this world." Then, lacking the sustenance of "vital food," they saw Christians engaged in God's work, and the heathen then "remember[ed]" that God was their Father. They returned to the father to receive "again" what they had lost through the transgression of Adam and to feed on the "'fatness' of the Lord's body,—the Eucharist" (chap. 9, in *ANF* 4:83). It is thus the heathen who returned to God and who become objects of envy: "Of course it is immediately over the *first* calling of the Christian that the Jew groans, not over his *second* restoration: for the former reflects its rays even upon the heathen; but the latter, which takes place in the churches, is not known even to the Jews" (chap. 9, in *ANF* 4:84).

Parables, in their literal and metaphorical interpretations, serve as an important resource in Tertullian's rhetorical arguments. He is an exceptional apologist for Christianity, interpreter of Scripture, and polemicist against those he perceives to be heretics. Through his interpretations of parables and other Scriptures, Tertullian advocates a rigorous, uncompromising Christianity, and his writings advise Christians to separate themselves from pagans to avoid contaminating themselves with pagan idolatry and immorality.

Origen (ca. 185–254)

Many scholars consider Origen of Alexandria to be the church's first systematic theologian and one of the foremost interpreters of the Bible. In addition, Origen's voluminous writings increased the church's intellectual interaction with its Greco-Roman contexts. Origen was no stranger to controversy, however, and his works were later condemned as heresy (e.g., in 400 CE at a church council in Alexandria; MacCulloch 2009, 150).

Jerome reports that Origen's father was martyred for being a Christian when Origen was a teenager. The family—Origen, his mother, and his six brothers—subsequently lived in poverty, because the family's property was confiscated. Jerome speaks approvingly of Origen's fame and brilliance, especially in the study of Scripture. Origen was one of the few Christian interpreters who learned Hebrew, for example, so he could work with the Hebrew scriptures and not just the Septuagint, the Greek translation of the Hebrew Bible. Although Jerome later renounces Origen's theology as heretical, he praises Origen's "immortal genius" in understanding "dialectics, as well as geometry, arithmetic, music, grammar, and rhetoric" (*Lives of Illustrious Men*, chap. 54, in *NPNF*[2] 3:374; cf. Eusebius, *Church History* 6.2.5–9).

Origen believes that behind the simple, obvious, and literal meaning of a word or text exists a deeper, concealed, and spiritual connotation that one should strive to determine, one that can be seen only through the wisdom granted by the Holy Spirit:

> The Scriptures were written by the Spirit of God, and have a meaning, not such only as is apparent at first sight, but also another, which escapes the notice of most. For those (words) which are written are the forms of certain mysteries, and the images of divine things. Respecting which there is one opinion throughout the whole Church, that the whole law is indeed spiritual; but that the spiritual

meaning which the law conveys is not known to all, but to those only on whom the grace of the Holy Spirit is bestowed in the word of wisdom and knowledge. (*On First Principles* 1.preface.8, in *ANF* 4:241)

The Scriptures are divinely inspired—the Holy Spirit infuses every verse, word, and letter—and we cannot trust their interpretation to the human senses alone, since sometimes "it was the design of the Holy Spirit, in those portions which appear to relate the history of events, rather to cover and conceal the meaning," just like Jesus says the kingdom of heaven is "like a treasure hid in a field" (*On First Principles* 4.1.23, citing Matt. 13:44, in *ANF* 4:373). When, for example, the literal sense of a text cannot be true (e.g., the account in Genesis 1 is physically impossible: the first three days of creation have evenings and mornings before the sun, moon, and stars were created; 4.1.16), interpreters must understand the text on a deeper, symbolic level. This spiritual interpretation is especially necessary, he says, when Scripture attributes human emotions to God, such as when God is described as angry or destroying a city with fire (as in the parable of the wedding feast, Matt. 22:1–14): "We do not take such expressions literally, but seek in them a spiritual meaning, that we may think of God as he deserves to be thought of" (i.e., "God . . . is to be regarded as wholly free from all affections of that kind"; 2.4.4, in *ANF* 4:278).

Most biblical texts have a literal sense, but every biblical text has a deeper, hidden truth, and allegory is Origen's primary means to ascertain this deeper, spiritual meaning (and, to some extent, explain difficult or apparently ethically unappealing passages). Thus Origen is especially concerned about the spiritual meaning of biblical texts—and he sometimes mocks "simple," literal understandings—but he does not ignore the literal sense. He most often starts with the "literal" meaning before he interprets a text's "spiritual" meaning.

Origen's commentary on Matthew illustrates his typical pattern of interpreting parables. In his discussion on the treasure hidden in a field, for example, Origen first distinguishes between a *parable* and a *similitude*, because this saying and the two that follow (concerning the pearl and the net) actually are similitudes:

Some one will then say, "If they are not really parables, what are they?" Shall we then say in keeping with the diction of the Scripture that they are similitudes (comparisons)? Now a similitude differs from a parable. . . . The similitude seems to be generic, and the parable specific. And perhaps also as the similitude, which is the highest genus of the parable, contains the parable as one of its species, so it contains that particular form of similitude which has the same name as the genus. (*Commentary on Matthew* 10.4, in *ANF* 9:415–16)

Origen notes that the text says that Jesus told parables to the multitudes and did not explain to them "the secrets of the kingdom of heaven" (Matt. 13:11). Jesus, though, tells these three similitudes to explain things clearly to the disciples. The field in the parable of the treasure in the field, for example, signifies Scripture, since the words of wisdom planted in it (e.g., the law and the prophets) are "concealed and lying under that which is manifest." But, according to Colossians 2:3, the real hidden treasure is Jesus, "in whom are all the treasures of wisdom and knowledge hidden" (*Commentary on Matthew* 10.5, in *ANF* 9:416).

Origen's discussion of the second similitude, the pearl of great value, illustrates how seriously he can interpret a text's "literal" meaning, because he begins with a detailed examination of how pearls are formed. He then carefully delineates differences between types of pearls and concludes that the best pearls are from India, especially ones that are "rounded off on the outer surface, very white in colour, very translucent, and very large in size" (*Commentary on Matthew* 10.7, in *ANF* 9:417). Origen's lengthy examination allows him to conclude that Jesus was well informed about the differences in pearls, a fact that helps us understand the similitude better. The deeper spiritual import, according to Origen, is that the Hebrew Bible prophets are symbolized by the "mussels which conceive the dew of heaven, and become pregnant with the word of truth from heaven, the goodly pearls which, according to the phrase here set forth, the merchantman seeks. And the leader of the pearls . . . is the very costly pearl, the Christ of God, the Word which is superior to the precious letters and thoughts in the law and the prophets" (10.8, in *ANF* 9:417–18). The other types of less valuable pearls, however, such as cloudy or darkened ones, are the words of the "heterodox," and "perhaps the muddy words and the heresies which are bound up with works of the flesh, are the darkened pearls, and those which are produced in the marshes, not goodly pearls" (10.8, in *ANF* 9:418). Human beings, to progress into spiritual maturity, must have instruction "corresponding to the very costly pearl" (10.9–10, citing Phil. 3:8, "the excellency of the knowledge of Christ," in *ANF* 9:418).

Origen begins his interpretation of the third similitude—the parable of the net (Matt. 13:47–50)—by noting that the two things being compared in similitudes are not alike in every respect, but only in "those features which are required by the argument in hand" (*Commentary on Matthew* 10.11; cf. 10.13, in *ANF* 9:419: "Parables and similitudes are not to be accepted in respect of all the things to which they are likened or compared, but only in respect of some things"). Therefore, Origen argues, the words about the net catching "fish of every kind" do not symbolize the holy and the evil. "All the

Scriptures" oppose that reading, because human beings have free will, and "we are responsible" for our "voluntary choice" to be good or evil.

How, then, should this similitude be interpreted? Origen declares that it not only incorporates the "varied character" of the actions of human beings, both of virtue and vice, but that it also refers to the "Old and the New Scripture which is woven of thoughts of all kinds and greatly varied" (e.g., the "prophetic net" of Isaiah, Jeremiah, or Daniel; the "gospel net"; or the "apostolic net"). Jesus, the "master of the net," is the one who casts the net into the sea, in which swim "the bitter affairs of life" (10.12, in *ANF* 9:420). It was only after Jesus's ministry that this net was filled, and it now includes the "calling of the Gentiles from every race." Jesus and the angels will draw out the net, and, as the parable of the wheat and the weeds demonstrates, "the angels are to be entrusted with the power to distinguish and separate the evil from the righteous" (10.12, citing Matt. 13:42, in *ANF* 9:420).

Origen's quest for the deeper meaning of parables can be illustrated by his fascinating interpretation of the parable of the laborers in the vineyard. Similar to Irenaeus's approach, Origen's involves first identifying the different agreements the owner makes at different times with laborers for the vineyard; these different agreements represent different dispensations in history, specifically the covenants made with Adam, Noah, Abraham, Moses, and now Jesus Christ (*Commentary on Matthew* 15.32).

Origen then adduces that the various agreements in the parable also represent the hierarchy of one's spiritual senses: touch (Adam's covenant and the "touch" of Gen. 3:3), smell (Noah's covenant and the smell of Gen. 8:21), taste (Abraham's covenant and the meal of Gen. 18:8), hearing (Moses's covenant, where Moses hears God speaking to him in Exodus), and sight, the highest of the senses (the covenant of Jesus and the disciples seeing him; e.g., Matt. 13:16; *Commentary on Matthew* 15.33). After identifying the five covenants/agreements with the five human senses, Origen, as he tends to do, develops additional aspects of this interpretation. The workers hired at different times, for example, need specific skills for their particular dispensation. The most recent workers are critical, because their work in the last dispensation demands a fresh new calling to the "work of the new covenant"—completing "the remaining work of the vineyard" (15.34, cited by Heine 2010, 248). All the workers, no matter when they were called, receive a denarius, the "coin of salvation." But all the ones called must do the work of the kingdom to receive the denarius of salvation; no one "who fails to do the works of the kingdom" is sent into the vineyard (the kingdom of heaven; Heine 2010, 248).

The fact that some workers stand idle in the marketplace until they are called at five o'clock (Matt. 20:9) gives Origen the opportunity to postulate that this aspect of the parable hints at the preexistence of the soul (*Commentary on Matthew* 15.34–35). Origen disassociates himself, however, from the doctrine of reincarnation or transmigration of souls (16.17; cf. *Homily on Jeremiah* 16.1; see Hanson 1959, 217). He then applies the parable to the life of the church, where the vineyard represents the church, and the time of day the workers are hired could represent their ages when they become Christians (cf. John Chrysostom below): those workers hired at dawn symbolize people who converted in childhood; those hired later symbolize, respectively, those converted during adolescence, during young adulthood, during old age, and at the point of death (or apostates returning to the church; *Commentary on Matthew* 15.37; see Daniélou 1955, 197–99; cf. Heine 2010, 249).

Origen's allegorical approach to the parable of the good Samaritan is especially significant, because it influences many later interpreters. In Homily 34 on Luke, for example, Origen observes that Jewish law has many precepts but Jesus in Luke prescribes only two: to love God with all your heart, soul, strength, and mind, and to love your neighbor as yourself. Similarly, in the parable, the only person who proved to be a neighbor was the Samaritan, who "willed [himself] to keep the commandments and prepare himself to be a neighbor to every one who needs help" (*Homilies on Luke* 34.2, trans. Lienhard 1996, 138).

Origen then summarizes how one of the "elders" interpreted the parable symbolically: the injured man is Adam, Jerusalem is paradise, and Jericho is the world. The robbers are hostile powers, the priest is the law, the Levite the prophets, and the Samaritan is Jesus. The wounds symbolize our disobedience, the animal is Jesus's body, the inn/stable is the church, and the innkeeper is the head of the church, to whom the two denarii (symbolizing the Father and the Son) are given. This interpretation also includes some additional symbolism not found previously in Irenaeus and Clement, such as the Samaritan's promised return symbolizing the forthcoming return (Greek: *parousia*) of Jesus (Homily 34.3). Another key difference is that the innkeeper represents the head of the church in this interpretation, instead of the Holy Spirit (Irenaeus) or angels (Clement), but the basic similarity (Christ = Samaritan) remains.

Origen finds much of the "elder's" allegorical interpretation to be reasonable, but he notes that it cannot apply to every human being, since not everyone "goes down from Jerusalem to Jericho" (*Homilies on Luke* 34.4, trans. Lienhard 1996, 138). Origen observes that the name Samaritan means "guardian" (cf. his *Commentary on John* 22.316–20), which implies that the Samaritan designates Jesus (he cites, as does Augustine later, Ps. 121:5 as evidence: "The Lord is your guardian"). Like Clement before him, Origen notices that the Samaritan, unlike the priest and Levite, did not travel the road by chance (Luke 10:33). The Samaritan, therefore, intentionally went to save the man, and he came prepared with bandages, oil, and wine, but not for that one man alone. The Samaritan also carried those items "on behalf of others who, for various reasons, had been wounded and needed bandages, oil, and wine" (*Homilies on Luke* 34.5–6, trans. Lienhard 1996, 139–40). After spending a day and night with the wounded man, the Samaritan entrusted the innkeeper, who symbolizes "the angel of the church," to bring the man fully back to health (34.8, trans. Lienhard 1996, 140).

Origen closes by exhorting his hearers "to imitate Christ and to pity those who 'have fallen among thieves.' We can go to them, bind their wounds, pour in oil and wine, put them on our own beasts, and bear their burdens." Jesus encourages us to do so, because his words to the lawyer to "go and do likewise" are meant for all human beings, not just that lawyer, so they may "obtain eternal life" (*Homilies on Luke* 34.9, trans. Lienhard 1996, 141).

In all of his biblical interpretations, including those of the parables, Origen labors diligently to find the spiritual treasures hidden in Scripture. He uses the allegorical method extensively to unearth those spiritual treasures, and that approach—commonly used but usually not as imaginatively as Origen—became the preferred one for many interpreters for centuries afterward, long after Origen himself fell out of favor.

John Chrysostom (ca. 347–407)

John Chrysostom was born in Antioch (in Syria) and studied law with the great pagan orator Libanius, but then felt drawn to Christian monasticism and studied with a Syrian monastic for four years. During this period he practiced severe austerities (e.g., living in a cave for two years), which undermined his health for the rest of his life. Chrysostom was ordained as deacon in 381, ordained as priest (presbyter) in 386, and, against his wishes, was appointed bishop of Constantinople in 398. As bishop, Chrysostom set out to reform the corruption he saw in Constantinople. He also became embroiled in imperial and ecclesiastical controversies and eventually was condemned to exile (in 404), where he died in 407 (Kelly 1995, 285).

Over nine hundred of Chrysostom's exegetical homilies are extant. In these sermons, he rails against the abuses of the wealthy and speaks words of comfort to the poor. A gifted orator—*chrysostōmos* in Greek means "golden-mouthed"—Chrysostom was the greatest preacher and one of the foremost expositors of Scripture in the patristic era. Two concerns are primary in his homilies: discerning the will of God through a rigorous reading of Scripture and urging his congregation to follow those biblical teachings, especially by taking care of the less fortunate within society.

Most of Chrysostom's parable expositions are found in his homilies from the Gospel of Matthew, and they usually follow a similar format. He begins by discussing the historical setting of Matthew and its author, as well as the major themes and overall structure of the book. Individual homilies on particular passages begin with a reading and detailed exposition of the passage, including placing the passage into its literary context. He then focuses on the flow and logic of the passage, such as key terms and its meaning in its historical context. Finally, Chrysostom turns to his own audience, exhorting his congregation to apply the text's meaning in their daily lives (McKim 2007, 572).

Chrysostom's understanding of the parable of the sower, for example, first places the parable within its literary context. Matthew says that Jesus told the people "many things in parables" (Matt. 13:3), whereas in the earlier Sermon on the Mount, Jesus spoke more clearly and plainly. That is because, Chrysostom says, the audience for the Sermon on the Mount was "simple people," whereas this audience for the sower parable also included scribes and Pharisees (cf. Matt. 13:12–15 concerning the parables and those who "do not understand"). Jesus begins with the sower parable to make "the hearer more attentive," to "rouse" hearers' minds, and to "make his discourse more vivid, and fix the memory of it in them more perfectly, and bring the things before their sight." This approach, Chrysostom adds, is similar to the approach of the prophets (*Homilies on Matthew* 44.3, in NPNF[1] 10:281).

Chrysostom basically follows an interpretation of the sower parable similar to what is found in Matthew 13:18–23: Jesus is the sower who sows the "word of godliness" (his "doctrine") on the land, the "souls of men." Three parts of the sown seed perish, and one part is saved, but Chrysostom absolves the sower (Jesus) of blame for the seeds that perish by focusing on the seeds: the parable does not say that the sower cast the seeds "by the way side" but that the seeds "fell," which places the responsibility upon the type of ground on which the seeds fell, not on the actions of the sower.

Chrysostom connects this parable to Jesus's audience in Matthew, by saying that Jesus taught the parable to everyone "without grudging," just as the sower makes no distinction in the types of land on which he sows the seed: "[The sower] simply and indifferently casts his seed; so [Jesus] too makes no distinction of rich and poor, of wise and unwise, of slothful or diligent, of brave or cowardly; but he discourses unto all, fulfilling his part, although foreknowing the results; that it may be in His power to say, 'What ought I to have done, that I have not done?' (Isa. 5:4)." Obedience to Jesus's commands is the key to producing fruits of the kingdom (*Homilies on Matthew* 44.4, in *NPNF*[1] 10:281).

Thus Jesus's disciples should not despair if their hearers fail to respond positively to their gospel message, because the same thing happened to Jesus. He (fore)knew that many would not respond, but kept on sowing the seeds of the kingdom anyway. Chrysostom then admits that it is reasonable to question why a sower would sow seed on soil among thorns, on rock, and on the wayside, all of which seem never likely to produce fruit. The reason is that Chrysostom believes that soil can change, just like human beings can change and respond positively to the good news of the kingdom:

> There is such a thing as the rock changing, and becoming rich land; and the wayside being no longer trampled on, nor lying open to all that pass by, but that it may be a fertile field; and the thorns may be destroyed, and the seed enjoy full security. For had it been impossible, this Sower [Jesus] would not have sown. And if the change did not take place in all, this is no fault of the Sower, but of them who are unwilling to be changed: He having done his part: and if they betrayed what they received of him, he is blameless, the exhibitor of such love to man. (*Homilies on Matthew* 44.4, in *NPNF*[1] 10:281–82)

Chrysostom concludes that the parable teaches that one's faith must be put into practice: people who hear the word and respond must become free from gluttony, envy, lust, pride, and the deceitfulness of riches. We also must cultivate virtues, "striking our roots deep" (44.7, in *NPNF*[1] 10:290).

The parable of the wheat and weeds explains what happens to the seeds in the sower parable that survive and flourish—even those fruitful seeds suffer great damage because of the weeds the devil plants in the field. Chrysostom then connects a third "nature" parable in Matthew 13 to explain the larger meaning: Jesus tells the parable of the mustard seed to encourage his hearers, since that parable demonstrates that God's message will be victorious in the end, that "the gospel shall be spread abroad" (46.2, in *NPNF*[1] 10:289).

Once again, Chrysostom focuses on the positive. Jesus uses nature to illustrate his message so often because nature follows a set course: the sower sows, crops appear, and then comes the harvest. Such parables imply that the same inevitability applies to Jesus's message about the kingdom; certain events "cannot fail to take place" (46.2, in *NPNF*[1] 10:289).

In his next homily Chrysostom notes that although Jesus's parables are designed to perplex his audience and to stimulate them to inquire further, some people, such as the scribes, do not pose a single question or follow Jesus to "his house" to learn more (*Homilies on Matthew* 47; cf. Matt. 13:36).

Jesus explains further only after his disciples ask him questions, and Jesus's interpretation of the parable of the sower illustrates that parables, because of their nature, "must not be explained throughout word for word, since many absurdities will follow" (47.1, in *NPNF*[1] 10:292). Chrysostom thus permits a limited amount of allegorical speculation on the meaning of the parables, and he usually does not travel far beyond the allegorical paths the Gospel authors themselves provide.

The parable of the laborers in the vineyard (*Homilies on Matthew* 64) is puzzling at first, according to Chrysostom, because the saying before and after the parable (first/last; Matt. 19:30; 20:16) seems to be at odds with what happens in the parable (where all are equal; 64.3). Chrysostom then offers a restrained (compared to Augustine and others) allegorical reading of the parable. The vineyard denotes the commandments of God, the time worked signifies one's life span, the various laborers indicate the different ways to follow those commands, and the hours at which the laborers are hired indicate those "who at different ages [i.e., from young to old] have drawn near to God." The first workers, who complain about their pay, are like the elder son in the parable of the prodigal son, who complains about the father's reception of the younger son. Those who complain, then, serve as a warning for longtime Christians not to envy how "latecomers" are treated. Once we learn the reason why the parable was composed this way, however, we should not speculate about anything further ("we must not be curious about all the points in the parables"; 64.3, in *NPNF*[1] 10:394). Chrysostom therefore seeks to ascertain the central and essential points of the parables, tries to focus on those elements alone, and cautions against overspeculating about other details of the parables.

Since Matthew's parable of the wedding feast clearly exhibits allegorical elements not found in Luke's version, Chrysostom decides that it "proclaims beforehand both the casting out of the Jews, and the calling of the Gentiles; and it indicates together with this also the strictness of the life required, and how great the punishment appointed for the careless" (*Homilies on Matthew* 69.1, *NPNF*[1] 10:421). Both the literary context (e.g., Matt. 21:33) and the symbolic elements within Matthew's version (e.g., the king, son, wedding banquet, troops burning the city, and the addition to the story in verses 11–13) lead to Chrysostom's conclusions, as do other verses from the Gospels (e.g., Jesus's commands before the resurrection for the apostles to preach to the Jews and after the resurrection to preach to "all nations"; 69.2).

A notable element in Chrysostom's parable interpretations is the necessity of almsgiving and other righteous deeds, such as in his homily on the parables of the wise and foolish virgins and of the talents:

> These parables are like the former parable of the faithful servant, and of him
> that was ungrateful and devoured his Lord's goods. For there are four in all, in
> different ways admonishing us about the same things, I mean about diligence in
> almsgiving, and about helping our neighbor by all means which we are able to
> use, since it is not possible to be saved in another way. But there he speaks more
> generally of all assistance which should [be] rendered to one's neighbor; but as
> to the virgins, he speaks particularly of mercifulness in alms, and more strongly
> than in the former parable. (*Homilies on Matthew* 78.1, in *NPNF*¹ 10:470)

In the parable of the talents, the servant was punished for committing evil
deeds, but in the parable of the wise and foolish virgins punishment comes
upon those who sin by omission, specifically not helping the needy. Here, perhaps because of his commitment to Christians' responsibility to aid the poor,
Chrysostom is more willing to include allegorical readings, such as equating
the "lamps" in the parable with the "gift itself of virginity, the purity of holiness," and the oil for the lamps symbolizing "humanity, almsgiving, succor to
them that are in need" (78.1, in *NPNF*¹ 10:470). This line of interpretation,
also suggested by Jerome, connects faith with works. All the virgins have
"faith," but the ones who have enough oil exhibit their faith through works,
which means that only those Christians whose works demonstrate their faith
will be admitted into the kingdom of heaven (see Wailes 1987, 179).

The parable of the talents reinforces Christians' responsibility to help the
poor and needy, as Chrysostom seeks to show:

> Knowing then these things, let us contribute alike wealth, and diligence, and
> protection, and all things for our neighbor's advantage. For the talents here
> are each person's ability, whether in the way of protection, or in money, or in
> teaching, or in what thing soever of the kind. Let no man say, I have but one
> talent, and can do nothing; for you can even by one approve yourself. For you
> are not poorer than that widow; you are not more uninstructed than Peter and
> John, who were both "unlearned and ignorant men"; but nevertheless, since they
> showed forth a zeal, and did all things for the common good, they attained to
> heaven. For nothing is so pleasing to God, as to live for the common advantage.
> For this end God gave us speech, and hands, and feet, and strength of body,
> and mind, and understanding, that we might use all these things, both for our
> own salvation, and for our neighbor's advantage. (*Homilies on Matthew* 78.3,
> in *NPNF*¹ 10:472)

Jesus commands us to help our neighbors in need, so the mere fact that our
neighbors are in need should be sufficient reason for us to help them. But
Chrysostom points to the parable of the sheep and goats to construct what

should be the strongest reason of all: when you help someone in need, you are helping Jesus, the one who gave his life to save you (79.2).

Chrysostom is an excellent example of the more "restrained" exegesis of what is called the "Antiochene" school, in contrast with the more allegorical interpretations of the "Alexandrian" school (e.g., Origen). As this chapter illustrates, however, that general distinction should not be overdrawn. Although allegorical readings were more extensive in places like Alexandria, most scholars now acknowledge that "figural representation belonged to all forms of early Christian exegesis" (F. Young 1997, 259). Some allegorized interpretations of parables are already found in the Gospels themselves, so even those interpreters who, like Chrysostom, focus more on literal meanings will include some allegorized, "spiritual" interpretations. Chrysostom in particular focuses on how the ethical teachings of Jesus should be applied concretely in one's life.

Augustine (354–430)

Augustine was the most influential theologian of Western Christianity in antiquity. Born at Thagaste (in modern Algeria), Augustine traveled a long, complex journey to Christianity. His *Confessions* is the first Christian autobiography, and, among other things, the narrative covers his early, "muddy cravings of the flesh" and the awakening of his spiritual aspirations by reading Cicero's *Hortensius*, which led to his nine years as a Manichaean. Augustine relates his decisive turning to Christianity, which occurred in Milan, where in a garden in July 386 he heard a voice tell him to "take up and read" the New Testament (he specifically read Rom. 13:13). When Augustine returned to Africa, he organized a lay ascetic community in Thagaste with some of his friends. Four years later, against his will, Augustine was ordained a priest in the nearby town of Hippo, and in 396 became bishop of Hippo. He would never leave Africa again (Gowler 2014, 9).

Augustine wrote voluminous numbers of letters, sermons, commentaries, and other books (e.g., *On the Trinity*) that exerted a tremendous influence throughout the history of the church. He also engaged in numerous controversies with such groups as the Donatists, Arians, Manichaeans, and Pelagians, and his parable interpretations are part of his repertoire in these debates.

Most of Augustine's parable interpretations are found in his homilies on the Gospels, such as his interpretation of the parable of the laborers in the vineyard. Like Origen, Augustine agrees that the calling of the workers at different times of the day is symbolic of times during human life spans. Those called at the first hour designate those "who begin to be Christians fresh from their mother's womb." Those called at the third hour symbolize youth, and so forth, until those who are "altogether decrepit" are called at the eleventh hour. All people, then, no matter the stage of life at which they become Christians, receive "the one and the same denarius of eternal life" (Sermon 37.7, in *NPNF*[1] 6:375). People should never seek to delay conversion, however, because people never know whether they will live to see that later hour.

Augustine's spiritual interpretation of the parable, however, is more complex, and it also incorporates his reading of the parable of the wicked tenants to speak of dispensations of God's interactions with humanity (Matt. 21:33–41). The vineyard was "planted," Augustine explains, when God gave the law to the Jewish people, who killed the prophets and then Jesus, the only heir of the householder: "They killed him that they might possess the inheritance; and because they killed him, they lost it" (37.3, in *NPNF*[1] 6:374). As Matthew 25:34 shows, the denarius is eternal life (37.5–6), which means that workers called at the "first hour" (e.g., Adam and Noah), workers called at the "third hour" (e.g., Abraham, Isaac, and Jacob), those called at the "sixth hour" (e.g., Moses and Aaron), prophets called at the "ninth hour," and Christians called at the "eleventh hour" will be equal with respect to the gift of eternal life.

Augustine's interpretations of parables often reflect his belief that biblical exegesis should be based on the two greatest commandments: love of God and love of neighbor: "Whoever, then, thinks that he understands the Holy Scriptures, or any part of them, but puts such an interpretation upon them as does not tend to build up this twofold love of God and our neighbour, does not yet understand them as he ought" (*On Christian Doctrine* 1.36.40, in *NPNF*[1] 2:533).

This understanding frequently leads Augustine to connect physical and spiritual aspects in his interpretations. The sheep and goats parable, for example, means that giving to those in physical need results in God giving you the gift of eternal life (Sermon 36.5–6). But Augustine declares that love of God and neighbor must underlie those actions, or those actions are in vain. Similarly, the wedding garment in the parable of the wedding feast symbolizes that a garment of love/charity is required for salvation (Sermon 40.4–9): "So then, have faith with love. This is the 'wedding garment'" (40.9, in *NPNF*[1] 6:395; cf. 43.5, where the oil in the lamps in the wise and foolish virgins parable symbolizes love/charity).

Augustine also finds the imperative to love God and neighbor in the parable of the unmerciful servant, which serves as a warning to "save us from perishing," since every person is in God's debt and, in some sense, is owed a debt by another (Sermon 33.2). Jesus, however, provides the way out of our debts: "Forgive and you shall be forgiven," and "Give, and it shall be given unto you" (i.e., doing kindnesses; Luke 6:37–38):

> Again, as to the doing kindnesses; a beggar asks of you, and you are God's beggar. For we are all when we pray God's beggars; we stand, yes rather we fall prostrate before the door of the Great Householder, we groan in supplication wishing to receive something; and this something is God himself. What does the beggar ask of you? Bread. And what do you ask of God, but Christ, who says, "I am the living Bread which came down from heaven" (John 6:51)? Would you be forgiven? Forgive. (Sermon 33.2, in *NPNF*[1] 6:363)

Augustine's most famous parable interpretation is his allegorical reading of the parable of the good Samaritan, one that follows those by Irenaeus, Origen, and Ambrose, who see the Samaritan as symbolizing Christ healing the wounds caused by sin and who detect numerous other allegorical details in the parable. Less well known, however, are Augustine's nonallegorical citations of the parable in which he interprets the parable as a moral example of the universal nature of Christian love: "Every human being is a neighbor to every other human being" (*Exposition 8 of Psalm 118*, in Augustine 2003, 373). Likewise, Augustine's Sermon 299 interprets the parable as a moral example to teach that every human being should be a neighbor to every other human being and to act as the Samaritan acted. In addition, Augustine discusses the moral application of the parable to admonish his readers that Christians must speak the truth, even to non-Christians, because we are "neighbors" of every human being, Christian or non-Christian (Sermon 299, in Augustine 1994, 257; cf. *Against Lying*, section 15, discussing Eph. 4:25).

Augustine notes that this love for our neighbors also extends to our enemies (*On Christian Doctrine* 1.30.31) but then moves to the "deeper" meaning of the parable: "For our Lord Jesus Christ points to himself under the figure of the man who brought aid to him who was lying half-dead on the road, wounded and abandoned by the robbers" (1.30.33, in *NPNF*[1] 2:531). Augustine elaborates this symbolic aspect of Jesus as the good Samaritan in several other texts, because he believes that the attacked man's descent from Jerusalem to Jericho necessitates a spiritual interpretation in addition to the moral one. We should desire to "ascend" in contrast to the man who "descended" and then fell among thieves (Luke 10:30), but Jesus, as the good Samaritan, "slighted us not: He healed us, he raised us upon his beast, upon his flesh; he led us to the inn, that is, the church; He entrusted us to the host, that is, to the apostle [Paul]; he gave two pence, whereby we might be healed, the love of God, and the love of our neighbor" (*Exposition on the Psalms* 126.11, in *NPNF*[1] 8:606).

An extensive example of Augustine's spiritual interpretation of the good Samaritan parable is found in his *Questions on the Gospels* (2.19):

> *A certain man was going down from Jerusalem to Jericho*. He is understood to be Adam himself, representing the human race. *Jerusalem* is that city of peace from whose blessedness he fell. *Jericho* is translated as "moon" and signifies our mortality, because it begins, increases, grows old, and sets. The robbers are the devil and his angels, *who stripped him* of immortality, *and having beat with blows*, by persuading him to sinfulness, *left him half alive*, because the man was alive in the part by which he could understand and know God, and he was dead in the part in which he was wasting away and weighed down by sins. And for this reason he is said to be half alive. But the priest and the Levite who saw him and passed him by signify the priesthood and ministry of the Old Testament, which could not be of benefit toward salvation. *Samaritan* is translated as "guardian," and for this reason the Lord himself is signified by this name. The binding of the wounds is the holding of sins in check. The oil is the consolation of good hope because of the forgiveness given for the reconciliation of peace. The wine is an exhortation to work with a fervent spirit. His beast of burden is the flesh in which he deigned to come to us. To be placed on the beast of burden is to believe in Christ's incarnation. The stable is the Church where travelers are refreshed from the journey as they return to the eternal fatherland. The following day is after the resurrection of the Lord. The two denarii are the two commandments of love that the apostles received through the Holy Spirit in order to bring the Gospel to others, or they are the promise of the present and future life. . . . The innkeeper, then, is the Apostle [Paul]. The extra expense is either the counsel he gave . . . or the fact he even worked with his own hands, so that he would not be a burden to anyone in the newness of the Gospel. (Augustine 2014, 388–89)

In Augustine's interpretation, almost everything has a symbolic meaning. *Jerusalem*, for example, designates the physical city of Jerusalem *and* the spiritual "heavenly city of peace." Like Origen, Augustine also appeals to the etymology of *Samaritan*, notes its connection to "guardian," and specifically connects it to Jesus as "guardian" in this parable (cf. Ps. 121:5), a claim, he argues, made by Jesus himself. Thus this parable, for Augustine, becomes symbolic of Jesus's incarnation and the process of redemption of human beings, which explains the identifications Augustine makes in the rest of the parable's details (Augustine 2014, 388–89; Teske 2001, 350; cf. *Tractate on John* 41.13; 43.8.2; Sermon 69.7; Sermon 81.6).

Thus Augustine's interpretations of the parables both build upon and expand the interpretations of those who preceded him. Like Origen and others, Augustine also uses allegorical interpretations of the Bible to explain and affirm "troublesome" passages, such as some ethically questionable actions of biblical patriarchs (see *City of God* 3.29, "The Knowledge of Tropes Is Necessary"). Most notably, Augustine's insistence that biblical interpretation should be based on love of God and love of neighbor is an important interpretive "lens" through which he and others have interpreted Scripture. Overall, it is hard to overestimate the influence that Augustine had on subsequent theology, doctrine, and the interpretation of Scripture, including the interpretation of the parables.

Macrina the Younger (ca. 327–380)

Macrina the Younger (her paternal grandmother is known as Macrina the Elder) was the older sister of three men who would become bishops and saints of the church: Basil the Great, Gregory of Nyssa, and Peter of Sebaste. Macrina would also be canonized as a saint, and many details of her life are found in her brother Gregory's hagiography of her, *Life of Saint Macrina*.

Macrina was born into a wealthy family in Cappadocia (in modern Turkey). Her father died when she was twelve, and, as the oldest daughter, Macrina played a significant role in raising her nine siblings. Her brother Gregory, for example, just four years her junior, repeatedly calls her "teacher" in his writings, and in his *Life of Saint Macrina* says that she was "father teacher, guide, mother, counsellor in every good" (Gregory of Nyssa 1989, 37).

When Macrina's fiancé died before their marriage, Macrina and her mother retreated to a family estate in Pontus, where they followed a strict regimen of prayer, frugal diet, and manual labor. Macrina, as a "consecrated virgin," became head not only of the household but also of a community of female ascetics.

In his *On the Soul and the Resurrection*, Gregory describes the conversation he had with his sister while she was on her deathbed (cf. *Life of Saint Macrina* 41–42). In many respects, this treatise functions as a Christian *Phaedo*, since it is reminiscent of the death of Socrates in Plato's more famous work. Gregory plays a student's role similar to that of Plato, and Macrina resembles Socrates on his deathbed arguing for the immortality of the soul.

In this work, Macrina presents the case for the resurrection of the dead, and she and Gregory discuss the nature and the immortality of the soul (e.g., the soul is "an intellectual essence which imparts to the organic body a force of life by which the senses operate"; *On the Soul and the Resurrection*, in NPNF[2] 5:438). She states that it is incorrect to include aspects such as desire or anger as being consubstantial with the soul. The contrast here is with

Plato's allegory of the chariot, in which a person's reason seeks to guide the soul/chariot to truth, with two winged horses pulling the chariot: one horse is immortal and represents the soul's moral/rational impulse; the second horse is mortal and symbolizes the soul's immoral/irrational impulse (see Plato, *Phaedrus* 246a–254e). Macrina observes, however, that desire and anger are also found in animals, which do not possess souls. Therefore, she argues, the connection between the soul and such emotions cannot be made; passions must be separated from the soul's essence, and, depending on how they are controlled, emotions can lead to virtue or vice.

Macrina builds on this argument by interpreting the parable of the wheat and weeds. In this parable, the good and bad seed represent the corresponding natures of the soul, a reflection of Origen's view of the nature of evil. The weeds that corrupt the harvest of the field represent the "weeds" of the heart:

> Now we think that Scripture means by the good seed the corresponding impulses of the soul, each one of which, if only they are cultured for good, necessarily puts forth the fruit of virtue within us. But since there has been scattered among these the bad seed of the error of judgment as to the true Beauty which is alone in its intrinsic nature such, and since this last has been thrown into the shade by the growth of delusion which springs up along with it . . . on account of this the wise Husbandman leaves this growth that has been introduced among his seed to remain there, so as to secure our not being altogether stripped of better hopes by desire having been rooted out along with that good-for-nothing growth. . . . Therefore the Husbandman leaves those bastard seeds within us, not for them always to overwhelm the more precious crop, but in order that the land itself (for so, in his allegory, he calls the heart) by its native inherent power, which is that of reasoning, may wither up the one growth and may render the other fruitful and abundant. (*On the Soul and the Resurrection*, in NPNF[2] 5:442–43)

In their discussion of the existence of the soul, Gregory asks his sister to explain the location of the "much-talked-of and renowned Hades" (*On the Soul and the Resurrection*, in NPNF[2] 5:443). Macrina answers that Hades does not exist in a particular location; instead, the soul migrates from "the seen to the unseen." Hades is invisible, and any passages from the Bible that suggest otherwise are allegorical (e.g., Phil. 2:10). But how can this view cohere with the teachings of Jesus, who clearly speaks of the existence of Hades, such as in the parable of the rich man and Lazarus? Macrina responds that the parable itself gives many hints that it is allegorical; these hints lead "the skilled inquirer to a more discriminating study of it" (*On the Soul and the Resurrection*, in NPNF[2] 5:446). A nonallegorical reading is "superficial," since such aspects as the "great gulf" between Lazarus in the bosom of Abraham and the rich man being in torment in Hades should not be interpreted literally. How can the rich man, for example, lift up his eyes to heaven, when his bodily eyes remain in his tomb? Both men's bodies physically are in a tomb, and disembodied spirits cannot feel the heat of a flame or have a tongue cooled by a drop of water: "And so it is impossible to make the framework of the narrative correspond with the truth, if we understand it literally; we can do that only by translating each detail into an equivalent in the world of ideas. Thus we must think of the gulf as that which parts ideas which may not be confounded from running together, not as a chasm of the earth" (*On the Soul and the Resurrection*, in NPNF² 5:447).

The many figurative elements of the parable, though, speak important truths about the soul. The chasm in the parable, for example, represents the decisions human beings make in their earthly lives between good and evil. On the one hand, those who choose evil dig for themselves the "yawning impassable abyss" that nothing can breach. Lazarus reclining in Abraham's bosom, on the other hand, represents those who choose the virtuous life:

> As then figuratively we call a particular circuit of the ocean a "bosom," so does Scripture seem to me to express the idea of those measureless blessings above by the word "bosom," meaning a place into which all virtuous voyagers of this life are, when they have put in from hence, brought to anchor in the waveless harbor of that gulf of blessings. Meanwhile the denial of these blessings which they witness becomes in the others a flame, which burns the soul and causes the craving for the refreshment of one drop out of that ocean of blessings wherein the saints are affluent; which nevertheless they do not get. If, too, you consider the "tongue," and the "eye," and the "finger," and the other names of bodily organs, which occur in the conversation between those disembodied souls, you will be persuaded that this conjecture of ours about them chimes in with the opinion we have already stated about the soul. Look closely into the meaning of those words. . . . If one, then, thinks of those atoms in which each detail of the body potentially inheres, and surmises that Scripture means a "finger" and a "tongue" and an "eye" and the rest as existing, after dissolution, only in the sphere of the soul, one will not miss the probable truth. (*On the Soul and the Resurrection*, in NPNF² 5:447–48)

The lesson of the parable, Macrina concludes, is that during their earthly lives, Christians should free themselves as much as possible from the attachments of this life "by virtuous conduct." The rich man in the parable symbolizes inordinate attachment to matters of the flesh, something that Christians must avoid.

The depth and complexity of Macrina the Younger's interpretations of the parables and other biblical texts amply illustrate why she deserves to have a more significant place in scholarly discussions of fourth-century Christianity. Her importance extends well beyond the profound influence she had on her three more-famous brothers.

Ephrem the Syrian (ca. 306–373)

Ephrem (also Ephraim or Ephraem) the Syrian was a prolific poet, hymnist, teacher, theologian, polemicist, and biblical interpreter. Ephrem lived in Nisibis (in the southeast of modern Turkey) for most of his life, writing hymns, serving in the catechetical school, tending to the poor, and performing other duties in episcopal service. In 363 CE, however, Emperor Jovian surrendered Nisibis to the Persians, causing Ephrem and other Christians to flee the city. Ephrem settled in Edessa, living a life of poverty and asceticism in a cave, until he died on June 9, 373.

Jerome's brief biography of Ephrem tells us that he "composed many works in the Syriac language" (a dialect of Aramaic) and exhibited the "incisive power of lofty genius" (*Lives of Illustrious Men*, chap. 115, in *NPNF*[2] 3:382). Ephrem wrote hundreds of hymns, and many of them were sung/recited in the church's liturgy, complementing—as Jerome notes—the chanting of Scripture in worship services. These hymns (*madrāshē*) are sometimes called "teaching songs," because they are intended to be chanted and accompanied by a lyre in the style in which Christians envisioned King David performing them in the Hebrew Bible (Griffith 2004, 1399; cf. the *kontakion* during the Byzantine era). As a result of Ephrem's influence, the liturgy of the Eastern church is still more based on poetry and hymns than is the liturgy of other church traditions (MacCulloch 2009, 183).

Ephrem's mode of biblical interpretation also became the approach adopted by Syriac Christian writers, and his writings were translated into a number of languages. His prose works include commentaries on the Bible and the *Diatessaron* (a harmony of the four New Testament Gospels compiled into a single narrative by Tatian around 150–160 CE), as well as polemical texts against the followers of Marcion and others.

Ephrem's commentary on the *Diatessaron* does not treat the whole text, and it spends more time on certain passages than others. Some of Ephrem's interpretations of the parables in this commentary focus exclusively on their literal, nonallegorical meaning (e.g., the parable of the laborers in the vineyard, *Diatessaron* 15.14–17; the Pharisee and the tax collector, 15.24; the unjust judge, 16.16). Ephrem also, however, uses significant amounts of typology and symbolism in his commentaries, and he elaborates the themes he discovers in the parables and compares those themes to types and symbols from Hebrew Bible narratives that, in his view, reflect on the passage (Griffith 2004, 1406). Ephrem indicates, for example, that the lost coin could symbolize not only someone who strayed from the "righteousness of nature" but also "the image of Adam" and Adam's fall (14.19; cf. the unjust steward, 11.21).

Ephrem's concern for the poor permeates his commentary on the *Diatessaron*. His comments on the parable of the sower, for instance, include an admonition to the rich not to let the thorns of wealth hinder their faith (11.16). He also devotes extended sections to the rich man—who, "confident in his earthly wealth," asks Jesus what he must do to inherit eternal life (e.g., Luke 18:18–25)—before explaining the meaning of the rich man and Lazarus parable. After the rich man and Lazarus died, the rich man's agony while he was being tortured in Hades was increased because he could also see Lazarus with Abraham. The context of the passage suggests, Ephrem argues, that Jesus was comparing the rich man to the Jewish priests and comparing Lazarus to his disciples (15.12). Ephrem then, however, discusses the moral implications of the parable:

> See then! The more the rich man lived sumptuously, the more [Lazarus] was humbled. The more Lazarus was made low, the greater was his crown. Why was it, therefore, that he should have seen Abraham above all the just, and Lazarus in his bosom? It was because Abraham loved the poor that he saw him, so that we might learn that we cannot hope for pardon at the end, unless the fruits of pardon can be seen in us. If then Abraham, who was friendly to strangers, and had mercy on Sodom, was not able to have mercy on the one who did not show pity to Lazarus, how can we hope that there will be pardon for us? (15.13; Ephrem 1994, 235–36)

Ephrem interprets the parable in a similar way in *Hymns on Paradise* by noting how Abraham, "who even had pity on Sodom," has no pity for the rich man "who showed no pity" (1.12; cf. 1.17). In Hymn 7, Ephrem elaborates that we should learn about God's justice from this parable:

> And may I learn how much I will then have received
> > From that parable of the Rich Man
> Who did not even give to the poor man
> > The leftovers from his banquet;
> And may I see Lazarus,
> > Grazing in Paradise,
> And look upon the Rich Man,
> > In anguish,

> So that the might of justice outside
>   May cause me fear,
> But the breath of grace within
>   May bring me comfort. (7.27; Ephrem 1990, 129)

Ephrem's interpretation of the good Samaritan parable also stresses God's command to extend mercy to everyone in need. He argues that the historical context (e.g., the logistics of travel from Jerusalem to Jericho) indicates that the wounded man was a Jew, which means that he "became a reproach to the priests and the Levites on account of the Samaritan, because they did not take pity on the son of their people." The law commands the priests and Levites to show compassion; they did not, but the Samaritan did. Therefore, Jesus's parable declares that one's neighbor is anyone of any race in need, even from among one's enemies, not just "the son of one's [own] race" (*Commentary on Tatian's Diatessaron*, trans. McCarthy 1993, 255).

Ephrem's *Hymns on the Pearl* focuses on the parable of the pearl of great value and develops the image of salvation as a precious pearl (Ephrem 1989, 11). He begins:

> On a certain day a pearl did I take up, my brethren;
> I saw in it mysteries pertaining to the Kingdom;
> Semblances and types of the Majesty;
> It became a fountain, and I drank out of it mysteries of the Son. (1.1,
>   in *NPNF*² 13:293)

Ephrem moves beyond the image of the parable as symbolizing the kingdom of heaven to other "mysteries." The primary focus of these mysteries—which include truth (1.1; 2.1; 3.4; 5.4; 6.2; 7.3), faith (3.5), the church (1.1; 6.7; 7.7), the Eucharist, Mary (1.1), baptism, and virginity—is also symbolized by the parable of the wise and foolish virgins:

> Thee He used as a parable of that kingdom, O pearl!
> As He did the virgins that entered into it, five in number,
> Clothed with the light of their lamps!
> To thee are those bright ones like, thou that art clad in light! (3.4, in
>   *NPNF*² 13:296)

In these hymns about salvation, Ephrem includes warnings about falling into heresy; he employs the wheat and weeds parable in one such admonition: true faith is continuous from Abraham, the prophets, and the apostles (7.1), but heretics, deceived by Satan, cannot understand the Father, Son,

Holy Spirit, and the true faith. Therefore, they subvert orthodox teachings (7.2):

> Satan saw that the Truth strangled him,
> And united himself to the tares,
> And secreted his frauds,
> And spread his snares for the faith,
> And cast upon the priests the darts of the love of preeminence. (7.3, in
>   NPNF[2] 13:299–300)

> He sowed tares,
> And the bramble shot up in the pure vineyard!
> He infected the flock,
> And the leprosy broke out,
> And the sheep became hired servants of his!
> He began in the People,
> And came unto the Gentiles, that he might finish. (7.4, in NPNF[2] 13:300)

Ephrem declares that these heretics incorrectly believe that Jesus is "only a Son of man" and envision him as either a "creature or of a thing made." They refuse to recognize that Jesus himself "was the Maker" (7.5, in NPNF[2] 13:300).

Ephrem writes that the pearl "became a fountain, and I drank out of it mysteries of the Son" (1.1, in NPNF[2] 13:293). For Ephrem, then, symbols are polyvalent and multifaceted; one meaning does not exhaust their potential, and one meaning does not exclude another meaning. The pearl symbolizes the kingdom of heaven, but the image of the pearl also serves as a door that opens and reveals many facets of the "truth" and symbolizes not only the kingdom but also Christ, faith, the virgin birth, Christ's crucifixion, and many other things. As the first stanza indicates (1.1), the symbol of the pearl serves as an invitation to—and as the starting point for—meditation (Brock 1992, 56).

Ephrem's legacy—especially the influence of his hymns and the musical precedents they set—is tremendously important for Syriac Christianity. He deservedly is the most celebrated voice within the Syriac tradition of Christianity—Sebastian Brock even calls Ephrem "the finest poet in any language of the patristic period" (1987, xv)—and one of the most revered Christians of late antiquity.

The Good Shepherd in Early Christian Art

Unlike scenes from the infancy narratives, the passion narratives, and miracles in the Gospels, depictions of Jesus's parables rarely appear in early Christian art. One of the first and most common images used by Christians is the popular Greco-Roman image of the ram bearer (*kriophoros*). This image can be traced back to 1000 BCE in reliefs at Carchemish (in modern southern Turkey), where it symbolizes an animal about to be sacrificed (Milburn 1988, 30). When the image appears in Greco-Roman environments, however, it represents such things as philanthropy, the happiness of rural life (Rutgers 2000, 89–90), or an allusion to paradise in the afterlife (Spier 2007, 6). In the late second or early third century CE, Christians began to use this image, since the Gospel of John represents Jesus as the Good Shepherd who lays down his life for his sheep (John 10:11–16; cf. Ezek. 34:1–4). That figurative language in John is usually not considered a parable, but the image of the ram bearer also came to represent the parable of the lost sheep in Luke 15:3–7, where the shepherd goes out to find and bring back one lost sheep out of the hundred in his flock.

Oil Lamp (Third Century)

One of the earliest Christian uses of this image is an early third-century oil lamp with images of the Good Shepherd, Noah's ark, and Jonah on it. The representation of the Good Shepherd dominates the circular image that is stamped between the handle on one side and the spout of this reddish clay lamp. The shepherd is a young man in a short tunic who faces the viewer with the sheep over his shoulders. A flock of seven sheep surrounds him on the bottom half of the plate, and the sun, moon, and seven stars are above him. There are additional figures on the left side of the image, such as the dove on top of Noah's ark (the ark here symbolized by a small box; see Gen. 8:6–12) and Jonah having been "vomited out" of the large fish (see Jon. 1–2). Both stories speak of God's preservation of humans from destruction in difficult times, but Jonah's three days in the belly of the large fish specifically came to symbolize the "three days" of the death, burial, and resurrection of Jesus (Matt. 12:40). On the right side of the image Jonah is found sleeping under a set of gourds (see Jon. 4). The use of the Good Shepherd in conjunction with the images from the Hebrew Bible—including their Christian symbolism— makes it clear that this lamp was made specifically for/by Christians (Spier 2007, 172).

Roman Catacombs (Fourth Century)

Catacombs are underground cemeteries that contain numerous tombs, often consisting of intricate and sometimes extensive networks of burial chambers. Such subterranean burial places were used by Jews, Christians, and others in the ancient world, and they can be found in many areas of the Mediterranean world. The most famous and extensive catacombs are the Christian catacombs that have been discovered around Rome.

The Christian catacombs in Rome include many of the earliest Christian works of art, well preserved in subterranean chambers. They give us valuable information about early Christianity and the genesis of Christian art, and the image of Jesus as the Good Shepherd is found approximately 120 times in the Roman catacombs (e.g., the Callisto, Priscilla, and Domitilla catacombs).

The Domitilla catacomb contains over nine miles of subterranean passages, and it is especially famous for its wall paintings, some of which date back to the third century. A wall painting of the Good Shepherd that dates from the late fourth century is painted on an apse in a *cubiculum* (i.e., a large room) that is often called *Pistores* (Latin for "bakers") since there are images depicting bread making in the room. The Good Shepherd stands in a garden, with one sheep over his shoulders and four sheep around him (figure 1.1). Two sheep are on his left, and two are on his right. The closest two sheep look up at him, but the two other sheep are turned away from him and peacefully graze on the grass in front of them. Even farther away on each side are two predatory animals (lions?) from which the Good Shepherd lovingly protects his sheep (Nicolai et al. 2009, 90).

Scala / Art Resource, NY

Figure 1.1 Domitilla catacomb, Good Shepherd

Figure 1.2 Dura-Europos house church, Good Shepherd

Yale University Art Gallery

Dura-Europos House Church (Early Third Century)

Another early example of Christian use of the image of the Good Shepherd is found in an early third-century fresco at Dura-Europos, an ancient city on the south bank of the Euphrates River in eastern Syria that was a Roman military outpost in the eastern border of the empire (*Limes Arabicus*). Among the important archaeological discoveries at Dura-Europos, beginning in the 1920s, are a fragment of Tatian's *Diatessaron* (fourteen fragmentary lines with words from all four canonical Gospels), paintings in the Temple of Palmyrene Gods, a Mithra temple in the Roman camp, an astonishing third-century Jewish synagogue whose four walls are covered with paintings with images from the Hebrew Bible, and a Christian house church with images on the walls of its baptistery.

The early date of the Christian images makes them unique, since they are in a place of worship and baptism, instead of in a tomb. The baptistery is one rectangular room of the house that consists of eight rooms, another of which was a meeting or assembly room for worship. Portions of frescoes line the walls, including images of Jesus healing the paralytic, the Samaritan woman at the well, the three women/Marys at the tomb of Jesus, Jesus and

Peter walking on the water, and, from the Hebrew Bible, David and Goliath. On the west wall of the baptistery is a decorated curved arch and pillars. On the wall behind/within the arch and over the baptismal font is a painting of the Good Shepherd that follows the curved outline of the arch (figure 1.2). On a red background, the Good Shepherd carries a rather large (in proportion) sheep on his shoulders, and a number of his flock walk before him. A representation of Adam and Eve, much smaller, is in the bottom left of the painting.

Obviously the juxtaposition of these two images makes a statement about the sins of human beings and the forgiveness of those sins signified through Christian baptism. The aptness of the shepherd imagery is also reinforced by such Hebrew Bible passages as Psalm 23, including Jesus as Lord being "my shepherd"; by the baptismal waters as the "still waters"; by the "prepared table" and the "cup" prefiguring the Eucharist; and by the imagery of dying/rising with Christ being associated with baptism and the forgiveness of sins (see Jensen 2000, 39).

Illuminations from the Rossano Gospels (Codex Purpureus Rossanensis, Early Sixth Century)

An illuminated manuscript is a text that has been illustrated or decorated in some way. Some ancient papyrus scrolls were illuminated, as Pliny the Elder notes concerning his own work (*Natural History* 35.4.8, about the color illustrations of plants) and the works of others (e.g., *Natural History* 35.2.11), although very few illustrated papyri have survived (e.g., a third-century CE Heracles poem). The invention of the codex, however, with flat sheets of parchment bound together, served as a catalyst for an increased amount of manuscript illumination. Not only were the materials more durable, but they also permitted more and thicker layers of paint to be applied to the pages. Thus such miniature painting became an advanced art form in the fourth century CE. The most popular illuminated manuscripts were of epic poems such as Homer's *Iliad* and *Odyssey* or Virgil's *Aeneid* (Weitzmann 1977, 10).

The Rossano Gospels (Codex Purpureus Rossanensis) is the oldest extant illuminated manuscript of the New Testament Gospels. The codex is named Purpureus Rossanensis because the parchment pages were dyed a purple-reddish color and the manuscript was housed at the cathedral in Rossano, Italy. The text is written in uncials (all capital letters), primarily with silver ink, with incipits (opening words) in gold ink. The current manuscript contains only the Gospels of Matthew and Mark (up to Mark 16:14), but it is distinctive because fourteen miniature full-page illustrations—which cover elements of all four Gospels—are placed together at the front of the manuscript in a coherent cycle. This placement allows the story told by the pictures to be viewed in sequence without any interruption by a written text (Weitzmann 1970, 93–94). In this case, the primary images are scenes from the life of Jesus, with ten illustrations, each of which includes depictions of four Hebrew Bible/Septuagint figures who prophesy the coming of Jesus and the events depicted above them.

The Rossano Gospels portray two parables: that of the good Samaritan (figure 1.3) and that of the wise and foolish virgins (figure 1.4). The image of the good Samaritan is placed in the cycle of pictures depicting the passion of

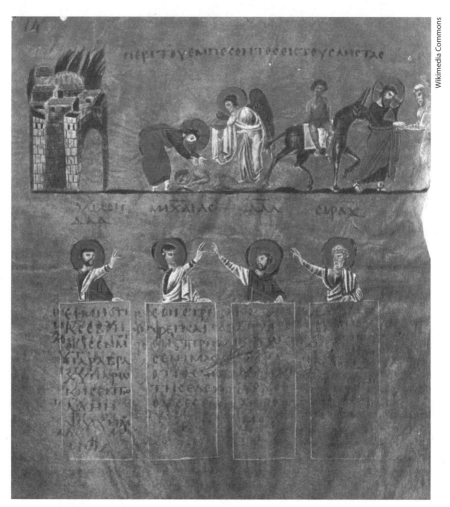

Figure 1.3 Rossano Gospels, Good Samaritan

Figure 1.4 Rossano Gospels, Wise and Foolish Bridesmaids

Jesus: between Jesus's prayer in the garden of Gethsemane and healing of two
blind men, on one side, and Jesus's trial before Pilate, on the other. The good
Samaritan image's placement in the cycle indicates its connection to the death
of Jesus, spiritual conversion (symbolized by the healing of the blind), and
redemption (through the passion of Jesus). In the illustration itself, the bottom
half of the page includes two pairs of figures from the Septuagint with their
names inscribed above them—David and Micah and David and Sirach. All
four figures have a nimbus/halo, but King David has a jewel-studded crown,
darker clothes, and possibly a breastplate (Milburn 1988, 300) in both of his

representations. The four figures each stand holding a brief text from the Septuagint relevant to the story. At the top left of the page a city is depicted (scholars debate whether it is Jerusalem [e.g., Brubaker 1999, 77] or Jericho [e.g., Weitzmann 1977, 93]; Jerusalem is more likely), and the miniature then depicts from left to right two scenes from the parable. The first scene is the good Samaritan ministering to the wounded, bloody man with an angel assisting him. The second is the good Samaritan paying the innkeeper to take care of the wounded man, who sits on the Samaritan's animal.

Perhaps the most interesting aspect of this illumination is that it incorporates an allegorical interpretation of the parable. Jesus is the good Samaritan, as is evident by the cross nimbus around his head. Jesus bends at a ninety-degree angle over the beaten man, who is lying on his right side, his head resting on his right arm. An angel stands just on the other side of the man; the angel, in a white robe and with blue wings, holds some sort of bowl draped by a white cloth. The second scene is pictured just to the right. Continuing from the left to the right, viewers encounter the wounded man, still covered with blood and without clothes, sitting sidesaddle on the Samaritan's animal—another indication that the man is injured or disabled. The man looks to his left, and following the man's (and the animal's) gaze, viewers next see Jesus paying the innkeeper, whose image does not completely fit on the page. Jesus looks at the money he is giving the innkeeper; the innkeeper's gaze is directed either to Jesus or to the wounded man now in his care.

The allegorical portrayal of the Samaritan as Jesus ensures that the Samaritan (Jesus) is the primary focus of attention in the illustration. Jesus is the one who ministers to beaten and broken human beings, takes them to the inn/church, and pays the price for them to be healed/saved.

The other parable depicted in the Rossano Gospels is that of the wise and foolish bridesmaids. This miniature is placed in the cycle of pictures after Jesus's entry into Jerusalem and the driving of the money changers from the temple, and before the Last Supper and Jesus washing the feet of the apostles. Once again, at the bottom of the page, four characters from the Hebrew Bible stand holding scrolls with selections from their writings that predict the event pictured above. King David appears three times. The two representations of King David on the left side, both of whose right arms are raised in the direction of the wise bridesmaids, connect the wise bridesmaids to Psalm 45:14–15 (where the princess and her virgin companions "with joy and gladness . . . enter the palace of the king"). On the right, David is paired with the prophet Hosea, and they both characterize the foolish bridesmaids, since their right arms are raised in the direction of the foolish bridesmaids above. David holds a scroll that cites Psalm 53:5 (God rejects the ungodly;

they are put to shame and are in "great terror"), and Hosea holds a scroll that quotes Hosea 7:13 (which pronounces woes and destruction on those who have strayed from God).

The parable is depicted at the top of the page. The foolish bridesmaids stand on the left side; Jesus and the wise bridesmaids stand on the right, with Jesus closing the door between them. The foolish bridesmaids each wear different-colored clothes. Only two foolish bridesmaids carry unlit torches, and they also carry three upside-down, empty small jars for their oil. One empty-handed bridesmaid is either knocking or attempting to open the door, but Jesus, dressed in gold and dark blue, stands on the other side with his hand raised, signifying that the door is closed to them forever. The five wise bridesmaids stand with Jesus on the right, all of them dressed in white and gold; all five carry lit torches and upright jars that still contain oil. Behind them is a forest of fruit-bearing trees that represents the garden of paradise, which is also symbolized by the four streams of water that flow from the right side of the picture. These four streams merge into one larger stream and end just on the paradise side of the door, with a small tree planted at the end of the stream, near the feet of Jesus.

The illuminations in the Rossano Gospels present interpretations of these two parables in two ways. Each image not only offers a distinct interpretation individually, but its placement is significant as well. Although the illuminations are placed together so they form a coherent cycle without "interruption" from the text they represent, text and image still interact to form a more coherent story, since the artist selects Septuagintal texts to place the images into particular contexts the artist deems important.

Byzantine Mosaics (Early Sixth Century), *Christ Separating Sheep from Goats*, Sant'Apollinare Nuovo (Ravenna, Italy)

Mosaics consist of a number of tesserae (small pieces of stone or glass) placed together to render a work of art. Pliny the Elder gives the Greeks credit for inventing the mosaic form of art (*Natural History* 36.31), but the earliest extant mosaics, from around 700 BCE, are found in Gordion in Phrygia (in modern Turkey). Almost no mosaics with Christian motifs are extant from the period before Emperor Constantine's Edict of Milan (313 CE), which granted religious toleration throughout the Roman Empire. The surviving Christian mosaics before 313 tend to be found in tombs (Poeschke 2010, 9–12).

Two early sixth-century mosaics depicting parables are found in the nave of the basilica Sant'Apollinare Nuovo in Ravenna, Italy (an early fifth-century

Figure 1.5 Sant'Apollinare Nuovo (Ravenna, Italy), Fifth-century mosaic, Sheep and Goats

mosaic of Jesus as the Good Shepherd is found in the mausoleum of Galla Placidia, also in Ravenna). The basilica was built by Theodoric the Great (454–526), who lived in Ravenna. Since Sant'Apollinare Nuovo served as the palace church, the mosaic decorations are extensive, originally covering the nave's side walls, the inner façade, and the apse (some mosaics, such as the one in the apse that was damaged by an earthquake, were replaced). The mosaics of the parables included in the Theodoric-era mosaics are found in the upper sections of the walls of the nave. These mosaics include representations of sixteen prophets, all of whom hold scrolls or codices and have halos. Just above those mosaics of the prophets are found twenty-six smaller (approximately 50 × 40 inches) mosaics that depict events from the life of Christ. The mosaics on the north wall primarily depict parables and miracles, and the ones on the south wall mostly depict events during the passion (Poeschke 2010, 144–47).

Among the mosaics on the north wall, barely discernible from the church's floor, is a depiction of Matthew's parable of the sheep and goats (figure 1.5). The primary focus of the mosaic, in the middle of the image, is Jesus in a purple robe and seated on the judgment seat. Jesus's halo also distinguishes him, since it includes a cross nimbus embedded with three blue jewels. His right hand is slightly raised, guiding our eyes to the three white sheep on his right. On his left (and our right) are three goats of darker color; Jesus does not acknowledge their presence. These goats are placed at a level lower than the sheep on the other side of the panel, and they are situated closer together, which also highlights the greater importance of the sheep. Two angels stand beside Jesus, both with their right hands raised in blessing. The angel on Jesus's right is clothed in orange and red, and his wings and halo are also orange and red. The clothes, wings, and halo of the angel on Jesus's left are blue. Jesus stares straight ahead—into the eyes of the viewer, if the viewer were at the same level as the mosaic—which serves as a warning to viewers who call Jesus "Lord" but do not do what he commands them to do: feed the hungry, give drink to the thirsty, welcome the stranger, clothe the naked, and visit the imprisoned (Matt. 25:31–46; cf. Luke 6:46).

Romanos the Melodist (ca. 485–555)

Romanos the Melodist is the greatest Byzantine liturgical poet and hymn writer—perhaps the most famous liturgical poet of the Orthodox Church—and, as such, was often called the "Christian Pindar" (Trypanis 1971, liii). Romanos was born in Emesa (Syria), was educated and became a deacon in Beirut, and later moved to Constantinople, where he spent most of his life serving the church during the reign of Emperor Justinian. Beyond those few details, little else is known about Romanos other than his creation, according to tradition, of around one thousand *kontakia* (although only about eighty-nine extant *kontakia* are attributed to him, and probably only about sixty of them are authentic). A *kontakion* is a chanted sermon that combines dramatic dialogue and theological teachings (Cunningham 1999, 70). Such *kontakia* consist of at least one prelude and usually between thirteen and twenty-four stanzas (each called an *ikos*) in the same meter; each stanza ends with the same refrain. *Kontakia* encourage participation from the congregation both in form and content (Romanos 1995, xv–xxix). Only the texts of these *kontakia* survive; the accompanying music has not.

Romanos's *kontakion* "On the Prodigal Son" (Romanos 1995, 99–111) incorporates elements of two sacraments: the Eucharist and baptism. The *kontakion* begins with the speaker/singer identifying with the prodigal. Since all have sinned and fallen short of the glory of God, this opening implies that everyone hearing the sermon also should identify with the prodigal, in the sense that they have sinned and are in church to repent and seek God's forgiveness:

Prelude 1

I have rivaled the prodigal by my senseless deeds
and like him I fall down before you and I seek forgiveness, Lord.
Therefore do not despise me,
Master and Lord of the ages.

The *kontakion* then identifies the feast with which the father celebrates his son's return with the Eucharistic table. Since the Greek term for the Last Supper is *to mystikon deipnon*, the English term "the mystical table" is used for both the Last Supper and the Eucharist (see Romanos 1995, 101):

Prelude 2

Of your mystical table, O Immortal,
Count me worthy, who have been corrupted by living as a prodigal.

This reference to the Eucharist is immediately followed by a reference to baptism, which also signifies the forgiveness of sins. Baptism is symbolized as "the first robe of grace," which designates the "first robe" given to Adam before the "Fall" (Romanos 1995, 103), thus connecting baptism to the robe that the father gives the returning son:

And the first robe of grace,
which I have befouled, wretch that I am, by the stains of the passions
in your unattainable mercy give me once again,
Master and Lord of the ages.

The focus of the *kontakion* then turns to imagining the celebratory supper prepared by the father as symbolizing God's love for humankind, God's receiving all repentant prodigals, and identifying the sacrificed calf with Jesus's sacrificial death for the sins of humankind. This emphasis is reinforced in the second stanza, where the food at the banquet (i.e., Eucharist) is bread—the body of Jesus—and the "holy blood" of Jesus.

The third stanza explores the meaning of the Eucharist by starting with the supper celebrating the prodigal's return:

What is the banquet? Let us first learn of the supper
from the Gospels, so that we too may celebrate.
I will therefore recall the parable of the Prodigal.
For he was formerly stripped bare of every grace,
having squandered all his substance,

and he runs to his father with many lamentations crying, "Father, I
have sinned."
So the one who sees all things saw, hurried,
and met him and kissed him,
flung his arms around the neck of the one who had returned,
for he is the God of the repentant.
In his compassion he had mercy on his son who had fallen, he the
Master and Lord of the ages. (Romanos 1995, 102–3)

"The Saviour of all," upon seeing his son dressed in "filthy apparel," tells his
slaves to bring his son the "first robe" (i.e., the baptismal robe, the "first robe"
of Adam before the fall), which "the enemy" (i.e., Satan) had stripped from
him (Romanos 1995, 103). Here the *kontakion* echoes elements of Genesis
1–3 (1:26; 2:1–15; 3:7) to connect the sin of the prodigal with the sin of all
humankind against their Creator. God cannot bear to look at the prodigal's
(i.e., Adam's) nakedness, because it reflects God's image (Gen. 1:26); God
thus commands that the repentant prodigal be clothed "with the robe of
grace." Just as God offered the obedient and sinless Jesus as the sacrifice for
the redemption of sinful humankind (stanza 8), likewise the priests reenact
this sacrifice of Jesus in the Eucharist and give "all who are worthy of [God's]
supper . . . the spotless calf" (Romanos 1995, 105).

Stanza 12 turns to the story of the elder brother, who is out in the field when
his brother returns and, when he hears what has happened, refuses to join the
celebration (stanza 13). The narrator's voice then reminds the hearers of the
"compassion and measureless pity" of God, who "wishes all to be saved" (1 Tim.
2:4). God loves both brothers and listens to the lengthy complaint of the elder
brother (stanzas 16–17). God then, however, makes clear to the elder son, who
symbolizes Christians who "have not separated from the Church," that his place
is with God, but that the younger brother has come home in shame, lamentation, and repentance. God asks the older brother: "How could I not have pity
and save my son as he grieved and wept?" (stanza 19; Romanos 1995, 110).

The *kontakion* then addresses the apparent problem in the parable that the
younger son has already received his inheritance, so, upon his return, whatever
is given to him comes (unfairly) from the older brother's inheritance. Not so,
God says in stanza 20:

Understand what I say, my son. All that is mine is yours,
and to him I wanted to grant some of my goods.
The property which you have is not any less,
for I did not take from it to give to your brother;
I provided for him from my own treasures. (Romanos 1995, 110)

How that can be true is left unexplained, but the father (God) then invites the older son to the supper, where he will "celebrate and sing with all the angels" the return of his brother who was lost but now is found. Stanza 21 records the older son's response:

> When he heard these words he was persuaded
> and shared the gladness with his brother. And he began to sing and say,
> "All of you shout with praise,
> that blessed are they whose every
> sin is forgiven, and whose iniquity
> has been covered and wiped away." (Romanos 1995, 111 [cf. Ps. 32:1;
>   Septuagint Ps. 31:1])

The singer/preacher of the sermon concludes with a message that also alludes to the parable of the Pharisee and the tax collector (publican):

> O Son and Word of God, Creator of all things,
> we your unworthy servants ask and implore you:
> have mercy on all who call upon you.
> As you did with the prodigal, spare those who have sinned.
> Accept and save through compassion
> those who in repentance run to you, O King, crying "We have sinned."
> Give us tears, as you did the harlot,
> and pardon for the sins we have committed.
> And, as you did the publican, take pity on us all,
> At the intercessions of the Mother of God.
> Make us partakers of your supper, as you did the prodigal,
> *Master and Lord of the ages.* (Romanos 1995, 111)

In his *kontakia*, Romanos skillfully interweaves biblical imagery into his poetry—his liturgical storytelling—whether narrating the story of Jesus's healing of a leper (Matt. 8:2–4) or Jesus's encounter with the Samaritan woman (John 4:4–42), or telling Jesus's parable of the prodigal son. The *kontakion* on the prodigal son stresses that God is a loving parent who celebrates a great feast when a sinner returns home. In addition, the sermon goes even further than the Lukan parable, since it provides the answer to a question that the parable itself leaves open: the loving Father persuades the indignant elder brother to join the celebration and to welcome his brother home with love and gladness. In this way, the *kontakion* urges its hearers both to identify with the repentant prodigal and also to celebrate as the elder brother when other prodigals repent and return home to God.

2

The Afterlives of Jesus's Parables in the Middle Ages (ca. 550–1500 CE)

> Trying to assess the place of the Bible in medieval culture is like trying to apprehend the oxygen in the air we breathe. In the liturgy, in proverbs and idioms of common speech, in the language of the law and of political thought, through dramatic performances in churchyards and in village squares, in the art of the cathedrals and of parish churches, for highborn and lowborn alike, the Bible was everywhere; it was a constant component of the mental life of medieval men and women. (Besserman 1988, 4)

The Bible was the most studied book in the Middle Ages—its study represented the "highest branch of learning"—and knowledge of the Bible was not restricted to specialists. Teachers regarded the Bible as a textbook par excellence (Smalley 1984, xxvii–xxx). As Lawrence Besserman notes, the language and content of the Bible permeated medieval thought, including most literature, art, and music. This environment brought rich and expansive developments in the afterlives of parables, with four parables receiving the most attention: the prodigal son, the good Samaritan, the rich man and Lazarus, and the wise and foolish virgins.

Most biblical interpretations during this period believe that Scripture must be explained in a fourfold way—according to the four "senses," as suggested by John Cassian (360–435)—the historical-literary, allegorical/typological, anagogical (which prophesies the future), and tropological (the ethical/moral), in order to "ascertain what everlasting truths are there intimated" with the

65

guidance of the Holy Spirit (Bede 1985, x–xi; cf. Ward 2002, 15–16, 81; Gowler 2014, 9–10).

In the later centuries of this era, however, the allegorical method began to decline, as is illustrated in this chapter with Thomas Aquinas's approach to biblical interpretation. Thomas emphasizes the literal sense of biblical texts, and although he supports allegorical interpretation of parables, he also urges restraint in its use: it adds nothing "necessary to faith" (Kissinger 1979, 42; Grant 1963, 125).

This chapter includes some of the most influential readings of the parables during this era (e.g., that of Gregory the Great), as well as some interpretations that are not as familiar. Comparing the interpretations of the parable of the wheat and weeds from Wazo of Liège and Thomas Aquinas is instructive, but so are the interpretations of parables in commentaries (e.g., of Theophylact, Bonaventure), literature (e.g., writings of John Gower), plays (e.g., of Antonia Pulci), art (e.g., illuminated manuscripts, stained-glass windows, and engravings), and sermons (of Gregory the Great and Hildegard of Bingen). Particularly interesting are the interpretations of Jesus's parables in Islamic literature, so several readings of the parable of the laborers in the vineyard from *Sahih al-Bukhari* are included in this chapter as well.

Gregory the Great (ca. 540–604)

Gregory the Great was born into an aristocratic family in Rome. His father was a Roman senator, and Gregory initially followed his father in an administrative career. After his father's death, however, Gregory became a monk and used his inheritance to found seven monasteries on his family's lands. In 579, Pope Pelagius II compelled him to be one of the seven deacons of Rome and then appointed him as papal ambassador to the imperial court in Constantinople. Gregory returned to Rome in 586 and, after Pope Pelagius's death in 590, became the first monk to be selected as pope.

Gregory was an influential pope who extended his duties to secular and even military roles, negotiating, for example, peace with the Lombards who besieged Rome in 592–593. He is also famous for the evangelization of England, sending approximately forty missionaries to Canterbury in 597. Gregory vigorously defended the authority of the bishop of Rome, promoted monasticism, and made significant changes to church liturgy and music (e.g., the Gregorian chant is attributed to him). In addition, Gregory devoted vast sums to charity to help those in need, and he combated "heretics" such as the Pelagians, Donatists, and Arians (see McKim 2007, 486).

Gregory's contributions to the interpretation of the parables primarily stem from his homilies on the Gospels that he wrote during the first three years of his papacy. His homilies are directed to both clergy and laity, so they are less complex than many of his other works. His homily on the parables of the treasure in the field and of the net, for example, combines allegorical interpretations with ethical exhortations. The treasure stands for our desire for heaven, the field in which the treasure is hidden "signifies the conduct by which we achieve" heaven, and the actions of the man who finds the treasure demonstrate how we are to achieve our longing for heaven: the man sells all that he has and buys the field, which denotes our renouncing the pleasures of the flesh, restraining our earthly desires, and delighting in the observance of God's instruction. The treasure has to be hidden in order to preserve it, because the desire for "celestial happiness" is in itself not a sufficient shield against the evil forces that attack like robbers (Gregory the Great 1960, 16–17). Likewise the parable of the pearl of great value represents the soul that has attained, as far as humanly possible, "a perfect knowledge of the heavenly life" and therefore is willing to give up the love of temporal things on earth: "Aflame with love for the things of heaven, it cares for nothing upon earth and considers as deformed all that once seemed so beautiful, for in the soul shines only the splendor of that priceless pearl" (17).

Similarly, in the parable of the net, the fishing net symbolizes the church, and the fish symbolize "the whole human race." Once the net is filled, it will be brought to the shore, and the separation of the fish into good and bad symbolizes the separation of good and wicked human beings that is performed by angels at the last judgment. After the fish are brought to shore, they have no opportunity to change, so Gregory concludes with an exhortation to his congregation to make sure they are prepared to reach the "shore" of the last judgment by choosing to flee the temporal delights of the world and to correct their behavior by "stringent discipline."

Origen's interpretation of the parable of the laborers in the vineyard established the parameters that others such as Augustine would follow, and Gregory's interpretation is similar as well, including a twofold allegorical interpretation. The different hours of the day when the workers are hired represent not only the different dispensations (Adam to Noah, Noah to Abraham, Abraham to Moses, Moses to Jesus, and Jesus to the end of the world) but also the different stages in human life (childhood, adolescence, youth, old age, and senility). Then, as usual, Gregory turns to moral exhortation: "As some are drawn to a good life in childhood, others in adolescence, others in youth, others in old age and some in decrepitude, it is as if the labourers were summoned at differing hours to the vineyard. Examine your behavior then, brethren, and see whether you are yet God's labourers. Let each one think over his conduct and see whether he is working in the vineyard of the Lord" (Gregory the Great 1960, 25).

In his homily on the wedding feast parable, Gregory argues that the version in the Gospel of Matthew is a separate parable from the version found in Luke. Matthew's parable is about a marriage "dinner," where a person is expelled after entering, whereas Luke's parable is a "supper," and no one is expelled. Gregory concludes that salvation is the main topic in Luke's parable, but the church is the focus of Matthew's (105–21; Wailes 1987, 155). Gregory also further develops the allegorical interpretations of the parable by Origen and Augustine, such as the wedding symbolizing the incarnation of Jesus, since God the king gave his son Jesus in marriage when God "united him to human flesh in the womb of the Virgin" (Gregory the Great 1960, 35). The marriage also represents the church, since the "wicked mingle with the good" in the wedding feast, a combination in the church that will continue until the last judgment. God allows us to enter the "holy church," where this marriage takes place, but the expulsion of the man without a wedding garment should cause "fear and trembling": the wedding garment does not symbolize baptism or faith, since both are needed to enter the church. Instead, like Augustine before him (although not citing Paul as a reason), Gregory argues that the wedding garment denotes "charity" (i.e., love), so the man without a wedding garment represents those in the church who have faith but lack love (42). Christians must obey the two precepts of charity: to love God and to love their neighbors: "It is necessary to observe these two precepts of charity if we desire to be found wearing the wedding garment" (43). Otherwise they will be condemned at the last judgment.

Gregory's interpretation of the parable of the talents as representing the differing gifts/capabilities of the recipients sets the standard for almost all the other interpretations that follow in the next few centuries. The man in the parable who goes on a journey is Jesus, who has ascended into heaven and has distributed "spiritual gifts to the faithful who believed in him." The five talents given to the first man symbolize the five senses of the body, which means "external knowledge." The giving of two talents represents understanding and action, and the one talent denotes the giving of understanding alone. Unlike the first two servants, the third servant hides his talent in the earth; this means that he does not seek spiritual profit but focuses his understanding only on matters of the world. The first two servants are rewarded with the prize of eternal life, and, as always, Gregory reflects on the moral implications:

> We should note that the worthless servant says that his master is hard, and nevertheless refuses to serve him. . . . This servant is a figure of many in the

church, who are afraid to lead a better life, but not afraid to continue in the quagmire of their inertia; because they consider themselves to be sinners, they tremble to approach the way of sanctity, but they are not afraid to persist in their vices. (Gregory the Great 1960, 62)

Those who are given the gift of wealth, for instance, should practice almsgiving, but the foundation for all good works must be charity/love:

> But he who has not the gift of charity will lose even those gifts which he seemed to have. So it is necessary, brethren, that charity should be the motive of all your actions. It is true charity to love your friend in God, and your enemy for God's sake. He who has not charity loses all the good he had; he is deprived of the talent he was given and, in the words of Christ himself, he is cast into exterior darkness. (64–65)

Gregory exhorts his congregation to recognize that Jesus will demand an accounting for all the gifts they had received. They should watch carefully to make sure that they use their talents as best they can, so that they will receive Jesus's approval at the last judgment (66).

Gregory even allegorizes the parable of the rich man and Lazarus. The rich man represents the Jewish people, "who made a cult of exterior things" (i.e., the law). Lazarus—covered with sores—denotes the gentiles, who are not afraid to confess the "open sores" of their sins. Lazarus longed to eat from the crumbs that fell from the rich man's table, but the rich man/Jewish people would not share the knowledge of the law (i.e., the food in the parable) with Lazarus/the gentiles. The dogs that came to lick Lazarus's wounds symbolize preachers of the gospel—since Scripture sometimes uses *dog* to denote a preacher (Gregory cites Ps. 68:23). The dogs helped cure the sores by licking them, just as "when the holy doctors instruct us in the confession of our sins . . . they touch the ulcer of our mind with their tongue" (146). Lazarus, symbolizing gentile believers, received his reward in heaven. The rich man, however, was punished in hell, which depicts the punishment of the Jewish people who do not believe Moses's words about Jesus (John 5:46) and therefore do not believe in Jesus (149).

After this discussion of the "hidden significance of the allegory," Gregory devotes a significant amount of the homily to the moral of the parable. The rich man was condemned not for overt evil deeds but for failing to help Lazarus and for "being attached" to his possessions (149). He used his possessions only for his own pleasure "in the service of his pride," and "he did not attempt to redeem his sins" through a just use of his abundant riches. He had no excuse: Lazarus had lain at his gate, and the rich man had "passed before him daily"; he thus knew about Lazarus's dire situation yet did nothing to help (151).

Gregory also observes that it is striking, since the names of the rich are usually more widely known than those of the poor, that the parable gives only Lazarus's name. This detail tells us that God "knows and approves of the humble." Just as the rich man denied Lazarus even a morsel of food, now God denied the rich man even a drop of water to cool his tongue. Gregory also argues that the tongue of the rich man is highlighted because, even though Jesus never mentions it, the man must have sinned through "loquacity" or "verbosity" (i.e., those who feast frequently also usually talk too much) and thus "justly suffered a special torment in his tongue" (153–54).

In addition, the rich man suffering in hell after receiving good things during his life "is sufficient in itself to inspire terror": Christians should beware of being perverted by riches and also should be forgiving of the poor, even when they sin, since they, like Lazarus, may be "purified by poverty" (155). Gregory then exhorts his congregation:

> My dear brethren, now that you know the glory of Lazarus and the punish-
> ment of the rich man, act with extreme caution; seek out the poor, that in the
> day of judgment they may be your intercessors and advocates. You have many
> brothers of Lazarus lying at your doors, in want of those crumbs which fall
> daily from your table when you have well satisfied your appetite. The words we
> have been reading should teach us to fulfill the law of mercy. Every minute we
> find a Lazarus if we seek him, and every day without seeking we find one at our
> door. Now beggars besiege us, imploring alms; later they will be our advocates.
> Rather it is we who should beg, and yet we are besought. Ask yourselves whether
> we should refuse what we are asked, when those who ask us are our patrons.
> Therefore do not lose the opportunity of doing works of mercy; do not store
> unused the good things you possess. (158)

Gregory concludes by urging his congregation to despise the transient honors of earth and to seek eternal glory. A key element is respecting the poor and sharing one's riches with them. As Jesus said in Matthew 25, everything you give to someone in need on earth, you are giving to Jesus in heaven (see Wailes 1987, 197–98).

Gregory's interpretive approach to Scripture establishes a typical pattern for medieval interpreters in the West. He insists that the historical or literal meaning of Scripture is foundational, but he prefers to move on to the alle-gorical sense of Scripture, which reflects the divine mystery and the limits of human understanding, and then to progress to moral practices. Scripture, he believes, nurtures Christians at many levels: it is like a river in which a lamb could walk and an elephant could swim (*Moralia; Letter to Leander*). The proper response to this divine mystery is to ascend from the "simpler historical sense to the more obscure spiritual senses" (Hauser and Watson 2009, 2:96).

Sahih al-Bukhari (ca. 870)

The Qur'an indicates that God's verbal supreme revelation has been revealed in written form to humankind in four different collections:

- *Torah* (revealed through Moses; *Sura* 6:154)
- *Psalms* (revealed through David; *Sura* 17:55)
- *Gospel* (revealed through Jesus, which fulfilled what was revealed in the Torah; *Sura* 5:46)
- *Qur'an* (revealed through Muhammad, which confirms both the Torah and Gospel, explains them, and has greater authority than they; *Suras* 3:3–4; 5:48; 10:37; 12:111; see Moucarry 2002, 26)

The Qur'an includes traditions from the Hebrew Bible (e.g., Moses and Abraham) and the New Testament (e.g., Mary, John the Baptist, and Jesus). Further development of these traditions took place in the *hadith* ("recollections"; Arabic plural = *ahadith*), which are collections of traditions reporting a saying or action of Muhammad or, less often, one of his companions (Khalidi 2001, 25–26). Hadith literature includes Muhammad's reactions to various events, his opinions on numerous matters, and the reasoning he used to reach his decisions. Muhammad taught that Islam was not a new religion; instead, he proclaimed the religion that God had revealed through the prophets. Beginning with Adam, the succeeding stream of prophets, including Abraham, Moses, Jesus, and others, had proclaimed the unity of God, submitting to and worshiping God alone and following the entirety of God's law. Islamic teachings and practice are, in part, understood as corrections of Judaism and Christianity, the two monotheistic traditions that preceded Islam, which partly explains why Islamic traditions about previous biblical figures diverge from biblical traditions (Outcalt 2014, 95–98).

The Qur'an and the hadith collections constitute the two most important sources for Islamic faith and practice, and the *Sahih al-Bukhari* and the *Sahih Muslim bin al-Hajjaj* are the two most authoritative of the six "canonical" collections, with the *Sahih al-Bukhari* being considered the "most authentic" collection.

Whereas the Qur'an is more concerned about correcting doctrinal errors about Jesus (e.g., that he died on a cross or is part of a Trinity), hadith traditions include many more teachings and miracles. In these traditions, Jesus emerges as both an apocalyptic figure—central to the Muslim concept of the end of the world—and as a figure more closely connected to popular piety and moral discourse. In addition, Jesus in hadith literature is especially concerned about "the least of these," and he illustrates the Muslim virtues of poverty and humility (Outcalt 2014, 109). By the ninth century, sayings by Jesus in hadith traditions usually fall within five categories: (1) eschatological sayings and discussions of Jesus's return; (2) sayings reminiscent of sayings in the Gospels; (3) ascetic sayings and stories; (4) sayings that involve intra-Muslim polemics; and (5) clarifications of the relationship between Muhammad and Jesus, including details of what Jesus looked like (e.g., fair complexion, moderate height, and beautiful long hair that was neither too curly nor too straight; Leirvik 2010, 37–39; Khalidi 2001, 32–34).

Many of the traditions about Jesus in hadith literature stem from the Sermon on the Mount; parables appear infrequently. The parable of the laborers in the vineyard found in *Sahih al-Bukhari* is a prominent exception. This parable, which appears at least six times—although none of those instances ever indicates that the labor occurs in a vineyard—is significantly reworked to Islamicize its message (for a more extensive examination, see Elmostafa 2015). All versions follow the same basic story, but the occurrences in 3:468, 3:469, 4:665, and 6:539 (Bukhārī 1971) are more closely related, and the occurrences in 1:533 and 3:471, where the first two sets of workers quit the assigned task, closely resemble each other.

The version in *Sahih al-Bukhari* volume 4, book 56, #665 (4:665), is an example of the first category:

> Allah's Apostle said, "Your period (i.e., the Muslims' period) in comparison to the periods of the previous nations, is like the period between the 'Asr prayer and sunset. And your example in comparison to the Jews and the Christians is like the example of a person who employed some laborers and asked them, 'Who will work for me till midday for one Qirat each?' The Jews worked for half a day for one Qirat each. The person asked, 'Who will do the work for me from midday to the time of the 'Asr (prayer) for one Qirat each?' The Christians worked from midday till the 'Asr prayer for one Qirat. Then the person asked, 'Who will do the work for me from the 'Asr till sunset for two Qirats each?'" The Prophet added, "It is you (i.e., Muslims) who are doing the work from the 'Asr till sunset, so you will have a double reward. The Jews and the Christians got angry and said, 'We have done more work but got less wages.' Allah said, 'Have I been unjust to you as regards your rights?' They said, 'No.' So Allah said, 'Then it is My Blessing which I bestow on whomever I like.'"

In this version, Muhammad is explaining to Muslims their current situation. The employer—Allah, as we find out at the end of the story—hires the first group (i.e., the Jews) to "work" until midday for one Qirat—a weight measurement seen as equal to the weight of a seed from a carob tree (0.2053 grams)—in gold or silver; it is from this term that we get the English word "carat." At midday, the work for the Jews was over, and then the Christians were hired, also for one Qirat, to work the next period of the day. The Christians finished their work, and then Muslims were hired to finish the day/task, and they were paid twice the amount that the first two groups of Jews and Christians were paid. The reason for the doubling of pay is perhaps explained elsewhere in the *Sahih al-Bukhari*, in a hadith that envisions the doubling of pay for extra work/faithfulness: "Allah's Apostle said, '(A believer) who accompanies the funeral procession of a Muslim out of sincere faith and hoping to attain Allah's reward and remains with it till the funeral prayer is offered and the burial ceremonies are over, he will return with a reward of two Qirats. . . . He who offers the funeral prayer only and returns before the burial, will return with the reward of one Qirat only'" (vol. 1, bk. 2, #45). In the parable, there is an important difference between the first two assignments and the third. The first two are finished working, since Jews and Christians have completed their tasks. The third group's mission is still ongoing, since the labor of Muslims continues: "You . . . are doing the work."

This interpretation of the different groups of laborers representing different religious groups is similar to some earlier Christian interpretations. Irenaeus, Origen, Augustine, and Gregory, for example, all argue that the different agreements the owner makes at different times with workers represent the different dispensations God established throughout history (e.g., the covenants made with Adam, Noah, Abraham, Moses, and Jesus). In hadith traditions, the first two dispensations are Jews and Christians, but the final dispensation is that of Muslims. In other words, this parable is reworked to argue that even though God's revelations to Muhammad are reminders of what God had already conveyed to previous prophets like Abraham, they are also corrections to the errors of the Jews and Christians. Muhammad, the last and most important of those prophets, is able to correct those errors.

The other major version of this parable found in the *Sahih al-Bukhari* in volume 3, book 36, #471, makes this even clearer (cf. vol. 1, bk. 10, #533):

The Prophet said, "The example of Muslims, Jews and Christians is like the example of a man who employed labourers to work for him from morning till night for specific wages. They worked till midday and then said, 'We do not need your money which you have fixed for us and let whatever we have done be annulled.' The man said to them, 'Don't quit the work, but complete the rest of it and take your full wages.' But they refused and went away. The man employed another batch after them and said to them, 'Complete the rest of the day and yours will be the wages I had fixed for the first batch.' So, they worked till the time of 'Asr prayer. Then they said, 'Let what we have done be annulled and keep the wages you have promised us for yourself.' The man said to them, 'Complete the rest of the work, as only a little of the day remains,' but they refused. Thereafter he employed another batch to work for the rest of the day and they worked for the rest of the day till the sunset, and they received the wages of the two former batches. So, that was the example of those people (Muslims) and the example of this light of guidance they have accepted willingly."

In this version, the first workers (Jews) were hired to work from morning to evening. They worked only until midday, however, when they quit and stated that they did not need the man's money and wanted their work to be annulled. Even though the man asked them to continue, they refused. Likewise, the second group (Christians) was hired to finish the day's work, but they worked only until the 'Asr prayer time. These workers did not state that they did not need the man's money, but they likewise wanted their work annulled, told the man to keep the wages, and refused the man's entreaty to keep working, even though "only a little of the day" remained. Therefore, the man hired a third group (Muslims), who completed the task and received the wages of the first two groups (thus double what the other two groups were promised).

This version of the parable stresses the recalcitrance of Jews and Christians and their refusal to complete the task upon which they and God had agreed. The Muslims are the ones who complete the task and remain faithful to God's commands. In all versions of the parable, Muslims receive God's special blessing.

The differing versions in *Sahih al-Bukhari* illustrate how different trajectories in the traditions are developed. In this case, the message that many Christian interpreters had received from the parable—that the time of the Jews had passed—is now extended to mean that the times of both the Jews and Christians have passed and that Muslims are finishing God's assigned task faithfully. Thus Islamic teachings and practice correct the deficiencies in the responses of Jews and Christians to the work assigned to them by God.

Wazo of Liège (ca. 985–1048)

Wazo was educated at the cathedral school of Lobbes, became head of the cathedral school in Liège (in modern Belgium), later became provost at Liège, and finally was elected bishop in 1042. Wazo was involved in a number of conflicts. Even his biographer and admirer, Anselm of Liège (1008–ca. 1056), notes that his opponents called Wazo an obstinate troublemaker and hothead, and Anselm's biography indeed portrays Wazo as stubborn, contentious, and confrontational—but as "a supremely bold defender of the pure truth" (Jaeger 1994, 205–8).

Anselm's biography of Wazo reports that sometime between 1043 and 1048 Roger II, bishop of Châlons-sur-Marne (renamed Châlons-en-Champagne), wrote to Wazo for advice concerning some "countryfolk" in his diocese "who eagerly followed the evil teachings of the Manichaeans and frequented their secret conventicles" (Wakefield and Evans 1991, 90). They also had committed the unforgivable sin of blasphemy against the Holy Spirit, by asserting that the Spirit came through the laying on of hands through Mani (see Matt. 12:31–32), Roger indicated. These heretics abhorred marriage, were vegetarians against the killing of any animal, and, worst of all, were converting others to this heresy.

Roger asks Wazo whether he should turn these heretics over to the secular authorities for execution, since, if these heretics were not "exterminated," their (evil) leaven would corrupt the whole loaf (cf. Matt. 13:33; Luke 13:20–21; 1 Cor. 5:6; Gal. 5:9). In his response, Wazo argues that although Christians should despise the heresy promoted by these people, Christians should also emulate the example of Jesus, who was "mild and humble of heart" and who suffered abuse, torture, and even death. Christians likewise should bear with such things as this heresy: "Moreover, to be prepared for doing what the merciful and compassionate Lord, who does not judge sinners straightway but waits patiently for repentance, desires to be done about such persons, let us hearken to what he deemed fitting to teach his disciples—nay, rather us—when in his Gospel he expounded the parable of the wheat and the cockle [tare]" (Wakefield and Evans 1991, 91).

Wazo summarizes the parable: Jesus is the sower, the good seed is the children of God, the field is the world, the devil sows the bad seed, the cockle is children of the devil, the harvest is the end of the world, and the reapers are the angels. Wazo adds: "What, moreover, but the role of preachers is signified by the servants who wish to gather up the cockle when it first appears? Do not preachers, as they separate good from evil in Holy Church, attempt as it were to root out the cockle from the good seed of the field?" (Wakefield and Evans 1991, 91–92).

Wazo also notes that Jesus himself restrains his followers from attempting to gather up the cockle to prevent some of the wheat from being uprooted, and "what does the Lord reveal by these words but his patience, which he

wishes his preachers to display to their erring fellow men, particularly since
it may be possible for those who today are cockle, tomorrow to be converted
and be wheat?" (Wakefield and Evans 1991, 92). Wazo commends Roger's
spiritual zeal for the people being led astray by these heretics. That fact alone
demonstrates that Roger is a servant of Christ, but Wazo urges him to demonstrate his piety by obeying what Christ commands:

> Out of this zeal you strive with the hoe of judicial decision to rid the grainfield
> of cockle, that the good not be corrupted by evil. But lest you do this hastily, lest
> it be done before its time, the holy text is rather to be obeyed, so that although
> we think we are practicing righteousness by punishing transgressors, whose
> impiety is veiled under semblance of strict life, we do no disservice to him, who
> desires not the death of sinners nor rejoices in the damnation of the dying, but
> rather knows how to bring sinners back to repentance through his patience and
> long-suffering. Therefore, heeding the words of the Maker, let the decision of
> the area wait; let us not seek to remove from this life by the sword of secular
> authority those whom God himself, Creator and Redeemer, wishes to spare, as
> he has revealed, to the end that they may turn again to his will from the snares
> of the devil in which they were entrapped. (Wakefield and Evans 1991, 92)

Wazo hopes that perhaps some of what appears to be "cockle" will be revealed
as "wheat" at the great harvest at the end of time.

Wazo concludes by saying that bishops of the church do not receive the
"sword which belongs to secular power" when they are ordained. A bishop's
task is to bring people to life eternal, not to hasten their earthly deaths. What
a bishop should do, however, is to deprive heretics and all who associate with
them of a "Catholic communion" (Wakefield and Evans 1991, 93).

Anselm's biography then informs its readers that some people in Roger's
diocese were identified as heretics simply because they had a pale complexion,
since it was assumed both that vegetarianism was an indication of heresy
and that it produced a lighter complexion. Anselm concludes that this is an
example of the wheat being uprooted with the cockle: "Thus, through error
coupled with cruelty, many truly Catholic persons had been killed in the past"
(Wakefield and Evans 1991, 89–96, 670), something that both Anselm and
Wazo urged should be avoided, just as Jesus commanded.

The Golden Gospels of Echternach (ca. 1045–1046)

The community of monks at the Benedictine Abbey of Echternach (in modern Luxembourg) produced some of the finest illuminated manuscripts ever

created. The most important of these manuscripts is known as the Golden Gospels of Echternach (Codex Aureus Epternacensis), because of the 23½-karat gold lettering that makes up most of the text. The metalwork and ivory on the front cover, which includes precious stones and pearls set into gold, come from an earlier manuscript, and the 135 pages of the manuscript were apparently trimmed to fit into the current binding (Dodwell 1993, 144).

This manuscript is distinctive for its use of color and comparatively rare depictions of parables. The representations of parables and other narrative illuminations appear on full pages in three panels, explanations of which are written in narrow gold strips. Each Gospel is preceded by such illuminated pages, with three scenes on each page, but the images are not connected to specific Gospels (e.g., unique scenes from the Gospels of Luke and John are included in the pages before the Gospel of Mark), which accentuates the idea that the four Gospels present a unified vision.

Four pages that precede the Gospel of Luke depict four parables from the Gospels (for details, see Metz 1957, plates 67, 68, 69, and 70).

The Laborers in the Vineyard (Figure 2.1)

The inscription at the top of the first panel indicates that a landowner (labeled as *pater familias*) is hiring laborers "needed for the vineyard of the world," which indicates that the parable is interpreted allegorically. The left side of the top panel shows the landowner hiring the first group of (four) workers, with two of them holding hoes. The right side of this panel shows the landowner hiring the second group of (five) workers, and two of them hold hoes.

The second panel portrays eleven workers toiling away in the vineyard. Six of them are hoeing, four of them are tending the vines, and one on the far right is slumped over, apparently overcome by the "scorching heat" of the day (Matt. 20:12), which is apparently depicted by the yellow in the background (see Metz 1957, 77). The man raises his hand to his head, which allows viewers to discern his discomfort.

The third and lowest panel has a green background, which indicates that it is late in the day. On the left side of the panel, the landowner addresses three workers, two of whom look up into the sky, which denotes the parable's eschatological context and the first/last reversal of which Matthew (19:30; 20:16) and later Christian interpreters (e.g., Origen with his "coin of salvation") speak. On the right side of the panel, the workers receive their pay from the landowner's steward (a steward is not mentioned in Matthew's parable).

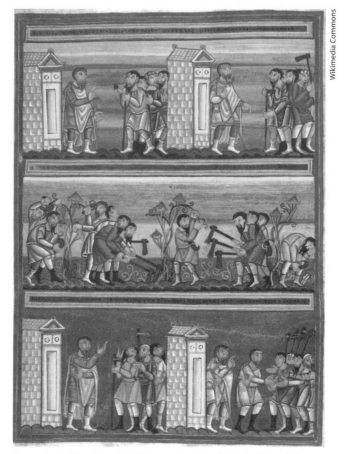

Figure 2.1 Golden Gospels of Echternach, Laborers in the Vineyard

Some of the workers remonstrate against the landowner, but he rebukes them (one of them in the parable) with strong words.

The Wicked Tenants (Figure 2.2)

The first panel includes a fenced-in vineyard with a winepress, a few vines growing inside the fence, and a magnificent building in the front. The landowner (who, labeled as *pater familias*, once again portrays God) appears along with three other people (labeled as *agricolae*/farmers) to whom he is entrusting the vineyard. He hands one of them a hoe and points to the vineyard. The second panel shows the man sending his slaves (*servi*) to collect the produce. At this stage, the vines have grown significantly and have produced abundant grapes. The tenants—six of them—are now armed with spears, shields, and

Figure 2.2 Golden Gospels of Echternach, Wicked Tenants

stones, and they are stabbing, beating, and stoning the landowner's slaves to death. The third panel shows the landowner sending his son (*filius*), and three of the tenants are depicted killing the son. One drags him by his legs out of the vineyard, and two stab the son to death with spears. The abundant grapes remain unpicked on their vines. Once again, the parable is depicted allegorically: God sends prophets, who are killed by Israel, and then finally God sends his son, Jesus, who is also killed.

The Great Dinner (Figure 2.3)

The representation of this parable is distinctive, because it does not portray the parable chronologically, and it depicts aspects of Luke's version instead of Matthew's. The top panel, for example, shows "paupers" being welcomed to

the table by the host, with a servant on the right starting to bring food to the
table. The middle panel depicts four men—representing the poor, crippled,
lame, and blind—crawling "upward" toward the top panel and being welcomed
by another man. In the middle, the man who has bought a piece of land tells
the messenger that he has to go examine it, and on the right the man who
bought oxen tells the messenger that he has to go try them out. The left side of
the bottom panel shows the messenger inviting the four men (poor, crippled,
lame, and blind) to the great dinner, and they start moving "upward." On
the right side of the panel the messenger watches as the man who just got
married rides away on a horse with his wife. The messenger points with one
hand to the man riding away and with his other hand to the four men crawling
or walking upward. The allegory in this illumination is not as obvious, but
it does signify the people whom God receives at the eschatological banquet.

Figure 2.3 Golden Gospels of Echternach, Great Dinner

The Rich Man and Lazarus (Figure 2.4)

The top panel shows the rich man (*dives*) wearing red/purple clothes and feasting at a table, with a servant bringing more food. Just outside the door crouches Lazarus, with his arm raised in supplication. Sores cover his entire body, and two dogs lick his wounds. On the left side of the second panel Lazarus lies dead. His body lies alone and abandoned, but two angels are taking his soul, which comes out of the corpse's mouth, and are wrapping the soul with a white cloth. The right side of the panel shows Lazarus sitting on Abraham's lap, and twelve other souls—six on each side—look at them with their hands raised in a prayer-like fashion.

The left side of the lowest panel shows the rich man having died. His body lies in his expensive house, with friends/family looking on. This scene shows

Figure 2.4 Golden Gospels of Echternach, Rich Man and Lazarus

two demons—their bodies are black, their wings red, and they have fearsome claws—taking his soul out of his mouth. One demon in the middle of the panel carries him away. The right side of the panel shows the rich man in the "inferno," looking up at Abraham and Lazarus, with both arms raised, begging Abraham to help him, but to no avail. Both Abraham and Lazarus look down at the rich man; their arms are raised, signifying that it is too late for anyone to help him. Luke's allusion to Jesus's resurrection (Luke 16:31) might also be reflected in the twelve souls (symbolizing the apostles?) that flank Abraham and Lazarus in heaven.

All the demons in hell are dark brown, with purple hair and with fire coming out of their mouths. Four demons face the rich man with their arms and menacing claws stretched out toward him. A fifth demon, larger than all the rest, lies helplessly bound with a rope around his neck, hands, and feet, perhaps signifying the day when the angels will bind Satan (Rev. 20:2). The faces of two other demons appear on the other side of the rich man, and they are flanked by seven other human figures—three on the left and four on the right—who also appear in supplication. The illumination thus offers a concise and terrifying portrait of what awaits those who act as the rich man did and the future comfort offered to the Lazaruses of the world.

Theophylact (ca. 1050–ca. 1125)

Theophylact was born in Euboea (an island in the Aegean Sea just north of Boeotia). He moved to Constantinople and studied under Michael Psellus, the eminent philosopher, theologian, and historian who was the first professor of philosophy at the University of Constantinople. Theophylact became the first teacher of rhetoric in the patriarchal school and was a royal tutor for Constantine Doukas, the future Byzantine emperor (reigned 1059–1067). Theophylact also served as a deacon in the Hagia Sophia in Constantinople, before he was appointed as archbishop of Ochrid in Bulgaria (ca. 1080–1090). Although he was archbishop in Bulgaria for about twenty-five years, in many ways Theophylact remained a citizen of his beloved Constantinople (e.g., in his letters, he writes about his "eternal exile" among the "barbarians"), but he also was a shepherd who looked after his flock and served as their protector and intercessor with the empire (Mullett 1997, 261–77).

Theophylact is best known for his biblical commentaries, and his parable interpretations exemplify his approach to the Bible. In his treatment of the dishonest manager (unjust steward) parable, for example, Theophylact notes:

Each parable indirectly and figuratively reveals the nature of certain things, but it is not similar in every respect to the things which it describes. Therefore it is not necessary to scrutinize in great detail every part of a parable; we should only draw benefit from that part of the parable which is central to its purpose. The other parts, which provide just the structure of the parable and do not contribute to its meaning, we should let alone. Such is the case with this parable. If we attempt to examine every part in detail—who is the steward? who is the one who made him steward? by whom was he accused? who are the debtors? why does one debtor owe wheat and another oil, why in measures of a hundred?—if we examine and belabor every such point, we shall render the entire discourse obscure and unintelligible. We may even make the explanation appear ridiculous because so much of it, by necessity, will be uncertain. Therefore we must attempt to receive from this parable just the benefit that it contains. (Theophylact 1997, 205)

The main point of this parable, Theophylact explains, is that we should use the wealth God gives us not for our own pleasures but to meet the needs of others. Theophylact thus urges his readers to distribute their "wealth of unrighteousness" to the poor and promises that all who do so will be welcomed as "righteous" into heaven by those poor whom they have aided in this life (208).

Other parables in Luke, Theophylact points out, have similar messages concerning the use of wealth. The Lukan context of the parable of the rich fool, which concerns a dispute over an inheritance, teaches us to disregard material goods and focus on things that benefit the salvation of our souls. Greed is idolatry; those who honor silver and gold are like those who worship idols, and Christians therefore should flee from abundance. The greed of the rich man in the parable is insatiable, as is evidenced by his decision to tear down his storehouses to build new, bigger ones. Theophylact asks: "But what need is there to pull down and build? You have available to you as storehouses the stomachs of the poor which can hold much, and are indestructible and imperishable. They are in fact heavenly and divine storehouses, for he who feeds the pauper, feeds God" (147). The rich man focuses on himself, not stopping to consider that "his" abundant harvest comes from and ultimately belongs to God. He also learns, too late, that "a long life is not a crop you can grow"; it too comes from God. Theophylact thus urges his readers "to be rich toward God," to trust in God, and to have God as their wealth. If they give all their material possessions away, they will not lack in the necessities to sustain their lives; God will provide them out of God's abundant "treasury of good things."

Theophylact's discussion of the parable of the Pharisee and the tax collector notes how Jesus ceaselessly teaches about the dangers of pride. Pride, like arrogance, stems from self-love, and it is the most destructive type of self-love. Pride is contempt for God because prideful people ascribe their accomplishments to themselves and not to God. Those who are prideful oppose God, in practice deny God's existence, and despise other human beings. Jesus therefore opposes pride and in this parable promises to heal the sin of pride.

The Pharisee's words initially sound full of gratitude to God ("God, I thank you . . ."), but his words are full of a foolish misunderstanding: "The Pharisee is proud, ascribing his deeds to his own strength, and that is why he proceeds to condemn others. By saying that the Pharisee *stood*, the Lord indicates his haughtiness and lack of humility." The Pharisee stresses his own good deeds, fasting twice a week and tithing, and Theophylact argues that Christians can learn from this Pharisee that avoiding evil is not enough; one must also do good. Theophylact then writes: "There is also another, more profound, explanation of this parable. Against the passion of adultery, the Pharisee boasted of his fasting, for lustful desires arise from eating and drinking to excess. By restraining his body through fasting on Mondays and Thursdays, as was the practice of the Pharisees, he kept himself far from such passions. He also resisted extortion and injustice by giving tithes of all his possessions" (236). The tax collector was the opposite of the Pharisee in every respect, Theophylact notes, not only in physical location but also in his demeanor, words, and heart. He, unlike the Pharisee, was too ashamed even to lift his eyes to heaven; he simply asked God for mercy. It was the tax collector, not the Pharisee, who went home "justified," because God resists the proud but gives grace to the humble (Prov. 3:34; James 4:6; 1 Pet. 5:5; Theophylact 1997, 237).

The parable of the wise and foolish builders (Luke 6:47–49) illustrates, for Theophylact, how important it is for Christians to match their deeds with their words, to obey the words of Jesus, and to model their lives after his actions: "The work of servants is to do what their master commands" (Theophylact 1997, 71). The man who built his house on the rock built his life's foundation on Jesus, since the rock signifies Jesus. On the one hand, digging deeply into that rock means searching out the depths of Scripture "with the aid of the Spirit." Then when the flood of persecution or temptation comes, it will not overcome Christians, who have built their foundation upon the rock of Christ. On the other hand, "the house falls when its builders do not do the words of the Lord, and great is the ruin of that house. It is those who hear, but do not do, what the Lord says, whose fall is *great*. For the sin of the man who heard but did not do what the Lord said is more grievous than the sin of the man who never heard the Lord at all" (171–72). In a similar way, the parable of building a tower (Luke 14:28–30) illustrates that before Christians decide to follow Jesus, they should not "lay down the foundation" of following Jesus "without being ready with sufficient zeal to finish the task." The foundation is the word of teaching, and the edifice consists of the deeds built upon that foundation, and that becomes "our strong tower of defence against the enemy" (188–89).

Theophylact also uses the parable of the two debtors to illustrate that all human beings are sinful. Simon the Pharisee may be less of a "debtor" than the sinful woman, but he is a debtor all the same. Then Theophylact turns to his readers: "The same is true for you, O reader. You may owe less than the sinful woman, but you are no more able to repay your debts than she, because in your pride you refuse to confess your indebtedness. And when both are forgiven, who will love more? Certainly that debtor who was forgiven more. By saying these things, the Lord shuts the mouth of that arrogant man" (80). As these examples demonstrate, although Theophylact uses allegorical interpretations, he also carefully investigates the literal meaning of the texts. He also stresses, like his model John Chrysostom, the moral application of the biblical texts: Christians should follow the teachings of Jesus, and their deeds should match their words.

Hildegard of Bingen (1098–1179)

Hildegard of Bingen is the first major German mystic and most famous twelfth-century female mystic. She writes not only about her visions (e.g., *Know the Ways*, or *Scivias*; *Book of Life's Merits*; *Book of Divine Works*) but also on numerous other topics, such as prophecy, poetry, medicine and science, music, ethics, and theology, as well as writing over three hundred letters, developing a secret coded language for her religious community, and preaching numerous sermons.

Hildegard was born in 1098 in Bermersheim, about a dozen miles southwest of Mainz. Hildegard reports that she started having visions in her early childhood (see Hildegard 1986, 2). At the age of eight, Hildegard was "tithed" (she was her parents' tenth child) into a religious life by her parents and entrusted to the care of a holy woman named Jutta (Judith). Both Jutta and Hildegard entered the Benedictine monastery of Disibodenberg, and a small number of women gathered into a religious community with Jutta as its head. After Jutta's death about thirty years later (1136), Hildegard succeeded her as the leader of the community.

In a powerful vision in 1141, Hildegard saw a "very great light," and a voice from heaven told her to "speak and write" about the secrets and mysteries revealed to her by God (Hildegard 1986, 1–2). This vision and subsequent ones in 1163 and 1167 were especially decisive in Hildegard receiving what she divined as a mandate to share what the Holy Spirit had revealed to her (Kienzle 2009, 7). Her visionary experiences gave Hildegard direct insight independent of an education usually reserved for males: "In that same [experience of] vision I understood the writings of the prophets, the Gospels, the works of other holy men, and those of certain philosophers, without any human instruction, and I expounded certain things based on these, though I scarcely had literary understanding, inasmuch as a woman who was not learned had been my teacher" (Dronke 1984, 145). Hildegard's biographer, Theodoric, writes that Pope Eugenius III, at the request of Bernard of Clairvaux, approved and blessed portions of Hildegard's *Scivias* and commanded her to finish it (Gottfried and Theodoric 1996, 39). This approval proved crucial to Hildegard's position, since it was extremely unusual during this era for a woman to produce such visionary writing and to have such authority (see Kerby-Fulton 2010, 344; Abigail Young 2012, 260).

Fifty-eight of Hildegard's homilies are collected in her *Homilies on the Gospels* (Hildegard 2011), and they establish her "as the only known systematic female exegete of the Middle Ages" (Kienzle 2009, 2). Fourteen homilies focus on seven parables (two homilies on each parable): one in Matthew (laborers in the vineyard) and six in Luke (great dinner, prodigal son, dishonest manager, rich man and Lazarus, Pharisee and the tax collector, and barren fig tree). Hildegard works through the text systematically, verse by verse, phrase by phrase, and even word by word.

Homilies 1 and 2 both discuss the parable of the dishonest manager, but they interpret it from different perspectives. Homily 1 envisions God as Creator as the foundational idea. The rich man symbolizes God, and the steward represents Adam, to whom God entrusted paradise and all creatures. As the steward of creation, Adam is "brought up on charges" by the angels and has to give an account to God, because Adam disobeyed God's command. The reviewing of the steward's accounts represents God's question in Genesis 3:11: "Who told you that you were naked?" Likewise, dismissing the steward symbolizes Adam's banishment from paradise. Other details of the parable also represent what happens to Adam in Genesis 3. The steward not being able to dig is equated with Adam no longer having the creatures subject to him; just as the steward makes deals with the debtors so they will receive him into their homes, Adam, after his banishment from Eden, arranges deals with the creatures who have been subject to him, assuring himself, "[They] *will receive me into their homes*, namely, into their cohabitations, so that we may live and dwell together on earth." Similarly, just as the master commends the unjust steward for the arrangements he has made with the debtors, so God also commends Adam for his arrangements with the creatures of the earth. By turning to God's creatures, Adam shows the prudence that will eventually lead him back to God (Hildegard 2011, 31).

The first homily concludes with Hildegard assuming the voice of Jesus to exhort her listeners with words that incorporate Jesus's words (in italics here and in subsequent Hildegard quotations) at the end of the parable:

> "*And I*," namely Christ, "*tell you*," human beings: "*Make for yourselves friends*," namely, good angels and humans, in justice and truth, so that they may hold you in esteem for good deeds. . . . They whom you have led in this age from unfaithfulness to faith, and from sin to righteousness and thus into eternal habitations, will hasten to you with extreme mercy and welcome you into the heavenly and unfailing homeland which you lost because of Adam. (Hildegard 2011, 33)

The obedience of the creatures in paradise to Adam (as their "superior") parallels the obedience human beings owe to God: "Proper work carried out in obedience to the superior"—including one's superior in one's religious community—"benefits all" (177).

The second homily interprets the parable as representing the soul's inner struggle between good and evil. The rich man still symbolizes God, but the steward designates the human will, which leads human beings either to obey or to disobey God. As in the first homily, Hildegard concludes with a direct exhortation to her audience: repent and "leave behind the burning lust of vices. In that way, when you lack vices, and you do not want to sin further, they will receive you, repentant and renewed in the good, into life's pastures, where there is no lack of security or fullness of eternal joys" (36).

Homilies 22 and 23 interpret the parable of the laborers in the vineyard, and the differences between them reflect the same concerns as Homilies 1 and 2, respectively: Homily 22 focuses on the creation story (including the history of salvation), and Homily 23 focuses on the soul (including moral explanations and exhortations).

Homily 22 again illustrates Hildegard's concern for the natural world, including her ideas about God's divinely appointed roles for all creatures (175). Although the details of the parable do not correlate exactly with the days of creation in Genesis 1, Hildegard's homily integrates them extensively. God is the householder of the parable, and Hildegard equates the householder going out early in the morning with the day that God created heaven and earth. Likewise, other aspects of the parable all designate aspects of the seven days of creation and the functions of all God's creatures. The agreement with the first laborers, for example, designates God's work on the second day of creation, when God divided "the waters from the waters" (Gen. 1:6–8), and the "eleventh hour" in the parable represents the sixth day of creation, when God created humankind, male and female (102).

The scene in the parable where the landowner pays the workers each a denarius signifies the creatures each receiving "particular functions according to their nature, with the result that wild creatures were in the forest but domestic ones in the farmland with humankind" (102–3). The laborers hired first in the parable correlate to the animals who were created first in Genesis 1; they have a greater opinion of themselves, according to Hildegard: "Led first to Adam were the ones who had come forth first in creation, such as birds and the like; in their opinion they would have greater potential in these things than would the herds, since they could both fly in the air and walk with humankind on earth" (103). These first creatures thus grumbled when the animals created after them, who fulfill only one function—fish only swim and other animals only walk—were given the same denarius for their work:

> *These last*, who were created after us, like the herds, *labored one hour*, because coming forth in their creation, they had supported no other creature to be created after them, as the prior creatures did; and *you made them equal to us*, in the full and not half function of their nature; *equal* on the pastures of the earth alone, because the birds, herds, and remaining creatures all feed at once from the earth alone. *We have borne the burden*, in our estimation, of flying and walking, what we were going to do, the time of our proceeding forth, and *the heat* of the sun, the moon, and the vicissitude of the other creatures following us. (103)

The laborers' complaint against the owner of the vineyard, then, represents the creatures' complaint against God for the extra burdens they had borne before the other creatures were created. God, however, replies that God had assigned duties to all creatures justly and according to the capabilities of each. In addition, God says, the Creator is allowed to do with creation whatever the Creator judges best, especially since the Creator has created them "rightly and beautifully" (104).

In a move reminiscent of Origen's exegesis of this parable, Homily 23 interprets the calling of the various groups of laborers with the human body's five senses and the struggle of the human soul. Like the householder "going out" to hire workers, the "rationality" in humankind goes out "in the knowledge of perception to lead the body's five senses into faith in the salvation of souls" (104–5). At the end of the day the five senses are given praise and honor according to what they have merited before God and human-kind: *from* those who repented from their evils, when knowing their sin they refused to sin, whereby they became innocent, *up to* those who, out of simplicity and innocence, did not know how to sin, or because they completed the righteous and upright deeds they began. *Therefore, when they who had arrived at about the eleventh hour came for remuneration, they each received a single denarius.* Clearly, those who failed to work and fell away to sin *"received"* only the hope of a heavenly reward. (105–6)

Those who had worked from the beginning were those who had not sinned because "they did not have the appetite for sin." Yet they received the same denarius as the others, because "*to give* to the one who knows how to sin, and stops sinning" (i.e., the later workers) is equivalent to giving to those "who do not know how to sin, due to the simplicity of innocence" (i.e., the first workers; 106).

Hildegard's homilies not only reveal the depth of her insights but also demonstrate her role as a visionary preacher and the resulting belief that her understanding of Scripture comes as a gift directly from God. Her visions did not, in her view, *authenticate* her message; instead, they were the *source* for her message. She spoke not with her own voice but with the voice "of the Living Light she saw in her visions" (Abigail Young 2012, 261).

Chartres Cathedral

Many medieval images reflect allegorical interpretations of the parable of the good Samaritan. Such symbolic elaborations are found, for example, in twelfth-century stained-glass windows in the Cathedral of Notre Dame in Chartres. These images physically and theologically integrate the parable with the fall of Adam and Eve: Jesus, as the true good Samaritan, restores fallen humanity (the wounded man), after humanity has been attacked by Satan (the thieves), to a right relationship with God that the old dispensation (the priest and Levite) cannot provide.

Chartres was a holy site for centuries before the construction of the cur-rent cathedral, and bishops are connected to Chartres as early as the fourth century. Chartres became a popular pilgrimage site, because of stories of healing miracles associated with a relic connected to the Virgin Mary—a linen garment (*Sancta Camisia*) that Mary allegedly wore when Jesus was born. The first mention of a cathedral, however, is a reference to the cathedral's destruction in 743, and a rebuilt cathedral was destroyed by Viking raiders in 858 (M. Miller 1996, 8–9).

The cathedral was also destroyed by fire in 1020/1030, rebuilt, damaged again when fire ravaged Chartres in 1134, and was almost completely destroyed by fire in 1194. The Romanesque church was rebuilt—some parts, such as the "Royal Portal" and the crypt, had not been destroyed—from 1194 to approximately 1260. This new edifice would be a magnificent Gothic cathedral, that is, one built in an architectural style that produced extremely tall naves and towers, airy interiors, and breathtaking stained-glass windows dominating the walls: "Gothic churches became the jeweled houses of God . . . glowing manifestations of Christian doctrines, and invitations to faithful living, encouraging worshipers to follow in the footsteps of the saints whose lives were frequently featured in the windows of Gothic churches" (Stokstad and Cothren 2010, 1:491).

The Gothic Chartres Cathedral is no exception. The walls serve almost as a bare skeleton for 176 massive stained-glass windows that cover approximately 22,000 square feet. One of the windows in the south aisle of the nave, created around 1210, visually narrates the parable of the good Samaritan and the story of Adam and Eve in Genesis in twenty-four separate but interrelated images. This window springs to life with the light of day, serving as a luminous sermon preached with pictures instead of words (Stokstad and Cothren 2010, 1:491). The story and its theological interpretation unfold as viewers work their way from the bottom to the top of the window (for more details of the description below, see M. Miller 1996, 64–65; for images of the scenes, see http://www.therosewindow.com/pilot/Chartres/w44-whole.htm).

At the bottom of the window are three scenes that portray shoemakers, the group that donated the money to pay for this window. The images, from left to right, depict:

1. A single shoemaker at work.
2. Two shoemakers working on soles of shoes.
3. Seven shoemakers presenting the panel of windows to the viewers.
   Some of the shoemakers are looking up and worshiping Jesus.

The Lukan parable is then depicted in nine different scenes. The first five scenes appear in a "medallion cluster" (quatrefoil panes):

4. The events in Luke 15:1–3.
   Pharisees and scribes grumble that Jesus "welcomes sinners and eats with them." Jesus is seated and has his hand raised, both of which indicate that he is teaching, and it appears that he is holding a red

book in his left hand. He is also portrayed with a cross nimbus (red background with a white cross) around his head. Two men appear on Jesus's right; one turns his head away from Jesus. The word *Fariseus* appears below the two men, so they are the ones to whom Jesus tells the three "lost" parables in Luke 15.

Viewers then encounter key events of the good Samaritan parable as their gaze continues to travel up and across the window:

5. A man leaving the walled city of Jerusalem through a red door in the wall.
6. A robber hiding.

    In the center of the quatrefoil, a robber, unseen by the man, hides behind a tree and begins to pull his sword out of its scabbard as the man walks by (some interpreters argue that both men are robbers about to attack).

7. Three robbers attacking the man.

    The one on the left has his sword ready to strike; the one in the middle attacks the man with a club; the third robber, dressed in red, strips the man of his clothes.

In many medieval stained-glass windows such as this one, there is not necessarily a consistency in the appearance of the characters. The robber with a sword, for example, wears green clothes in one scene and red clothes in the next.

8. The priest and the Levite passing by.

    Both the priest and the Levite, carrying books of the law, pass by the wounded man. Although the man is in obvious distress, his eyes are open and he is clearly not dead. Oddly, the robbed man already has bandages on his head, leg, and torso.

The next four scenes focus on the actions of the Samaritan, who sees the wounded man, has compassion on him, stops to help, and takes him to an inn:

9. The Samaritan binding the wounds.

    The Samaritan binds the wounds on the man's head (bandages already appear on his leg and torso). Although there is no halo/cross nimbus, the Samaritan clearly resembles Jesus.

10. The Samaritan taking the wounded man to an inn.

> The Samaritan (i.e., Jesus), having placed the wounded man on his animal, leads him to an inn. This image is connected to the next scene on the immediate right by the outstretched arm of the Samaritan/Jesus, who has coins in his hand that he will give to the innkeeper. Once again, there are inconsistent elements between scenes in the window. Here the Samaritan is dressed in blue and green; in the last scene his clothes were red and green. Likewise the wounded man is now (half) dressed in blue, whereas in the previous scene he was dressed in red.

11. The innkeeper accepting payment.

> The innkeeper accepts the money from the Samaritan to take care of the wounded man at the inn (there are four horses in his stable, depicted just below his outstretched right arm).

12. The Samaritan caring for the wounded man.

> This scene starts a new quatrefoil; it shows the Samaritan taking care of the wounded man at the inn. The man lies in bed while the Samaritan ministers to him.

13. God creating Adam.

> God creates Adam in this next scene of the quatrefoil. God has a cross nimbus and looks just like the Samaritan/Jesus.

One of the interesting aspects of this stained-glass window, therefore, is the way it theologically and physically integrates the parable with the story of Adam and Eve. Not only do the characters of the two narratives inhabit the same window, but the last scene of the parable depicted in the window (i.e., the Samaritan taking care of the wounded man) is also found in the same quatrefoil that begins the story of Adam and Eve. In this way, viewers understand how Jesus, as the true good Samaritan, restores fallen humanity to a right relationship with God. The story then continues:

14. Adam being placed in a garden (Gen. 2:15).
15. God creating Eve (Gen. 2:21–22).

> Situated just to the right of the center of the quatrefoil, with Adam alone in the garden, this scene shows Adam in a deep sleep (on the left) as God creates Eve by pulling her out of Adam's side.

16. The transition to the fall of Adam and Eve.

> This scene prepares the way for the "fall" story in Genesis 3: God (once again with a cross nimbus) shows Adam and Eve the tree of the

knowledge of good and evil and tells them not to eat from its fruit (cf. Gen. 2:15–17, where only Adam has been created at that point). The fruit also looks like red apples, a tradition that began at least by the thirteenth century. The serpent already appears. It is also red, entwined around the trunk of the tree, and its head points toward Adam and Eve.

17. The fall.

Eve persuades Adam to eat of the fruit of the tree (which is also an elaboration on the story in Gen. 3:1–7). A very happy red face (apparently of the serpent) is depicted just below them.

18. The moment after the fall.

Adam and Eve appear after eating the forbidden fruit. Adam clutches his throat, which most likely signifies the tradition that the male's Adam's apple was caused by a piece of the fruit sticking in Adam's throat.

19. Adam and Eve clothing themselves.

Adam and Eve, after their sin, clothe themselves and attempt to hide from God. God, however, finds them hiding behind some plants.

20. Adam and Eve being expelled.

Because of their disobedience, Adam and Eve are expelled from paradise, forced out through a red door (cf. the red door of Jerusalem in #5 above) by an angel brandishing a sword. The serpent is nowhere to be seen, although just behind the angel a tree with red fruit is visible, which most likely represents the tree of life, which God is concerned Adam and Eve might eat and therefore live forever (Gen. 3:22–24). Jesus, the good Samaritan, will later be the one to give fallen humanity the chance at eternal life.

21. Adam and Eve suffering God's punishments.

Some of the punishments that God gives to Adam and Eve in Genesis 3 are shown through depictions of Adam and Eve working. Adam digs the soil, and Eve spins thread (not mentioned in Genesis). They wear the clothes that God made for them.

The stained-glass window integrating the Good Samaritan and the story of Adam and Eve concludes with three final scenes.

22. God pointing down toward Adam and Eve.

God appears in the middle of the last quatrefoil. Once again, God is depicted as Jesus, the true good Samaritan, with a cross nimbus.

God's right arm points down toward the previous scene, where Adam and Eve, after their sin, clothe themselves and attempt to hide from God. Opinions differ as to what this scene signifies. Some argue that it portrays God/Jesus subjecting human beings to mortality. Others argue that the scene depicts God promising redemption to human beings. The latter seems more likely, although a combination of the two is possible, based on a Christianized reading of Genesis 3:15.

23. Sin continuing.

The pattern of sin continues, however, since this scene portrays Cain murdering Abel with a hoe, with his left foot on Abel. This scene depicts the predicament of human sin and the continuing struggle to choose between good and evil.

24. Jesus offering redemption.

But that is not the final answer or situation, because Jesus appears at the top of the window. He sits on a rainbow in between two angels who kneel before him. He, as the redeemer of the world, holds a globe of the world in his left hand and blesses the viewers with his right hand. Jesus/God is the one who offers the solution to the predicament of human sin, and the parable of the good Samaritan, when allegorically interpreted, gives that answer.

Other examples of stained-glass windows that allegorically combine the story of Adam and Eve with the parable of the good Samaritan are found in cathedrals in Bourges and Sens. These windows all relate the story of salvation history. The fall of Adam and Eve introduced sin into the world, and it continued through their offspring to future generations. The windows then reproduce in visual form the allegorical interpretations of the parable of the good Samaritan from such theologians as Irenaeus, Clement of Alexandria, Origen, Augustine, Gregory the Great, and others: the man leaving Jerusalem is Adam and is symbolic of fallen humanity leaving paradise (note the common red door in both scenes). The thieves who strip and beat him represent the devil and other hostile powers who attack fallen humanity and leave them half dead with sin. The priest and Levite represent the old dispensation and its inability to provide salvation. The Samaritan is Jesus, who rescues fallen humanity from their sin, brings them to the "inn" of the church, and promises to return again. The parable, then, remains symbolic of Jesus's incarnation and the process of redeeming human beings.

Bonaventure (ca. 1217/1221–1274)

Giovanni di Fidanza (Bonaventure), in his biography of Saint Francis of Assisi, recounts how his commitment to Saint Francis began when as a young boy he was healed from a serious illness after his mother prayed to Francis. Giovanni took the name Bonaventure after he entered the Franciscan order while a student at the University of Paris. He earned a doctorate in theology, was elected as the leader (general minister) of the Franciscan order in 1257, and became cardinal of Albano in 1274. He died just two months later, on July 15, 1274, and was canonized as a saint in 1482.

Many of Bonaventure's contributions to parable interpretations are found in his massive commentary on the Gospel of Luke. His exegeses include allegorical elements, since he believed that the Holy Spirit can lead interpreters to understand Scripture's depth in "the multiplicity of its mystical understandings" beyond the literal words. Bonaventure's approach is significant because he also includes nonallegorical interpretations of parables. In Bonaventure's interpretation of the parable of the great dinner, for example, he stresses the essential nature of physically helping the poor that is commanded in Jewish law. He also notes the "physical" nature of the excuses of the invited guests who, after accepting the invitation, decline to attend: pride (buying the country estate), avarice (buying oxen), and lust (getting married; Bonaventure 2001, 1354–72). In all cases, the goal of the Bible is to transform us morally, engaging both reason and emotions (see Bonaventure 2001, xx–xxxii; 2003, x–xii; McKim 2007, 203).

Bonaventure's ethical concerns led him to respond creatively to Jesus's apparent praise of the dishonest manager. In this case, Bonaventure argues that the parable "must be understood partly in a literal sense and partly in a parabolic sense" (Bonaventure 2001, 1470). Jesus would never praise the "detestable and fraudulent action of the steward"; instead, Jesus praises only the steward's prudence:

> So, although the steward has done something reprehensible in itself, nevertheless, his manner of providing for his future can be taken as an example for good people. For just as the serpent, in injecting poison, is detestable, but is to be imitated by perfect men in its prudence in protecting its head—for which reason it is said in Matthew 10:16: "Be prudent as serpents as simple as doves"—so the steward is to be despised because he has committed fraud, but praised because he prudently found a solution to the perilous situation in which he found himself. (1484)

Another notable aspect of Bonaventure's interpretations is his use of other biblical passages to explain the text he is interpreting. In his reading of the

parable of the rich fool, for example, he notes that the abundant harvest made
the rich man feel so secure that he became "anxious and restless," an anxiety
that stems from greed: "His barn was full but his heart was empty" (quoting
Eccles. 5:12, "The fullness of the rich does not allow him to sleep," and Sirach 14:9, "The eye of the avaricious person is insatiable"; Bonaventure 2001,
1160–61). Bonaventure argues that the parable highlights the wickedness of
the rich man, "since an abundance with security gives birth to the evil of moral
depravity" (citing such passages as Amos 6:1–6; James 5:5). God calls the man
a fool, because in his "earthly wisdom," he did not foresee the dangers ahead
(quoting Job 20:20–22; Prov. 27:1; Eccles. 2:14; 1 Tim. 6:7; James 4:14). The
man should have laid up treasure in heaven instead of on earth (citing Matt.
5:3; 6:19–20; 1 Cor. 1:5–7; 2 Cor. 6:10; 8:9; Phil. 4:18; 1 Pet. 1:3–4).

Bonaventure also makes abundant use of previous interpreters. His interpretation of the parable of the rich man and Lazarus includes not only over 120
citations of Jewish scriptures and over 45 citations of the New Testament but
also citations of over 30 earlier interpreters, such as John Chrysostom, Bede,
Boethius, Gregory the Great, and Peter of Ravenna (Bonaventure 2001, 1516–51).

Augustine had argued that the rich man allegorically symbolizes those
Jews who were filled with pride, Lazarus represents a poor tax collector or
the gentiles, the rich man's purple and linen clothes represent the kingdom
of heaven, which will be taken away from the Jews, the banquets denote the
Jews' boasting about the law, and so forth (see Wailes 1987, 255–56). Bonaventure, however, avoids all such allegorical interpretations: "This passage
has more the character of an *example* than of a *parable*," and it functions
as an "exemplum of punishment for a lack of mercy" (Bonaventure 2001,
1516). Bonaventure also emphasizes the physical reality of what occurs in this
"exemplum" to inform/warn his readers about the dangers of wealth, and he
finds three important lessons to learn (1516–51).

First, the rich man lacks mercy because he loves himself and is filled with
wicked desires: "For through its love for earthly things the spirit grows fat and is
weighed down, so that it cannot travel into the higher realms of heaven" (1517).
The rich man also takes excessive pride in the glory of his "handsome and precious garments," and his love of sumptuous banquets indicates his sin of gluttony.

Second, this sinful lack of mercy results in a "merciless and impious" indifference toward his neighbor, Lazarus, who is sick, abandoned, and starving. In
contrast, Bonaventure argues, Lazarus is holy and good. He shows patience, for
example, in spite of the cruelty of the rich man, but the ultimate evidence of his
piety is that he "*was borne away by the angels into Abraham's bosom*" (1527).

Third, the punishment for the rich man's merciless indifference to Lazarus
was "*being cast into the calamity of hell*" (1517). Even though the rich man

saw Lazarus's need, he did not have mercy. Agreeing with others such as Macrina the Younger (although he does not refer to her) that the soul is what is being tortured, Bonaventure says that the "flame was real, but the tongue was imagined" (1536). Bonaventure thus focuses on the physical reality of sin/ punishment and faith/blessing.

Bonaventure also balances the literal and allegorical in his interpretation of the good Samaritan (969–92). Primarily, the parable is "*an illustration that stimulates us to understand*" (980) the way of life that following the commandments of God entails—loving God with all one's heart, soul, strength, and mind, and loving one's neighbor as oneself (Luke 10:27). The majority of Bonaventure's interpretation focuses on the "literal sense" of the parable. The man was attacked, for example, because he traveled by himself on a dangerous road. Bonaventure also muses about why the priest and Levite ignore the wounded man, and he reaches a similar conclusion about them as he did about the rich man who saw but ignored Lazarus: "After a description of a person who was needy through a doubly miserable condition, the text introduces *a person who looks away because of his hardness of heart*. Now this person is displayed in two characters, namely, one who is *superior* and another who is *inferior* in ecclesiastical dignity" (982). Both men ignored clear commandments in the Scriptures, and because of their responsibilities to know and follow the law, their failure to help is even more reprehensible. The Samaritan, however, "was moved with mercy," and as a "good physician" offered the oil, wine, and bandages to restore the man to health and also the "means of transport and hospitality and food" (985).

The illustration of the good Samaritan offers "*learning on an intellectual level*," such as the fact that everyone who either is in need or can show mercy is indeed a "neighbor." The lawyer who asked the question also learned that being a neighbor is about love and compassion, not physical proximity or kinship:

> And the intellect of the lawyer was thus enlightened by wonderful instruction. For if the Lord had given a straightforward response to the lawyer's question, the lawyer would scarcely have believed it. Therefore, the Lord most wisely elicited the truth from his own mouth and formed him in this truth more by means of question and answer than by means of pronouncing opinions. In this he gives a lesson on how one must satisfactorily deal with the proud. (987)

The parable and Jesus's command to "go and do likewise" also appeal "*to the affections*," so that hearers may "extend mercy to every person" (987). God's mercy extends to all people, and followers of Jesus are to be merciful as God is merciful (e.g., Luke 6:35–36): "But genuine mercy does not reside solely in the affections, but *also produces effects*. . . . And in this the law of God is fulfilled, when a neighbor who is needy in whatsoever a way is assisted not only in word and mind, but also in deed" (987–88).

After this analysis of the parable's "*literal*" sense, Bonaventure turns to an analysis of the "*spiritual sense*" of the parable, one which includes allegorical elements suggested by previous interpreters, such as Origen and Augustine. The person in need could symbolize the human race, "which in Adam the sinner *went down from Jerusalem to Jericho*, that is, from paradise into the world." The robbers are demons who stripped the man of God's gifts and wounded his natural faculties. The people who passed by designate those whose hearts are hard with the "righteousness of the law." Bonaventure also identifies the Samaritan with Jesus and allegorizes remaining elements in the parable (e.g., the medications of the oil and wine are symbols for the sacraments, which "heal the wounds of sins"; the animal on which the wounded man rides symbolizes "*the grace of the virtues and gifts*, through which we are conveyed to *the inn* of the Church"; Bonaventure 2001, 990–92; see also 2003, xii).

Bonaventure's monumental commentary on Luke is a tremendous achievement, and one that creatively combines literal and allegorical interpretations of the biblical text as Bonaventure seeks to enlighten his readers with the depth of Scripture's insights. The literal meaning is never abandoned, but the allegorical meaning yields deeper "mystical" understandings.

Thomas Aquinas (ca. 1224/1225–1274)

Thomas Aquinas was an Italian priest, a philosopher, and the most influential Christian theologian of the Middle Ages. Thomas was born in Roccasecca (between Rome and Naples) into an aristocratic family and was sent at the age of five to be an oblate at the Benedictine abbey at Monte Cassino. Against his family's wishes, however, he entered the Dominican order in 1244. He studied at the universities of Paris and Cologne, where Albert the Great introduced him to the works of Aristotle, which would be very important to Thomas's later work. During his twenty-five-year career, Thomas wrote or dictated over eight million words, and one-fourth of them were biblical commentary. Although best known for his theological and philosophical treatises, such as his classic work *Summa Theologiae* (which remained unfinished at his death in 1274), Thomas viewed interpretation of the Bible as critical, because Scripture was God's primary source of revelation to human beings (Kerr 2009, 19–20).

Thomas explains in detail the approach one should take to Scripture, and in some ways he builds upon the modes of interpretation offered by Gregory the Great (see above). Since God is the author of Scripture and has the power to signify meaning not just by words but also by "things themselves," Scripture includes the first sense, the literal or historical, and a spiritual sense, which is based on the literal sense and presupposes it. The spiritual sense occurs in three aspects: the allegorical (e.g., events in the Hebrew Bible signifying events concerning Jesus in the New Testament), the moral (what we ought to do), and the anagogical (signifying what relates to eternal salvation). Thus what is written in the Bible may indeed, as Augustine and others argued, have several senses (*Summa Theologiae* I.1.10).

Thomas's key point is that this multiplicity does not produce equivocation or confusion of interpretation, because all these different senses are founded upon the literal sense of Scripture. Thus arguments about the meaning of a text have to be drawn solely from the literal sense, not from the allegorical sense, an extremely important move because it emphasizes the literal over the allegorical:

> Nevertheless, nothing of Holy Scripture perishes on account of this, since nothing necessary to faith is contained under the spiritual sense which is not elsewhere put forward by the Scripture in its literal sense. . . .
> The parabolical sense is contained in the literal, for by words things are signified properly and figuratively. Nor is the figure itself, but that which is figured, the literal sense. When Scripture speaks of God's arm, the literal sense is not that God has such a member, but only what is signified by this member, namely operative power. Hence it is plain that nothing false can ever underlie the literal sense of Holy Writ. (Thomas Aquinas 1947, I.1.10; all subsequent references in this section are to this work)

Thomas lived two centuries after Wazo of Liège, during an era when execution of heretics was more widespread (e.g., in 1215, canon 3 of the Fourth Council of the Lateran codified procedures for persecuting "heretics"). Thus Thomas's interpretations of the parable of the wheat and weeds/tares reach much different conclusions from those of Wazo. In *Summa Theologiae*, for example, Thomas cites the parable to discuss when people should be excommunicated from the church. The first question is, since people can band together in "wickedness," whether a whole group can be excommunicated. Thomas answers that individuals should be excommunicated only for mortal sins, and such sins are committed by individuals, not groups: "Therefore the Church, who should imitate the judgments of God, prudently decided that a community should not be excommunicated, lest the wheat be uprooted together with the tares and cockle" (III.Suppl.22.5, ad. 2).

Thomas discusses this parable several times in *Summa Theologiae*. In the "Treatise on the Theological Virtues," for example, Thomas addresses the question, "Whether unbelievers ought to be compelled to the faith?" The first "objection" Thomas discusses comes from interpreters like Chrysostom (*Homilies on Matthew* 46), who argues that the parable of the wheat and weeds teaches that "unbelievers ought by no means to be compelled to the Faith." Thus Chrysostom concludes that it is wrong to kill heretics, since innocent persons would be killed as well. Thomas replies to this objection by stating that unbelievers such as "heathens and Jews" should not be compelled, although they should be compelled not to hinder the faith of others by their blasphemies or persecutions (thus war against unbelievers is sometimes necessary). He notes, however, "there are unbelievers who at some time have accepted the faith, and professed it, such as heretics and all apostates: such should be submitted even to bodily compulsion, that they may fulfil what they have promised, and hold what they, at one time, received" (II-II.10.8, ad. 4).

Thomas also cites the parable when he addresses the question, "Whether heretics ought to be tolerated?" Thomas argues that it could be examined from two sides. First, heretics deserve to be excommunicated from the church and "severed from the world by death," because it is a worse offense to corrupt others' faith (and damage eternal souls) than to forge money (and damage earthly lives). The secular state condemns forgers to death, and heresy is a much graver matter, so "much more reason is there for heretics, as soon as they are convicted of heresy, to be not only excommunicated but even put to death." The church, however, has mercy; it seeks to convert the heretic. When heretics refuse to be corrected, though, the church has to keep in mind the salvation of others whom heretics might lead astray. Therefore the church should not only excommunicate heretics from the church but also deliver them "to the secular tribunal to be exterminated thereby from the world by death" (II-II.11.3).

But does not the parable teach that Jesus commanded his followers to allow the tares (i.e., heretics) to grow until the harvest (i.e., the end of the world)? Thomas rejects that argument, because excommunication by the church is not the same as "uprooting" the heretic and should be an attempt to save the heretic's soul (1 Cor. 5:5). Thomas also observes that the parable cautions against uprooting the tares since the wheat would also be uprooted. Killing a heretic, though, uproots the heretic but not anyone else; therefore killing a heretic "is not contrary to Our Lord's command, which is to be understood as referring to the case when the cockle cannot be plucked up without plucking up the wheat" (II-II.11.3).

Thomas later uses the parable to address a similar question: "Whether it is lawful to kill sinners?" Once again, interpreters had argued that Jesus's parable meant that God forbids killing sinners, but Thomas cites verses that state the opposite (e.g., Exod. 22:18 says that sorcerers should be put to death). Since the health of the whole body sometimes demands the excision of one of its parts if it is decayed beyond repair or infectious to the other parts of the body, it is "both praiseworthy and advantageous to have it cut away." Likewise, if a sinner is dangerous and "infectious" to the community as a whole, "it is praiseworthy and advantageous that he be killed in order to safeguard the common good, since 'a little leaven corrupteth the whole lump' (1 Cor. 5:6)":

> Our Lord commanded them to forbear from uprooting the cockle in order to spare the wheat, i.e. the good. This occurs when the wicked cannot be slain without the good being killed with them, either because the wicked lie hidden among the good, or because they have many followers, so that they cannot be killed without danger to the good, as Augustine says (*Contra Parmen.* iii, 2). Wherefore our Lord teaches that we should rather allow the wicked to live, and that vengeance is to be delayed until the last judgment, rather than that the good be put to death together with the wicked. When, however, the good incur no danger, but rather are protected and saved by the slaying of the wicked, then the latter may be lawfully put to death. (II-II.64.2)

God sometimes slays sinners to bring about the good; other times God allows them additional time to repent. God knows best, and human justice should do its best to emulate God, putting to death those persons who are dangerous and allowing time for repentance for those who sin but who do so "without grievously harming others" (II-II.64.2): "Our Lord forbids the uprooting of the cockle, when there is fear lest the wheat be uprooted together with it. But sometimes the wicked can be uprooted by death, not only without danger, but even with great profit, to the good. Wherefore in such a case the punishment of death may be inflicted on sinners." As Scripture says, all who sin are deserving of eternal death, so punishments incurred in life are "more of a medicinal character" (II-II.108.3).

As a comparison between Wazo of Liège, Thomas Aquinas, and Roger Williams (chap. 3) reveals, the interpreters' presuppositions and contexts often influence their interpretations just as much as, if not more than, the texts of the parables themselves do.

One of Thomas's more significant contributions to parable interpretation is his argument that the "literal" sense of a text is not the historical event "behind" it but is instead the intention of the biblical authors. This development means, for example, that parables could now be interpreted as poetic ways in which human authors could express their intentions. This literal sense, Thomas declares, is the "sole locus of authoritative sacred doctrine." The spiritual sense of Scripture, however, is directly authored by God (Thomas

Aquinas 2002, 167). Thomas thus defends and uses allegorical interpretations of parables, but he also cautions about an overemphasis on allegorization: it adds nothing "necessary to faith" (Thomas Aquinas 1947, I.1.10; Kissinger 1979, 42; Grant 1963, 125).

John Gower (ca. 1327/1330–1408)

John Gower was a medieval poet whose fame during his lifetime rivaled that of his friend and contemporary Geoffrey Chaucer. Until the seventeenth century, Gower was considered as influential as Chaucer (note, e.g., Shakespeare's use of Gower for a chorus before each act of *Pericles*, since Gower's *Confessio Amantis* was one of the two major sources Shakespeare used). Chaucer thought highly of Gower and dedicated his work *Troilus and Criseyde* (ca. 1385) to "moral Gower," because of Gower's concern for social mores and ethics. Gower's reputation eventually suffered by comparison to Chaucer, and he slipped into relative obscurity until the twentieth century (see Gower 2006, 1–41).

Gower most likely was born into a prominent and affluent family in Kent or Yorkshire. Records indicate that he bought an estate in Kent in 1365 and acquired a manor in Suffolk (other properties would follow), so he was certainly economically prosperous. Around 1377, Gower moved to St. Mary Overeys Priory, and he is credited with financing the repair of the damaged priory. Gower was buried in the priory's church—today's Southwark Cathedral, London—and the inscription notes that he has been called "the first English poet."

Gower is best known for writing three extended poems, all of which explore the responsibility of human beings within society: *Mirroir de l'Omme* ("Mirror of Man," later renamed *Speculum Meditantis*), *Vox Clamantis* ("The Voice of One Crying Out"; cf. John the Baptist, Mark 1:3–4), and *Confessio Amantis* ("The Lover's Confession"). The third work, *Confessio Amantis*, exists in three recensions (1390, with revisions in 1391 and 1393) and is an allegory based on the Christian sacrament of confession. The majority of the work focuses on the seven deadly sins, which are illustrated with a treasury of stories from different historical periods. The sixth book of *Confessio Amantis* treats the sin of gluttony, and the parable of the rich man and Lazarus is one of the stories used to illustrate it (6.975–1150). Because there are so many different types of gluttony, the text focuses on two main ones: drunkenness and delicacy (i.e., an immoderate attachment to sensual pleasure, especially the love of excessively fine or exotic food).

The book begins with the "Confessor" (Genius) noting that gluttony is "Sin's great and awful origin" (6.1; all quotes from Gower 2006), and he compares drunkenness and delicacy with love. The drunken person and someone in love, for example, could be described as having "loste his wit" (6.80–82), although drunkenness is a choice and being in love is not (6.90–92; cf. 6.117). The Confessor warns that drunkenness "turns a wise man to a fool" (6.18), and Amans (the lover to whom the Confessor is talking) admits that he is intoxicated, but he is drunk with love instead of alcohol (e.g., 6.112–32). The primary issue is not to allow (love) drunkenness to separate the mind and its thoughts from reality: "*Kep thi wittes that thou hast, And let hem noght be drunke in wast*" (6.314–16).

The second aspect of gluttony, "delicacy," also pertains to love, as well as to material possessions and pleasures (e.g., the one who is "delicate" [gluttonous] in love also is not faithful to his wife; no matter her excellent qualities, he is never satisfied; 6.677–86).

The attachment to excessively fine or exotic food is not possible for those in poverty (6.619), which makes delicacy easier to condemn than drunkenness. Such foods also are not good for one's health: "comun mete" (common meat) is better for one's "sustenance" and "governance" (6.649–52). To make sure that Amans understands what delicacy is, the Confessor illustrates delicacy with the parable of the rich man and Lazarus. The rich man was "delicate" in both clothing and food:

> Crist seith: "Ther was a riche man,
>   A mihti lord of gret astat,
>   And he was ek so delicat
>   Of his clothing, that everyday
>   Of pourpre and bisse he made him gay,
>   And eet and drank therto his fille
>   After the lustes of his wille,
>   As he which al stod in delice
>   And tok non hiede of thilke vice.

This mighty lord with a great estate ate and drank his fill. Then a deadly hungry Lazarus appeared at the rich man's gate and asked for food ("axed mete"), a direct request for help not mentioned in the Lukan parable:

> And as it scholde so betyde,
>   A povere lazre upon a tyde
>   Cam to the gate and axed mete:
>   Bot there mihte he nothing gete
>   His dedly hunger forto stanche;

The rich man, who had a full paunch from all the food and drink that he had lusted after, would not deign to speak a word to Lazarus and offered him not even a crumb. The man's lack of charity toward the poor is thus made even more explicit, because Lazarus could not survive without alms from the rich man:

> For he, which hadde his fulle panche
> Of alle lustes ate bord,
> Ne deigneth noght to speke a word,
> Onliche a Crumme forto yive,
> Wherof the povere myhte live
> Upon the yifte of his almesse. (6.986–1005)

The Confessor continues in greater detail than the Lukan parable does concerning the extent of impoverished Lazarus's distress; not only was he starving but he was freezing as well, so sick that he could no longer move from where he lay (6.1006–9). At that low point, the dogs came from the hall of the rich man to lick Lazarus's wounds as he lay dying:

> The houndes comen fro the halle,
>   Wher that this sike man was falle,
>   And as he lay ther forto die,
>   The woundes of his maladie
>   Thei licken forto don him ese.

The Confessor states that the dogs licked Lazarus's sores because they pitied him and were trying to help, but Lazarus was so "full of such desese [disease]" that even this gesture of help was not enough to save him. So his soul "passeth" from his body, and God, the one "whom nothing overpasseth" (6.1020), took Lazarus to heaven to Abraham's "barm" (bosom), where he had everything that his heart desired (6.1025).

Then it happened—"as it should," the poem says—the rich man suddenly died and went straight to hell. The "fiend" (i.e., Satan) dragged him into the fire, and, as he suffered immensely from the intense pain of the flames, he looked up to heaven and saw Lazarus enthroned with Abraham. In response, he "preide" (prayed) to Abraham to send Lazarus to cool his thirst:

> Send Lazar doun fro thilke Sete,
> And do that he his finger wete
> In water, so that he mai droppe
> Upon my tunge, forto stoppe
> The grete hete in which I brenne. (6.1041–45)

Although Abraham responds first by calling the rich man "Mi Sone" (my son), he is adamant that this great reversal occurred because Lazarus in his lifetime had done "gret penance" and that the rich man is deservedly punished with everlasting pain in hell for his sin of sating his bodily lusts, whereas Lazarus receives the reward of endless joy in heaven (6.1048–61).

The Confessor then delivers the moral of the story. On the one hand, the sin of delicacy/gluttony occurs when those who have do not share with those who have not, just like the rich man, who had grown rich from the labor of others, would not even share a crumb of bread with poor, starving Lazarus. Such gluttonous rich will "falle in gret destresse." On the other hand, a wise rich man—although he may clothe his body with the best clothes and partake of the finest food and drink—also "feeds and clothes" his soul (6.1111–50). Jesus's parable thus indicates that the sin of gluttony/delicacy involves the lack of sharing one's possessions with the poor, but the critical issue is not to "prize" (6.1130) those earthly possessions and to use them to help others in need.

As Peter Nicholson notes, Gower does not condemn wealth. Instead, he condemns the misuse of and lust for wealth. If the rich man had helped Lazarus and others in need, he would not have been condemned. Gower's interpretation indicates that renunciation of wealth is not necessary; neither is the complete avoidance of worldly pleasures ("bodily delices"). Wealth should be used wisely, however, with a concern not only for the needs of the body but also for the needs of the soul (Nicholson 2005, 323).

Gower's use of the rich man and Lazarus parable is not unique in this period. A comparable interpretation in the context of gluttony may be found in Robert of Brunne's *Handlyng Synne* (214.6635–6720), but interesting divergent interpretations are found in such texts as *The Pricke of Conscience* (84.3062–66), William Langland's *Piers Plowman* (B.16.252–71), and Geoffrey Chaucer's "The Summoner's Tale" (which uses the parable in a morally dubious way, with Friar John hypocritically citing the parable deceitfully to portray his life as one of poverty, abstinence, and fasting).

Antonia Pulci (ca. 1452/1454–1501)

Antonia Pulci was born around 1452 in Florence, Italy. Because of her family's financial comfort, Antonia received a good religious and literary education, most likely being tutored at home, although her written works demonstrate a familiarity with books common in the Italian "abacus school" curriculum. In these schools, students learned mathematical skills (including bookkeeping), how to read a series of religious and secular works, and how to write in Italian. In addition, Pulci shows a mastery of the various forms of Italian verse (see Pulci 1996, 12–13).

Antonia married Bernardo Pulci in 1470, and she and Bernardo probably collaborated on a number of works; both wrote sacred dramas for popular performances and for publication by the newly established printing industry in Florence (Pulci 2010, 21). After Bernardo's death in 1488, Antonia devoted herself to religious life, becoming associated with the Augustinian order and eventually founding the convent Santa Maria della Misericordia.

Pulci wrote at least seven one-act plays that were published numerous times over the next two centuries, three of which are on biblical subjects: Joseph, David and Saul, and the parable of the prodigal son. The structure of her plays varies, but all begin with a prologue narrated by an angel, which apparently serves as the voice and point of view of Pulci. Pulci's play is an early example of the plays about the prodigal son that began to proliferate in this era. In particular, Pulci makes use of an earlier Florentine play about the prodigal son by Piero di Mariano Muzi—just as hers served as a model for a later one by Castellano Castellani—but she significantly reworks the play and makes it her own (Pulci 2010, 47–54).

A major elaboration of the parable occurs immediately after the play's prologue. The prodigal son sins even before he leaves home: he gambles at cards and loses a large amount of money, which immediately highlights his irresponsibility. It is this loss at cards that spurs the prodigal to ask his father for his inheritance, and the prodigal's focus is solely on himself and his happiness:

> I don't think that beneath the moon before
> Was ever found with luck like mine a man
> Who of a thousand bets could not win one.
> "Unfortunate" I surely can be called—
> I am not paid up yet—I want to go
> And ask my father for my inheritance. (Pulci 1996, 137)

Pulci believed that asceticism helped lead to a virtuous life, so she wants the audience to reject the prodigal's view that money brings happiness. Ironically, even after saying that he could not win one bet out of a thousand, the prodigal declares that he wants "to go away and try [his] luck" using his "great inheritance" to travel and to seek earthly pleasures: people "with money travel without fear," he says, and the world is theirs for the taking.

A second major elaboration is that in Pulci's play both the prodigal's father and his elder brother beg him to stay after he asks for his inheritance. The prodigal continues to insist that he wants his inheritance, and the father repeatedly—in four separate speeches—states his "great love" for his "dear son," speaks of the "great pain" the son's leaving will cause him, and begs him to yield to his father's "great prayers" to stay home. The father's heartfelt pleas are to no avail, however. The prodigal takes ten thousand ducats from his father, and, after also rejecting the pleas of his brother to stay home, departs for a foreign land. One line sums up his state of mind: "Who has cash in this world has what he wants."

When he arrives at his destination, the prodigal encounters seven "boon companions" who say they will accompany him wherever he goes, promise to love him, and guarantee that he will always have his "every pleasure." The audience now discovers that the prodigal's new companions are the seven deadly sins—pride, avarice, envy, wrath, sloth, gluttony, and lust. "Pride" is the leader of the seven men, but he allows each one to introduce himself. Avarice, for example, says:

> My name is Avarice, and I can think
> Of nothing but increasing what I own;
> I value neither friendship nor my kin,
> As long as I can gather many goods.
> This is my goodness, this my every joy;
> To prosper more, I'd even hurt myself;
> I never have enough for future need;
> In gathering goods, I disregard my life. (Pulci 1996, 143)

Here the play transitions from emphasizing the son's comfortable life at home with a loving family to the son wanting to experience every pleasure. The seven deadly sins will oblige him. It is clear that the prodigal has already succumbed, to a certain extent, to many of these seven mortal sins, and he leaves the stage with these new companions. Ironically, he has been prophetically warned about his forthcoming downfall not only by his father, his brother, and the servant who counted out his ducats, but also by one of his new "boon companions," Gluttony:

> I know how to make famine out of wealth,
> Know how to turn great riches into nought,
> And of great poverty I am the cause—
> Now my condition you have understood. (Pulci 1996, 144)

Obviously, the prodigal does not yet truly understand, although he soon will.

The younger son leaves the stage with the seven deadly sins after they each give a speech, so at this point Pulci's play does not dwell on the prodigal's debauchery—the audience does not see it directly. Instead, the play transitions to a dialogue between the father and the elder son, in which they ardently declare their love and devotion for each other.

After the elder son leaves the stage, the prodigal son returns home, "exhausted, naked, quite abandoned, poor." When he reaches his father, he begs for mercy, says that he has repented and that he loves his father, and asks to be kept on as a servant. The father welcomes him back with great joy to the family's "safe harbor"—not as a servant but as a beloved son—and says he wants to host "a solemn, worthy feast" in the son's honor. At this point, however, another elaboration of the parable appears: the father cautions the younger son that he has to behave himself from now on (cf. the "Go your way, and from now on do not sin again" Jesus tells the adulterous woman in John 8:11):

> O my beloved son, I pardon you
> The injury you've done to me in the past.
> Your being pardoned is a blessed state,
> Be sure; see that no more into such sin
> You fall. You see I have been merciful to you,
> And I, since I have freely pardoned you,
> Wish to make it manifest to God,
> Because I cherish you so tenderly. (Pulci 1996, 147)

This speech is a crucial part of the universal sermon that Pulci is preaching to the play's audience.

It is only now, through delayed exposition, that the audience hears an elaboration on the sins of the prodigal. He wasted his inheritance, he says, on "women, taverns, banquets, games of chance, horses, falcons, on rich garments new." His seven companions who drained him of his money were world-renowned for their wickedness; they were his constant companions, leading him into every type of sin until his money ran out. Destitute, the son hired himself out as a servant to a cruel master, who forced him to eat acorns with the pigs during a great famine in order to survive (the play thus assumes that the prodigal, unlike in the parable, actually ate the food the pigs ate and that the food was acorns). It was then, the son told his father, that he came to his senses and decided to beg mercy of his father and to be received back as a servant.

The father instructs his servants to arrange a "splendid banquet" and to invite the family's relatives and friends. The guests rejoice in the return of the beloved prodigal—once again an aspect that is not found in the Lukan parable but that reflects the theme of the other "lost" parables of Luke 15 (that of the lost sheep and of the lost coin) about rejoicing with friends and neighbors when what was lost is found.

When the elder son returns home, however, he cannot understand why his father has prepared a feast for "this immoral wretch" who has gambled all his worldly goods away, while the father has never celebrated the goodness of the older brother. Now the elder brother himself, ironically, feels like a "wretch" and states that he—similar to his brother earlier—does not intend to come home again:

> O wretched me! They never even killed
> Some measly lamb—not once—to honor me!
> For this scapegrace, my brother, him who is
> The very pinnacle of vice and every sin,
> They've killed the calf to fatten up the feast.
> With sorrow, by my faith, my heart will break;
> Such a party I will not attend,
> Nor do I mean to come back home again. (Pulci 1996, 151)

The older son's reaction, though, is more in sorrow than anger, and, unlike in the parable, he still calls the prodigal "my brother" instead of "this son of yours." His father responds by declaring his love for his elder son, equating the younger son's return with "rising from the dead," and explicitly connecting his brother's physical return with his spiritual salvation:

> Belovèd son, obedient, reverent,
> Do not desire to say again such things,
> And from your mind all envy strip away,
> For love of me, do come home again,
> For you obeyed me ever, in the past,
> And in the future still so shall you do.
> Join with me now in happy celebration
> Of your brother's return to us, of his salvation. (Pulci 1996, 152)

The older brother is convinced by his father's words—unlike the prodigal, who rejected four entreaties by his father before leaving home, the elder son needs only two speeches to be convinced—and goes to the celebration, embraces his brother, and welcomes him back, calling him his "dear" and "sweet" brother:

> Dear brother, you are welcome back again!
> I surely never thought to see you more,
> And to the Son of Mary I give thanks!
> When I recall to mind, sweet brother, how

> You had departed without company,
> By night and day I used to sigh for you,
> But now may highest God by all be praised
> Because to this safe harbor you've returned. (Pulci 1996, 152–53)

The younger brother shows a little bit of concern about his older brother's compassion for him:

> If you but knew in what great grief and woe
> I've been since I departed, certainly,
> How much compassion you would feel for me. (Pulci 1996, 153)

But he reciprocates by also calling his brother "sweet brother," and he praises their father's "infinite goodness" in forgiving his "weighty sin."

The play concludes almost with an altar call. An angel returns to remind the audience of the lesson they should learn from the play: to give thanks to God, who is always ready to pardon them of their sins. No sinner is so wicked that Jesus will not forgive those sins and welcome the sinner into heaven, if the sinner repents. Pulci wants her audience to know what they should do, how they should treat one another as brothers and sisters, in order to inherit eternal life "when this brief life comes to its end."

Among the numerous prodigal son dramas of this era, Pulci's play is a prime example of incorporating the seven deadly sins into the story—a theme paralleled in many texts of this era, because the parable of the prodigal son is commonly used in the Middle Ages as an example of the importance of penitence (e.g., Chaucer's "The Parsons Tale"). In addition, Pulci's play/ sermon extends the theme of gambling, reconciles the two brothers, and explicitly applies the message to all humanity.

Albrecht Dürer (1471–1528)

Albrecht Dürer was the most famous Renaissance artist in northern Europe. He was born in Nuremberg, Germany, in 1471, the third of eighteen children. His father was a goldsmith, and Dürer began his career as an apprentice in his father's shop. After becoming fairly proficient in goldsmithing, however, Dürer decided that his talents were more suited for painting. In 1486, then, his father reluctantly agreed to allow Dürer to apprentice for three years with Michel Wolgemut, a local painter.

After his apprenticeship, Dürer traveled extensively (a *Wanderjahr* from 1490 to 1494) to learn from other artists and to improve his art, including a lengthy sojourn in Italy. He returned to Nuremberg a truly Renaissance artist, influenced by the classical revival in the Italian Renaissance (especially the work of Andrea Mantegna), but merged it with a northern European, more linear style and a concern for precise detail. He immediately became the city's leading artist, primarily making his reputation as a printmaker. Because of such works as his series of fifteen woodcuts of the Apocalypse (1498), his fame spread throughout Europe, so much so that during his second trip to Italy (1505–1507), he was received as a (minor) celebrity (Chilvers 2004, 224). After his return to Nuremberg, Dürer's reputation increased as he continued painting and printmaking, wrote a manual on painting for other artists, and received commissions—and a significant annual allowance, beginning in 1515—from Emperor Maximilian I and his successor, Charles V.

Dürer is best known for his engravings and woodcuts. They are stunning in their narrative power, vivid imagery, and layers of meaning. At his death, Dürer was acknowledged as the premier artist outside Italy, and only Rembrandt would later approach the brilliance of his engravings. The engravings also had a wide influence, because many prints could be made from one engraving, which made copies relatively cheap and easily transportable. Numerous Dürer prints spread over Europe, and they exerted a tremendous influence on other artists (Murray and Murray 1996, 147).

One of Dürer's greatest engravings was his 1496 *The Prodigal Son amongst the Pigs* (figure 2.5). The engraving depicts the prodigal kneeling in penance among the pigs. This scene is rare during this period, since most previous images of the son among the pigs portray him standing (D'Oench 1995, 4), although some earlier images, such as the one in the Chartres Cathedral stained-glass window, show him sitting or kneeling. Depictions of the parable of the prodigal son in art usually portray either the father welcoming the prodigal home or the prodigal carousing in a tavern or brothel, but Dürer's motif of the son kneeling among the pigs established a trend. It also influenced later images of the son returning home to his father and kneeling before him.

Twenty years after Dürer created this masterpiece, representations of the prodigal son would begin to illustrate the difference between Catholic and Protestant interpretations of the parable. Catholic interpretations emphasize the role of penance in the son's forgiveness, whereas Protestant interpreters emphasize the (undeserved) grace of God and salvation coming through the prodigal's faith, not actions of penance. Dürer would later show sympathy for the Reformation view of the salvation by faith, but this early, pre-Reformation work of art emphasizes the repentance of the prodigal, whose pose shows his remorse and repentance (Witcombe 1998, 7).

National Gallery, Washington DC

Figure 2.5 Albrecht Dürer, *The Prodigal Son amongst the Pigs*

The prodigal's repentance appears to take place not in a field, as in the parable, but near enough to a farm for the buildings to be clearly seen, although the perspective of the middle section of the engraving and the building that appears just above the prodigal's head are a bit unclear. The setting is the village of Himpfelshof, just west of Nuremberg, where Dürer lived. The dilapidated farm buildings are in a wretched state of disrepair. Part of the roof on one building is missing, and a vine is beginning to creep across other parts of the roof. Cracks appear in most of the buildings, with sections of the outside walls missing part of their covering; the dilapidation of the architecture mirrors that of the prodigal.

A number of other details make the scene even more lifelike, an aspect important in Renaissance art. Four birds perch on a roof with two more flying just above them. Two ducks appear in a pond just behind the prodigal—one, like the prodigal, apparently looking for food—and the hindquarters of a bull appears on the left (with perhaps a bit of "fertilizer" on the ground behind it). A rooster pecks in the hay just behind the prodigal on the right, and it seems to be searching for food as well. A turnip lies on the ground near the prodigal's kneeling leg—turnips were common fodder for livestock, especially in winter months—food for the pigs that the prodigal longs to eat.

The five large pigs look ferocious and aggressive. The search for food, once again, is a major theme, and, once again, it mirrors the prodigal's hunger. Four of the large pigs eat from the trough and in the process prevent the fifth one from reaching it. One of the smaller pigs has its front legs on the top of the trough, but it is too small to reach the food. Two other piglets are by a small bucket, and two others appear on the front left, apparently running to get food. At least one of the large pigs eyes the prodigal menacingly, and at least one of the large pigs and two of the piglets apparently look at the viewers of the print, perhaps silently asking whether viewers get the message.

The urgency of the pigs attempting to get food seems to be matched by the urgency of the prodigal's repentance. One's gaze is immediately drawn to the posture of the prodigal. He kneels on one knee—with legs perplexingly askew—with his hands clasped and his eyes raised to heaven or perhaps to a church in the upper right corner. The pose clearly portrays the moment when the prodigal "came to himself" (Luke 15:17). Dürer's work, then, represents the choices the prodigal has made. His decisions to demand his inheritance, leave his home, and squander "his property in dissolute living" (Luke 15:13) result in his being so hungry that he longs to eat the food that the pigs eat. Here, Dürer captures the moment the prodigal decides to go home, ask his father's forgiveness, and request to be treated as a servant.

As early as 1604, some interpreters, such as Karel van Mander, have argued that the physiognomy of Dürer's prodigal son demonstrates that it is a self-portrait (D'Oench 1995, 7). The image clearly resembles Dürer, including the long curly hair (although the prodigal has only a moustache, not Dürer's full beard, which he grew sometime after 1493). If it is a self-portrait, the engraving could be seen as the first example of an artist identifying himself with the prodigal, and some scholars also wonder whether this early print may thus contain a glimpse of Dürer's own spiritual life. There are hints in some of his later works, for example, of Dürer's religious struggles—that is, deliberations about the role of a Christian artist in the midst of his unshakable piety (e.g., in his *The Sudarium Held by Two Angels*). That view is tempting, but works of art, including parables, often tantalizingly refuse to answer such questions.

3

The Afterlives
of Jesus's Parables in the Sixteenth
and Seventeenth Centuries

The Renaissance, Reformation, and Counter-Reformation (i.e., Catholic Reformation)—including the advent of Humanism—all brought significant changes to biblical interpretation in general and the approach to parables in particular. The most significant development was the decline of the allegorical method of interpreting the parables. Martin Luther, for example, who early in his career used allegorical interpretations extensively, later railed against such "jugglery" with biblical texts—although he does interpret some parables allegorically. John Calvin represents an even clearer rejection of the allegorical method; his primary aim is to understand and explain the central point that Jesus seeks to make in a parable. In addition to the scholarly study of the Bible in its original languages, the advent of the printing press and the increasing availability of the Bible in translation for nonscholars (e.g., Luther's translation of the Bible into German) played important roles in how the parables were received during this time period. The depth and breadth of the Bible's influence on all aspects of life continued, but the importance of allegory declined, including in the interpretation and reception of the parables of Jesus.

In addition to two of the main voices of the Protestant Reformation (Luther and Calvin), this chapter includes a major voice (John Maldonatus) within the Counter-Reformation, the continuing efforts of reform within the Roman

Catholic Church. It also includes voices within "Radical Christianity," such as Anabaptists (e.g., Anna Jansz), English nonconformists (e.g., John Bunyan; Roger Williams, who immigrated to North America). Also included are interpretations of Jesus's parables in plays (e.g., William Shakespeare), literature and sermons (e.g., Bunyan), art (e.g., Rembrandt, Domenico Fetti), music (the story of Anna Jansz), and poetry (e.g., George Herbert).

Martin Luther (1483–1546)

Martin Luther, the leader of the Protestant Reformation in Germany, was born in 1483 in Eisleben, Saxony. His father, Hans Luther, was a miner, and he wanted his son to become a lawyer. After earning his bachelor's and master's degrees at Erfurt University, however, Martin Luther abandoned his studies in 1505, became a monk at the Augustinian Monastery at Erfurt, and was ordained a priest in 1507. After earning a bachelor's degree in biblical studies (1509) and a doctorate in theology (1512) at the University of Wittenberg, Luther was appointed professor of biblical exegesis at the university, where he would stay for the rest of his career.

Over the next five years, especially through his exegetical study of Paul's Letter to the Romans, Luther developed a theology of justification/righteousness by faith: righteousness cannot be earned through human efforts; it is given solely by God's grace to sinners through faith (and faith alone) through the atoning death of Jesus.

Luther's Ninety-Five Theses, which essentially began the Protestant Reformation, were founded upon this theology of justification by faith; they decried various practices of the church, such as the selling of indulgences—accepting money for the remittance of sins—and challenged the authority of the pope. The Ninety-Five Theses initiated a firestorm throughout Germany, and in 1520 Pope Leo X excommunicated Luther.

Luther also embarked on an ambitious number of writings that served as the foundation for a reform of the theology and practice of the church in Germany, including a translation of the Bible into German, numerous treatises, catechisms, hymns, sermons, commentaries on biblical texts, and other works.

Luther's approach to exegesis also changed significantly. Early in his career, for example, he used allegorization extensively in his interpretations of Scripture:

> When I was a monk, I was a master in the use of allegories. I allegorized everything. Afterwards through the Epistle to the Romans, I came to some knowledge

of Christ. I recognized then that allegories are nothing, that it's not what Christ signifies but what Christ is that counts. Before I allegorized everything, even a chamber pot. . . . Jerome and Origen contributed to the practice of searching only for allegories. God forgive them. In all of Origen there is not one word of Christ. (Luther 1955–1986, 54:46–47)

Luther uses even harsher language in his treatise *Against the Heavenly Prophets in the Matter of Images and Sacraments*. Allegorical interpretation is a "trifling art" and "is so stupid that it makes one feel like vomiting" (Luther 1955–1986, 40:188). Allegorical interpreters "juggle and play" with texts, and as long as they do not damage the message of Christ, Luther is content to leave such "prophets," as he sarcastically calls them, alone, but he adds about such "spiritual juggling":

I was thoroughly drilled in this method when I first began to study the Bible ten years ago, before I discovered the true method. . . . Brother, the natural meaning of the words is queen, transcending all subtle, acute sophistical fancy. From it we may not deviate, unless we are compelled by a clear article of the faith. Otherwise the spiritual jugglers would not leave a single letter in Scripture. . . .

In this manner even the great teacher Origen played the fool, and led St. Jerome and many others astray with him. In former times his books were justly forbidden and condemned on account of such spiritual tomfoolery. For it is dangerous so to play with the Word of God by which conscience and faith are to be guided. Therefore, interpretations of God's Word must be lucid and definite having a firm, sure, and true foundation on which one may confidently rely. (Luther 1955–1986, 40:189–90)

Interpreters must begin with the plain sense of Scripture and pursue the literal sense as far as possible. Only then may any symbolic meaning be considered, and the focus must continually be on Christ, who provides the context for all biblical interpretation (Kissinger 1979, 45).

Luther further explains why he moved from allegorical to literal interpretations in a *Table Talk* from October 1540:

When I was young . . . I dealt with allegories, tropologies, and analogies and did nothing but clever tricks with them. If somebody had them today, they'd be looked upon as rare relics. I know they're nothing but rubbish. Now I've let them go, and this is my last and best art, to translate the Scriptures in their plain sense. The literal sense does it—in it there's life, comfort, power, instruction, and skill. The other is tomfoolery, however brilliant the impression it makes. (Luther 1955–1986, 54:406)

Luther's approach to interpreting parables is seen in his 1525 sermon on the parable of the laborers in the vineyard (Luther 1995, 2:106–12). He moves away from allegorical interpretations of previous interpreters and argues: "We must not consider this parable in every detail, but confine ourselves to the leading thought, that which Christ designs to teach by it. . . . For such parables are never spoken for the purpose of being interpreted in all their minutia" (106–7). Instead, the parable seeks to portray God's unmerited mercy to sinners, including the fact that human beings cannot "storm their way into heaven by their good works" (those who try to do so are designated by those workers who "murmur against the householder," who signifies God; 108).

Even in his early sermons, Luther focuses on the ethical implications of the parables. In what is likely to be his earliest extant sermon (1510–1512), with the Golden Rule (Matt. 7:12) as the main text, Luther argues that salvation depends upon human beings actively helping one another, not just refraining from doing evil to one another (Luther 1955–1986, 51:7). As the parable of the rich man and Lazarus demonstrates:

> [The rich man] was not damned because he robbed or did evil with respect to these goods, for he feasted and clothed himself sumptuously every day with his own goods. He was damned rather because he did not do good to his neighbor, namely, Lazarus. This parable adequately teaches us that it is not sufficient merely not to do evil and not to do harm, but rather that one must be helpful and do good. It is not enough to "depart from evil"; one must also "do good" [Ps. 37:27]. (Luther 1955–1986, 51:7)

Luther then argues that the parable of the talents, with the "slothful servant," in Matthew 25:14–30 makes the same point: "He was not damned because he took something away from others, but because he did not give to others. So it will be with us." A similar message is found, Luther points out, in the parable of the sheep and goats: "It is therefore not enough to be innocent of harming one's neighbor; we must also do good as far as we are able" (Luther 1955–1986, 51:8–9). Luther's first extant sermon, then, uses the parables to focus on how Christians are called by Jesus to be active in helping others in words and both physical and spiritual "good deeds."

Luther stresses the primacy of faith in a 1522–1523 sermon about the parable of the rich man and Lazarus (Luther 1995, 4:17–32), where he argues that acts of love necessarily follow from authentic faith: "I hope you are abundantly and sufficiently informed that no human being can be pleasing to God unless he believes and loves" (18). Therefore, the rich man must have been an unrepentant sinner who might have outwardly led a holy life, but "if we judge this rich man according to the fruits of faith, we will find a heart and a tree of unbelief" (19). The man is not punished for his wealth; instead, he is punished because "he found in them all his joy, delight and pleasure; and made them in fact his idols" (19). Since he gratified only his own desires, he lived only for himself, and his inner sinfulness is displayed by the absence of his love and mercy for Lazarus: "From this now follows the other sin, that he forgets to exercise love toward his neighbor; for there he lets poor Lazarus lie at his door, and offers him not the least assistance" (20). In contrast, a person of faith knows the goodness and graciousness of God and responds to fellow human beings in a much different way: "Therefore he does not look after the healthy, the high, the strong, the rich, the noble, the holy persons, who do not need his care; but he looks after the sick, the weak, the poor, the despised, the sinful people, to whom he can be of benefit, and among whom he can exercise his tender heart, and do to them as God has done to him" (21).

In the same sermon, Luther's faith-centric theology also shines through when he declares that Lazarus must have had faith, because "without faith it is impossible to please God" (quoting Heb. 11:6); otherwise God would not have rewarded him (23). This parable demonstrates, for Luther, that "we all must like Lazarus trust in God, surrender ourselves to him to work in us according to his own good pleasure, and be ready to serve all men" (25).

Luther also did not avoid tackling some of the more problematic parables. In his sermon on the parable of the dishonest manager, for example, Luther notes how the steward artfully but deceitfully cheats his master of his property (Luther 1995, 4:294). The key point, for Luther, is that Jesus praises the steward for his shrewdness, not his dishonest actions:

> Just as when a flirt draws the whole world after her, and I say: she is a clever flirt, she knows her business. The Lord further concludes, that just as the steward is wise and shrewd in his transactions, so should we also be in obtaining eternal life. . . . As the unjust man acts shrewdly, though wrongly and like a rogue, so we also should act shrewdly but righteously in godliness. This is the proper understanding of this parable. (294–95)

A second difficulty of interpretation arises because Jesus then commands his followers, "Make friends for yourselves by means of dishonest wealth" (Luke 16:9), which some of Luther's "adversaries" (in the Roman Catholic Church) interpret as meaning that doing "works" is necessary for salvation. Luther responds:

If they thus attack us we must answer. Above all things it must be remembered that there is indeed no doubt whatever, that faith and love are the only source, as you have ever learned, that through faith we become inwardly pious, and we outwardly prove our faith by our works of love. . . . If I am to make for myself friends by means of mammon, I must first be godly. For compare these two statements: A corrupt tree cannot bring forth good fruit, and again, a good tree cannot bring forth evil fruit. From which judge for yourself: if I am to do good and give away mammon, I must indeed be first good at heart, for God looketh upon the heart, and as he finds the heart, so he estimates our works. . . . Hence the conclusion is, that I must first be good before I can do good. You cannot build from without inward, you do not commence at the roof, but at the foundation. Therefore faith must first be present. (296)

The "works" are outward signs of one's inner faith, and faith comes first. Works do not make anyone good; instead, works bear witness to the genuineness of one's faith (297). Christians do not earn salvation by doing good works; Christians must first believe, and good works will follow (299). That is the heart of Luther's theology of justification by faith and the implications of how one therefore should live.

Anna Jansz of Rotterdam (Anneken Jans; ca. 1509–1539)

Anna Jansz was born in an upper-class family in Briel, a Dutch city located on the island of Putten (near Rotterdam). She married a physician, Arent Jansz, and they soon converted to Anabaptism. Anabaptists (literally "re-baptizers") based their community of faith on what they believed to be the beliefs and practices of the earliest Christian congregations as found in the New Testament. Therefore, they rejected infant baptism, since the only true baptism documented in the New Testament, they argued, is of an adult who has undergone a conversion experience. Anabaptists also refused to take oaths (cf. Matt. 5:34) and believed in the separation of church and state, so they were often fined, imprisoned, and/or executed by both Catholics and Protestants (who believed in a state church; see Bradstock and Rowland 2002, 84).

Arent and Anna fled to England to escape persecution, but after Arent's apparent death in 1538, Anna returned home with her fifteen-month-old son, Isaiah, and a female companion (Snyder and Hecht 1996, 338–39, 341). The two women—after singing a hymn in public—were recognized as Anabaptists, reported to the authorities, and subsequently arrested. Anna and her traveling companion were put on trial in Rotterdam, convicted, and sentenced to death on January 23, 1539.

Over the years, the traditions about Anna were enhanced to portray her as a model martyr. Anna's moving testament to her infant son, for example, was included in a number of other works, such as the first edition of the 1562 Dutch martyr book *Het Offer des Heeren* (*The Sacrifice of the Lord*). Most famously, her testament is found in the massive *Martyrs' Mirror*, by the Mennonite Thieleman Jansz van Braght, a book that compiles stories of martyrdom since the beginning of Christianity. The second edition of this work became even more popular, since it contained 104 etchings by the Dutch poet and artist Jan Luiken, one of which immortalizes Anna as she hands her son over to the baker as she is taken to be executed.

> Anna's last ordeal belongs to the most moving scenes in martyr literature. On her way to the execution with her son in her arms the distraught mother offered her fortune to any of the spectators willing to adopt her son. A local baker responded, promising to raise the child as his own. According to a postscript in the *Martyrs' Mirror* the baker kept his pledge and was rewarded with divine favour. He was able to add two breweries to his possessions and his adopted son Isaiah rose to become mayor of Rotterdam. (Snyder and Hecht 1996, 341)

Another development in the tradition occurred in the 1670 edition of *Het Offer des Heeren*: Anna's testament to her son was reworked by an anonymous poet into a song of fourteen stanzas. A more expanded version of the song—in German with twenty-two stanzas—was published in the 1583 German *Ausbund*, the oldest Anabaptist hymnal (first published in 1564). The hymn is a martyrology that helps edify the faithful and fosters their "sense of history and identity" (Snyder and Hecht 1996, 342).

The song about Anna is the eighteenth hymn in the *Ausbund*, and it is sung to the tune of "Come Here to Me, Says God's Son." The first two stanzas set the stage for Anna's testament to her son by noting the joy that parents receive from instructing their children to follow God's teaching. "Annelein" (i.e., Anna), however, now receives one final chance to instruct her young son before she follows the path of the prophets to martyrdom. Like the prophets, Anna follows the example of Jesus:

> I am going on the path of the prophets,
> The martyrs' and apostles' way;
> There is none better.
> They all have drunk from the cup.
> Even as did Christ Himself,
> As I have heard and read. (stanza 3; all quotes are from Snyder and
>   Hecht 1996, 345)

The next stanza declares that all "the priests of the King" travel on this path of martyrdom, which demonstrates that they are "God's true sons and children" (stanza 4). The hymn partly moderates the apocalyptic fervor evident in Anna's own works; it employs the imagery of Revelation 6:9–11, but now the perspective expands and softens: "All the priests of the King" feel this persecution, and the delight in vengeance becomes a plea for justice:

> They cried out to God: O Lord!
> Righteous and Truthful One,
> How long until you bring order to the earth
> Among people everywhere?
> And take revenge on only those
> Who with great insolence (stanza 6)

> Have shed blood everywhere,
> Murdering innocent people?
> Are you willing to punish them
> So they no longer cause dishonour,
> Driving your own out of the land,
> Continuing in their sin? (stanza 7)

The next stanzas again note that all believers face persecution (e.g., "God gives to all [His children] a white robe"), but the hymn also assures its readers/singers/hearers that God's wrath will be calmed "once the number is fulfilled" (stanza 11). The hymn's reflection on the implications of Revelation 6:9–11 ends with stanza 11, and it switches to portraying Anna's final advice to her son. He should join with those who are despised, rejected, and persecuted; who follow God's word; and who "must carry Christ's cross" (i.e., suffer persecution; stanza 13).

The parable of the sheep and goats plays a key role in the hymn, because it demonstrates how faithful Christians are to live in order to follow Christ's "pure teaching" and to escape "the eternal fire." The most important aspects are what the faithful sheep do in the parable:

> Share your bread with the hungry,
> Leave no one in need
> Who professes Christ.
> Also clothe the naked,
> Have pity on the sick.
> Do not distance yourself from them. (stanza 17)

These actions of love commanded by Jesus in the parable, however, are apparently interpreted in the hymn to extend only to those in need who "profess

Christ," although that limitation is not explicitly stated in the other sections about the naked, sick, or imprisoned:

> If you cannot always be with them,
> Show your good will.
> Comfort the imprisoned,
> Welcome guests cheerfully into your home,
> And don't let anyone drive them out.
> Then your reward will be greatest. (stanza 18)

The hymn then connects this exhortation to identify with and help those in need with Jesus's prophetic proclamation of liberation in Luke 4:18:

> Both your hands should be ready
> To do the works of mercy,
> To give twofold offerings;
> This is spiritual and worldly work:
> To set the prisoners free, strengthen the weak;
> Then you will truly live. (stanza 19)

Anna urges her son, Isaiah, to follow the example of the parables and "to give always to God's people" (stanza 20) with the assurance that God will reward him if he follows her counsel (stanza 21). Anna thus exhorts her son and all others who listen to take the narrow path that few travel: to follow Jesus down the path of persecution and to minister to other fellow travelers who are in need, to love them, feed them, clothe them, and minister to the sick and imprisoned for the sake of Jesus.

The hymn concludes by presenting Anna as a "beautiful model" of what Christians should be:

> Annelein paid with her life,
> Which in virtue soft and mild
> Was for Christians a beautiful model,
> Given in death as well as in life. (stanza 22)

As victims of persecution and ostracism, Anabaptists could identify with the hungry, thirsty, stranger, naked, sick, and imprisoned in the parable of the sheep and goats. Like Jesus's parable, Anna's moving testament to her son focuses on where the kingdom is found—among the poor and those despised by the world—and how a person of faith should act to be a member of that kingdom:

But where you hear of a poor, simple, cast-off little flock (Luke 12:32), which is despised and rejected, by the world, join them; for where you hear of the cross, there is Christ; from there do not depart. . . . Honor the Lord in the works of your hands, and let the light of the Gospel shine through you. Love your neighbor. Deal with an open warm heart thy bread to the hungry, clothe the naked, and suffer not to have anything twofold; for there are always some who lack. (Matt. 26:11; Van Braght 1987, 454)

John Calvin (1509–1564)

John Calvin was a preeminent Reformed theologian and biblical interpreter. He was born in Noyon, France, and, according to his father's wishes, was educated in Paris. He initially studied theology and then, in 1528, started to study law at Orleans and Bourges. After a "sudden conversion," he changed course and became no longer "obstinately devoted to the superstitions of Popery" (Calvin, *Commentary on the Psalms*, preface). Calvin fled Paris in 1533 and France in 1534, due to a threat of persecution against Protestants, and he arrived in Basel in 1535. After publishing the first edition of the *Institutes of the Christian Religion*—Calvin's theological magnum opus—in 1536, he was offered a position as a lecturer and preacher in Geneva, where he stayed for the rest of his life, except for a three-year exile as a pastor to the French congregation in Strasbourg (1538–1541).

Calvin's biblical commentaries include rhetorical, philological, and historical insights and references to philosophers, orators, poets, historians, and rhetoricians, including previous and contemporary interpreters of Scripture. Calvin strives to ascertain the "original" meaning of the text—in its literary and historical contexts—before applying the text to contemporary life (see McKim 2007, 291).

In his *Commentary on Matthew, Mark, and Luke*, originally published in 1555, Calvin explains why Jesus used parables and how they should be interpreted:

Although similitudes usually cast light on the matter in hand, yet if they consist of one continual metaphor they are enigmatic. Hence when Christ put forward this similitude, He wanted to wrap up in an allegory what He could have said more clearly and fully without a figure. But when the explanation has been given, the figurative word has more power and effect than the straightforward. That is to say, it is not only more efficacious in affecting the mind but it is more perspicuous. It is important, therefore, both to consider how a thing is said and what is said. (Calvin 1972, 2:63)

Calvin recognizes the great power of parables, but he also realizes that such figurative language could be a two-edged sword: the truth of God could shine brightly upon the elect through the parables, but their obscurity leads to "the light," that is "the Word of God," being "quenched by men's darkness." Parables thus "might . . . only strike on [the reprobates'] ears with a confused and ambiguous sound" (Calvin 1972, 2:63, 64; see also Flaming 2006, 148).

In his commentary, Calvin begins interpreting a parable by stating the central point that Jesus seeks to make; Calvin quotes the text he seeks to interpret; then he speaks briefly about the parable as a whole and its overall meaning, before beginning a verse-by-verse exposition of the parable. His primary goal, once again, is to seek to explain Jesus's mind and intention. In Calvin's discussion of the parable of the wise and foolish virgins, for example, he first states that Jesus stresses perseverance and then notes (see also Flaming 2006, 148–49):

> Once the object of the parable is understood there is no reason to labour over minute details which are quite beside Christ's intention. There is great ingenuity over the lanterns, the vessels, the oil: the plain and natural answer is that keen enthusiasm for a short term is not enough unless accompanied by long unwearying effort. Christ makes the point with a most apt simile. Shortly before He had encouraged His disciples to be provided with lamps as they had to make a journey through dark and gloomy regions [Luke 12:35], but without a supply of oil the lampwick gradually dries up in the lanterns and the light fails. Christ says now that the faithful need constant replenishment of power to foster the light kindled in their hearts: otherwise their speed will give out on them halfway up the course. (Calvin 1972, 3:109–10)

Like Luther, Calvin usually rejects allegorical interpretations of the parables, and, like many interpreters, he often cites other biblical passages to explain the text he is interpreting. He does so not only because he believes in the unity of Scripture but also to explain difficult passages with more easily understood texts.

When Calvin discusses Jesus's intentions in the parables of the treasure in the field and of the pearl of great value, he argues that Jesus tells these parables to instruct Christians to deny themselves the desires of the flesh so that nothing will prevent them from obtaining the most valuable possession of all: the kingdom of heaven. Jesus shows us the "excellence of eternal life," first by comparing it to a hidden treasure:

> On the whole it is the things we can see which we prize; and so the new and spiritual life which is proclaimed in the Gospel seems too humble for us, because

it is hidden, enclosed in hope. The comparison to treasure is very apt; the value of it will never depreciate, even if it is buried underground and hidden from men's eyes. By these words we learn that the riches of God's spiritual grace are not to be assessed by the perception of our flesh or by their outward beauty but as a treasure which is preferred before all desirable riches, however hidden it is. (Calvin 1972, 2:82)

The parable of the pearl of great value conveys the same message in that a small pearl can be so highly valued that skillful merchants will sell all they have so they may purchase it. Once again, human beings tend not to see the real worth of life in heaven, since it cannot be seen "by the sense of the flesh"; we have to "renounce those things that shine before our eyes" and value God and God's kingdom above all: "Now let us get to the sum of both parables: Only those are capable of receiving the grace of the Gospel who set aside all other desires and devote themselves and their studies completely to making it their own" (Calvin 1972, 2:82).

Christians, however, do not have to abandon every possession in order to gain eternal life. The "straightforward meaning" of these parables, Calvin argues, is that Christians must prefer the kingdom of God to all that the world offers and be satisfied with the spiritual blessings that the kingdom promises. Christians have to "neglect everything that would draw us from" the gospel, "be freed from all hindrances," and "renounce the things that are contrary to godliness." But Christ still "permits God's temporal benefits to be used and enjoyed as if they were not used" (Calvin 1972, 2:83).

Calvin cautions his readers, though, not to forget that salvation comes only through God's grace. Buying a field or pearl in these parables does not mean that human beings can earn salvation; salvation is a free gift from God.

In many places Calvin reprimands Christians who judge others too severely and encourages them to be kind, merciful, and forgiving. The parable of the barren fig tree, for example, reinforces how Christians are "overstrict and severe critics of others while approving of [their] own sins." All Christians should examine themselves, and Calvin urges them to remember that God "is inviting us by this kindness and mercy to repentance" (Calvin 1972, 2:94).

Calvin also takes whatever opportunity he can to urge his readers to treat other human beings with kindness, mercy, generosity, and love. Such is the case with his exposition of the dishonest steward. Jesus is not telling his followers to advance themselves by fraud and extortion; instead, this parable demonstrates that we ought to treat others with kindness and generosity so that at the last judgment we will reap the benefits of our mercy. Jesus warns his disciples that, after having accepted the many gifts God gives them during their lifetimes, it is imperative to be both beneficent and merciful to others.

The parable itself "seems hard and farfetched," Calvin admits, but "those who investigate minutely every single part of a parable are poor theologians." The parable does not commend the unjust steward for his villainous actions but makes the point that "heathen and worldly men are more industrious and clever in taking care of the ways and means of this fleeting world than God's children are in caring for the heavenly and eternal life." Jesus thus seeks to arouse believers to be especially attentive to their eternal salvation. Thus acts of charity are essential, because "loving gifts bring us the favour of God, who promises that He will be merciful to the merciful and humane" (Calvin 1972, 2:112; cf. Ps. 18:25).

Another one of Calvin's favorite topics is the need for people to be humble, and the parable of the Pharisee and the tax collector exemplifies the contrast between the humility we should have and the arrogance we should avoid: "Now two causes are noted why the Pharisee suffered a repulse: he trusted in his own righteousness [i.e., "the merits of his works"], and he esteemed himself and despised others" (Calvin 1972, 2:128). Christians must come to God in prayer with humility and abasement, because arrogance is the most dangerous disease of all and the one that is deeply fixed in humanity down to the marrow of one's bones.

The Pharisee trusted in outward appearances, but Jesus cares about the inward uncleanness of the man's heart. The tax collector was humble, made an honest confession of guilt, acknowledged "that he was wretched and lost and betook himself to the mercy of God." From this, Jesus teaches that "he who begins by being convicted and guilty and yet asks for forgiveness is renouncing confidence in his works; and what Christ was aiming at was that God will only be entreated by those who flee trembling to His mercy alone." Calvin concludes by saying that God rejected the Pharisee but that the tax collector was able to stand before God because he could not rely on the merits of good works and had no other basis for hope than God's mercy. Such it is with all human beings, Calvin argues: "all in common are guilty"—some more than others—but "God is appeased only when we cease to trust in our works and pray to be reconciled freely" (Calvin 1972, 2:129–30). Christian faith needs nothing more than the assurance that God accepts human beings not because they deserve it but because of God's grace alone.

Calvin's influential commentaries, with their rhetorical, philological, and historical insights, in many ways anticipate modern historical-critical approaches. Calvin argues that interpreters should strive to determine the "original" meaning of the text, and his knowledge of philosophy, rhetoric, poetry, history, and previous interpretations of Scripture added greatly to his own interpretations. Although he believes that interpreters should aim for "lucid brevity" (Calvin 1973, 1), Calvin realizes that Jesus's parables are a figurative and sometimes obscure mode of discourse that has greater energy, force, and impact upon its hearers. To explain that impact, Calvin focuses upon the central point that Jesus, in his view, wants his hearers to understand and put into action in their lives.

John Maldonatus (ca. 1534–1583)

The term "Counter-Reformation" can be misinterpreted to mean that attempts at reform within the Roman Catholic Church occurred only as a reaction to the Protestant Reformation. Long before Luther, Calvin, and other Reformers, however, efforts of reform had occurred within Catholicism. The Protestant Reformation, though, provided a considerable catalyst for such reforms, culminating in the Council of Trent, which attempted to clarify the Catholic Church's essential doctrines and practices (Hastings 1999, 271–72).

The Jesuits, founded by Ignatius of Loyola and approved by Pope Paul III in 1540, are an educational, missionary, and charitable society created to help defend and revive Catholicism. Biblical interpretation played an important role in Jesuit theological education from the beginning, and the Jesuit John Maldonatus was one of the foremost interpreters of Scripture during this era and the "most significant Catholic biblical scholar of the sixteenth century" (Reventlow 2009, 3:201).

Maldonatus was born in 1533/1534 in Casas de Reina, about seventy miles north of Seville, Spain. He studied at the University of Salamanca and, after earning his doctorate, taught theology, philosophy, and Greek at the university. Maldonatus joined the Jesuits in 1562 and soon moved to Paris to teach theology at the new Jesuit institution, the Collège de Clermont. Maldonatus proved to be an extremely popular teacher, but in 1576 controversies caused him to leave for Bourges, where he wrote his acclaimed *Commentary on the Gospels*.

In this commentary, Maldonatus explains his conception of "parable" in the discussion of the parable of the sower in Matthew 13:3–8: "[Parables] are a kind of sermon, in which one thing is said and another meant, and are wrapped up in obscure comparisons. The word is so common among ecclesiastical writers that (as in some of the earlier ages) they call every word a parable. Why Christ pleased to speak not explicitly and openly, but in parable, He will Himself explain in verse 13" (Maldonatus 1888, 1:422). Maldonatus also cautions against forcing parables into a one-to-one correspondence with the aspect being illustrated. Instead, the whole of the parable should be compared to the whole of what is being illustrated. The kingdom of heaven, for example, is not to be compared to the man in the parable of the sower. Instead, the sower parable illustrates that the same thing happens in the kingdom of heaven as happens in a field if a man sows good seed in it: "There are numberless examples of the same kind; so that they lose their labour who endeavour to show how persons answer to persons, and parts to parts. We must look at the whole body of the sentence and extract the whole result from the whole parable, lest by division into parts it come to nothing and lose all its force" (1:372).

Maldonatus argues that Jesus tells the parable of the sower because of the large crowd that has gathered around him, many of whom can be designated in the parable: "Some like the stony places, some like the thorns, some like the good ground" (Maldonatus 1888, 1:422). As often is the case, Maldonatus turns to refuting the Protestant doctrine of salvation by faith. His interpretation of Jesus's explanation of the differing yields from the good soil responds directly to Luther and Calvin in particular. Maldonatus claims that when Jesus uses "fruits" he is referring to either good works or, more likely, to eternal life (citing 2 Cor. 9:6, 10; Gal. 6:7, 8; James 3:18). He concludes:

> Two errors of Luther and Calvin are over-thrown by these words, (1) They deny that we can merit eternal life; for the fruit answers not only to the quality of the soil, but to the diligence of the cultivator. Nay, each one of us, as S. Augustine says, can make himself a good or a bad soil. (2) They say that the reward of all the blessed will be equal, when we see some bring forth fruit a hundred-fold, some sixty, some thirty, as each cultivates his ground. (1:434–35)

Likewise, Maldonatus uses the parable of the net to argue against the "modern heretics," the followers of Luther and Calvin. He states that the term "kingdom of heaven" in Matthew 13:47 could be understood as designating either the gospel (as in the previous parables) or the church. Either understanding, however, provides a "strong argument against modern heretics":

> For, if we understand the Gospel, Christ signifies that not all who receive the Gospel, that is, the faith, will be saved, but they only who are the good fishes, that is, they who have not only faith, but also good works; for all are fishes, that is, all are Christians, all are faithful, but those are evil, these good. Against this, the heresy of the above teaches that all who have faith will be saved. (1:446)

The other possibility, that the "kingdom of heaven" denotes the church, makes the refutation against heretics even more explicit. Luther and Calvin are as wrong in Maldonatus's day as the Donatists were in Augustine's. Augustine had refuted the Donatists frequently, effectually, and completely, and, for Maldonatus, Augustine might as well have been writing directly "against the followers of Luther and Calvin long after. This is so great a matter, that whoever reads them may substitute for the word Donatists those of the followers of Luther and Calvin" (1:446).

Maldonatus battles against "heretics" such as Luther and Calvin, but he draws the line at physical combat or persecution. The parable of the wheat and weeds, for example, forbids such actions, because it teaches that the church will always have good seed (people) and bad seed (people) within it, with the bad seed being sown by the devil. Jesus insists that the church must patiently endure the bad seed until the final harvest (1:436). The church, however, does have the authority to excommunicate people—even the dead, by depriving them of the prayers of the church—or, in contrast, to free people in purgatory by prayers of the church (2:69).

In his analysis of the parable of the laborers in the vineyard, Maldonatus again stresses that interpreters should focus only on the essential elements and the primary message they convey. He believes the parable contains eight essential parts; the other, nonessential elements are "emblems, embellishments, and additions to complete the whole" (2:166–67). The essential points are:

1. The householder could designate either God or Jesus.
2. The day on which the householder hired the workers signifies history from creation to the end of the world (e.g., Irenaeus, Gregory). This opinion is confirmed by the fact that the parable uses "evening" to designate the final judgment. Maldonatus stresses, in contrast to Luther and Calvin, that each will receive "his reward according to works." Maldonatus also, however, sees merit in the interpretations of Jerome, Chrysostom, and the "preferred" interpretation of Origen, that the day signifies the time of "the entire life of each man" (2:167–68).
3. The vineyard represents the justice and commandments of God (e.g., Irenaeus and Chrysostom), our souls (e.g., Athanasius and Theophylact), or the church (e.g., Origen and Gregory); the last of the three seems most likely to Maldonatus.
4. The hours could signify the various ages from the beginning to the end of human time (e.g., Gregory) or the different stages of a human being's life (e.g., Bede). In this instance, Maldonatus argues that the hours signify the different stages of a person's life, since the parable's meaning is that some humans accomplish more in a short time than others do in

longer periods of time, although interpreters should not press the issue, "lest we narrow the meaning too much." In other words, the five hours/hirings are an "adornment"—per ancient forms of keeping the time of the day—not essential for understanding the parable: some were called by God earlier, and some later (2:168–69).

5. The marketplace denotes, as Origen and Augustine argue, the whole world outside the church. In that arena, humans are either idle or "absorbed in secular business," and they are called into the vineyard/church.

6. The "penny" (i.e., denarius) symbolizes salvation and eternal life, although Maldonatus cautions that Irenaeus's elaboration about the image of the king on the coin (that it symbolizes "immortality") is problematic, because "this [interpretation] seems allegorical." To understand why Jesus refers to a denarius in this parable, Maldonatus prefers the simpler reason that Matthew 18:28 implies: Jesus's reference to denarii in that other parable suggests that "the reason why a penny was given [in the parable of the laborers in the vineyard] rather than any other coin may probably have been that a penny was perhaps the usual payment for a day's labor" (2:170).

7. The evening when the penny is paid designates the final judgment, or perhaps the end of a human being's life. Either way, the meaning is the same: judgment has arrived.

8. The landowner commanding the workers who were called last to be paid first means that the workers who were called at the last hour are preferred to the workers who were called earlier, "because they had labored as much in one hour as the rest in the whole day" (2:171).

Maldonatus concludes by listing several nonessential "ornaments" that play no role in the parable's primary meaning (e.g., the steward). Speculation about such nonessential details can be dangerous, he says:

> If we enquire into these and other points of the same kind too closely, we shall not only lose our labour, but we shall incur the danger of following what is void of truth, or is without meaning, or at least is nothing to the purpose. For whoever seeks for that which does not exist, sometimes imagines what he is looking for, and will believe what is false rather than nothing. The human mind must be held in check or it will be led astray by its own subtlety, beyond all reason, and on matters of no consequence. (2:191)

More interesting is Maldonatus's claim that the workers who toiled for only one hour were so productive that they accomplished as much as the ones who worked all day. This argument allows Maldonatus to discredit the position of Luther and Calvin that salvation is bestowed by God's grace alone. Instead, Maldonatus claims, salvation "is not bestowed freely but according to merits" (2:163). Thus the ones who started working first in the vineyard "labored less, and therefore merited a less reward" (2:164; cf. *Sahih al Bukhari* in chap. 2). Maldonatus concludes, against Luther and Calvin: "The end of the parable is that the reward of eternal life answers not to the time each has laboured, but to his labour and work performed" (2:164). It is simply a matter of an equal amount of pay for an equal amount of work actually accomplished, a fact that the parable of the sheep and goats makes even more clear (2:325).

Maldonatus's commentary illustrates his erudition in a vast number of areas, including ancient languages, history, theology, previous interpreters (e.g., Augustine, Chrysostom, and Theophylact), and contemporary interpreters (e.g., Luther and Calvin). His interpretations seek to counter those of his Protestant adversaries and to counteract their growing influence, so his readings of the parables often include critiques of Protestant views on good works and justification. As Henning Graf Reventlow puts it, "Maldonatus considers himself a warrior who seeks to gain victory only through Scripture and theological tradition" (2009, 3:206).

William Shakespeare (1564–1616)

William Shakespeare was baptized at Holy Trinity Church in Stratford, England, on April 26, 1564. Like many details of his life, the exact date of his birth is unknown, but between his birth and his death on April 23, 1616, Shakespeare composed the greatest dramas ever crafted in the English language. The next certain official record of his life (unless he is the "William Shakeshafte" in Sir Thomas Hesketh's 1581 will; see Honan 1998, 61–62) is his marriage at the age of eighteen to Anne Hathaway in 1582. Except for the baptism of their children—Susanna, in 1583, and the twins Judith and Hamnet, in 1585—Shakespeare disappears from view for a number of years until he resurfaces in London as an actor and playwright. By 1594 Shakespeare had established himself as an actor, writer, and partner in the Lord Chamberlain's Men (later the King's Men), a successful acting company in London, a group that built the Globe Theatre (1599) and acquired the Blackfriars indoor theater (ca. 1608). Shakespeare published both plays and poetry (his first poem was published in 1593) and became wealthy enough to buy the second largest house in Stratford (the "New Place") before returning to

Stratford between 1611 and 1613. He thereafter spent most of his time in Stratford until his death in 1616.

Shakespeare's extant literary corpus includes thirty-nine plays—comedies, histories, and tragedies—with *Henry VIII* being his final play (ca. 1613). In those works Shakespeare refers to the Bible more than any other source. Although the number and types of allusions are vigorously debated (a recent volume cataloging such allusions consists of 879 pages; Shaheen 1999; cf. Wordsworth 1892 with 420 pages), every single play and many of his sonnets contain significant allusions to the Bible. On the one hand, the Bible is a rich storehouse of stories of drama, intrigue, and pathos. On the other hand, it also provides a rich variety of words and themes that would be easily recognizable to Shakespeare's audiences, since the Bible was the most familiar and important book in Shakespeare's England. Therefore, knowledge of the Bible is critical for understanding Shakespeare's plays, especially such plays as *The Comedy of Errors*, *The Merchant of Venice*, and *Hamlet* (Hamlin 2013, 3, 225).

One problem, however, is that it is often difficult to determine whether a play may refer (intentionally) directly or indirectly to a biblical text in general or to a parable in particular. An allusion, like beauty, is often in the eye of the beholder (cf. *Love's Labour's Lost* 2.1.15). Does, for example, the Duchess of York in *King Richard II* refer to the Pharisee and the tax collector parable when she says the following of Aumerle?

> His prayers are full of false hypocrisy,
> Ours of true zeal and deep integrity;
> Our prayers do outpray his—then let them have
> That mercy which true prayer ought to have. (5.3.105–8; all quotes are
> from Shakespeare 2011)

The connection to prayer and mercy seems to indicate that Shakespeare alludes to the parable (Luke 18:13 in particular), but the different context lessens the connections (e.g., Aumerle, unlike the tax collector, "prays but faintly"; 5.3.101). Likewise, does the Duke in *The Merchant of Venice* (4.1.88) explicitly allude to the parable of the unforgiving slave when he says to Shylock, "How shalt thou hope for mercy rend'ring none?" Similarly, does the same play refer to the parable of the laborers in the vineyard (Matt. 20:15) when Shylock argues that it is his decision what he should do with his possessions: "And all for use of that which is mine own" (1.3.111)? In contrast, *Timon of Athens* clearly incorporates the parable of the talents (e.g., Timon pays the "five talents" of Venditius's debt, which Venditius repays "doubled with thanks and service";

1.1.103–6; 1.2.4–7) and the parable of the dishonest manager (2.2.179–81; 4.3.497–509; Shaheen 1999, 675–78; cf. *Cymbeline* 3.4.118).

Numerous other allusions to parables in Shakespeare's works are also exceedingly evident. *The Merchant of Venice*, for example, clearly refers to the prodigal son's leaving home and returning bedraggled after his dissolute living (2.6.14–19; cf. the use of "younker" by Falstaff in *Henry IV, Part 1*, 3.3.79–80):

> How like a younger ["younker"] or a prodigal
> The scarfed bark puts from her native bay—
> Hugg'd and embraced by the strumpet wind!
> How like the prodigal doth she return
> With over-weather'd ribs, and ragged sails—
> Lean, rent, and beggar'd by the strumpet wind!

Gratiano, who utters this speech, himself echoes aspects of the prodigal's story (e.g., his drinking and desire for "mirth and laughter," 1.1.80–81; he also is "too wild, too rude, and bold of voice," 2.2.172). This speech echoes the parable not only in using the word "prodigal" and showing the character in a bedraggled state of return; it also, by twice using the term "strumpet," may subtly bring to mind the "strumpets" (i.e., prostitutes) with whom the prodigal (allegedly) consorted (Luke 15:30). This prodigal, like the one in Luke 15, departs to be "hugg'd and embraced" by a strumpet and returns "Lean, rent, and beggar'd." In addition, Shylock in this play may serve as one illustration of an elder son, one who, in this interpretation, refuses the invitation to join in the celebration of forgiveness (see Tippens 1988, 61–64, 72).

The prodigal son story, more than any other parable of Jesus, significantly influences a number of Shakespeare's plays. The prodigal son narrative was almost omnipresent in Shakespeare's world, especially in Protestant areas, where it was often used to portray the primacy of faith (the younger son) over works (the elder son). Prodigal son plays became exceedingly common in England, becoming "the oldest, most prevalent, and most important species of English Renaissance drama" (Tippens 1988, 59–60; see Alan Young [1979, ix, 318–20], who lists thirty-five prodigal son plays extant in England before 1642), an emphasis that continued through the Elizabethan era (see Helgerson 1976). A play directly based on the parable of the prodigal son, *The London Prodigal*, was even incorrectly attributed to Shakespeare in the first edition of the Third Folio of Shakespeare's works.

The first scene of *As You Like It* is a good example of how Shakespeare uses the prodigal son parable in a powerful way. Orlando and his older brother, Oliver, are at odds over an inheritance. Their father had passed away, and

Oliver received the vast bulk of the inheritance, whereas Orlando received a mere one thousand crowns. Oliver is supposed to provide for Orlando's education, but he refuses to do so. Instead, he provides for the education of their other brother, Jaques, and keeps Orlando "rustically at home" (i.e., like a peasant, not like the nobleman he is). Orlando complains that Oliver takes better care of his animals than of Orlando and "begins to mutiny against this servitude" (1.1.1–24). Orlando exclaims to his brother, "Shall I keep your hogs and eat husks with them? What prodigal portion have I spent that I should come to such penury?" (1.1.36–38). The use of "husks" suggests that Shakespeare here depended on the Geneva Bible (most translations available when Shakespeare wrote this play use "cods" instead of "husks"; Shaheen 1999, 216). The dispute turns violent (1.1.51–54), and Orlando again alludes to the parable by stating that Oliver must either allow him to "train" to become a gentleman or give him "the poor allottery my father left me by testament; with that I will go buy my fortunes" (1.1.69–72). Oliver retorts that dispensing the inheritance would do little good: "And what wilt thou do? Beg when that is spent?" (1.1.73).

The prodigal son parable also permeates *King Lear*, both in its primary plot (with Lear and his daughters Cordelia, Goneril, and Regan) and in its subplot (with the Earl of Gloucester and Edgar, his son, and Edmund, his illegitimate son). The story itself depends upon earlier works (e.g., the anonymous play *The True Chronicle History of King Leir*, ca. 1605), but Shakespeare incorporates numerous biblical references not found in his sources and, it seems, a story that in many respects parallels that of the prodigal son: "The protagonist starts by rejecting the one who loves him most [i.e., Lear rejects Cordelia], embarks on a reckless course which brings him eventually to suffering and want—and, paradoxically, to the self-knowledge he lacked before—and finally is received and forgiven by the rejected one" (Snyder 1979, 362–63). Although specific textual allusions to the parable in the play are sparse (e.g., Lear "hoveling" with swine may not be a specific reference; 4.7.39), many other broad parallels are evident, such as the premature granting of an inheritance, the resulting drama of broken family relationships, and the restoration of some relationships (see Snyder 1979).

Allusions to the prodigal son abound in Shakespeare's Henry IV plays. Prince Hal is the archetypal prodigal who "comes to his senses" just in time to help save the day. Both Prince Hal and Falstaff indulge in dissolute living, although we find out later that Prince Hal's behavior was not as debauched as previously thought. The prince returns to his father, asks his forgiveness, and pledges his determination to live responsibly. Falstaff, who has a particular propensity to allude to the parable (and to that of the rich man and Lazarus), can be seen as an "inverted prodigal" (cf. Lear) who has to repent and beg forgiveness from someone younger than he is (Tippens 1988, 64).

Falstaff's life sometimes seems a parody of the parable (see Hamlin 2013, 244). *The Merry Wives of Windsor* (4.5.8), for example, says that Falstaff's room in the inn is decorated with an image of the prodigal son parable, which is one of three allusions to the parable connected to Falstaff. When Hostess Quickly complains in *Henry IV, Part 2*, "I must . . . pawn both my plate and the tapestry of my dining-chambers," Falstaff refers to images of the parable on "bed-hangers" and fly-bitten tapestries (2.1.140–47). Falstaff also refers to the prodigal son parable in *Henry IV, Part 1* (4.2.33–35). In his lengthy description of the miserable state of his conscripted soldiers, he first alludes to the rich man and Lazarus ("slaves as ragged as Lazarus in the painted cloth, where the glutton's dogs licked his sores"; 4.2.24–26; cf. 4.3.31) and then combines it with an allusion to the prodigal son ("You would think that I had a hundred and fifty tattered prodigals lately come from swine-keeping, from eating draff and husks"; cf. 3.3.79–80; cf. Tippens 1988, 68).

Allusions to the prodigal son appear in numerous other plays (e.g., *Comedy of Errors* 4.3.17–21; *Love's Labour's Lost* 5.2.64; *King Lear* 4.7.36–40; *Timon of Athens* 3.4.12; 4.3.278–81; *Twelfth Night* 1.3.23–24; *The Winter's Tale* 4.3.92–98; etc.), but a brief reference in *Two Gentlemen of Verona* (2.3.3–4) is notable because Shakespeare uses it for great comedic effect (cf. the humorous parody of the parable of the lost sheep in the opening scene of *Two Gentlemen of Verona*; 1.1.69–110). Launce humorously confuses "portion" (Luke 15:12) with "proportion" and "prodigious" with "prodigal": "I have received my proportion, like the prodigious son." This form of pun is also used by later authors such as Charles Dickens (*Pickwick Papers*, chap. 43; Jeffrey 1992, 641). Finally, Launce leaves with his money amid the great lamentation of his family and even the family cat: "my mother weeping; my father wailing; my sister crying; our maid howling; our cat wringing her hands, and all our house in a great perplexity" (2.2.6–9).

Darryl Tippens rightly notes how important the prodigal son parable is to Shakespeare's works. The "prodigal plot" features a number of themes Shakespeare found compelling, such as generational conflicts; rivalries between siblings; thankless or rebellious children; the relationship of justice, love, and mercy; the loss and restoration of community; and many others: "The parable in fact comprehends the dramatist's most universal interest: what David Bevington describes as the romance pattern of 'separation, wandering, and reunion' and the morality pattern of 'fall from grace, temporary prosperity of evil, and divine reconciliation.' In one sense, then, the Prodigal story is the poet's *ur-plot*" (Tippens 1988, 60). The importance of the parables in

Shakespeare's plays is not just reflected in the quantity of allusions; the critical nature of those allusions is also seen in the depth of interaction, especially with the parable that Shakespeare evidently found most compelling: that of the prodigal son.

Domenico Fetti (1589–1623)

Domenico Fetti was born in Rome in 1589. He apprenticed with his father, Pietro, a painter about whom little is known, before probably working with Andrea Commodi and then Lodovico Cigoli. Fetti became the court painter for Cardinal Ferdinando Gonzaga, who moved him and his family to Mantua (ca. 1613–1622). Fetti relocated to Venice under duress (after a violent argument following a soccer match), where he died in 1623 (Safarik 2007–2015).

Fetti began his career in Rome during the emergence of Baroque art, a style associated with the Catholic Counter-Reformation. Baroque art is diverse, but it tends to include a forceful, emotional intensity. Although not necessarily religious, Baroque art often, as the Council of Trent urged, served the church and its teachings. Fetti's work is clearly influenced by more famous Baroque masters—the color, vitality, and opulence of Rubens; the realism of Caravaggio; and the landscapes of Elsheimer—but his work attained its fullest expression once he moved to Mantua and then Venice, when he had increased contact with the sixteenth-century masters of northern Italy, such as Titian, Tintoretto, and Veronese (Askew 1961, 21).

Fetti's reputation largely depends upon the series of parable paintings he created in Mantua near the end of his career (1618–1621). He painted at least eight and possibly twelve parables (some works attributed to Fetti were primarily created by his workshop). These small paintings display Fetti's mature style, one that employs rich colors, expressive use of chiaroscuro (strongly contrasting light and shade), and, in later stages, Venetian-style landscapes. These paintings are his most original and most popular works. Like the parables of Jesus, they are rich with mundane details of everyday life—with some surprising elements included—and can proclaim religious truths with a tender concern for the welfare of human beings (Safarik 2007–2015).

One of Fetti's earliest paintings in this series, *The Mote and the Beam* (figure 3.1), portrays a proverbial saying that is sometimes categorized as an "aphoristic parable" and is labeled a parable by the author of Luke (along with the passage concerning the blind leading the blind; 6:39–42). Jesus's humorous hyperbole makes the point that human beings tend to criticize various faults in others while minimizing their own.

Figure 3.1 Domenico Fetti, *The Mote and the Beam*

The Mote and the Beam uses satire, so, unlike most of Fetti's parable paintings, this image strikes an overall note of unreality. A bearded older man sits
at the top of a small set of steps. He raises his right hand and points his index
finger at a younger man on the right, apparently lecturing the younger man
energetically. The younger man stands, leans slightly toward the older man,
and rests his arms on a small wall between them. His left hand, in response
to the older man's gesture, is slightly raised, much less energetically, with its
index finger pointing back at the older man.

Their interaction takes place outdoors, and most of the image is dominated by a deep blue sky with white clouds. The wall behind the older man
has a decorated urn at the top, and the stucco of the wall has deteriorated,

revealing bricks underneath. A taller wall behind the younger man is similarly dilapidated, with a plant growing out of the wall at the top of the painting. A few bricks stick out of the taller wall, but what first grabs the viewers' attention is a massive beam that juts out of the wall on the right, stretches three-fourths of the way across the center of the painting, and almost touches the left eye of the older man. In contrast, a splinter from that beam juts out in almost the opposite direction and comes close to if not touches the younger man's eye.

The older man comically seems nonplussed by the beam nearing his eye; he continues his stern lecture of the younger man, who, in contrast, seems surprised by the splinter in/near his eye. Tellingly, the older man is almost completely in shadows, with only his right hand, upper arm, and part of his right knee in the light. The face and upper body of the younger man are, besides some brilliant white clouds in the background, the brightest part of the painting. It is almost as if a spotlight shines upon him. The older man is in both physical and metaphorical darkness, and Jesus's humorous yet deadly serious warning is clearly and comically conveyed (cf. Askew's interpretation of another version of this painting, that it "represents the argument as a youth's challenge to his elder" and that the painting overall is "a fundamentally Baroque resolution of fact and fancy"; 1961, 27).

In contrast, Fetti's painting *The Parable of the Lost Coin* (figure 3.2) takes place indoors in a darkened room illuminated by a single lamp. The stone-and-stucco room is simple, unadorned, and showing its age. The focus is almost entirely on the woman holding the lamp, as she bends over and diligently searches for her lost coin. An overturned basket sits in the corner of the room, and an open chest stands on the right, with articles of cloth(ing) scattered on and beside it. A pitcher and a bowl appear in the right foreground. In most representations, such as the one by John Everett Millais (see chap. 4), the woman holds a broom (or it leans against a wall) to illustrate her sweeping the house as she looks for the lost coin (per Luke 15:8). Here, perhaps, the bowl and pitcher are meant to convey another form of cleaning the house.

A stool lies on its side in the left foreground, close enough so that viewers can count the nine coins on top of the stool that are still in the woman's possession. In the middle foreground is a rather large crack in the floor. As viewers look carefully, they can see the lost coin lodged in that crack. The question remains: Is the coin lodged deep enough in that crack so that, even though viewers can see the coin, the woman does not yet see it (but soon will)? Or has the woman just now caught her first glimpse of the lost coin, and does she now, as a result, begin to set the lamp down on the floor so she can retrieve the coin? In that case, the rejoicing over finding the lost has just

bpk, Berlin / Gemäldegalerie Alte Meister / Hans-Peter Klut / Art Resource, NY

Figure 3.2 Domenico Fetti, *The Parable of the Lost Coin*

begun, which might explain the apparent smile that begins to spread on her face (cf. Zuffi 2003, 223).

Some interpreters (e.g., Tertullian) argue that, in Luke 15, the man searching for the lost sheep, the woman searching for the lost coin, and the father welcoming the lost son home all represent God either searching for lost sinners, as in the first two parables, or welcoming sinners home. Other interpreters (e.g., Cyril of Alexandria) suggest that those who search for the lost sheep and coin actually symbolize Jesus, who seeks and finds lost sinners. In the Catholic Reformation—and in Fetti's representation of it—the woman instead represents the church (cf. Hornik and Parsons 2013). Some interpreters take the symbolism even further by arguing that the lamp with which the woman/church searches "is symbolic of the word of God" and that the scene stresses the repentance of the sinner, "a dominant theme in the Counter Reformation" (e.g., Askew 1961, 25). If indeed the lamp symbolizes the Word of God, that would explain why the painting, in its portrayal of this simple domestic scene, merges the real with the unreal: How, for example, could one small oil lamp illuminate the room and the woman so brilliantly?

Fetti's painting of the unforgiving slave (unmerciful servant) parable presents a much different message (figure 3.3). It depicts the scene when the servant who has been forgiven the ten-thousand-talent debt comes across his fellow servant who owes him one hundred denarii, seizes him by the throat—with the fellow servant falling down on his knees to beg for patience—and drags him off to prison. This painting draws its viewers into the drama with a sense of action, pathos, and contrasts. At the top of the stairway, one sees a bright and cheerful

bpk, Berlin / Gemäldegalerie Alte Meister / Hans-Peter Klut / Art Resource, NY

Figure 3.3 Domenico Fetti, *The Unmerciful Servant*

sky. Yet the action takes place at the bottom of the stairway, through an arch and in a darker, more sinister place, although the two men at the bottom of the stairs have swathes of light upon them. A large vine, which grows across most of the painting horizontally, provides another visual barrier between the upper area, with its light, openness, and hope, and the lower area, which is dominated by darkness, anger, and despair (cf. Askew 1961, 28).

At the bottom of the stairs, the unmerciful servant—bearded, dressed in red and yellow, and wearing a white turban—has both his hands around the other man's throat. The bearded man is clearly older and larger than the other servant, and he stands over the other servant, with his right leg in front of the other man and his left leg across him. The younger servant is dressed mostly in white and is forced by the older servant into almost a reclining position. His right hand touches/holds the older man's right arm in supplication, and his left arm braces against the stone below him, trying to prevent the older servant from forcing him into what most assuredly is the (debtors') prison below. He will not be strong enough, it appears, to prevent the older man from pushing him down into the prison.

As a final appeal to the viewers' emotions, the older man's mouth is open in anger, and his eyes look upon his victim's face; the younger man's mouth is open in terror, and his eyes look out at the viewers, appealing for help, for mercy, and for forgiveness—and silently reminding viewers not only that Jesus told them to forgive people over and over and over again (Matt. 18:22) but also that the king of the parable will later say, "Should you not have had mercy on your fellow slave, as I had mercy on you?" (Matt. 18:33).

Parables can create pictures in the minds of their hearers/readers, and this painting, like the others in Fetti's series of parable paintings, illustrates that visual works of art can have much in common with these narrative works of art, including their power and sometimes enigmatic nature. Fetti interprets Jesus's parables within the context of the Catholic Reformation, and these visual teachings reflect the spiritual instruction of the church with simplicity and clarity but in personal, not dogmatic, terms (cf. Askew 1961, 21; Safarik 2007–2015).

George Herbert (1593–1633)

George Herbert, one of the greatest English poets, was born into an aristocratic family on April 3, 1593, in Montgomery, Wales. His father died when Herbert was three, and the family moved to Eyton (1596), Oxford (1599), and then London (1601). An accomplished musician and brilliant student, Herbert enrolled at Trinity College, Cambridge, in 1609, and he became a Fellow of the

College in 1614. While at Cambridge, Herbert wrote his mother that, in his view, poetry about the love of God was significantly better than poetry about the love between men and women. He considered love poems, perhaps like the ones published by Shakespeare the year before, as "vanity." Herbert, in contrast, declares: "My resolution [will] be that my poor abilities in poetry shall be all and ever consecrated to God's glory" (Drury 2013, 85). Herbert included in the letter two sonnets, his earliest known poetry, as examples of his vow.

Herbert was named university orator in 1620 and was elected to Parliament in 1624, the same year that he changed his professional trajectory: he was ordained a deacon (1624), became canon of Lincoln Cathedral (1626), was ordained a priest (1630), and was named rector of Fugglestone with Bemerton (near Salisbury). He served as a parish priest for three years, until he died from tuberculosis on March 1, 1633.

Although Herbert wrote poetry for most of his life, he published very little during his lifetime. As he lay dying from tuberculosis, though, Herbert sent a collection of over 160 poems to his friend Nicholas Ferrar, requesting that he read the poetry and decide whether to publish it or destroy it. The collection of poems, titled *The Temple*, was published in Cambridge a few months after Herbert's death.

Many of Herbert's poems in *The Temple* make passing allusions to parables, but most references are minor ones, such as to the parable of the sower in "The Church-Porch" (line 98) or to that of the sower and that of the talents in "Grace" (line 1). Other poems make more extensive use of parables, however. The parable of the great dinner, for example, serves as the foundation for "Love (III)," a poem that Simone Weil calls "the most beautiful poem in the world" (Herbert 2007, xxi):

> Love bade me welcome: yet my soul drew back,
>> Guiltie of dust and sinne.

"Love" here signifies God, and the poem features a dialogue between (a) the loving God who welcomes sinners home and invites them to share the feast and (b) sinful human beings who feel unworthy to be called. At a deeper level, the traveler represents a soul who arrives in heaven only to be convinced that he does not deserve to be with God in heaven. His sins weigh his soul down and cause him to hesitate, but God ("Love") responds (cf. Vendler 1975, 58–60, 274–76; Ray 1995, 104–5; Herbert 2007, 661–63):

> But quick-ey'd Love, observing me grow slack
>> From my first entrance in,

> Drew nearer to me, sweetly questioning,
>> If I lack'd any thing.
>
> A guest, I answer'd, worthy to be here:
>> Love said, you shall be he.
> I the unkinde, ungratefull? Ah my deare,
>> I cannot look on thee.

God quickly sees the guest's reticence and immediately, as the perfect host, comes near to see if the guest lacks anything (Herbert often uses forms of "sweet" to convey his experience of God's redemptive love). The guest's self-evaluation leads him to explain that he is not worthy to be a guest, because of his sinful shortcomings (Herbert 2007, xliv–xlv). In the parable of the great dinner, the previously invited guests give various excuses as to why they will not come to dinner. Their refusal is not reflected in this poem; instead, the hesitation to enter stands closer to the viewpoint of the prodigal son when he declares that he is no longer worthy to be declared his father's son because of his sins (Luke 15:21). A similar hesitation may be reflected in the poor, crippled, blind, and lame in the parable of the great dinner, since they must be "compelled" to come in (Luke 14:23).

The guest feels unworthy, but God responds, without explaining why (yet), that he is indeed worthy to enter God's house. The guest describes himself as unkind and ungrateful, and he cannot even bear to look upon God because of his shame. It is possible that the 1559 *Book of Common Prayer* for the Church of England, for which Herbert was a devoted advocate, may provide some perspective on this section of the poem. The *Book of Common Prayer* includes an exhortation, which also alludes to the parable of the great dinner, that priests should use when people are negligent about coming to Holy Communion: God lovingly calls all sinners to the "feast" of Holy Communion because of the atoning sacrifice of Jesus on the cross (Booty 1976, 254–55). For Herbert the parish priest, the loving invitation of God to come to the eucharistic table is always present and urgent.

> Love took my hand, and smiling did reply,
>> Who made the eyes but I?
> Truth Lord, but I have marr'd them: let my shame
>> Go where it doth deserve.

God is love, Herbert proclaims, and what better way to portray God's love than for God to take the hand of the sinner, smile lovingly, and say, "I know who and what you are; I am your Creator."

The guest recognizes who God is ("Lord") but does not (yet) obey the Lord's command. The guest believes that his eyes are too "marred" by sin to be worthy, and his shame persists, even in the face of God's love and care. This sin and shame, the guest apparently feels, mean that he deserves to be sent away from God's presence and into damnation (Ray 1995, 105).

> And know you not, sayes Love, who bore the blame?
>> My deare, then I will serve.
> You must sit down, sayes Love, and taste my meat:
>> So I did sit and eat.

The best example of God's love for humanity, Herbert believes, is Jesus's sacrifice on the cross. God thus reminds all who feel unworthy to enter God's dinner that through Jesus God bore the blame and paid the price for human sin so that all would be welcome. Herbert's God is a God of love, akin to the father of the prodigal son and the man in the parable of the great dinner who invites the poor, crippled, blind, and lame to his feast. Although the guest first insists that he should be the one to serve at the dinner, this ultimate act of love—the sacrifice of Jesus on the cross—is what finally convinces the guest that he truly deserves to be in God's presence and to participate in that holy meal of and from the "heavenly host" (cf. Luke 12:37).

The pearl of great value parable is the primary source for Herbert's poem "The Pearl," one of only five of his poems that incorporate biblical texts in their titles (Herbert 2007, 323). As the first lines of the first three stanzas indicate, the voice in the poem is a person of great learning, honor, and pleasure, but desires foremost to "flie" and "climbe" to God.

The first stanza discusses intellectual pride. It appreciates the attraction of knowledge and catalogs its sources, such as discoveries in geography or astronomy. Knowledge, it seems, is given its due (Vendler 1975, 182–83), and it is readily available to the poet, who has the keys:

> I know the ways of learning; both the head
> And pipes that feed the press, and make it run;
> What reason hath from nature borrowed,
> Or of itself, like a good huswife, spun
> In laws and policy; what the stars conspire,
> What willing nature speaks, what forc'd by fire;
> Both th' old discoveries and the new-found seas,
> The stock and surplus, cause and history;
> All these stand open, or I have the keys:
>> Yet I love thee.

The last line of the stanza possibly speaks to the love that the poet has for knowledge—which will be surpassed in the fourth stanza. More likely, however, it (already) speaks to the poet's love of God and indicates that intellectual pride is one of the things that this "merchant" is willing to sell to "buy" (or to fly, climb, and enter into) the kingdom of heaven. Strikingly, the "I know" in the first line of each of the first three stanzas is symmetrically contrasted with the "I love" in the last line of the first three stanzas, and "thee" (i.e., God) is the last word in all four stanzas: "The love of God overpowers all worldly knowledge, an idea inherent in the structure of the first three stanzas that is fully explicated in the last stanza" (Ray 1995, 120).

In the second stanza, the poet turns to ways of honor. The poet also knows about the life, etiquette, and intrigue of the social and political life at the royal or noble court, the necessity of witty repartee, the striving for fame and glory, and the importance of minute expressions or gestures in that society. What the poet argues is that such a life is actually burdensome ("bear the bundle") and possibly enslavement ("To sell my life"; see Herbert 2007, 324). Winning the favor of the king or nobleman can be compared to the wooing of a lover ("true-love-knot"; Ray 1995, 121). This description of honor seems decidedly more negative than the description of knowledge, and the stanza ends the same way as the first: "Yet I love thee."

The third stanza combines many musical terms (e.g., "strains") with sexual allusions (e.g., "relishes," "propositions") and sense experiences (e.g., "sweet," "my senses live," "five") to build a comprehensive description of pleasure that builds and builds ("unbridled store"). The senses grumble that they outnumber, five to one, the thing that curbs or controls them. Is it reason that controls them, or conscience, or the soul, or the Holy Spirit? That is unclear, although reason seems most likely, given the context; what remains clear, again, is that the poet loves God.

The poet has full understanding of the value of learning, honor, and pleasure, and the superior value of the kingdom of God, so the terms related to buying and selling bring readers back to the parable itself: the poet "sells" all that he has (learning, honor, and pleasure) to "buy" the pearl of great value (God and God's kingdom). It is possible, though, that "at what rate and price I have thy love" could also refer to the price that Jesus "paid" on the cross for the remission of human sin:

> I know all these and have them in my hand;
> Therefore not seeled but with open eyes
> I fly to thee, and fully understand
> Both the main sale and the commodities;

> And at what rate and price I have thy love,
> With all the circumstances that may move.
> Yet through the labyrinths, not my grovelling wit,
> But thy silk twist let down from heav'n to me
> Did both conduct and teach me how by it
>   To climb to thee.

The "ways" of learning, honor, and pleasure of the first three stanzas—which the poet has in his "hand"—give way to the fourth stanza's "labyrinths" through which the poet's "grovelling wit" cannot navigate. It takes the grace of God, the "silk twist" that permits him to climb upward to God. The last three lines also contain a surprise for the reader. Until now, the poem used present tense verbs. Now, however, readers learn that this silk twist "did both conduct and teach" the poet to "climb" to God. Apparently, the poet has already made his way out of the labyrinth of earthly desires for learning, honor, and pleasure (Herbert 2007, 326).

Herbert is considered the greatest devotional English poet, and his piety shines through these poetic conversations with God. Although a brilliant rhetorician with advanced learning in classics and theology, Herbert in his poems eschews sophisticated language for a more unadorned simplicity and human immediacy. As he declared to his mother years before, the subject of all of his poems is God, whether they are arguing, complaining, grieving, celebrating, praising, or singing to God (Herbert 2007, xxi–xxii; cf. Drury 2013, 72).

Roger Williams (ca. 1603–1683)

Roger Williams was born in England around 1603. After serving as an apprentice to the famous jurist Sir Edward Coke, Williams earned a scholarship to Cambridge University, studied to become a minister, and then served as chaplain on the estate of William Masham from 1628 to 1630. Pressures to conform to the Church of England increased after Charles I ascended to the throne in 1625, so Williams and his wife left to join the Massachusetts Bay colonists in North America in 1630 (J. Davis 2004, 6).

The governor of the Bay Colony, John Winthrop, welcomed Williams's arrival, calling him "a godly minister," but things soon changed. When Williams was offered the prestigious position of teacher in the Boston church, he refused, because the church had not separated from the Church of England. A number of other controversies followed, and in 1635 Williams was ordered to leave the Massachusetts Bay Colony. Williams made his way south, bought some land from Narragansett Indians, and founded a settlement that he named Providence, which a few years later, along with other nearby settlements, was chartered as Rhode Island and Providence Plantations. Notably, the charter issued by Charles II in 1663 decreed that the colony would have "full liberty in religious concernments" (Gaustad 2005, 70). Rhode Island thus became a refuge for all types of dissenters—believers and nonbelievers.

Many Puritans in New England envisioned themselves as a "New Israel" and interpreted some Hebrew Bible texts about ancient Israel as applying typologically to them (Gordis 2003, 125), including the idea that God would bless or punish the "New Israel" for obedience or disobedience to God's will. Church and state were interdependent, and the state was responsible, for example, for compelling, by force if necessary, conformance to religious obligations.

Williams disagreed strongly with identifying anything but the church with a "New Israel" and argued that the church should use only spiritual weapons (e.g., Scripture, prayer, and persuasion), not physical ones (e.g., a sword). Ancient Israel and its "National Religion" was a unique phenomenon in history, Williams declared, with Jesus proclaiming a different way: Jesus refused to use violence, and the new covenant he inaugurated means that neither the state nor the church can use violence or religious coercion (Williams 2008, 29).

Williams's theological and scriptural arguments for liberty of conscience are most evident in his ongoing debate with John Cotton, the eminent Puritan minister in the Massachusetts Bay Colony. The parable of the wheat and weeds (Williams and Cotton used the older word, "tares") plays a major role in their debates, because Williams believes this parable is central to Jesus's advocacy of religious liberty. He also argues that it has been tragically misinterpreted over the centuries to justify the persecution of those believed to be heretics (Byrd 2002, 88), a misapplication that resulted in the "spilling of the blood of thousands" (Williams 2001, 55).

Cotton argues that the field in the parable symbolizes the church. The wheat designates faithful Christians, the servants represent God's ministers, and the tares, since they look so much like wheat, symbolize hypocrites within the church. Therefore, those tares should not be "rooted out"; Jesus commands toleration, since, just as tares look similar to wheat, so do these people look similar to faithful Christians. Sinners and heretics, however, are stubborn, prideful people who, even though they know better, rebel on purpose. They are easily discerned from Christians; Cotton compares them to "briars and thorns." If these sinners are warned, given opportunities to repent, and still refuse to change their ways, they should be punished, either by the church by censure or excommunication or, if they corrupt others, then by the "Civil

Sword" of the state (Byrd 2002, 106). Otherwise, Cotton declares, these sinners would expose others in society to "a dangerous and damnable infection" (Williams 2001, xxxi).

Williams responds that any such persecution is a perversion of the teachings of Jesus. Jesus clearly says that the field represents the world (Matt. 13:38), not the church, and the tares symbolize all sorts of dissenters, separatists, heretics, and even nonbelievers in society, not Cotton's hypocritical sinners within the church. The *wheat* plants are "children of the kingdom" who must coexist in society with the followers of Satan until the end of the world. The *servants* denote messengers or ministers of the church, and the crucial point is that Jesus's parable commands Christians to advocate religious liberty and oppose any coercive policies of the state concerning religion, even when those policies concern "heretics and pagans" (Byrd 2002, 117). Jesus warns against civil persecution of those deemed heretics, because it is impossible in this fallen world always to distinguish between God's people and those opposed to God. The weeds will be collected when Jesus returns, and then they will receive the punishment they deserve at the hands of God, not human beings. Like Jesus commands, it is better to allow the wheat and tares to coexist in the world until he returns than to risk the damage that uprooting the sinful ones would do.

To Cotton's argument that tares are so similar to wheat in appearance that they must designate hypocrites within the church, Williams responds by examining the Greek text of the parable. The word for tare (*zizania*) designates all sorts of weeds, so the term signifies people who are "manifestly different from, and opposite to, the true worshippers of God." In addition, in the parable the servants easily recognize the difference between the wheat and the tares very early in their development (Williams 2001, chap. 20; all subsequent chapter references in this section are to this work), and Williams later insinuates that Cotton, ensconced in his "soft and rich saddle" of city life in Boston, may not be the best judge of agricultural practices (Williams 1963, 304).

The church, Williams argues, is a beautiful garden within the sinful world but distinguishable from it. The garden of the church should remain pure with its righteous wheat, but the field of the world in which it finds itself includes sinful tares. The parable demonstrates that Christian rulers and ministers should not confuse the garden of the church with the field of the world. Constantine, the first Roman emperor to be identified as a Christian, began this horrible confusion within the history of Christendom with terrible results. Such "holy men" intended to exalt Christ but did not follow Christ's commands "to permit the tares to grow in the field of the world." In their zeal, they sometimes persecuted "good wheat instead of tares" (chap. 64).

Jesus uses the field, Williams observes, to symbolize the entire world, not just the church, because the world is an extremely wicked place. The problem is that as soon as "the Lord Jesus had sown the good seed, the children of the kingdom, true Christianity, or the true church, the enemy, Satan, presently, in the night of security, ignorance, and error, while men slept, sowed also the tares which are anti-Christians, or false Christians" (chap. 21). People like Cotton incorrectly desire to call down fiery judgments upon these people "and to pluck them by the roots out of the world. But the Son of man, the meek Lamb of God—for the elect's sake which must be gathered out of Jew and Gentile, pagan, anti-Christian—commands a permission of them in the world until the time of the end of the world, when the goats and sheep, the tares and wheat, shall be eternally separated from each other" (chap. 21).

In addition, the parable of the sower, just previous to this parable, includes four varieties of ground upon which the true messengers of Jesus sow their message of the kingdom. The four types of ground (symbolizing various "hearts of men") also represent people in the entire world, not just inside the church. The good soil represents people in the church, and the "proper work of the church concerns the flourishing and prosperity of this sort of ground, and not the other unconverted three sorts; who, it may be, seldom or never come near the church, unless they be forced by civil sword, which the pattern of the first sower never used" (chap. 22). Thus the parable of the sower similarly demonstrates that Jesus commands the church to tolerate unbelievers and not to use coercion against them. This toleration does not mean approval or acceptance of their errors, however: "The Lord Jesus, therefore, gives direction concerning these tares, that unto the end of the world, successively in all the sorts and generations of them, they must be (not approved or countenanced, but) let alone, or permitted in the world" (chap. 22). Offenders against "the civil state and common welfare" certainly should be punished by the state (Williams includes adultery with offenses "against the civil state": "robbery, murder, adultery, oppression, sedition, and mutiny"), but Jesus's command "Let them alone" means that ministers of the gospel should have no civil power or authority, and civil authorities should not be permitted to punish religious dissenters or offenders (chap. 27).

Yet, Williams argues, the church should not be passive against these tares, such as the ones who "with perverse and evil doctrines labor spiritually to devour the flock, and to draw away disciples after them" (chap. 19). Williams agrees that their "mouths must be stopped" but stipulates that, as Jesus taught, "no carnal force and weapon [are] to be used against them; but their mischief [is] to be resisted with those mighty weapons of the holy armory of the Lord Jesus Christ." Until Jesus returns at the end times, all such (evil) people must be tolerated, as Jesus commands: "*Let them alone until the harvest*" (chap. 19; emphasis original).

The implications are dramatic and shocking to Puritans like Cotton: there are no "holy commonwealths" such as Puritans in Massachusetts sought to create; there are only "holy churches." Jesus's parable of the wheat and weeds actually undermines the Puritan use of Scripture to create a godly society or "New Israel" (Byrd 2002, 113). Against the commonly held view that a state-sponsored church is necessary to promote an orderly society, Williams proclaims that freedom of religion and the separation of church and state are necessary to promote order, peace, and a just society: "Obedience to the command of Christ to let the tares alone will prove the only means to preserve their civil peace, and . . . without obedience to this command of Christ, it is impossible . . . to preserve the civil peace" (chap. 26). Christians should not promote or support or even acquiesce to religious persecution; they should instead speak fervently and prophetically against all such religious coercion.

Williams steadfastly practiced what he preached concerning religious liberty, as his treatment of the Society of Friends (Quakers) demonstrates. Although he emphatically denounced Quaker beliefs (e.g., his last published work, the 1676 *George Fox Digg'd Out of His Burrowes*), Williams adamantly rejected requests to help "stamp out" this new religious movement. Unlike neighboring Massachusetts or Connecticut (where Quakers could be fined, whipped, disfigured, burned, or even hanged), Williams permitted no Quaker to be punished by the government in Rhode Island (Gaustad 2005, 60, 107–8). In addition, Williams's arguments about religious liberty and the separation of church and state are one of the pillars upon which Thomas Jefferson and others built (e.g., Jefferson's "wall of separation" in his letter to the Rhode Island Baptists).

Rembrandt Harmenszoon van Rijn (1606–1669)

Rembrandt was born on July 15, 1606, to an upper-middle-class family in Leiden. Unlike his older brothers, who were apprenticed to become craftsmen and tradesmen, Rembrandt was sent by his parents first, at age seven, to Leiden's Latin school and then, in 1620, to Leiden University. Soon after his enrollment, however, Rembrandt left the university and apprenticed to a local painter, Jacob Isaacszoon, for about three years, and then with Pieter Lastman in Amsterdam for about six months. Rembrandt worked in Leiden for a few years before returning to Amsterdam (ca. 1632), where he would live for the rest of his life.

In 1634, Rembrandt married Saskia van Uylenburgh, who appears in a number of Rembrandt's paintings, etchings, and drawings. Saskia died in 1642, the same year Rembrandt completed his famous (and mistitled) *The Night Watch*. Although Rembrandt earned significant income during these years, his extravagant spending led to financial difficulties. In 1656 he was declared insolvent, his collections were sold, and he moved to a poorer part of town. Rembrandt remained, however, a respected figure and painter, and he created some of his greatest masterpieces during the 1660s (Chilvers 2004, 583).

Approximately one-third of Rembrandt's extant works interpret biblical subjects, but his paintings depict surprisingly few parables, all of which are from Luke's Gospel: the parables of the good Samaritan, of the prodigal son, and, possibly, of the rich fool (his depiction of the last is likely not actually about the parable; see Gowler 2012, 199–217; *The Parable of the Laborers in the Vineyard*, in the Hermitage Museum, is now considered a product of his workshop).

Rembrandt had a special affinity for the parable of the prodigal son, which he depicted many times over his long career. Rembrandt's earliest treatment of the parable is a 1632/1633 drawing, *The Departure of the Prodigal Son*, which is notable because the prodigal's mother is depicted attempting to persuade the prodigal to remain home. Rembrandt also sometimes self-identifies with the prodigal. For example, one of his early paintings (*Self-Portrait with Saskia in the Guise of the Prodigal Son*; 1634–1636) portrays him as the prodigal son and Saskia as a prostitute. The slate order board at the top left (to keep track of drinks ordered) and the peacock pie on the table are standard elements in representations of the prodigal son's dissolute life in a tavern (Wetering 2008, 91; Gowler 2016).

Around the same time he created that painting, Rembrandt produced an etching of the prodigal son kneeling before his father upon his return home (*The Return of the Prodigal Son*; 1636; see figure 3.4), which has been called "one of his most intense expressions of human anguish" (D'Oench 1995, 7). The abject son kneels before his father, his hands clasped in supplication. His body is emaciated, his clothes ragged, and his face utterly disconsolate (figure 3.5). His only possessions are the clothes around his waist, a knife tied at the waist, and the walking stick that lies on the steps beside him. His father bends over him—with the son's right foot partly coming out of its shoe—tenderly touching his son's back with his right hand. Two servants rush out the door, bringing the robe and sandals, and they appear to avert their faces at the tender reconciliation. Another servant looks out the window at the reunion, apparently also with eyes diverted from the pathos-filled reunion. The elder brother, however, is still out in the field in the background, as of yet unaware of his father's forgiveness of the prodigal.

Rembrandt's most famous representation of the parable is one of his last paintings: *The Return of the Prodigal Son* (1667–1669), a work that also conveys the impression that Rembrandt found the parable's story of dissipation and redemption autobiographically significant. As Henri Nouwen wrote after seeing the painting: "I knew that Rembrandt deeply understood this spiritual homecoming. I knew that, when Rembrandt painted his *Prodigal Son*, he had lived a life that had left him with no doubt about his true and final home" (1994, 6).

In the painting the father lovingly leans over the prodigal who kneels before him, and both of the father's hands rest upon the boy's shoulders. One figure appears in the back left of the painting, most likely the prodigal's mother, her response hidden in the darkness. Three figures appear on the right. In the center of the background, next to a pillar, a younger woman stands—most likely a young servant—her eyes gazing at the viewers of the

Figure 3.4 Rembrandt, *The Return of the Prodigal Son*

Personal photo from Amsterdam

Personal photo from Amsterdam

Figure 3.5 Rembrandt, *The Return of the Prodigal Son* (detail)

painting, perhaps encouraging them to respond. The middle figure of the three is seated, with his right leg crossed over the left, his arm drawn across his chest. On the right, another man stands, holding a walking stick in front of him. He, like the father, is dressed in fine clothes, mostly in red. Perhaps this is the elder brother, who at this point observes the scene with little emotion. The entire focus of the painting, however, is the reunion of the prodigal and his elderly father and the absolution the prodigal receives. As Gary Schwartz notes, the painting itself has been interpreted allegorically, especially in Russia, where the painting now finds its home; according to this interpretation, the father's embrace of the returning prodigal—whose tired head finds rest and solace upon his father's chest—symbolizes the final return home to God at the end of one's earthly sufferings (2006, 370), an illustration that others besides Rembrandt tend to identify with the prodigal son (see Gowler 2016).

Rembrandt's etching *The Good Samaritan Bringing the Wounded Man to the Inn* (1633) is an especially intriguing and enigmatic image. This (fourth-state) etching has produced varied receptions, from criticisms about the figures being "ungraceful," with "lumpish shapes" that "hang from one another like a string of potatoes" (Clark 1966, 12), to praise that it is "among the most beautiful of Rembrandt's works" (Goethe 1986, 66).

The image itself collapses two scenes in the last part of the Lukan parable: (a) the arrival of the Samaritan and the wounded man at the inn and (b) the Samaritan's departure, payment, and instructions to the innkeeper the next day.

The horse, in profile, is in the center foreground with its left eye apparently looking at the viewer. A young boy with a feather in his cap holds the reins, as an older servant helps the wounded man off the horse. The servant's face is emotionless, but the strain is apparent on his face, as he assists the man, and

Metropolitan Museum of Art, New York, NY

Figure 3.6 Rembrandt, *The Good Samaritan Bringing the Wounded Man to the Inn*

his left leg does not match the placement of his torso. The wounded man is shirtless, with a bandage wrapped around his head, and his face—especially the mouth—vividly portrays the pain he feels. At the top of the stairs, we see the back of the good Samaritan as he speaks to the elderly innkeeper, who apparently is putting the denarii into his purse. He looks intently at the Samaritan, and the Samaritan gestures with his left hand as he explains what he wants the innkeeper to do.

A man appears on the left looking out a window. He also has a feather in his cap, and his face also bears no emotion; perhaps not quite uninterested, but certainly noncommittal. His gaze seems to focus on the wounded man being lifted off the horse, and the wounded man returns his gaze and turns his body to the man as well. Who is this apparently uninterested man at the window? Johann Wolfgang von Goethe provides a fascinating possibility:

We for our part are convinced that the victim recognizes in the youth at the window the malicious leader of the band of robbers who attacked him a short time before. At this moment the poor man is seized by the fear that he is being taken to a den of thieves and that the Samaritan himself is part of the plot to kill him. In brief, he finds himself in a desperate situation: he is weak and helpless. (1986, 68)

Other aspects of the image are more certain. The inn is in a state of serious disrepair. Deep cracks appear in the outside wall, and in places bricks show through. Some of the boards on the railing of the steps are broken, perhaps rotten; the wooden eaves are in the same shabby state. It is in this decaying and perhaps disturbing world that the Samaritan's surprising act of mercy takes place, a place where everyday life continues as normal. A woman gets water from a well. Two birds are in the tree above her, two leaves drift down to earth, and two chickens stand just in front of the well. The woman does not notice the good Samaritan's act of kindness and mercy, and in fact no one else seems to care. And, in the right front foreground, a central location nearest the viewer, a dog, with its back to us, defecates upon the ground.

Why do we only see the back of the good Samaritan at a distance but see the back of the defecating dog so prominently? Dogs appear in at least fifty-five of Rembrandt's biblical subjects (Durham 2004, 48), including similar characterizations in unexpected places, for example, in his *John the Baptist Preaching* (1634/1635). Among the diverse audience of John the Baptist is another defecating dog, although in this painting the dog partly functions as a silent rebuke to the nearby Pharisees and Sadducees (Matt. 3:7–10). Other dogs appear as well—some fighting, others copulating—and the defecating, fighting, and copulating dogs, it appears, help illustrate the sinfulness of the world, which largely ignores John's preaching (Bruyn et al. 1982, 85). Defecating dogs in religious or other scenes are also found in a number of other Dutch paintings of this era (e.g., Emanuel de Witte, *Interior of the Oude Kerk, Delft, During a Service*, 1641; cf. the urinating dogs in churches in de Witte and van Vliet; Philips Wouwerman, *Cavalrymen Halted at a Sutler's Booth*, ca. 1655; Herman Breckerveld, *Winter*, 1626).

Like the dogs in *John the Baptist Preaching*, the provocative image in the good Samaritan etching seems designed, at least in part, to shock a polite audience, and many critics take offense at Rembrandt's seeming vulgarity in this and other works (see Kuretsky 1995, 150). Kenneth Clark, with perhaps an unintended pun (*dog*-matic?), calls the dog "repulsive," arguing that it functions as part of "Rembrandt's dogmatic sermon against the frivolity of elegance." The dog is there to remind us, he claims, "that if we are to practice the Christian virtues of charity and humility, we must extend our sympathy to all natural functions, even those that repulse us" (1966, 12). In a similar way, Nigel Spivey wonders whether this is an attempt by Rembrandt to "out-Caravaggio Caravaggio" to highlight those down-to-earth, everyday elements of the world that God seeks to redeem through Jesus: "It is rather the claim of Rembrandt's art that it sees and portrays the world as it is. No special and sanitary preserve labeled 'art' should exist. Dogs lead their doggy lives. Humankind is humankind" (2001, 164). Others, to absolve Rembrandt from responsibility, tried to blame one of Rembrandt's students or assistants for adding the dog later.

The centrality of the dog is striking; one's eyes instinctively travel to that part of the image first, whereas the hero of the story, also with his back to us, appears farther away, and it takes awhile for our eyes to travel to him. The structure of the painting tends to lead us from the dog, to the servant boy holding the reins of the horse, to the horse itself, to the servant lifting the wounded man, to the wounded man himself—with perhaps a side trip to the man at the window, since we might be directed to go there by the wounded man's gaze—and, finally, up the flight of stairs to the good Samaritan giving instructions to the elderly innkeeper. Only a small part of the Samaritan's face is revealed to us, and even it appears in shadow. We are led, it seems, from the bottom right of the painting—where the dog performs one of the most rudimentary bodily functions common to all animals—along a diagonal to the left and back—where the Samaritan performs one of the most selfless acts of kindness and mercy to another human being. Such acts, the parable of the sheep and goats reminds us, are necessary for human beings to enter into the eternal kingdom of heaven.

If that is the case, perhaps the open door of the inn symbolizes the door of heaven that opens for those who perform such acts of mercy. As Kuretsky points out, Rembrandt's biblical images commonly parallel home and church in this way, using doors to symbolize the passageway to eternal salvation. Likewise, if the woman at the well alludes to the Samaritan woman of John 4 (and the setting of Rembrandt's etching of that scene, *Christ and the Woman of Samaria, among Ruins* [1634], is very similar in many ways), then the conversation between her and Jesus about "eternal life" may be incorporated as well (Kuretsky 1995, 150–51). Kuretsky also notes, however, that imagining such symbolism might be "overthinking" this true-to-life image of a dog relieving itself, oblivious to all around it. The dog could be due to Rembrandt's adherence to verisimilitude, "rigorous naturalism" (Westermann 2000, 115), an attempt to "humanize" the narrative (Durham 2004, 48), or it could be Rembrandt rather playfully and amusedly including this bodily function as an example of what is commonly ignored or concealed in polite society (Kuretsky 1995, 151).

Thus the dog simply could inject an aspect of realism. Life inherently includes the sublime and the everyday, the unusual and the banal, the sacred and the profane, with the latter—in each of these polarities/dialectics—often being more prevalent than the former.

John Bunyan (1628–1688)

John Bunyan was born in Elstow (near Bedford, England) most likely in 1628, since he was christened in November of that year. Bunyan began training with his father as a brazier or tinker, but when he turned sixteen he joined the Parliamentary Army in the English Civil War against the Royalists. Bunyan returned home in 1647, resumed life as a tinker, and got married in 1649, the same year that Charles I was put on trial and executed, the monarchy and the House of Lords were abolished, and a republic (the Commonwealth) was proclaimed. Although his marriage and other events caused him to consider "religion" (Bunyan 1998, 8–9), Bunyan notes that his sins included a great propensity for swearing (he also confesses to dancing and bell-ringing). His life changed when he encountered "three or four poor women" in Bedford who spoke of a "new birth" (par. 37). Bunyan's heart "began to shake," and he started to visit them regularly (par. 39–41). He joined an independent congregation in Bedford and later began to preach.

The political turbulence of this era is reflected in the radical religious movements that challenged the status quo in England. These struggles went beyond those who were Catholic, Anglican, or Presbyterian. Now other groups of "dissenters" had arisen who were independent of those established churches, such as the Quakers (Society of Friends), Baptists, Levellers, and other groups, such as those Bunyan joined. Oliver Cromwell died in 1658, Cromwell's Protectorate collapsed in 1659, the monarchy was restored in 1660, and Charles II returned to England. In that volatile atmosphere, Bunyan was imprisoned for twelve years (1660–1672) for the offense of preaching without a license. He wrote his autobiography, *Grace Abounding to the Chief of Sinners* (1666), while in the Bedford jail and also the first part of *The Pilgrim's Progress*. He was released in 1672 and became pastor of the nonconformist congregation in Bedford. Bunyan's reputation grew along with his literary production, and when he died in 1688 he was buried in the nonconformist Bunhill Fields Burial Ground in London like other, later prominent nonconformists such as Daniel Defoe and William Blake.

Bunyan's literary genius was the triumph of a humble believer over the educated scholar, and he believed that his Spirit-taught understanding of the Bible was vastly superior to a formal education. Scripture is primary for Bunyan: it is the Word of God, which contains the only source for knowledge of salvation that must be applied in people's lives. Like many previous interpreters, Bunyan views the Bible as a unified narrative in which one text should be interpreted in light of other texts (Bradstock 2009, 287, 293, 295) and believes that the Bible should be interpreted typologically, with an understanding that words or passages may contain deeper spiritual meanings that can be discovered by a careful, Spirit-filled interpreter (Owens 2010, 46).

The full title of *The Pilgrim's Progress*, for example, is, *The Pilgrim's Progress from This World to That Which Is to Come: Delivered under the Similitude of a Dream*, and the allegory includes both a narration of the dream and a running commentary on what it means, with a key focus being on a correct interpretation (Pooley 2010, 81). Bunyan defends the form of *The Pilgrim's Progress* by arguing that parables and other biblical texts justify allegorical interpretations of the Bible:

> All things in parable despise not we,
> Lest things most hurtful lightly we receive,
> And things that good are, of our souls bereave.
> My dark and cloudy words they do but hold
> The truth, as cabinets inclose the gold.
> The prophets used much by metaphors
> To set forth truth: yea, who so considers
> Christ, his apostles too, shall plainly see,
> That truths to this day in such mantles be.
> . . . .
>
> Sound words, I know, Timothy is to use,
> And old wives' fables he is to refuse;
> But yet grave Paul him nowhere doth forbid
> The use of parables, in which lay hid
> That gold, those pearls, and precious stones that were
> Worth digging for, and that with greatest care. (Bunyan, n.d., 23–24)

A key question that Bunyan asks his readers in the prologue of *The Pilgrim's Progress* is: "Would'st thou see a truth within a fable?" Bunyan hopes that they do.

Bunyan addresses this issue directly in his lengthy exposition of the rich man and Lazarus parable, *A Few Sighs from Hell*. In the introductory "The Author to the Reader," Bunyan responds to an anticipated objection that "Parables are no realities":

I could put thee off with this answer, that though it be a Parable, yet it is a truth, and not a lie, and thou shalt finde it so too, to thy cost, if thou shalt be found a slighter of God, Christ, and the salvation of thy own soul.

But secondly, know for certain, that the things signified by Parables, are wonderful realities. O what a glorious reality was there signified by that Parable! The kingdom of heaven is like unto a net that was cast into the sea, &c. Signifying, that sinners of all sorts, of all nations, should be brought into God's kingdom, by the net of the gospel. And O how real a thing shall the other part thereof be, when its fulfilled, which saith, And when it was full they drew it to shore, and put the good into vessels, but threw the bad away, Matth 13.47, signifying the mansions of glory that the Saints should have, and also the rejection that God will give to the ungodly, and to sinners. . . . O therefore, for Jesus Christs sake, do not slight the truth because it is discovered in a Parable; For by this argument thou mayest also, nay, thou wilt slight almost all the things that our Lord Jesus Christ did speak; for he spake them for the most part (if not all) in parable. Why should it be said of thee as it is said of some, These things are spoken to them that are without in parables, that seeing they might not see, and that hearing they might not understand Luke 8.10. I say, take heed of being a quarreller against Christ's parables, lest Christ also objecteth against the salvation of thy soul at the judgement day. (1976, 246–47)

Salvation by grace is the key element for Bunyan, and parables are "wonderful realities" that contain deep spiritual truths about the kingdom of heaven, salvation, and damnation (Davies 2002, 194).

Bunyan uses parables in many of his works, and a particularly noteworthy example is his 1673 sermon "The Barren Fig Tree." This sermon primarily attacks the "barren" or "fruitless" members of the church, including those who hypocritically feign piety. Bunyan begins by noting that two aspects must be explored when interpreting parables: the *metaphors* that are used and the *doctrine* or *mysteries* "couched" in those metaphors. Bunyan lists six metaphors in this parable; a certain man (God the Father), a vineyard (the church), a barren fig tree (a fruitless "Professor," i.e., one who "professes" to be a Christian), a dresser (Jesus), three years (the patience of God), and digging and dunging (God's willingness to help). The doctrine, then, is that God planted the church, which has members who bear no fruit. God has been patient but commands Jesus to destroy those barren members. This destruction is just and deserved, but Jesus intercedes to defer the execution of the barren church members, and he also works to try to make the church members start bearing fruit. If those church members continue to be barren, however, their end is unavoidable and eternal damnation results (Bunyan 1986, 5).

The foolish virgins in the parable of the wise and foolish virgins are a prime example of such barren church members. It is one thing to be *in* the church but quite another thing to be *of* the church (Bunyan 1986, 15). Another example is found in the ending of the parable of the wedding feast, when the king (God) commands a man not wearing a wedding garment (hypocrites within the church) to be thrown "into the outer darkness." God demands that church members forsake their sinful pasts and begin to bear the fruit of the Spirit (e.g., righteousness; 24). God cannot stand a barren fig tree (32), so at some point God finally declares that an unfruitful tree must be cut down. Since God's forbearance eventually ends, Bunyan argues, the time to repent is now, while there is still time. If repentance does not ensue, God's ax is laid to the root of the barren fig tree, and the fig tree is thrown into the fire. Bunyan urges his readers to recognize the truth of the parable:

> Barren Fig-tree, *Dost thou hear*! the Ax is laid to thy roots, the Lord Jesus prays God to spare thee; Hath he been *digging* about thee? Hath he been *dunging* of thee? *O Barren Fig-tree, Now* thou art come to the point; if thou shalt *now* become good, if thou shalt after a gracious manner suck in the Gospel-dung, and if thou shalt bring forth fruit unto God, **Well**; But if not, *the fire is the last.* Fruit or the Fire. Fruit or the Fire, *Barren Fig-tree. If it bear fruit, well.*
>
> And if not, then after that
> thou shalt cut it down. (Bunyan 1986, 42–43; emphasis original)

A second theme emerges when one explores the historical context in England when this sermon was published (1673). Bunyan had recently been released from prison, but now nonconformists in Britain had suffered a setback: Charles II rescinded the Declaration of Indulgence, and dissenters were once again suppressed in some areas of England. Bunyan wrote *The Barren Fig Tree* in the context of the renewed attack on nonconformists such as him. Bunyan first claims that the barren fig tree can symbolize the Jewish people who were eventually punished by God (e.g., the destruction of Jerusalem). Bunyan then claims that England fits the same pattern: England did not meet God's standard of bearing good fruit, and its claim to be a Christian nation would not save it, because it was filled with barren fig trees who merely embraced outward signs of Christian practices (e.g., worshiping according to the *Book of Common Prayer*). Bunyan uses the parable to speak a prophetic warning: England faces divine retribution unless it repents. The only conformity that matters is not to the king or the Church of England and its liturgy; it is to the demands of God and to the precepts of Christ (Greaves 2002, 307–9).

Likewise, Bunyan pens *A Discourse upon the Pharisee and the Publicane* (1685) in the midst of oppression of dissidents during the last few months of Charles II's reign. Bunyan's analysis of the Pharisee makes it clear that his primary target is the Church of England, such as its hypocritical concern for outward piety and ritual:

> Great is the formality of Religion this day, and little power thereof. . . . Nor can much of the power or savour of the things of the Gospel be seen at this day upon Professors. . . . How proud, how covetous, how like the world in Garb and Guise, in Words and Actions, are most of the great Professors of this our day! but when they come to Divine Worship, specially to Pray, by their words and carriages there, one would almost expect them to be Angels in heaven. (Bunyan 1988, 129)

Pharisees, in this context, are emblematic of those who are concerned about external rituals, not real piety. Such people may be found in the dissenting churches, Bunyan admits, but the outwardly religious but inwardly corrupt members of the Church of England are Bunyan's primary target (Greaves 2002, 307–9).

The tax collector ("publican") was a "notorious" sinner, and the Pharisee was a "notorious" righteous man, but "they were both found sinners" (Bunyan 1988, 122–23). The Pharisee was deficient in righteousness—he was a hypocrite whose "holiness" was grounded in "ceremonies" such as tithing. But, Bunyan argues, even so, this Pharisee "was better than many of our English Christians; for many of them are so far off from being at all partakers of Positive righteousness, that all of their Ministers, Bibles, good Books, good Sermons, nor yet God's Judgements, can persuade them to become so much as Negatively holy; that is, to leave off evil" (128). In addition, like the Pharisee, people in the Church of England "own Rules, Laws, Statutes, Ordinances and Appointments *before* the Rules, Laws, Statutes and Appointments of God" (143). The Pharisee, as the text of Luke reveals, was an "utter stranger" to the "things of the Spirit," one who neglected "Faith, Judgement, and the love of God" (130). Many so-called Christians in England, Bunyan argues, do the same.

The most important battles, Bunyan believes, are not military, political, or economic; they are spiritual battles concerning eternal salvation, and Bunyan uses the "wonderful realities" of parables effectively as a weapon in that battle for the salvation of souls by God's grace.

4

The Afterlives
of Jesus's Parables in the Eighteenth
and Nineteenth Centuries

A few years ago I taught a course, Portraits of Jesus, in Emory University's British Studies Program at Oxford University. The six-week course examined how Jesus and the New Testament Gospels were portrayed in visual art, and we used the National Gallery in London as our "laboratory" for exploring various artistic interpretations of Jesus and the Gospels. The National Gallery organizes its collection by eras (1250–1500; 1500–1600; 1600–1700; 1700–1900), and what students quickly discovered as they walked through the museum is that religious (Christian) images declined significantly at the beginning of the eighteenth century (cf. the Enlightenment's stress on reason, including the scientific method, and not tradition or religion) and even more so during the nineteenth century. This decline of biblical and religious images in art mirrors the overall decline of the use and influence of the Bible in society and culture during the modern era, and it also corresponds with increasing lack of knowledge about the Bible. In 1854, for example, Henry David Thoreau complained about the ignorance, religious and otherwise, of those people living in Concord, Massachusetts:

> The best books are not read even by those who are called good readers. . . . Even the college-bred and so-called liberally educated men here and elsewhere have really little or no acquaintance with the English classics; and as for the recorded

163

wisdom of mankind, the ancient classics and Bibles, which are accessible to all
who will know of them, there are the feeblest efforts anywhere made to become
acquainted with them. (Thoreau 2004, 85)

Such biblical illiteracy had a significant impact on how—and how much—the
parables of Jesus were received and interpreted.

The eighteenth and nineteenth centuries are especially significant within
biblical scholarship because of the advent of the modern "historical criticism" (or historical-critical method). This term denotes a number of related
methods or approaches, all of which influenced the study of the parables.
One such effort is source criticism, the attempt to discern what sources or
materials Gospel authors used to compose their narratives. Historical criticism attempts to use the "scientific method" to obtain more "objective" interpretations of these texts in their "original" contexts—such as the author's
intended meaning or the various stages of the traditions before they reached
their final form—interpretations not influenced by dogmatic, theological,
ideological, or ecclesiological presuppositions. Ultimately, purely "objective"
interpretations are impossible to obtain, but the goal remains to be as objective as humanly possible.

Although parable scholars are not the focus of this volume (for an introduction to and analysis of parable scholarship, see Gowler 2000), Adolf Jülicher
is included in this chapter as an important example of a historical-critical
scholar who revolutionized parable interpretation in modern scholarship. He
argues, for example, that the parables of Jesus were significantly transformed
by the time the New Testament Gospels were written (including changes by
the Gospel authors themselves).

The other major interpreters in this chapter are chosen to illustrate the
increasing diversity of responses to the parables during this era. These responses include developments in art (William Blake, John Everett Millais),
music (Fanny Crosby), literature (Leo Tolstoy), poetry (Emily Dickinson),
philosophy (Søren Kierkegaard), the church (Charles Spurgeon), and political
discourse (Frederick Douglass).

William Blake (1757–1827)

William Blake was an English poet, printmaker, painter, and radical Christian
mystic whose work is striking for its originality, independence, and prophetic
vision. Blake claimed to have seen a vision of angels as a young child, and he
considered himself a kindred spirit to and in the same tradition as biblical

prophets (for details of Blake's life, see Bindman 1977; Bentley 2001; J. King 1991). After a seven-year apprenticeship with James Basire (1772–1779), Blake enrolled as an engraver in the Royal Academy, where he exhibited seven watercolors. Soon thereafter, he became a commercial engraver, primarily creating illustrations for books.

Blake's works *There Is No Natural Religion* and *All Religions Are One*, both published in 1788, are the first published examples of Blake's "illuminated printing." This brilliant innovation unifies images and written text; images serve as metaphors that "put flesh upon the bones" of the written text (see Hults 1996, 360). These tracts proclaim that prophecy and imagination ("Poetic Genius") are the foundation of all religions and philosophies (although the Bible has a special place as an "original derivation"), thus denigrating empiricism or reason that stems from mere sense perception. Art thus has a "divine mission" (Bindman 1977, 53–54).

Blake struggled financially during his prolific career. He was largely ignored or dismissed as eccentric, and his works were bought and known only by a small circle of people, although the patronage of John Linnell made the last decade of Blake's life relatively free from financial difficulties. Blake also later gained some admirers, such as the "Ancients," a group of young painters who held both Blake and his work in esteem near the end of his career. It was not until after his death, however, that Blake was more widely recognized as one of the era's greatest poets and most brilliant artists (Chilvers 2004, 80–81).

The Bible permeates Blake's thought and works. His words and images interact with, critique, and interpret biblical texts in unconventional ways. Although there is a development in Blake's views on the Bible (he becomes more positive after 1800), Blake insists that the Bible is not a handbook of moral virtue divinely ordained by God that can be used as a means of social control: "The Whole Bible is filld with Imaginations and Visions from End to End & not with Moral virtues" (Blake 2008, 664). Blake's Christianity does not consist of obedience to a list of commands; it is the practice of the forgiveness of sins, and the immediate apprehension of God that comes through visions (Rowland 2010, 2–4; cf. Hults 1996, 360).

Blake approaches the Bible "allegorically." He does not search for the single "true" meaning of a text; instead, Blake envisions a biblical text "as a gateway to perception, a stimulus to the imagination" (Rowland 2010, 10). Blake's three extant images titled *The Parable of the Wise and Foolish Virgins* amply demonstrate this approach. The first was in a series of biblical subjects that he painted for Thomas Butts around 1805, a work that is now in the New York City's Metropolitan Museum of Art (available at http://www.metmuseum.org /art/collection/search/340853). Blake created the second version for John Linnell

Yale Center for British Art

Figure 4.1 William Blake, *The Parable of the Wise and Foolish Virgins* (ca. 1825)

around 1822, and it is now housed in the Fitzwilliam Museum in Cambridge, England (available at http://data.fitzmuseum.cam.ac.uk/id/object/17531). The third is a watercolor similar to the 1822 version, which Blake painted for William Haines around 1825, and it is currently in the Yale Center for British Art, in New Haven, Connecticut (figure 4.1; also available at http:// collections.britishart.yale.edu/vufind/Record/1670866).

In the third image, an angel flies above the ten maidens. It fills the entire width of the painting and blows a trumpet as it flies from right to left at the top of the page. The face betrays a hint of red, which reinforces the power of the trumpet blast. The five wise virgins stand on the left side of the painting. They all stand in a dignified way, and all hold oil lamps with burning wicks. We see the first and third virgins from left to right only in profile; they face away from the foolish virgins as they prepare to leave to go meet the bride-groom. In between them, another wise virgin raises her right hand, with her palm facing the viewers. She looks directly at the viewers, perhaps silently asking them about their own preparedness for the bridegroom. The fourth wise virgin (from the left) raises her left hand, in the same fashion as the second wise virgin, which bookends the wise virgin who looks at the viewers and gives more symmetry to the five wise virgins. She also looks up into the sky, to the top right of the painting, either at the feet of the angel who blows the trumpet or in anticipation of what follows the angel, which serves to give a sense of progression to the five wise virgins as well. The body of the fifth wise virgin is directed toward the viewers, but her head and face turn toward the five foolish virgins as she raises her arm and points dramatically with her left hand to the top right of the painting, possibly to the same area at which the fourth virgin directs her gaze.

This gesture also portrays the dramatic answer of the five wise virgins to the pleas of the foolish ones to give them some oil for their lamps: "No! there will not be enough for you and for us; you had better go to the dealers and buy some for yourselves" (Matt. 25:9). The fifth virgin's face is calm; it paradoxically betrays the hint of a smile, whereas the arm with which she points is strikingly powerful and muscular, which seems mismatched with the rest of her body. The power of her pointing gesture is also reinforced by the fact that she is the only one of the barefoot wise virgins who stands on her tiptoes.

The stately posture of the five caryatid-like women, with "the precisely contrapuntal movements of their heads and feet," greatly contrasts with the groveling, desperate, and disheveled five foolish virgins (Klonsky 1977, 107). Even the coloring of the wise virgins is less pronounced and more homogeneous; their clothing is limited to various shades of blue, whereas the color of the foolish virgins' clothing includes one in a shade of red, another in blue, and the three others in less distinct shades. The animation of the foolish virgins is also in stark contrast to the courtly presentation of the five wise virgins. The first foolish virgin kneels in front of the closest wise virgin, beseeching her for help. She raises her right arm in supplication but is not allowed to touch her. In her left hand is the cord holding her worthless lamp. Two others kneel in shock and horror over their fate, one with her hands on the side of her face and the other with arms raised and holding a lamp. Another stands with uplifted arms, looking up to heaven at the trumpeting angel, her right hand holding both a lamp and her head covering enmeshed in her hair. The last stands with her back to the wise virgins; she bows her head and holds her face in her hands. The expressions on their faces run from plaintive pleading to shock to utter dismay to horror, but every one of the five foolish virgins recognizes that all is lost.

Most interpreters argue that the angel blowing a trumpet heralds the imminent approach of the bridegroom in the parable (cf. Bindman 1970, 45, on the Fitzwilliam Museum image). Christopher Rowland, however, suggests another intriguing possibility. In the Gospel of Matthew, the parable is preceded by Jesus's eschatological discourse, which describes the appearance of "the Son of Man coming on the clouds of heaven" (Matt. 24:30; see also vv. 29–44). This Son of Man comes at an unexpected hour, and the parable of the wise and foolish virgins is the first of seven parables in Matthew 24–25 that progressively depict the need for being prepared and what human beings specifically are to do to be prepared (culminating in the parable of the sheep and goats). Part of the eschatological discourse in Matthew—missing in Mark 13 and Luke 21 (cf. 1 Thess. 4:16)—includes angels gathering the elect "with a loud trumpet call." Rowland notes that Blake was a keen interpreter of biblical texts, so the angel blowing the trumpet in this image may also connect this parable to the end times, just like the Gospel of Matthew. Thus the buildings (one with a spire) in the background that appear over the heads of the foolish virgins may represent the promised celestial city (Rowland 2014, 319). This interpretation is bolstered by the fact that the parable itself says only that a "shout" denoted the arrival of the bridegroom (Matt. 25:6), and it also helps to explain another intriguing element of this painting: Why, given his concern for mercy and forgiveness, would Blake choose to depict this parable, since the wise virgins display a marked lack of charity and mercy? The answer may be that Blake wants to convey the sense that within every person there exist "contrary states" and that at some point a decision must be made and action must be taken.

As Rowland observes: "In his images and writing Blake wants to stir his readers and viewers much as the Matthean Jesus does in his parables" (2014, 319). Both Blake's works and Jesus's parables "rouze the faculties to act," since they challenge their hearers to engage imaginatively with the story being presented. They do so by not merely attempting to impart knowledge or information; instead they, often urgently, strive to influence, persuade, and challenge their audiences (see Gowler 2000, 38–39, 101–3).

Søren Kierkegaard (1813–1855)

Søren Kierkegaard was born in Copenhagen on May 5, 1813, and went on to study theology, philosophy, literature, and history at the University of Copenhagen. In his studies he encountered the work of the German philosopher Georg Hegel (1770–1831), which initiated a lifelong intellectual quarrel with Hegel's influential philosophy (Kierkegaard 2004, xxiii). Kierkegaard published an astounding number of works from 1843 to 1846, and, in 1846, he abandoned his quest to become a Lutheran minister and instead devoted his life to writing (Evans 2009, 6).

Kierkegaard's voluminous writings eventually earned him status as one of the nineteenth century's greatest thinkers, but his location (Copenhagen) and language (Danish) prevented his fame from spreading during his lifetime. Even people in Copenhagen often ridiculed him because of his idiosyncratic behavior and awkward gait and appearance (e.g., the satirical magazine *The Corsair*), which led to Kierkegaard's increasing isolation (Collins 1983, 13).

Kierkegaard's writings became progressively more polemical against Denmark's Lutheran Church, especially after 1854, when there was a change in the church's leadership. He was convinced that the church had domesticated true Christianity, and he believed that the Lutheranism of his day used the Bible to enumerate doctrines instead of envisioning Scripture as "the object of faith" that proclaims "radical demands" for Christian life (McKim 2007, 609, 612). Despite his polemics against the church, however, Kierkegaard esteemed the Bible greatly, referring to it at least 1,500 times in his writings. In addition, no philosopher made more use of parables and metaphors than Kierkegaard—both the parables of Jesus and parables that he created—who embeds them in many of his works, using them as effective weapons in his philosophical debates: Kierkegaard "takes delight in leading his readers along a path, only to arrive at an unexpected junction where he suddenly leaves them to make a decision about a set of events" (Kierkegaard 1978, xi). Since, for Kierkegaard, "the truth exists only in the process of becoming, in the process of appropriation," then the communication of truth must be indirect, unlike the "objective presentation of data or information." Such indirect communication requires what Kierkegaard calls "double reflection," because indirect communication presents alternative possibilities, an "either-or" decision in the "appropriation process," where human beings grasp their own human possibilities. Parables thus function as indirect communication because they engage their readers and challenge them to "untie a knot" and choose between possibilities of self-understanding (Kierkegaard 1978, xii–xiii): "If anyone is to profit by this sort of communication, he must himself undo the knot for himself" (Kierkegaard 2004, 117–18).

This process of personal "appropriation" is extremely important for Kierkegaard's understanding of the Bible: "The divine authority of the Gospel does not speak to one person about another, does not speak to you, my listener, about me, or to me about you—no, when the Gospel speaks, it speaks to the single individual. It does not speak *about* us human beings, you and me, but speaks *to* us human beings, you and me, and what it speaks about is that love is to be known by its fruits" (Luke 6:44; Kierkegaard 1995, 14).

An excellent example of Kierkegaard's interpretative approach is his 1849 sermon on the Pharisee and the tax collector (or publican) parable (in *Three Discourses at the Communion on Fridays*; Kierkegaard 1971, 361–86). Kierkegaard begins with a prayer that exhorts his hearers/readers to emulate the repentant stance of the tax collector, and the discourse/sermon itself opens by observing, "The Pharisee represents the hypocrite who deceives himself and would deceive God, whereas the publican represents the sincere man whom God justifies" (371). The tax collector is usually portrayed as the "model of a sincere and Godfearing churchgoer," but Kierkegaard connects him with the repentance necessary for partaking in Holy Communion. The fact that the tax collector stood far off is also important because when one is alone with God, one is actually closer to God; it takes solitude for one to realize that one is estranged from God: "He was alone, alone with the consciousness of his guilt and crime, he had entirely forgotten that there were in fact many other publicans beside him, it was as if he were the only one. He was not alone with his guilt in the face of a righteous man, he was alone before God—ah, that is to be afar off. For what is farther from guilt and sin than God's holiness?" (373). The Pharisee, on the contrary, pridefully compared himself to the men around him, thanking God that he was not like them. The tax collector, though, "was alone with the consciousness of his guilt and crime" (373). He would not look up into heaven, and he did not look at the others around him: "but he with his eyes cast down, turned *in*ward, had only *in*sight for his own wretchedness" (374).

Kierkegaard notes that the Pharisee deceives himself that he is in a right relationship with God, but the tax collector suffers no such illusion: he recognizes that he is a sinner who must depend upon the mercy of God, so he cries out for God's mercy, because he is "alone in individuality . . . and face to face with God's holiness" (374). Thus, according to Kierkegaard, when we are alone before God's holiness, with no one else to help us, then in terror we discover, as sinners, that we must cry out for God to have mercy upon us. The Pharisee, however, felt no such terror, felt no danger, and—full of pride and secure self-satisfaction—uttered no cry for forgiveness. He did not understand that he was standing before the abyss, and he was not really, Kierkegaard argues, standing "before God" (375).

Only the tax collector went home "justified." His previously averted eyes had seen God; he was exalted, and the Pharisee suffered "annihilating abasement" from God. The results of their two attitudes, Kierkegaard says, are as established as the law of gravity: "As little as water changes its nature so as to run up hill, so little can a man succeed in lifting himself up to God . . . by pride" (376).

In his conclusion, Kierkegaard identifies the actions of the tax collector with the actions of model participants in Holy Communion as they move from confession to Communion to going home (Barrett and Stewart 2010, 2:120). To make confession in the Eucharist is to stand, like the tax collector, far off in order to be nearer to God, to cast one's eyes downward and therefore inward, to smite one's breast in sorrow for one's sin, and to exclaim, "God be merciful to me a sinner." By condemning one's self at the altar of Communion and praying for grace, one can indeed go home "justified by God" (Kierkegaard 1971, 377).

The third sermon in *Three Discourses at the Communion on Fridays* again pits a sanctimonious Pharisee against a sinner who receives forgiveness: Simon the Pharisee against the woman who enters his house (Luke 7:36–50). Kierkegaard repeatedly portrays the woman as a sinner who "loved much." The strongest expression of loving much "is to hate oneself," and the woman not only risks coming into the presence of "the holy One" (i.e., Jesus); she also does so in the house of a "proud" Pharisee, where he and other Pharisees will roundly condemn and cruelly mock her (Kierkegaard 1971, 380).

The woman, who hated herself but loved much, Kierkegaard says, "went straight ahead to the banquet . . . and to confession," a frightful admission of sin, not just to herself, but in front of others. She wept at the feet of Jesus, and, Kierkegaard writes, those tears caused her to forget her terrible surroundings and herself (382):

> He who at the moment when he is most occupied, the moment which to him is the most precious, forgets himself and thinks of the other, he it is who loves much; he who being hungry himself forgets himself and gives to the other the meager provision which is sufficient only for one, he it is who loves much; he who in mortal danger forgets himself and leaves to the other the only plank of safety on the waves, he it is who loves much. So also he who at the moment when everything within him and everything about him not only reminds him of himself but would compel him against his will to remember himself—when nevertheless he forgets himself, he loves much, as she did. (383)

The woman, Kierkegaard observes, says not a word, and Jesus, perhaps to make the point clearer to the other guests at the banquet, does not speak to her; he speaks about her, almost as if she were absent. Jesus turns her almost into a parable, and Kierkegaard tells the story as if Jesus were telling it in

Kierkegaard's text; he replaces the parable of the two debtors with a retelling of the story of Simon and the woman as a parable:

> Simon, I have somewhat to say unto thee. Once upon a time there was a woman, she was a sinner. When one day the Son of Man sat at table in the house of a Pharisee, she too came in. The Pharisees scoffed at her and condemned her as a sinner. But she sat at his feet, anointed them with ointment, wiped them with the hairs of her head, kissed them, and wept—Simon, I would say somewhat unto thee: Her many sins were forgiven her because she loved much. (383)

Kierkegaard declares that this sinful woman becomes an eternal example: "This woman who was a sinner—yet she became and is a pattern; blessed is he who resembles her in loving much! The forgiveness of sins which Christ offered while He lived on earth, continues to be, from generation to generation, offered to all in Christ" (385). Kierkegaard points out that the sinful woman entered a Pharisee's house, a place where she was unlikely to find forgiveness and where she was most unwelcome; participants in Holy Communion, however, enter into where they are most welcome and, upon repentance, receive forgiveness. Kierkegaard concludes with this exhortation, once again making this woman a prototype: "Oh, forget the orator who has been speaking, forget his art, if so be he has displayed any, forget his defects, which perhaps were many, forget the discourse about her—but forget her not; along this road she is a guide, she who loved much, and to whom therefore her many sins were forgiven" (386). Thus, for Kierkegaard, the sinful woman is a positive prototype for Christians, even though no one, except Jesus, deigns to speak with her, and she herself is not allowed to speak except through her actions: "And hence a complete, honest, deep, utterly true, entirely unvarnished confession of sin is the perfect love, to make such a confession of sin is to love much" (385–86; Barrett and Stewart 2010, 2:130).

One of Kierkegaard's 1843 "edifying discourses" heightens the role of the sinful woman by elevating her as a "teacher," although she still remains silent. Kierkegaard discusses, for example, how the silent sinful woman might have responded to Jesus's parable of the two debtors, which he addresses to Simon the Pharisee:

> So she listens to Him as He talks with those present at the banquet. She understands very well that He is speaking about her when He speaks about two debtors, that one owed five hundred pence, and the other fifty, and that it is reasonable, when both are forgiven, that the first shall love more than the other. She understands well enough how the one thing, about the debtor, applies, alas, to her, and how the other thing, about forgiveness, praise God, applies to

her also. But at the same time she perfectly understands that she is able to do nothing at all. She therefore does not mix in the conversation, she keeps silent, keeps her eyes to herself or upon the work she is attending to, she anoints His feet and wipes them with the hairs of her head, she weeps. Oh, what a mighty, what a true expression for "doing nothing"! (Kierkegaard 2004, 251)

What we learn from this woman, Kierkegaard concludes, is that human beings can do nothing to merit the forgiveness of sins. That forgiveness comes only through "infinite grace," and we, as sinful debtors who are forgiven, should, as did the woman, "love much" (Kierkegaard 2004, 252).

Kierkegaard stresses that parables, whether constructed by Jesus or by Kierkegaard himself, do not aim to impart a "casual illumination"; instead, they challenge their hearers to become participants—the parables promote the capability in their hearers not only to "understand" the parables but also to serve as catalysts for self-examination, for understanding themselves better, for greater moral and spiritual awareness, and to affect how they make fundamental choices (Kierkegaard 1978, xv).

Frederick Douglass (ca. 1818–1895)

Frederick Douglass was a prominent abolitionist, orator, and advocate for human equality, civil rights, and women's rights. Douglass, who was born as a slave named Frederick Bailey, fled to New York City in 1838 and then to New Bedford, Massachusetts. After he courageously delivered an eloquent extemporaneous address at an antislavery convention in Nantucket, Douglass became one of the most important voices for the abolition of slavery. As William Lloyd Garrison, a prominent editor of an abolitionist newspaper who heard Douglass speak at that meeting, wrote in the preface to Douglass's autobiography: "As a public speaker, he excels in pathos, wit, comparison, imitation, strength of reasoning, and fluency of language. There is in him that union of head and heart, which is indispensable to an enlightenment of the heads and a winning of the hearts of others" (Douglass 1845, viii).

After publishing his autobiography, Douglass could no longer hide as an "anonymous" escaped slave, so he left for a speaking tour of England and Ireland, and the publication of those speeches made him internationally famous. He returned to the United States two years later, having earned enough money to purchase his freedom from slavery. For the rest of his life, Douglass diligently worked for human equality and justice for all human beings. His writings and speeches are notable for their cogency and prophetic character (see Gowler 2014, 14–15).

Douglass underwent a religious conversion in his youth and became a licensed lay preacher; although his religious thought developed significantly over the course of his life, he read the Bible carefully and quotes, paraphrases, and alludes to it frequently (Aymer 2008, 1). Douglass's famous "What to the Slave Is the Fourth of July?" speech, for example, given on July 5, 1852, in Rochester, New York, thoroughly deconstructs "slaveholding religion" and prophetically denounces the type of Christianity in the United States that systematically oppresses the downtrodden (47–48). The parable of the sheep and goats is a key element of Douglass's address:

> A worship that can be conducted by persons who refuse to give shelter to the house-less, to give bread to the hungry, clothing to the naked, and who enjoin obedience to a law forbidding these acts of mercy, is a curse, not a blessing to mankind. . . .
>
> But the church of this country is not only indifferent to the wrongs of the slave, it actually takes sides with the oppressors. . . . Many of its most eloquent Divines, who stand as the very lights of the church, have shamelessly given the sanction of religion and the Bible to the whole slave system.
>
> They have taught that man may, properly, be a slave; that the relation of master and slave is ordained of God; that to send back an escaped bondman to his master is clearly the duty of all the followers of the Lord Jesus Christ; and this horrible blasphemy is palmed off upon the world for Christianity. (Douglass 1982, 377–78)

Douglass challenges proslavery interpretations of the Bible and also uses Bible passages to demonstrate what he believes is "true religion." He both offers a critique of the improper use of Scripture and states the positive moral implications of the Bible for a just society in which all human beings are equal (cf. Williamson 2002, 85).

In a similar way, Douglass often cites the good Samaritan parable to urge others to behave with compassion as the Samaritan did (i.e., to oppose slavery) and to denounce those who act as the priest and Levite did (i.e., support slavery). In 1852, for example, Douglass delivered four addresses at an antislavery convention in Cincinnati, Ohio. In his opening address on April 27, Douglass denounced the clergy who supported slavery and claimed that it was a "Divine institution":

> In this connection I am always forcibly reminded of the incomparable illustration of the principle of brotherly love in the New Testament. When the stranger fell among thieves and was left alone on the highway to perish, there came along three persons, severally representing the classes in society. First came the Priest—evidently all *Priest* and no humanity—who passed entirely "on

the other side," and his successors appear to have remained on the *other* side to this time. (Laughter.) Then came another, a Deacon, probably; he seemed half man and half priest, for he took a middle course, and seemed wavering; but, unfortunately, the *Priest* predominated, and he followed "in the footsteps of his illustrious predecessor" on the *other* side??? (Great laughter.) But, my friends, there next came that way a man, nothing but a MAN; yes a regular *human*! (renewed laughter); and he went straight up to the suffering stranger, bound up his wounds, and attended to all his wants. (Douglass 1982, 344–45)

Douglass stressed, therefore, that Christians are required to love both God and other human beings in word and in deed, especially those who are oppressed and in need. As he noted in a later address, in Pittsburgh on August 11, 1852, the parable of the good Samaritan also demanded that Christians oppose the Fugitive Slave Law (which required that all escaped slaves, if captured even in "free states," must be returned to their masters) in that the parable insisted that Christians are to "do right," "show Mercy," and "follow the example of the good Samaritan" (Douglass 1982, 391; cf. his eulogy of William Jay, whom he sees as a paradigm of a "Good Samaritan"; Douglass 1985, 254).

Douglass denounces those who call themselves Christians who not only actively support slavery but claim divine sanction for it: How can the horrors of slavery exist in a "Christian" country that dutifully prints Bibles and tracts and sends missionaries all over the world to convert people to Christianity? he asks. Douglass notes that his denunciations of slavery, since it was so closely identified with religion, generated accusations that Douglass was undermining religion (Douglass 1979, 269–99). In his defense, in a speech in Syracuse, New York, Douglass alludes to the good Samaritan, documents the complicity of the American church with the institution of slavery, and defends his view of Christianity:

I dwell mostly upon the religious aspect, because I believe it is the religious people who are to be relied on in this Anti-Slavery movement. Do not misunderstand my railing—do not class me with those who despise religion—do not identify me with the infidel. I love the religion of Christianity—which cometh from above—which is pure, peaceable, gentle, easy to be entreated, full of good fruits, and without hypocrisy. I love that religion which sends its votaries to bind up the wounds of those who have fallen among thieves. By all the love I bear to such a Christianity as this, I hate that of the Priest and Levite, that with long-faced Phariseeism goes up to Jerusalem and worships, and leaves the bruised and wounded to die. I despise the religion that can carry Bibles to the heathen on the other side of the globe and withhold them from heathen on this side—which can talk about human rights yonder and traffic in human flesh here. I love that which makes its votaries do to others as they would that others should do to them. I hope to see a revival of it—thank God it is revived. I see revivals in the absence of the other sort of revivals. (Douglass 1982, 99–100)

Then Douglass alludes to the parable of the great dinner (Luke 14:16–24, where the host of the dinner commands his slave to bring "the poor, the crippled, the blind, and the lame" to dinner) to argue what "true religion" is and does:

There is another religion. It is that which takes off fetters instead of binding them on—that which breaks every yoke—that lifts up the bowed down. The Anti-Slavery platform is based on this kind of religion. It spreads its table to the lame, the halt, and the blind. It goes down after a long neglected race. It passes, link by link till it finds the lowest link in humanity's chain—humanity's most degraded form in the most abject position. It reaches down its arm and tells them to stand up. This is Anti-Slavery—This is Christianity. It is reviving gloriously among the various denominations. It is threatening to supercede those old forms of religion having all of the love of God and none of the man in it. (Douglass 1982, 99–101; cf. 1979, 269–99)

For Douglass, Christianity inherently involves performing good deeds, caring for those who are in need (he often cites the parable of the sheep and goats), and following the Golden Rule (Aymer 2008, 41).

Douglass delivered the speech "Black Freedom Is the Prerequisite of Victory" at New York City's Cooper Institute on January 13, 1865, just two weeks before Congress would pass the Thirteenth Amendment to the U.S. Constitution—which would abolish slavery—and send it to the states for ratification. In addition, in just under three months, on April 9, 1865, General Robert E. Lee would surrender his Confederate Army to General Ulysses S. Grant at Appomattox Court House.

Douglass knew that the end of the war was at hand, and he realized that the issue of slavery was settled (Douglass 1991, 54). At this stage of the war, Douglass saw the parable of the rich man and Lazarus being acted out:

We all know who the rich man is in this country, and who the poor man is, or has been, in this country. The slaves in the South have been the Lazaruses of the South, lying at this rich slaveholder's gates; but, it has come to pass that the poor man and the rich man are dead, for both have been in dying condition for some time, and the poor man is said to be some where very near in Abraham's bosom. (Loud laughter and applause.) And the rich man is now crying out, "Father Abraham, send Lazarus." (55)

Douglass identified the black slaves with Lazarus and the slave owners with the rich man; as Douglass noted ironically, the rich man, after death, called out to Abraham, a name that—he assumed the audience realized—also happened to be the first name of President Lincoln. A major question facing the postwar United States, Douglass observed, was what place the five million blacks would hold within society and what condition they would occupy (58).

Just ten days before Abraham Lincoln would be shot on April 14, 1865, Douglass returned to the rich man and Lazarus parable during an address in Boston that celebrated the fall of Richmond, the Confederacy's capital, the day before. Douglass began by noting: "I, for the first time in my life, have the assurance, not only of a country redeemed, of a country regenerated, but of my race free and having a future in this land" (Douglass 1991, 71). Douglass rejoiced, because now he and other blacks were "*citizens*" (72; emphasis original): "What I want, now that the black men are citizens in war, is, that they shall be made fully and entirely, all over this land, citizens in peace" (73). And then Douglass evoked the parable of the rich man (traditionally called Dives) and Lazarus to explain the current historical situation, this time even more clearly invoking Abraham Lincoln's role in this "parable":

> I tell you, the negro is coming up—he is rising—rising. Why, only a little while ago we were the Lazaruses of the South; the Dives of the South was the slaveholder; and how singular it is that we have here another illustration of that Scripture! . . . But now a change has taken place. That rich man is lifting up his eyes in torments *down there*, and seeing Lazarus afar off in Abraham's bosom (tumultuous laughter and applause), is all the time calling on Father Abraham to send Lazarus back. But Father Abraham says, "If they hear not Grant nor Sherman, neither will they be persuaded though I send Lazarus unto them." (Prolonged and vociferous applause.) I say we are way up yonder now, no mistake. (73–74)

Years later, in 1888, Douglass again invoked the parable of the rich man and Lazarus to argue for another form of emancipation: that of women, which he said was an even greater cause, since it involved the liberation of "one-half of the whole human family" (Douglass 1992, 379). Douglass saw the women's suffrage movement as a continuation of the abolitionist movement, seeking human rights for all and opposing the same types of bigotry and oppression (381).

His major address to the 1888 annual convention of the New England Woman Suffrage Association was titled, "I am a Radical Woman Suffrage Man." Douglass had been for women's suffrage, he said, since he "brushed the dust of slavery from [his] feet and stepped upon the free soil of Massachusetts" (1992, 383). The equality of women is not a "privilege"; it is a right, and Douglass supposed that the same antislavery arguments are applicable to the women's suffrage movement. Douglass then reinterpreted his former invocations of the rich man and Lazarus parable to begin his arguments for women's emancipation:

> Woman's claim to the right of equal participation in government with man, has its foundation in the nature and personality of woman and in the admitted doctrine of American liberty and in the authority and structure of our Republican government. When the rich man wanted someone sent from the dead to warn his brothers against coming where he was, he was told that if they heard not Moses and the prophets, neither would they be persuaded though one rose from the dead. Now our Moses and our prophets, so far as the rights and privileges of American citizens are concerned, are the framers of the Declaration of American Independence. If the American people will not hear these, they will not be persuaded though one rose from the dead. (384)

Douglass then offered a detailed argument for women's suffrage (e.g., from the Declaration of Independence, from nature, etc.) and expressed the following hope for the near future: "When this battle for woman suffrage shall have been fought and the victory won, men will marvel at the injustice and stupidity which so long deprived American women of the ballot" (387).

The polyvalency and power of the parables allowed Douglass even to use the same parable in new and striking ways. His interpretations were ensconced in history—since he often identifies characters in the parables with people in his own era—and he brings the full force of his prophetic critique against those who, in his view, represent the negative if not evil characters in the parables. He also brings words of encouragement and liberation to those who, in his view, represent the oppressed or downtrodden in Jesus's parables.

Fanny Crosby (1820–1915)[1]

Frances Jane (Fanny) Crosby wrote lyrics for over eight thousand hymns, which makes her in all likelihood the most prolific hymnist in history. Crosby became blind as an infant, which her family attributed to incompetent medical care for an inflammation of the eyes. Although she could perceive some light, Crosby remained blind for the rest of her ninety-five years.

Crosby entered the New York Institution for the Blind in 1835, and, because of her talent, soon became a spokesperson for the school. Her poems were also published in such magazines as *Saturday Evening Post*, and she published

---

1. All the hymns cited in this section can be found at http://www.hymnary.org/person/Crosby _Fanny or http://www.hymntime.com/tch/bio/c/r/o/crosby_fj.htm.

her first book of poetry in 1844, *The Blind Girl and Other Poems*, a book that served primarily as a fund-raising vehicle for the Institution (Blumhofer 2005, 62–65; Aufdemberge 1997, 675).

After graduation, from 1847 to 1858, Crosby served on the school's faculty, where she met and became friends with a young Grover Cleveland, who taught at the school, served as secretary to the superintendent, and often took dictation of Crosby's poetry (Blumhofer 2005, 87). Crosby began attending revivals at Methodist Broadway Tabernacle, and in the fall of 1850 had a dramatic religious experience, the culmination of which occurred during the fifth stanza of Isaac Watts's hymn "Alas and Did My Saviour Bleed?" (Ruffin 1976, 68).

Crosby left the Institution for the Blind in 1858, when she married Alexander van Alstyne, and the couple moved to an economically disadvantaged area of Lower Manhattan so they could work in rescue missions and contribute their "superfluous" money to others. After Alexander's death in 1902, Crosby moved to Bridgeport, Connecticut, where she lived until her death in 1915. One of her last public appearances was at Carnegie Hall in New York City at the age of ninety-one (Aufdemberge 1997, 675).

Although a talented musician—she played the piano, organ, harp, and guitar, as well as singing—Crosby focused on writing lyrics for hymns. She collaborated with a number of composers, most notably George Root, William Bradbury, William Doane, and Ira Sankey, and she published hymns under more than two hundred pseudonyms (see a partial list in Blumhofer 2005, 358–60).

Crosby's hymn "All Is Ready" (1889) specifically alludes to Jesus's parable of the wedding feast but interprets the parable allegorically and generalizes it into an altar call for all human beings. The first stanza quotes the king's invitation to his invited guests for his son's wedding banquet: "All is ready" (Matt. 22:4). This quote comes from the king's second invitation, after the invited guests have already spurned his first call to come to the wedding feast, so the hymnist wonders how many will spurn this call:

> All is ready, the Master, said,
> All is ready, the feast is spread;
> Sweet His message of love to all,
> Yet how many will slight the call!

> Refrain

> Why, why, why will you die?
> Ask, and the Savior will freely forgive;

> Why, why, why will you die?
> Only a look, and your soul shall live.

The second stanza repeats that "all is ready" and urges people to come and bring their burdens of doubts, fears, sorrow, cares, and tears. The offer of salvation is the focus, and the hymn exhorts its hearers to respond and accept the invitation before it is too late. Instead of focusing directly on the man who lacked a wedding garment and was thrown "into the outer darkness" (Matt. 22:11–13), the hymn advises its hearers to wear "the garment of praise":

> Though His mercy prolongs your day,
> Time is precious, no more delay;
> Now He listens to hear your prayer,
> Haste the garment of praise to wear.

The hymn ends with another exhortation to accept Jesus's offer of pardon so that the waters of eternal life can begin to flow.

Some of Crosby's hymns integrate multiple parables, such as "Will Jesus Find Us Watching?" (1876). The first stanza echoes elements of the parable of the wise and foolish virgins—with its reference to trimmed lamps, for example—but it also includes elements of the waiting (watchful) slaves parable, which symbolizes Jesus's return at the end of the world (Mark 13:33–37; Luke 12:35–38; cf. 12:41):

> When Jesus comes to reward His servants,
> Whether it be noon or night,
> Faithful to Him will He find us watching,
> With our lamps all trimmed and bright?
>
> Refrain
>
> O can we say we are ready, brother?
> Ready for the soul's bright home?
> Say, will He find you and me still watching,
> Waiting, waiting when the Lord shall come?

The second stanza incorporates a third parable, that of the talents, which, at first, might seem a rather disjointed way to continue the hymn. This stanza, however, builds upon the first because the parable of the talents (Matt. 25:14–30) immediately follows that of the wise and foolish virgins (Matt. 25:1–13). More important, however, is the reason it immediately follows the parable of the wise and foolish virgins: both Matthean parables symbolize Jesus's return. The parable of the wise and foolish virgins allegorically explains that people should be ready for Jesus's return, and the parable of the talents allegorically begins to explain what people are to do in order to be prepared. So the second stanza of the hymn asks if Jesus will tell us, "Well done," and the third stanza explains that if people do their best to live according to the will of Jesus, then he will reward them when he returns:

> If, at the dawn of the early morning,
> He shall call us one by one,
> When to the Lord we restore our talents,
> Will He answer thee—Well done?

> Refrain

> Have we been true to the trust He left us?
> Do we seek to do our best?
> If in our hearts there is naught condemns us,
> We shall have a glorious rest.

The final stanza reiterates the message of the previous one:

> Blessèd are those whom the Lord finds watching,
> In His glory they shall share;
> If He shall come at the dawn or midnight,
> Will He find us watching there?

Crosby's lyrics for the hymn "Have You Sought?" (1891) also connect two parables, this time in order to integrate evangelism, salvation, and Christians' responsibilities to people in need—primarily spiritual need but including physical need. Crosby collaborated on this hymn with Ira Sankey, the musician/singer for the evangelist Dwight L. Moody. The popularity of a hymn Sankey sang at revivals, "The Lost Sheep," led Crosby and Sankey to create a hymn on the lost sheep parable that would have a more "practical application" (Blumhofer 2005, 239–40).

The "The Lost Sheep" hymn Sankey originally sang opens with these words:

> There were ninety and nine that safely lay
> In the shelter of the fold.
> But one was out on the hills away,
> Far off from the gates of gold.
> Away on the mountains wild and bare.
> Away from the tender Shepherd's care.

In this hymn, there is one sheep lost, and it is Jesus who goes out to search for it and to return it to the flock. Compare how Crosby changes the focus in the opening stanza of her lyrics to the new hymn, "Have You Sought?":

> Have you sought for the sheep that have wandered,
> Far away on the dark mountains cold?
> Have you gone, like the tender Shepherd,
> To bring them again to the fold?
> Have you followed their weary footsteps?
> And the wild desert waste have you crossed,
> Nor lingered till safe home returning,
> You have gathered the sheep that were lost?

The lost sheep now are plural, and they symbolize all those sinners who are lost. In addition, the sheep are not just lost; they have "wandered," and the ones responsible for bringing them back are Christians who follow Jesus's example as the Good Shepherd. This opening stanza and the two stanzas that follow each contain a series of four questions that focus on Christians' responsibility to seek out and save the lost and bring them "again to the fold."

The second stanza slightly increases the pathos by stressing the desperate situation of these lost sheep; they are sad and lonely with heavy burdens, and the Christians' task is to share with them the good news of the salvation that Jesus died to bring them. The third stanza further develops the theme about the responsibility of all Christians to search and save the lost sheep by beginning to switch the focus from the parable of the lost sheep to the parable of the sheep and goats, specifically by including caring for the sick and imprisoned (Matt. 25:36):

> Have you knelt by the sick and the dying,
> The message of mercy to tell?
> Have you stood by the trembling captive
> Alone in his dark prison cell?
> Have you pointed the lost to Jesus,
> And urged them on Him to believe?
> Have you told of the life everlasting,
> That all, if they will, may receive?

At first hearing, the hymn may seem to connect the two parables simply because both involve sheep in their imagery. Yet it quickly becomes clear that the hymn develops the theme by now emphasizing that if Christians follow the example of the Good Shepherd Jesus—to seek and save the lost, to take care of those in spiritual and physical need—then Jesus will reward them with eternal life in heaven:

> If to Jesus you answer these questions,
> And to Him have been faithful and true,
> Then behold, in the mansions yonder
> Are crowns of rejoicing for you;
> And there from the King eternal
> Your welcome and greeting shall be,
> "Inasmuch as 'twas done for My brethren,
> Even so it was done unto Me."

Crosby's hymns are filled with words of comfort and encouragement, with exhortations for Christians to live lives worthy of the gospel and with warnings for Christians to work for the kingdom. Yet her hymns do not focus on fire, brimstone, and the terrors awaiting sinners in hell; instead they describe the lives of human beings who are lost and afraid, adrift on the waters of a storm-tossed sea (e.g., "Dark Is the Night"), and announce the comforting promises of Christ's guidance for the lost, comfort for the afraid, and rest for the weary (e.g., "Blessed Assurance"). Crosby's hymns also declare that every Christian has a role to play in building the Christian community and a duty to be faithfully committed to the cause of Christ (e.g., "I Am Thine, O Lord"). In her thousands of hymns, Crosby sticks to a small number of familiar themes: salvation, consecration, service, and heaven. The parables of Jesus are not found extensively in Crosby's lyrics, but there are notable examples that do help her illustrate those themes. Her lyrics are simple and often sentimental, but, for millions of people, they are poetic and moving and powerful (Blumhofer 2005, 194, 252–80), as is her use of Jesus's parables.

Leo Tolstoy (1828–1910)

Leo Tolstoy, the author of classic novels such as *War and Peace* and *Anna Karenina*, was born in a Russian aristocratic family at Yasnaya Polyana, his family's estate about 120 miles south of Moscow. Tolstoy's mother died when he was two years old, and his father died just seven years later. Both deaths were devastating losses that affected Tolstoy for the rest of his life.

Tolstoy lived a rather dissolute life—parts of his family's estate, for example, were sold to pay his gambling debts—and suffered from an often-overpowering guilt (Tolstoy 2006, 15–16). He joined the army in 1851, following in the footsteps of his brother Nikolai, and his first published novel,

Childhood, appeared in the magazine *The Contemporary*, where it gained the favorable attention of other Russian authors, such as Fyodor Dostoevsky and Ivan Turgenev.

Tolstoy became more famous after he published several other works during the five years he served in the army. He often reflected on religious issues, became an ardent pacifist, and even contemplated starting a new religion based on "the religion of Christ, but purged of dogma and mystery, a practical religion, not promising future bliss but providing bliss on earth" (Bartlett 2010, 113).

Tolstoy left the army in 1856, traveled extensively, moved back to Yasnaya Polyana, and then married Sofya Behrs in 1862. He published *War and Peace* in 1869 and *Anna Karenina*, a book he never liked, in 1878 (Tolstoy 2006, 23). A spiritual crisis led him to reevaluate his religious beliefs, and in his *A Confession* (1882), he concluded that God did indeed exist. This work represents a shift in Tolstoy's writings; the novelist developed into a moralist, prophet, and evangelist preaching the ethics of Jesus. Tolstoy's *The Kingdom of God Is within You*, for example, argues that nonresistance to evil as espoused by Jesus in the Sermon on the Mount is the foundation upon which humanity must build its house (citing the wise and foolish builders parable; Matt. 7:24–27; Tolstoy 1894, 185–86).

Tolstoy's understanding of Christianity was unorthodox, and he was excommunicated from the Orthodox Church in 1901 after his book *Resurrection* harshly criticized the church. He refused to accept traditional Christian doctrines, such as the virgin birth, the resurrection, or the Trinity. Tolstoy's Christianity focused on the love commandment (Matt. 22:37–39), the Golden Rule, and social action based on the Sermon on the Mount. Christianity, he argues, is not about the worship of God or doctrines; it is instead a way of life based on the teachings of Jesus that changes the whole structure of society.

One of the best examples of Tolstoy's view of Christian morality is found in his 1885 short story "Where Love Is, God Is." It is a poignant and somewhat sentimental tale, but it gets to the heart of Jesus's teachings, most notably focusing on what the parable of the sheep and goats teaches about human relationships and the will of God.

The story begins by describing the main character, a cobbler named Martin Avdeitch, who lived in a village in Russia. Martin's wife died when their son was three years old, and their son died a few years later, so Martin was filled with overwhelming grief. He expressed his pain, loss of hope, and desire to die to an older holy man, who told him that he must live for God despite his pain. The story continues:

Martin was silent for awhile, and then asked, "But how is one to live for God?"

The old man answered: "How one may live for God has been shown to us by Christ. Can you read? Then buy the Gospels, and read them: there you will see how God would have you live." (Tolstoy 1907; all subsequent references in this section are to this work)

Martin began to read the Bible occasionally, but as time went by, he read it every night after dinner. The narrator then relates how Martin sat up late one night reading Luke's Gospel, including the wise and foolish builders parable. Martin wondered whether he had built his own "house" on the rock, and he recommitted himself to trying to follow God's commands in every aspect of his life. He went on to read about the sinful woman and Simon the Pharisee in Luke 7:36–50, including the two debtors parable, and reflected on it: "He must have been like me, that Pharisee. He too thought only of himself—how to get a cup of tea, how to keep warm and comfortable; never a thought of his guest. He took care of himself, but for his guest he thought nothing at all. Yet who was the guest? The Lord himself! If he came to me, should I behave like that?" After reading that story, Martin fell asleep, but then thought he heard a voice speaking to him: "Look out into the street tomorrow, for I shall come."

The next day Martin kept looking out his window, because he wondered whether Jesus might visit him. Once when he looked out the window he saw Stepanitch, a retired soldier from the czar's army who was now so poor that he did odd jobs in the neighborhood just to make ends meet. Stepanitch was shoveling snow but had paused to rest, so Martin invited him inside to warm up and have a cup of tea. As they talked, Martin shared with Stepanitch what the voice the night before had told him about Jesus coming to visit Martin, as well as many stories about Jesus. The conversation ends this way:

Stepanitch forgot his tea. He was a very old man, easily moved to tears, and as he sat and listened the tears ran down his cheeks.

"Come, drink some more," said Martin. But Stepanitch crossed himself, thanked him, and moved away his tumbler, and rose.

"Thank you, Martin Avdeitch," he said, "you have given me food and comfort both for soul and body."

"You're very welcome. Come again another time. I am glad to have a guest," said Martin.

Martin returned to work but kept looking out his window in anticipation. Soon he saw a peasant woman, dressed in tattered summer garments, who carried a baby in her arms. Martin asked her to come inside to warm up. As he fixed the woman some lunch, the woman told him that she had pawned

her winter shawl to buy food. Martin gave her an old cloak to keep her and
the baby warm, and then

> [Martin] told the woman his dream, and how he had heard the Lord's voice
> promising to visit him that day.
>
> "Who knows? All things are possible," said the woman. And she got up and
> threw the cloak over her shoulders, wrapping it round herself and round the
> baby. Then she bowed, and thanked Martin once more.
>
> "Take this for Christ's sake," said Martin, and he gave her six-pence to get
> her shawl out of pawn. The woman crossed herself, and Martin did the same,
> and then he saw her out.

Martin's words "for Christ's sake" foreshadow how the story will end.

Martin returned to work, and as it grew dark he looked out his window
and saw an elderly woman walking by. She carried a heavy sack of woodchips
and a small basket of apples, and, as Martin watched, a boy grabbed one
of her apples and tried to run away. The woman grabbed him, however, and
threatened to take him to the police. Martin rushed out the door, separated
the woman and the boy, and calmed them both down. He told the boy to ask
the woman for forgiveness and to promise never to take anything that didn't
belong to him ever again. After the boy did so, Martin gave him an apple
and told the woman he would pay for it. Then Martin told the parable of
the unforgiving slave to the woman to help persuade her to forgive the boy:

> And Martin told her the parable of the lord who forgave his servant a large
> debt, and how the servant went out and seized his debtor by the throat. The
> woman listened to it all, and the boy, too, stood by and listened.
>
> "God bids us to forgive," said Martin, "or else we shall not be forgiven.
> Forgive everyone; and a thoughtless youngster most of all." . . .
>
> "Of course, it was only his childishness, God help him," said she, referring
> to the boy.
>
> As the old woman was about to hoist her sack on her back, the lad sprang
> forward to her, saying, "Let me carry it for you, Granny. I'm going that way."
>
> The old woman nodded her head, and put the sack on the boy's back, and
> they went down the street together, the old woman quite forgetting to ask
> Martin to pay for the apple. Martin stood and watched them as they went
> along talking to each other.

It had grown dark, so when Martin returned to his basement room, he
lit his lamp, finished his work, and got the Gospels from the shelf. Before he
started to read, though, he heard a noise, turned around, and thought he saw
some people standing in the dark corner:

And a voice whispered in his ear: "Martin, Martin, don't you know me?"

"Who is it?" muttered Martin.

"It is I," said the voice. And out of the dark corner stepped Stepanitch, who smiled and vanishing like a cloud was seen no more.

"It is I," said the voice again. And out of the darkness stepped the woman with the baby in her arms, and the woman smiled and the baby laughed, and they too vanished.

"It is I," said the voice once more. And the old woman and the boy with the apple stepped out and both smiled, and then they too vanished.

And Martin's soul grew glad. He crossed himself, put on his spectacles, and began reading the Gospel where it had opened; and at the top of the page he read: "I was an hungred, and ye gave me meat: I was thirsty, and ye gave me drink: I was a stranger, and ye took me in." And at the bottom of the page he read: "Inasmuch as ye have done it unto one of the least of these my brethren, ye have done it unto me" (cf. Matt. 25:35, 40). "And Martin understood that his dream had come true; and that the Saviour had really come to him that day, and that he had welcomed him."

The entire structure of the story's plot is based upon the parable of the sheep and goats, and it uses several other parables to highlight the importance of how God expects human beings to treat one another. This story and its use of parables clearly reflect Tolstoy's view of Christianity: the importance of loving God and loving others. Tolstoy believed that if everyone behaved the way Martin did, with ethical actions based on Jesus's teachings, the kingdom of God would be created on earth (cf. Tolstoy's *What I Believe* [1882], which discusses the principles—based on the Sermon on the Mount—that Tolstoy wants to follow in his daily life; see also Bartlett 2010, 309, 342).

John Everett Millais (1829–1896)

John Everett Millais was born in 1829 in Southampton, England. A child prodigy, Millais worked at the British Museum before he was ten and won a Silver Medal from the Society of Arts for a drawing. At age eleven, Millais was the youngest student ever allowed to enroll in the Royal Academy Schools (1840), and he quickly became a star pupil who won medals both for drawing (1843) and for painting (1847). While still a teenager, he also had a painting exhibited at the Royal Academy (1846; *Pizarro Seizing the Inca of Peru*; Walker Art Gallery 1967, 5–15).

In 1848, Millais was one of the founding members, along with William Holman Hunt and Dante Gabriel Rossetti, of the Pre-Raphaelite Brotherhood

(PRB), a group of disenchanted young artists and writers—aged nineteen to twenty-two—who believed that contemporary art was incorrectly seeking beauty through idealization, resulting in an artificial and sentimental aesthetic. The PRB attempted to return to the sincerity and simplicity of fourteenth- and fifteenth-century Italian (pre-Raphael) mode of painting, which they believed was truthful and natural (Rosenfeld and Smith 2007, 10–20). Hunt sums it up this way: "In short, what we needed was a new and bolder English art that turned the minds of men to good reflection" (Cars 2000, 23). This philosophy resulted in works of art that illustrated a fidelity to nature through detailed (if not literal-minded) representations, a "clear, bright, sharp-focus technique," and a "moral seriousness" in the choice of themes to portray (Chilvers 2004, 563).

Millais's first religious work of art, *Christ in the House of His Parents*, was controversial because it deviated from idealized portraits of Jesus and his family. The painting incorporates the symmetry of early Renaissance works with an abundance of realistic details, such as the wood shavings on the ground, dirty toenails of the bare feet, and bulging veins in Joseph's arms. *The Times* of London called the painting "revolting" and "disgusting." Charles Dickens was particularly offended: the depiction of Jesus was "hideous," Mary was "horrible in her ugliness," and the painting itself was "mean, odious, revolting, and repulsive" (Cars 2000, 98; Millais and Dickens would later become friends).

The PRB was important for Millais's early development as an artist, but he continued to experiment with other modes of artistic expression, such as a broader and more fluid style of painting. In the 1850s he became the most popular artist of his day, although some critics claimed that he had sacrificed artistic authenticity for fame and fortune; Millais himself noted that he now needed enough income to support his family. His subjects increasingly became more sentimental and told a "good story" that would appeal to the broader public, such as charming portraits of children and scenes of family life (Chilvers 2004, 468; Rosenfeld and Smith 2007, 50).

By the late 1850s, Millais had become the foremost illustrator of books and magazines in England, and in 1857 he accepted a commission from the Dalziel brothers (actually three brothers and a sister) to illustrate the book *The Parables of Our Lord*. Millais agreed to produce thirty images in a few months, but—even after the project was reduced from thirty to twenty images—the project took Millais six years to complete. The book finally appeared in 1863, and Millais explained the delay in this way: "I can do ordinary illustrations as quickly as most men, but these designs can scarcely be regarded in this same light—each Parable I illustrate perhaps a dozen times before I fix, and the hidden Treasure I have altered upon the wood at least *six* times" (Rosenfeld and Smith 2007, 95). The prints were created through a process of Millais producing a design onto boxwood—a hard wood that lasted longer in the printing process. It is the reverse of the "intaglio process" of engraving on metal; in this process the engraver gouges out (with a sharp-edged tool like a "burin" or "graver") all the parts that are *not* to appear in the print, and the areas that are left create the printed image. Millais usually drew his designs in reverse right on the block of boxwood, and the Dalziels did the carving (Millais 1975, ix–xii).

Millais began the project with three parables: those of the good Samaritan, the Pharisee and the tax collector, and the prodigal son. All three images include striking if not haunting details: the wounded man's arm curls around the Samaritan as the Samaritan begins to assist him. The tax collector bows his head in shame in the shadows of a column, while the Pharisee stands proudly

Metropolitan Museum of Art, New York, NY

Figure 4.2 John Everett Millais, *The Pharisee and the Publican*

in the bright sunlight looking up toward heaven (figure 4.2). The prodigal returns home to his father. He kneels, barefoot and dressed only in a fur loincloth, while the father, clad with sandals and dressed in a finely engraved robe, bends over to embrace him. The reclining cattle in the background ensure the presence of a fatted calf and reflect the comforting fact that the son is indeed welcomed back home by his father. Millais even strove to represent the fingernails on their hands with great "Delicacy," although, oddly enough, the heads of the father and the son are almost indistinguishable (Millais 1975, xix; one assumes that the head with white hair is indeed the father's).

Millais was especially proud of his work on the parable of the unjust judge/importunate widow (figure 4.3). In an 1859 letter to the Dalziels, he wrote: "Nothing can be more exquisitely rendered than the 'Importunate Widow.' . . . It appears to me even better cut than any of the others I have ever seen" (Millais 1975, xix–xx).

In the image, the judge sits with his legs crossed at the ankles on a throne-like cushioned chair. He wears fine clothes, pointed slippers, and an apparently bejeweled hat. His right hand pushes the woman away, and his left hand is upraised, in effect telling her to stop, that he has heard enough, and that his answer is no. His head turns from her, and his face reflects a haughty, superior disdain; he smiles or perhaps even derisively laughs at her desperate pleas.

The woman kneels by his feet on the right side of his chair, her hands clasped in supplication, and her right arm reaches over the judge's right knee. Her face reveals her humble pleas, and her eyes remain steadily focused on the unjust judge, a hint that she will persevere, no matter how much he mocks or ignores her.

The faces are what stand out the most in the image, especially the mocking, contemptuous dismissal of the woman reflected in the judge's face, and the pleading, desperate yet insistent face of the woman for whom the judge is her last recourse. There is no sign yet that the judge will relent, but the woman will not be deterred, even with the guard trying to drag her away in light of the judge's dismissal of her. She kneels alone; no one, it appears, is willing to take her side, which accentuates her isolation and desperation.

In the foreground, on the right side, we see a secretary sitting on a cushion on the floor just to the left of the judge's chair. He holds a tablet on his lap and a writing instrument in his right hand. He looks up at the woman expectantly and, perhaps, sympathetically—an emotion lacking from most of the others in the image—waiting to see what, if anything, will happen.

A guard on the far left looms over the woman and grabs her with both hands to pull her away from the judge. Just to the right of the guard is a servant holding a fan; the judge has every comfort available to him. The servant

Metropolitan Museum of Art, New York, NY

Figure 4.3 John Everett Millais, *The Importunate Widow*

looks at the judge, and he shares the judge's amusement at the woman's pre-dicament, although his smile is not as pronounced as the judge's—his teeth do not show. There is no trace of sympathy in his smiling face. Another man stands just beside him. He also smiles with some amusement, but instead of looking at the judge, he looks at the woman. His hand is raised, seemingly to direct the woman to leave the judge's presence.

Another young man peers over the top of the judge's chair. We see only his face and one hand on the top of the chair. Apparently he has to struggle to gain a peek at the scene, and his face also betrays a slight sense of amuse-ment. No one yet shows any interest in helping the poor widow.

Two men, however, stand in the background, both with full, long beards and neither with a trace of amusement on his face. One man stands in profile, and he apparently looks at the widow as she attempts to plead her case, or perhaps his eyes merely look down in sadness. The other man looks directly at the viewers, in effect challenging if not accusing them: "What will you do?" he seems to ask. "How will you respond to the unjust treatment of this woman?" Or he may be reminding viewers that they too must be persistent, which eventually results in a happy resolution for the widow in the parable of the unjust judge: God brings justice to those who cry out for it "day and night" (Luke 18:6–8).

Millais's representations of the parables were not universally acclaimed, and some of the criticisms of the images reflect dialogues about how "authentic" (i.e., historically accurate) such representations should be. Unlike his former PRB colleague William Holman Hunt, who traveled to the Holy Land and painstakingly recorded the sites and people of the area, Millais did not venture beyond Scotland and London for his models, landscapes, and other contexts (Rosenfeld and Smith 2007, 127). The women usually appear in contemporary clothing (e.g., *The Lost Piece of Silver*). Even images that are expertly crafted with intricate detail, such as *The Wicked Husbandmen*, contain anachronistic elements. Note the outstanding craftsmanship of the vines—their leaves and tendrils—as well as the detail of the rope around the heir's neck. Yet the wall of the vineyard is a representation of the wall of Balhousie Castle in Perth (Millais 1975, xxviii; cf. the building in the background of *The Unmerciful Servant*, which resembles St. Paul's Cathedral in London).

A contemporary review in the *Athenaeum* (December 1863), for example, argues that Millais could have attempted either to represent the parables in their original settings (and suggested that a trip to the Holy Land would have been helpful in this regard) or to (re)interpret the parables consistently in contemporary contexts. As Mary Lutyens notes in her introduction to the 1975 reprinting of *The Parables of Our Lord*, for the most part Millais was content to give these parables a contemporary context in "authentic Scottish backgrounds," but even though he read the parables closely and followed the stories carefully, he "never attempted to penetrate their mysteries." Only in three works—*The Pharisee and the Publican*, *The Unjust Judge*, and *The Pearl of Great Price*—did Millais attempt a realistic first-century context (for which he may have been indebted to some of Hunt's sketches; Millais 1975, xxxiii).

Others, however, found the images to be haunting and full of power, suggesting that anachronistic elements in such images do not detract from the impact of Jesus's parables. Eugene Benson, for example, argues that the images are "positive, singular, full of interest," and profound in their interpretations (Casteras 1990, 92). Even a cursory look at the images (http://www.tate.org .uk/search/Millais%20parable) is enough to demonstrate their beauty, power, and insight, no matter what deficiencies some of them may contain.

Emily Dickinson (1830–1886)

Although Emily Dickinson authored at least 1,789 poems and over a thousand letters, her life and work in many ways remain enigmatic. Her poetry invites but intimidates, dazzles but baffles, and has left "a trail of editors, readers, and scholars perplexed by her idiosyncratic use of meter, rhyme, capitalization, and punctuation" (W. Martin 2007, vii). Yet her usually brief poems continue to influence and inspire their readers. As Dickinson wrote:

> The Poets light but Lamps—
> Themselves—go out—
> The Wicks they stimulate
> If vital Light
>
> Inhere as do the Suns—
> Each Age a Lens
> Disseminating their
> Circumference— (Dickinson 1999, 397–98)

Unlike poets, who are mortal beings, poems can achieve a form of immortality by continuing to shed their light and stimulating other poetic lights, as is the case with Dickinson's transformative poems (although Dickinson [1999, 232] also warned of such delusions of grandeur in her poem "The Spider holds a Silver Ball").

Dickinson was born in Amherst, Massachusetts, to a prominent New England family. She attended Amherst Academy (a secondary school for young women) and Mount Holyoke Female Seminary. She excelled as a student and had a circle of close friends, but as more and more of her friends and family became committed Christians during a series of revivals that swept the area, she felt increasingly isolated. She resisted converting or even attending church, despite significant pressure to do so (see Leiter 2007, 8). As Dickinson notes in a letter to her friend Abiah Root after their mutual friend Abby Wood became a Christian, Dickinson herself was unable to hear the "still small voice" that led to Abby's conversion. Dickinson then speaks of her resulting isolation: "I am one of the lingering *bad* ones, and so do I slink away, and pause, and ponder, and ponder, and pause, and do work without knowing why—not surely for *this* brief world, and more sure it is not for Heaven" (letter 36; Dickinson 1986, 98–99).

A certain agnosticism concerning Dickinson's personal religious beliefs seems justified, however. Various poems can be marshaled to support portrayals of Dickinson as agnostic, skeptical, heretical, or even Christian in religious matters. There certainly is "a baffling array of religious attitudes" in Dickinson's poems that reflects a struggle "between traditional religious belief and American modernity" (Ladin 2008, 198, 202). In a similar way, a case can be made for development in Dickinson's thought and religious outlook.

The dialogues with the Bible in Dickinson's poetry are extensive and complex. She can apparently dismiss the Bible as "an antique volume written by faded men" ("The Bible is an antique Volume" in Dickinson 1999, 581). This apparent mockery, however, is directed toward such things as the image of a condemning, wrathful God from her Calvinist background, as the last line of the poem suggests: "Orpheus' sermon captivated, it did not condemn." Dickinson alludes to the Bible constantly—Bennett's list of biblical references in her poetry is 498 pages (Bennett 1997). Capps notes that of the thirty-eight books of the Bible to which Dickinson refers in her letters and poems, references to the Gospels of Matthew, Luke, and John count for over half of her allusions, with Matthew counting for over half of those references. Matthew is a favorite biblical text when Dickinson looks for the promise of mercy—often manifest in the love of children, birds, and flowers—as well as for confirmation for the apparently paradoxical view that the first will be last and the last will be first, that the "least of these" will ultimately triumph (Capps 1966, 30, 41).

Both Dickinson's poems and her letters allude to the parable of the sheep and goats numerous times, sometimes merely mentioning the "Lord's right hand" of judgment. The poem "I bring an unaccustomed wine," however, focuses on the act of mercy in Matthew 25:35: "I was thirsty and you gave me something to drink":

> I bring an unaccustomed wine
> To lips long parching, next to mine,
> And summon them to drink.
>
> Crackling with fever, they essay;
> I turn my brimming eyes away,
> And come next hour to look.
>
> The hands still hug the tardy glass;
> The lips I would have cooled, alas!
> Are so superfluous cold,
>
> I would as soon attempt to warm
> The bosoms where the frost has lain
> Ages beneath the mould.

Some other thirsty there may be
To whom this would have pointed me
Had it remained to speak.

And so I always bear the cup
If, haply, mine may be the drop
Some pilgrim thirst to slake,—

If, haply, any say to me,
"Unto the little, unto me,"
When I at last awake. (Dickinson 1999, 65)

What first appears as a simple act of charity, giving wine for a fellow traveler's parched lips, becomes more potent when read in the context of Dickinson's other poems. More than 10 percent of her poems use images of food or drink, but these references give few or no details about their appearance, aroma, or taste. Instead, food and drink appear to represent other things, such as a hunger or thirst that only God can satisfy (C. Wolff 1988, 209):

We thirst at first—'tis Nature's Act—
And later—when we die—
A little Water supplicate—
Of fingers going by—

It intimates the finer want—
Whose adequate supply
Is that Great Water in the West—
Termed Immortality— (Dickinson 1999, 334–35)

In addition, most of the references to food and drink are to water, wine, and bread—the elements of the Eucharist (in many traditions a small amount of water is added to the wine). The question in this poem is not only whether this act of mercy makes a person more Christlike but also whether it takes on a transcendent quality and has eternal consequences, as the last three lines intimate (C. Wolff 1988, 213). Amid human desolation and despair, perhaps there is some eternal hope in the "sacrament" of love and charity for the "least of these" (Matt. 25:40; cf. Jesus's gracious invitation to the "least of these," despite their human frailties, to "occupy his house" in paradise in Dickinson's [1999, 363] poem "'Unto Me?' I do not know you").

At first glance, Dickinson's poetry may appear to interact with Jesus's parables only minimally. Dorothy Huff Oberhaus, however, argues that Dickinson's fortieth and final booklet, Fascicle 40 (or F-40), demonstrates just how important both Jesus's parables and the parabolic mode of expression are to Dickinson. This collection of poems, Oberhaus writes,

> shows that the Bible was not simply a rich tropic source, it was essential to her poetics, structure, and meaning. F-40's tropes and rhetorical figures are those of biblical writers: the metonym, the kenning, parallelism, the chiasm, the envelope structure, and key words to link related poems. . . . No F-40 poem is without biblical allusions, most of them to the New Testament, with particular emphasis on the Gospel of Matthew and Jesus' parables. (1995, 12)

On another level, then—the way in which her parables function—Dickinson's poetry interacts with parables in even deeper ways than allusions in specific poems, including how her poems can operate in a riddle-like manner similar to the description of parables in Mark's Gospel: enigmas that those "outside" cannot perceive or understand (Mark 4:11–12). Dickinson as the outsider often adopts this strategy, where the poem "poses a riddle that with each line is complicated and questioned, recomplicated and requestioned; with each articulation, the darkness is intensified, but, as in one of Mark Rothko's dark canvases, there is much to see in the blackness" (Barnstone 2006, 61).

The role of poet merges with that of prophet in Dickinson's poetry, and her poetry incorporates numerous biblical literary forms, their rhythm and artistry, including parallelism and paradox, with Jesus and his parables as important models, among others:

> Like Christ's parables, in which his indirection often baffled, even frustrated, his audiences, Dickinson's prophetic lines often have the form of riddle or enigma because she relies on paradox and indirection as basic techniques. Thus, although some scholars might read her poetry as "private" or "eccentric," the lines are no more private than the sayings of Christ and the other biblical prophets. Christ, the earlier Scriptural prophets . . . and Dickinson all focused on an audience of initiates; the prophetic tradition of writers presumes this kind of audience to be familiar with an indirection that rests most often on a contrast of spiritual reality with a more mundane experience of perception. Dickinson's poetry presumes this kind of audience of initiates, an audience itself paradoxical in its simultaneous potential openness and resistance to prophetic revelations of spiritual truth. (Doriani 1996, 118)

Dickinson's "riddle poems" see their task as not solving a riddle but discovering it, discerning it, and presenting it to the reader "in all its irreducible mystery" (Leiter 2007, 51). As one of her most famous poems says:

Tell all the truth but tell it slant—
Success in Circuit lies
Too bright for our infirm Delight
The Truth's superb surprise
As Lightning to the Children eased
With explanation kind
The Truth must dazzle gradually
Or every man be blind— (Dickinson 1999, 494)

This poem describes the nature of poetry: instead of telling the truth in a way that conceals from outsiders, Dickinson, in kindness, tells all the truth in a circuitous fashion, because the truth's brightness must dawn gradually or it blinds its viewer with its brilliance. Dickinson's poetry, like the parables of Jesus, can be indirect, polyvalent, and circuitous. Such indirectness is not just a rhetorical strategy; it is born of necessity—our own protection—and it is inherent in the nature of poetry, metaphor, and parable. Perhaps it is even at their heart, as Dickinson's poetry demonstrates (cf. Doriani 1996, 107–18; Peterson 2008, 1–5).

Charles Haddon Spurgeon (1834–1892)

Charles Spurgeon was a Baptist minister in Victorian England who was renowned for the eloquence of his sermons. Spurgeon was born in Kelvedon, Essex. He was the son and grandson of Congregational pastors and underwent a conversion experience at a Primitive Methodist Church in 1849. Spurgeon became a Baptist in 1850 because he was persuaded that faith, repentance, and immersion were essential elements of biblical baptism. Shortly thereafter, he began a preaching career that would last forty years, beginning as a lay preacher at St. Andrew's Baptist Church in Cambridge and then, at the age of seventeen, becoming pastor of the Baptist Church in Waterbeach. His sermons were so powerful that the tiny congregation quickly grew from approximately forty people to over four hundred. Spurgeon already was exhibiting the gift for preaching that would lead to him being called the "Prince of Preachers" (Dallimore 1984, 25–35).

Spurgeon became pastor at New Park Street Baptist Church in London, and soon all 1,200 seats in the chapel were filled during services, with people also sitting in the aisles and standing in other areas of the church to hear his sermons. The congregation expanded the building and also held some services at Exeter Hall, which accommodated 4,000–5,000 people (Dallimore 1984, 47–50). Even then, hundreds were still turned away, so just six years after

Spurgeon's arrival, the congregation moved to a new building that held 6,000 people, the Metropolitan Tabernacle.

Printed versions of Spurgeon's sermons also became so popular that as many as 350,000 copies were sold every week, and his sermons were printed in many major newspapers in the United States. In addition, Spurgeon applied his faith to social issues of the day, such as denouncing war, British imperialism (e.g., actions in India), and racial discrimination, including slavery (Bradstock and Rowland 2002, 186). Spurgeon also founded a college to train pastors (Pastors' College, later renamed Spurgeon's College), an orphanage, and other charitable institutions. A prolific author, Spurgeon wrote books, religious tracts, and other writings, including over 3,500 sermons.

A sermon Spurgeon preached on the parable of the two debtors at the Metropolitan Tabernacle on September 16, 1883 (titled "Bankrupt Debtors Discharged"), illustrates how he understood and interpreted the parables. The sermon focused on the central theme of Spurgeon's preaching: the doctrine of atonement. In brief, for Spurgeon, all human beings are sinners who fall short of God's expectations. As sinners, they deserve eternal damnation but can do nothing on their own to merit salvation. Their redemption comes by the free gift of grace from God through Jesus's "substitutionary" death—Jesus takes the place of sinful humans—and resurrection.

Spurgeon begins the sermon by discussing the obvious differences between the two debtors. The debtor who owed the greater amount could be compared to those who have transgressed more seriously: "The man who is moral, sober and industrious is only a fifty-pence debtor as compared with the vicious, drunken blasphemer whose debt is written at 500 pence" (Spurgeon 1883; all subsequent references in this section are to this work). Spurgeon illustrates these differences with an allusion to the parable of the sower, because these differences are clearly evident in people even before their conversion to Christianity: "The soil, which was none of it yet sown with the good seed, yet varied greatly, and some of it was honest and good ground before the sower came to it. Sinners differ from each other."

All sinners, like these two debtors, however, are similar in three ways, Spurgeon argues. First, both men were sinners, which illustrates that all people have sinned against God. Second, neither one could pay his debt, which denotes that sinful human beings cannot earn salvation. Third, both were freely forgiven of their debt, just as sinners may be forgiven by God's grace through the death and resurrection of Jesus: "There is forgiveness with God! He delights in mercy! He can cast all our sins into the depths of the sea that they may not be mentioned against us any more forever!" Spurgeon then discusses three aspects and applications of this parable.

(1) *The two debtors are bankrupt and unable to repay the debt.* The debtors, Spurgeon posits, had searched diligently to find assets they could use to repay their debts, but to no avail. Their creditor was demanding that they settle their debts, and they could not. This difficult problem is the heart of the text, and it parallels the situation of sinful human beings, because we owe God "the debt of obedience," the obligation to worship and serve God dutifully. Yet no human being is able to obey God completely; all have broken God's law and deserve eternal punishment: "That is where we stand—can any man be at rest while this is his condition before God? We are debtors—the debt is overwhelming—it brings with it consequences tremendous to the last degree!" Just like a fine alabaster vase is ruined by one chip or flaw, even a person guilty of one sin is guilty "in all points" of breaking God's law. That is the ultimate tragedy: to be banished from God's presence and glory and to be "cast away from all hope and light and joy forever!"

In addition, no human being can earn or merit salvation (pay our "debt"), because we owe everything to God:

> [Our] debt is immense and incalculable! Fifty pence is but a poor representation of what the most righteous person owes. Five hundred pence is but an insignificant sum compared with the transgressions of the greater offenders. Oh, Friends, when I think of my life, it seems to be like the sea, made up of innumerable waves of sin; or like the seashore, constituted of sands that cannot be weighed nor counted! My faults are utterly innumerable and each one deserving eternal death! . . . Now, to think that we can ever meet such a debt is, indeed, to bolster up ourselves with a notion that is utterly absurd—we have nothing with which to pay!
>
> If the Lord does not work salvation in us, we cannot work it out!

Human beings, however, try various ways to escape acknowledging that they are "bankrupt sinners." Some people attempt to forget their very dire spiritual situation altogether, but, Spurgeon warns, "God does not forget your sins." Other people put on a show of (self-)righteousness, but, although they profess to be religious, they are deceiving only themselves; they cannot deceive God. Still others attempt to bargain with God and put off their "payment," not realizing that there is a time when the bill comes due. Some ask God for more time to pay their debts, an effort that is also doomed to fail. Here Spurgeon points to the parable of the unforgiving slave (Matt. 18:23–35), who asks for additional time to pay his debt of ten thousand talents. Eventually, time runs out, and Spurgeon advises his listeners not to procrastinate and to own up to their desperate, "bankrupt" situation: "Your soul-matters are the most important things you will ever have on hand, for when your wealth must be left and your estate shall see you no more—and when your body is dead—your soul will still be living in eternal happiness or endless woe! Therefore, do not neglect your state in reference to God. It is the most important matter! Give it the first place. Settle this business before you attend to anything else." Nothing is hidden from God; God sees all for who they really are, so honesty not only is the best policy; it is also the only policy that works before God. All human beings must plead their absolute bankruptcy and ask for God's mercy and grace. That is their only hope.

That leads Spurgeon to the second major point of the parable of the two debtors: (2) *The creditor freely forgives both debtors*. As a result, the debtors who go to meet their creditor with trepidation "come out with light hearts, for the debt is all disposed of; the bills are receipted; the records are destroyed! Even thus the Lord has blotted out the handwriting that was against us and has taken it out of the way, nailing it to his cross. . . . Oh, the goodness of it! Oh, the largeness of the heart of God!" Here Spurgeon discerns not only the goodness of God, who freely discharges our debts of sin, but also God's mercy and kindness. The debtors do not have to beg, and the creditor, like God, freely forgives them:

> This is a fair picture of the grace of God! When a poor bankrupt sinner comes to him, he says, "I forgive you freely—your offense is all gone. I do not want you to earn a pardon by your tears, prayers and anguish of soul. You have not to make me merciful, for I am already merciful and my dear son, Jesus Christ, has made such a propitiation that I can be just and yet can forgive you all this debt. Therefore, go in peace."

Not only that, Spurgeon notes, but the debt was fully and completely paid:

> The creditor did not say, "Come, my good fellow, I will take 50 percent off the account if you find the remainder." As they had nothing with which to pay, they would not have been a bit the better if he had reduced them 90 percent! If he had reduced the debts by half, the one would have owed 250 and the other 25, but their cases would have been hopeless, since they had not a farthing of their own.
>
> Now the Lord, when He blots out His people's sin, leaves no trace of it remaining. My own persuasion is that when our Lord Jesus died upon the Cross, He made an end of all the sins of all His people and made full and effectual atonement for the whole of those who shall believe in Him. . . . The Lord has frankly forgiven their debt and He has not done so in part, but as a whole.

Only God can forgive sinful human beings, and, through "the precious blood of Christ," their sins can be forgiven for eternity, both the sins of those who have sinned a little and of those who have sinned greatly: "A bird held by a string is as much a prisoner as a bull that is tied by a rope!"

Spurgeon concludes with the third major point he gleaned from the parable: (3) *There is a connection between the bankruptcy of the debtors and the free discharge of their debts.* God will not forgive sinners until they acknowledge their dire situation, honestly confess their debt, and admit their incapacity to pay; otherwise people would not cherish the depths of God's mercy and forgiveness:

> Under conviction, a poor soul sees the reality of sin and of pardon!
>
> My dear Hearer, you will never believe in the reality of forgiveness till you have felt the reality of sin! I remember when I felt the burden of sin and though, but a child, my heart failed me for anguish and I was brought very low. Sin was no bugbear to scare me—it was a grim reality—as a lion, it tore me in pieces. And now, today, I know the reality of pardon—it is no fancy, no dream—for my inmost soul feels its power! I know that my sins are forgiven and I rejoice because of that belief, but I should never have known the real truth of this happy condition if I had not felt the oppressive load of sin upon the conscience.

Spurgeon joyfully proclaims the parable's assurance that both debtors/sinners are forgiven by God, and he urges his hearers to respond accordingly—to join hands in faith with Christ, who is the savior of sinners; receive God's forgiveness; and become "saved forever."

This sermon, as are most of Spurgeon's sermons, is notable for its earnestness, clarity, plainspokenness, Calvinist theology, and strict morality. It also, as do many of Jesus's parables, stresses the urgency of the present moment and calls for an immediate decision.

Adolf Jülicher (1857–1938)

Adolf Jülicher was born in Falkenberg, Germany, in 1857. He attended the University of Berlin, where he earned a doctorate in 1880, and then served as a Lutheran pastor at Rummelsburg. He also worked as a private lecturer (*Privatdozent*) in Berlin, and during that time wrote the first volume of his seminal work, *Die Gleichnisreden Jesu* (*The Parables of Jesus*), which was published in 1886. As a result, Jülicher was invited to join the faculty at the University of Marburg, where he remained until he retired in 1923 (the famed New Testament scholar Rudolf Bultmann was one of his students).

Die Gleichnisreden Jesu is the most famous and influential scholarly book on the parables ever written, and it inaugurated a new era in the modern research of the parables. The first volume of the work discusses interpretative issues, and the second volume, published along with a revised first volume in 1888–1889, gives detailed interpretations of all the parables found in Matthew, Mark, and Luke. Although many of Jülicher's categories have been superseded by subsequent interpreters, some of his discussions still influence current debates (for much of the following, see Gowler 2000 and the sources listed there).

For example, Jülicher argues that scholars must distinguish between the parables as told by Jesus and the parables as they are found in the Gospels. Jesus uttered his parables perhaps as much as fifty years before the Gospels were written, and the Gospel authors creatively reworked those traditions. For Jülicher, the major problem is that the Gospel authors obscured the parabolic message of Jesus with an overgrowth of allegory, descriptive supplementation, and interpretive application, with the "incontrovertible" (*Unangreifbar*) result that the Gospels actually in some ways conceal the meaning and function of the parables as Jesus had uttered them: "The authenticity [*Echtheit*] of the Gospel parables is not absolute. They did not emerge from the mouth of Jesus as we now read them. They are translated, displaced, and internally transformed. . . . Without careful examination, one can nowhere identify the voice of Jesus with voices of the Gospel authors" (Jülicher 1963, 1:11; unless otherwise indicated, all quotations from this source are my translation).

In addition, in a survey of previous interpretations of the parables, Jülicher demonstrates that, with a few exceptions such as John Calvin and John Maldonatus, virtually all interpreters imposed allegorical interpretations far exceeding those found in the Gospels themselves. As Joachim Jeremias observes, "It is positively alarming to read . . . [Jülicher's] story of the centuries of distortion and ill-usage which the parables have suffered through allegorical interpretation" (1972, 18).

Jülicher sets out to prune the allegorical overgrowth found in the Gospel versions of the parables. Thus he assumes not only that such an allegorical overgrowth exists—some clearly does—but also that scholars armed with proper sets of shears and trained eyes can pare back the allegorical overgrowth in the Gospels to uncover the parables of Jesus as he spoke them, thus uncovering more authentic elements of Jesus's teachings. Jülicher finds that Jesus used parables to "illustrate the unfamiliar by the commonly familiar, to guide gently upwards from the easy to the difficult" (1963, 1:146). Jesus's "original" parables are not allegorical, not meant to obscure his message, not (intentionally) created to be difficult puzzles to solve, and do not serve as stumbling blocks for "outsiders" (cf. Mark 4:11–12). Instead, the parables as told by Jesus before they were distorted by the Gospel authors are always straightforward discourse (*immer eigentliche Rede*) in clear language that is "meant to inform, clarify, and persuade" (McKim 2007, 586). Jülicher declares:

> So far as I see, we cannot escape explaining the meaning and understanding of the evangelists [Gospel authors] as a misunderstanding of the essence of Jesus' parables. The difference can be expressed as follows: *According to the theory of the evangelists, the "parables" are allegories, and therefore figurative discourse that to some extent requires translation, while in fact they are—or, we should say, they were, before they came into the hands of zealous redactors—something very different: parables, fables, example paradigmatic stories, but always literal discourse.* (Jülicher 1963, 1:49, quoted in Kümmel 1972, 187; emphasis original)

Jülicher thus argues that even though centuries of interpreters have considered the parables of Jesus to be allegories—including the Gospel authors themselves—the evidence points to Jesus's parables not being allegorical (1963, 1:61).

Jülicher explores the form and nature of parables and, depending primarily on Aristotle's *Rhetoric* (book 3, part 4), argues that parables are similes, not metaphors. Metaphors are indirect, enigmatic speech; they say one thing but mean another; they can remain incomprehensible without proper context and interpretation. An example borrowed from Aristotle is that "A lion rushed on" (*der Löwe stürmt los*) can function as a metaphor for "Achilles rushed on," depending on the context. Metaphors thus easily and naturally extend into allegories, something that Jülicher argues Jesus never used.

Similes, though, are direct, simple, and self-explanatory speech, such as the clear comparison also used by Aristotle: "Achilles rushed on like a lion" (*der löwenmutige Achill stürmt los*; 1:52). Jülicher concludes that Jesus used similes and that they develop into three categories:

1. similitude (*Gleichnis*): A similitude reflects a typical or recurring event in daily life, and it has two components—the "picture" (image part: *Bildhälfte*) created by the story and the "object" (or reality part: *Sachhälfte*) contained in the story. The details of the similitude merely provide a colorful context for the "object/reality" that the "picture" portrayed, and a single point of comparison (the *tertium comparationis*) connects the two parts with "like" or "as." The similitude's *tertium comparationis* challenges its readers with the necessity of either forming a judgment or making a decision (1:58–80). The saying about the children playing in the marketplace (Matt. 11:16–19; Luke 7:31–34) and the parables of the lost sheep (Matt. 18:12–14; Luke 15:4–7), the lost

coin (Luke 15:8–10), and the seed growing secretly (Mark 4:26–29) are all similitudes.

2. parable or fable (*Parabel*; *Fabel*): The parable is a fictional story that has all of the attributes of a similitude and functions the same way. The "resemblance" in the parable refers readers to an external reality; it is different from a similitude in that the parable is a story that takes place in the past. Jülicher considers this form to be a fable, but, since fables are often confused with stories that involve animals, he prefers the term "parable" (1:92–111). The majority of Jesus's parables, Jülicher adds, are fables similar to the fables attributed to Stesichorus or Aesop. The narratives about the laborers in the vineyard (Matt. 20:1–16), the prodigal son (Luke 15:11–32), and the sower (Matt. 13:1–9; Mark 4:1–9; Luke 8:4–8) are all parables, although the allegorical interpretation of the parable of the sower (Mark 4:13–20; Matt. 13:18–23; Luke 8:11–15) does not stem from Jesus.

3. example story (*Beispielerzählung*): An example story is a fictional narrative—like the parable—but it differs from the similitude and the parable because it actually illustrates the reality/truth it is meant to demonstrate; it doesn't just refer to an external reality (1:112–15). Jülicher lists only four example stories from the Gospels: the good Samaritan, the rich fool, the rich man and Lazarus, and the Pharisee and the tax collector. The distinctive feature of parables of this type is that they present examples that are supposed to be emulated by others. The good Samaritan, for instance, is an example story because it illustrates the moral principle of loving one's neighbor. God esteems loving compassion, so even a despised Samaritan demonstrates through his compassion what it means to be a neighbor in contrast to the priest and Levite (2:596). Thus all the allegorical interpretations by people like Origen completely miss the point. The injured man does not symbolize Adam, the Samaritan does not denote Jesus, the inn does not designate the church, Jerusalem does not symbolize paradise, and Jericho does not denote "the world." Attempts to find symbolism in such elements are doomed to fail because details like Jerusalem and Jericho are used only to give local color to this example story. Instead, Jülicher contends, interpreters should focus on the one basic point of comparison—the neighborly actions of the Samaritan—to understand the meaning of the parable as Jesus intended it: the compassion we should have for our fellow human beings (2:585–98).

The problem, for Jülicher, is that a parable's pictorial elements (*Bildhälfte*) *must* be understood literally (*eigentlich*), whereas the pictorial elements of an allegory must be understood figuratively (*uneigentlich*), and "this contrast allows no mixing of forms" (1:76). The parables, after they have been examined and restored to the form taught by Jesus, are "masterpieces of popular eloquence" that are "wholly unpretentious" and give their readers an overpowering feeling of the exalted nature of Jesus: "As far as we know, nothing higher and more perfect has ever been accomplished in this area" (Jülicher 1963, 1:152, quoted in Kümmel 1972, 187).

Jülicher attempted to remove the allegorical accretions in the Gospel parables and situate the parables in concrete situations in the life and ministry of Jesus, who uttered them in particular contexts and in response to particular challenges: "Jesus's parables were designed to make an immediate effect, children of the moment, deeply immersed in the particularity of the present moment" (Jülicher 1963, 1:91). Parables are not riddles; they are self-evident and do not need to be explained (Jones 1964, 17). Yet in stripping away all traces of allegory, Jülicher's interpretations of the parables, since they focused on one single idea, often with the broadest application, are frequently bland generalities. The parable of the rich man and Lazarus, for example, was supposed to produce joy (*Freude*) in a life of suffering and to inculcate fear (*Furcht*) of a life of wealth and pleasure (Jülicher 1963, 2:638). Likewise, the parable of the unjust steward encourages its hearers to make wise use of the present to ensure a happy future (2:511).

Scholars since Jülicher have noted the groundbreaking nature of his work, but many have pointed to weaknesses in his approach. Do parables always have one point, and is there an "essential" (*wesentlich*; 1:52) difference between simile and metaphor? Many have answered no to both those questions. Even Aristotle's *Rhetoric*, on which Jülicher depended, notes: "The simile also is a metaphor; the difference is but slight" (*Rhetoric* 3.4). In addition, Jülicher was criticized for being too dependent upon Aristotle and not appreciative enough of the Jewish context of Jesus and his parables (e.g., see the discussion of David Flusser in chap. 5). Some recent scholars suggest that Jesus's parables can include allegory or even be allegorical, so they contest Jülicher's rigorous exclusion of allegorical elements from the original parables of Jesus. It is true, however, that post-Jülicher scholars would never completely resuscitate the allegorical method.

5

The Afterlives
of Jesus's Parables in the Twentieth
and Twenty-First Centuries

The decline of the use of the Bible and of its impact on society and culture that is evident in the eighteenth and nineteenth centuries continued during the twentieth and twenty-first centuries. Biblical literacy declined precipitously, even among evangelical Christians (see Prothero 2007, 1–121). This increasing lack of use, knowledge, and impact of the Bible in general and the parables in particular had three major implications for the reception and interpretations of the parables.

First, interpretations of the parables—whether in art, music, literature, plays, or anywhere else outside the church—became less common. Second, even as interactions with the parables became less frequent, interpreters became more varied in their responses (e.g., less religious in orientation): the diversity of approaches and interpretations continued to expand. Third, the impact of various interpretations of the parables of Jesus diminished as well because of biblical illiteracy. Only a small number of parables, for example, are well known enough today to have some salience in contemporary culture. Even the terms "good Samaritan" and "prodigal son" are likely to elicit only a general sense of their intended meanings; the details of these and other parables are often not common knowledge. People may not even realize that these titles are given to parables from Jesus.

For example, in the early stages of my research for this book, my son sent me a link to an article from the *Boston Globe* titled, "LeBron James, the Prodigal Son" (https://www.bostonglobe.com/sports/2014/07/11/lebron -james-prodigal-son/Ak2mlhvsHjraYDAOjEs6RK/story.html). The article itself makes no mention of Jesus's parable. One wonders how much readers of an article in the sports pages of the *Boston Globe* will understand or fully recognize that the narrative of James's return home to Ohio and his former NBA team, the Cleveland Cavaliers, is placed into the context of Jesus's parable. (As a comparison, a 1990 Gallup survey indicated that only half of the people in the United States could even name one of the four New Testament Gospels; Gallup and Bezilla 1990, 17; cf. Thoreau's lament of biblical illiteracy in Concord—just outside Boston—at the beginning of chap. 4 above.) Such biblical illiteracy heightens the importance of a book such as this one, which documents the continuing importance of Jesus's parables by explaining how much, in both overt and subtle ways, they have become embedded in multiple aspects of (primarily Western) culture. The breadth and depth of their influence is surprising even to those familiar with Jesus's parables. For those not as familiar with Jesus's parables or the Bible, these explorations can be truly eye-opening, such as the connection of the wheat and weeds parable to religious liberty in the United States, the critical nature of the prodigal son parable in understanding many of Shakespeare's plays, and so forth.

As in previous chapters, this chapter seeks to include perspectives on the parables from a diverse range of worldviews, people, and media. Parables continue to play a key role in literature, as a novel by Flannery O'Connor and a science fiction novel by Octavia Butler demonstrate. O'Connor's *The Violent Bear It Away* and Butler's *Parable of the Sower* both use Jesus's parable of the sower as a guiding metaphor for their stories, but in very different ways.

Interpretations from two New Testament scholars are included: David Flusser and Elsa Tamez. Flusser highlights that Jesus was a first-century Jewish sage whose parables share a common narrative tradition with rabbinic parables. Tamez illustrates how Jesus's parables can be interpreted in light of Latin American liberation theology, from a feminist perspective, and in the context of oppression. Sermons by Dr. Martin Luther King Jr. on the parables also include a prophetic concern for basic human rights and economic justice for all people. In addition, excerpts from a commentary by the "peasants of Solentiname" in Nicaragua offer "grassroots" perspectives of nonscholars about the "good news to the poor" that Jesus proclaims (Luke 4:18).

The chapter includes representations of visual art: a painting by one of the peasants of Solentiname, José Arana, on the rich man and Lazarus parable, contrasts in several ways with the lithograph *Prodigal Son* by the American

"Regionalist" painter Thomas Hart Benton, although both images evoke contexts of difficult economic circumstances. Other works of art include a blues song by Robert Wilkins and the film *Godspell*, which is based on a 1970s play by the same name.

The chapter concludes with a contribution to an interfaith dialogue between Buddhism and Christianity from a Buddhist monk, Thich Nhat Hanh, whose "Engaged Buddhism" involves active, nonviolent civil action. Using Jesus's parable of the mustard seed, Nhat Hanh argues that the kingdom of God is within all human beings and that the living Jesus, like the living Buddha, is a door into that path of enlightenment, the kingdom of God.

Thomas Hart Benton (1889–1975)

The influential American painter Thomas Hart Benton was born in Neosho, Missouri. After studying at both the Chicago Art Institute and the Fine Arts Academy in Paris, Benton eventually settled in New York City, where he taught at the Art Students League (one of his students was Jackson Pollock, who would become a leader in abstract expressionism). In 1935, Benton moved to Kansas City, Missouri, to chair the painting department at the Kansas City Art Institute. He lived in Kansas City until his death in 1975 (see Benton 1983).

As Benton's success grew in the 1920s, so did criticism of his work. Some critiques were aimed at the content of his images. His 1933 mural for the State of Indiana was controversial, for example, because it included the Ku Klux Klan in its depiction of the historical development of Indiana. Likewise, Benton's mural for the Missouri State Capitol building, *A Social History of Missouri*, generated controversy because it included Huckleberry Finn with Jim the slave, a lynched slave, the outlaws Frank and Jesse James, and Tom Pendergast, a corrupt political boss from Kansas City. In addition, other critics thought Benton's works were sentimental caricatures or cartoon-like. Yet for many people in the United States, especially in the late 1920s and 1930s, Benton "spoke their language, painted their lives, and believed wholeheartedly in the significance of their experiences" (J. Wolff 2012, 4–11, 13, 197; cf. Benton 1983, 248).

In his autobiography, *An Artist in America*, Benton writes that he "was moved by a great desire to know more of the America" that he had glimpsed back home in Missouri in 1924, while visiting his father before his father's death (1983, 77). Benton began traveling throughout the United States, as "he began to search for signs of distinctly American elements in the environments he discovered" (Gruber 1998, 18). He created a distinctive style that stresses that art should represent life as it is experienced in a specific time and place as it is "known and felt" by people he called "ordinary Americans" (Benton 1983, 318). Benton thus abandoned the abstract styles with which he had experimented for a dynamic and realistic style that was called (initially by critics) *regionalism*, and Benton was one of the "regionalist triumvirate": Benton, John Steuart Curry, and Grant Wood.

Religion did not play a dominant role in Benton's work, but he was convinced that historically all great art was inspired by religion or culture and that its meaning emerged from the way in which people lived (Burroughs 1981, 49). Much of his art, therefore, included an interest in the history, culture, and lives of the people he sought to represent (Benton 1983, 74–80), especially those experiences not usually documented by artists. Religion is a central element, for example, in what Benton says was his first regionalist painting on Martha's Vineyard, titled *The Lord Is My Shepherd* (1926), which depicts George and Sabrina West sitting at the table in their farmhouse. These New England Yankees symbolize for Benton not only reliance on God but also self-reliance, frugality, perseverance, strength, and independence—qualities Benton valued (Gambone 1989, 73).

Before he moved to Kansas City, Benton started a fifteen-year project, a series of lithographs called "The American Scene" that capture many of Benton's experiences on his travels around the United States. Some of these lithographs chronicle the religious lives and practices of Americans, such as a pastor preaching to his small white congregation in the mountains of West Virginia (*The Meeting*, 1941), African Americans headed to their small country church in southern Arkansas (*Sunday Morning*, 1939), and people headed to an evening prayer meeting in a small country church somewhere in the Bible Belt (*Prayer Meeting* or *Wednesday Evening*, 1949).

One of the lithographs in this project is the 1939 *Prodigal Son* (figure 5.1), which was a study for his later painting of the same name (now found in the Dallas Museum of Fine Arts). Benton's description of the lithograph is as follows: "Study for a painting—owned by Dallas Museum. Picture of the belated return of the 'son.' The house was at the foot of the Boston hill in Chilmark, Martha's Vinyard [*sic*]. It has long since hit the ground" (Benton 1979, 78). Benton first painted the house in 1921 (*The Flanders' House*), but in the intervening years the abandoned house had collapsed and was a suitable site to depict the desolation awaiting the return of this prodigal son, a desolation that is captured more brilliantly by the black-and-white lithograph than by the warm, subtle hues of the painting.

The lithograph presents an idiosyncratic and haunting view of a prodigal son who has waited far too long to "come to himself" and return home. His

Figure 5.1 Thomas Hart Benton, *Prodigal Son* (1939)

hair has turned white, and his left hand touches his white/gray beard as he ponders what has been and what is now. His old truck is off in the distance, and his suitcase—tied together with ropes—sits on the ground just behind him. There is no longer any father to run out, throw his arms around him, and kiss him. No best robe, ring, or sandals are forthcoming either, and, as the bottom right of the lithograph makes clear, there will be no feast with a fatted calf: the sun-bleached bones of a cow are all that's left of what could once have been a fatted calf, if only the prodigal had returned earlier. The dead tree branch at the man's feet also reflects the death and devastation that have come upon his home in his absence. The house stands as only a ramshackle shell of its former self, completely deserted and dilapidated—not only with no father inside to greet the prodigal, but also no servants to attend to him and no elder brother to complain about him. The sun sets in the sky behind him as well, another indication that he has waited too late; all he loved is gone.

Perhaps some people in the churches that Benton visited on his travels would interpret this image as a sermon of warning, one that says, "Do not wait too long to return to the father. Some day it will be too late." This warning, like some of Jesus's parables, urges prodigal sons and daughters to return home to their father while there is still time. Such an interpretation, for many

Christian interpreters, might be attractive, although it does not follow the story line of the parable.

Benton's own interpretation of the image is unclear, but some scholars postulate that the prodigal son reflects Benton himself at this stage of his life, as he reflects on what seems to have been the downward trajectory of his career and his contentious return home to Missouri. The choice of the Chilmark farm on Martha's Vineyard, where Benton's career started in earnest, could bolster the interpretation that Benton is implying that he, like the prodigal, had squandered his career and was, at that time, depressingly devoid of hope (Gambone 1989, 83–88). Benton's homecoming to Missouri after years in New York City was not as welcoming as he had expected. A campaign had already begun in 1938 to oust Benton from his position at the Kansas City Art Institute—he would be fired in 1941—and he felt estranged from many of his artistic contemporaries. Regionalism itself was often discussed already in the past tense. As Ellen D'Oench argues, "For Benton, like his prodigal son, going home to find resolution was an aspiration without hope" (1995, 26).

In addition, this image was clearly influenced by Benton's experience during the Great Depression and Dust Bowl in the United States. A comparison with other works he created in 1939 illustrates Benton's understanding of the economic realities in the United States during that era. Benton was commissioned to create a series of drawings of the characters of John Steinbeck's *The Grapes of Wrath* for the 1940 Twentieth-Century Fox film adaptation of the novel, which, in spite of its controversial subject matter, had just won a Pulitzer Prize. Benton's *The Departure of the Joads* (1939), which depicts the Joads loading their beat-up Hudson truck for their journey down Highway 66, is hauntingly similar to the lithograph of the *Prodigal Son*; it evokes some of the same feelings of loss and barrenness. Both images depict dispossessed refugees: one where people leave their ravaged home, the other where the prodigal returns to his ravaged home. In addition, the novel depicts a similarly bleak homecoming: when Tom Joad first returns to his childhood farm home, he finds it deserted, because the banks have evicted all the farmers from their land (Steinbeck 1996, 251–73).

Not only, then, does the *Prodigal Son* lithograph likely reflect Benton's autobiographical context; it also likely addresses the political, economic, and social contexts in which he lived. Benton could be described as a 1930s populist whose art was sympathetic to the plight of "common" human beings, critical of special interests, and supportive of moderate reforms. Benton also thought that the "American character was formed by hard-working non-intellectual people who were sometimes victimized by their circumstances" (J. Wolff 2012, 4–11). Beginning in the 1930s, Benton pilloried urban politicians, big business, and big industry and their effects on the "common person," including the "moral, self-sufficient, self-supporting rural individual" (Baigell 1984, 23, 27). One of his major concerns was that the exploitative business practices of modern industries "would ravage the land and destroy the culture he was trying so hard to record and preserve" (Marling 1985, 67).

As Erika Doss points out, when Benton created the lithograph of the prodigal son, he was undergoing "a profound lack of faith in the tradition he had celebrated throughout the [1930s]" (1991, 253). Benton also writes of the political and economic divisions that President Roosevelt was struggling to overcome. The reforms of the New Deal were faltering within the United States, and clouds of war were gathering (1983, 296–97). Thus it is possible if not likely that this image combines self-identification with the prodigal (as did works by Rembrandt and Dürer) with trenchant socioeconomic commentary.

Parables and the Blues: Rev. Robert Wilkins (1896–1987)

The first published blues music appeared in the early 1900s, but its roots extend to Africa. The horrific slave trade to the Americas meant that human beings from Africa were torn from their homes, chained like animals in the holds of slave ships on brutal voyages, auctioned to the highest bidders, separated from family members, and often subjected to merciless treatment at the hands of their owners (see Awmiller 1996, 14–15). Many slave owners also attempted to convert their slaves to Christianity in the belief not only that the slaves' eternal salvation could be obtained but that conversion would increase slaves' contentment and obedience: heaven, after all, awaited them after their suffering on earth, if they would be patient. The music called "spirituals" that was created in their segregated places of worship often merged Christian salvation with liberation, freedom from captivity—not only from sin but also from political and economic oppression—with often subtle critiques of their bondage, including frequent themes of faith, hope, patience, weariness, and the struggle for freedom (Dowley 2011, 191–93).

Blues music incorporated some aspects of spirituals, but also assimilated elements of "field hollers," an early form of black work-music. Field hands "whooped, moaned, and sang in sudden and completely improvised ways" (Guralnick et al. 2003, 15). These work songs fooled many slave owners into thinking that their slaves were fairly content with their fate, but in reality these songs were filled with lamentation and protest. Slaves could communicate their misery, anger, and desire for liberation in ways not easily understood by outsiders. These work songs were an outlet for expressing a subversive message of resistance from a position of utter powerlessness (Awmiller 1996, 16). Many of these work songs were of the "call and response" variety, with a leader singing a line and the other workers following in response. Early blues music followed a similar format, often with the guitar "answering" the lines sung by the blues musician (Rolf 2007, 14).

Even after slavery officially ended, the social isolation and economic oppression of African Americans made it virtually impossible for them to escape dire poverty. Most forms of relief could be found either on Saturday night (in a "juke joint" or bar) or on Sunday morning (in church). The latter primarily offered ultimate release in heaven after death, and the former primarily spoke of the disappointments in everyday life or offered cathartic, albeit temporary, relief from suffering (Iglauer 2012, xi). The deceptively simple form of blues music—often a strophic song with a repetitive three-line stanza (A-A-B pattern) followed by a refrain, in twelve measures of 4/4 rhythm—masks its complexity, power, subtlety, and depth. Even from the outside looking in, the power of the blues to stir one's heart, soul, and mind can be almost magical (Iglauer 2012, x).

Blues artists often existed at the periphery of the church (see Cone 1972), but a host of early blues artists also sang gospel music. Robert Wilkins, for example, was a popular blues artist during the 1920s and 1930s in Memphis, but he quit in the mid-1930s to become an ordained minister. A Delta bluesman who fused gospel music and the blues, Wilkins was a talented composer as well as a guitar player and singer. Wilkins, originally from Mississippi, became the first black songwriter to perform live on the radio in his adopted home of Memphis. He also was the first to record a blues song, titled "Rolling Stone," a primitive, one-chord song recorded in 1928. Reports vary as to why Wilkins quit his life as a secular blues artist to become a minister, but he was "rediscovered" in the blues revival of the early 1960s and performed gospel songs intermittently until his death in 1987 (F. Davis 1995, 113–14).

Wilkins's "The Prodigal Son" was originally not a religious song; it was a classic blues lament, "That's No Way to Get Along," in which a young man complains to his mother about "These low down women" who "treated your poor son wrong":

> I'm going home, friends, sit down and tell my, ah, mama (repeat)
> That that's no way to get along
>
> These low-down women, mama, they treated your, ah, poor son wrong
>   (repeat)
> And that's no way for him to get along

> They treated me like my poor heart was made of a rock or stone
> (repeat)
> And that's no way for me to get along (Wilkins 1994)

After Wilkins became a minister, he would sing only religious music, so he rewrote the lyrics and, using the same tune, retitled the song "The Prodigal Son." The only original lyrics that remain in this Christianized version are the key words of the refrain, "That's the way to get along" in various forms, depending on the stage of the prodigal's journey.

The song begins with the prodigal planning how to improve his position in life by asking for his inheritance and leaving home. In particular, the variations in the lines about how the prodigal and others "will get along" are especially significant:

> Now the prodigal son left home by himself
> Home by himself
> Now the prodigal son left home by himself
> The prodigal son left home by himself
> And that's the way for me to get along
>
> And the last words that I heard him say (repeat)
>
> Said I'm gonna tell my father to give me all of mine today (repeat)
> And that will be the way for me to get along (Wilkins 1964; all quotes
>   from this song come from this source)

The focus is on how the son will prosper on his own by using his inheritance. The lyrics then hint that all would not turn out well for the prodigal, since he was already a "poor boy":

> And the poor boy got all he had and he started on down the road
> (repeat)
> And that's the way for me to get along

The prodigal son, like Jonah in the Hebrew Bible, even attempted to escape the knowledge and presence of God. He did not need God to succeed in life (cf. Pulci's prodigal son in chap. 2 saying, "Who has cash in this world has what he wants"):

> Said I'm going somewhere out in this world and God never will know
>   it (repeat)
> And that will be the way for me to get along

The "poor boy's" plans went awry, however, because he spent all that he had, and the narrator now explicitly informs us that the son's leaving home with his inheritance actually was not the way "for him to get along." The sermon intervenes:

> And the poor boy got away from home and spent all that he had
>   (repeat)
> And that was no way for him to get along
>
> Spent all that he had and a famine come in the land (repeat)

After the famine, the prodigal son came up with another way for him "to get along," hiring himself out to another man with the focus, once again, on himself: how he could "get along." The man's conception of how best for the prodigal "to get along" was a far cry from what the prodigal envisioned, however:

> And the man told him I'll give you a job for to feed my swine (repeat)
> And that'd be the way for you to get along

The "poor boy" responded in tears and shame, and he came up with yet another way for him "to get along"—but the focus was still on himself:

> And the poor boy stood there and he hung his head and cried (repeat)
>
> Said I believe I'll ride, and I believe I'll go back home (repeat)
> And that'd be the way for me to get along

His father saw the son from a distance, and the father changed the focus from a first-person singular to a first-person plural: in the language of the song, the "me" getting along is dramatically changed to "us" getting along, which signals that the prodigal's self-centered focus on himself was beginning to be corrected:

> And as far down the road as far as his father could see (repeat)
>
> He said I believe that's my son, he's coming home to me (repeat)
> And that'd be the way for us to get along

The song apparently then heightens the love and compassion of the father. The voices merge together, and it seems that the father was the one who not only ran to his son, but also fell on his knees before his son, cried and prayed for mercy, and expressed thankfulness for God sending his son back to him (cf. The Rolling Stones truncated version of the song on their 1968 *Beggars Banquet*):

> And his poor father run to him and he fell down on his knees (repeat)
>
> And he was cryin' and praying, Lord have mercy on me (repeat)
>
> And I'm so glad the Lord sent my son home to me (repeat)
> And that's the way for us to get along

The father and son still did not agree on the best way for them "to get along," because the father was rejoicing that his son had returned, and the son now said that the best way for them "to get along" was for his father not to "own" him as a son. The son was at least now focused on their familial relationship and also used the first-person plural. His father responded, however, by calling the entire family together and restoring family relationships between "his" son and the rest of the family.

> And his father stood there and he called the family round (repeat)
>
> Said my son was lost but now he is found (repeat)

Even in this ten-minute song that includes many details of the story, the elder brother was not allowed to stay outside the celebration or protest to his father about the welcome his younger brother received. The father instead instructed the elder son to go and kill the fatted calf himself. The stress, once again, is on familial relationships, and it appears that the elder son joined the banquet. The message of this blues sermon is universal: treating one another in this forgiving and welcoming fashion is indeed "the way for us to get along."

Wilkins's song is another example of how the prodigal son parable was used to preach repentance and reconciliation. In the context of blues, however, the prodigal son parable plays a larger role and demonstrates also how people identify with the prodigal and how the "prodigal son pattern"—the redemption that comes after returning home from leading a life of sin—provides a well-traveled bridge between the sacred and profane in African American music.

Churchgoers often criticized those who played or enjoyed blues (i.e., the "devil's") music as "sinners." As Jon Michael Spencer notes, some early blues artists could identify with the prodigal son and envision their lives as a reenactment of the parable: their own sinful lifestyles were similar to the prodigal's debauchery in a foreign land. Christianity in the Protestant South celebrated dramatic conversion stories, and when blues artists became preachers of the gospel, they reenacted this prodigal son pattern by "returning home" from the "devil's life," often with dramatic conversion experiences (see Spencer 1993, 26–31, 64–65).

Even "The Prodigal Son" song by Robert Wilkins follows this pattern, since it started as a secular blues song but was converted into a gospel sermon about the prodigal son parable and the way for all human beings to "get along." Although Wilkins was always religious and never fell into the stereotype of a prodigal returning home, his story is of a blues artist turning to full-time Christian service, and his song "The Prodigal Son" exemplifies this transformation from secular to holy.

Flannery O'Connor (1925–1964)

Flannery O'Connor was born in a prominent Irish Catholic family in Savannah, Georgia, on March 15, 1925. O'Connor's family moved to Atlanta and then Milledgeville, Georgia, where she enrolled in the Georgia State College for Women. After graduation, O'Connor joined the Writers Workshop at the University of Iowa and earned a master of fine arts degree in 1947. Her first novel, *Wise Blood*, was published in 1952, and during her career she published a second novel, numerous short stories, and countless letters and essays.

O'Connor was diagnosed with lupus in 1950, and poor health forced her to move back to Milledgeville, where she lived at the family farm, Andalusia. The disease limited her mobility and her ability to write—by 1956, she walked using crutches, and she could work only three hours a day (Simpson 2005, 22). Despite her physical condition, she remained active in life around Milledgeville, and she also traveled around the country, primarily to give lectures. She also entertained numerous people in her home and exchanged hundreds of letters with others (see O'Connor 1979). In February 1964, surgery to remove an ovarian tumor reactivated her lupus, and she died on August 3, 1964, at the age of thirty-nine.

O'Connor's *The Violent Bear It Away*, first published in 1960, is her second and last novel, and it is generally considered a better written and richer story than *Wise Blood*. The title for the book comes from the Douay-Rheims Bible (a Catholic English translation of the Latin Vulgate) translation of Matthew 11:12: "From the days of John the Baptist until now, the kingdom of heaven suffereth violence, and the violent bear it away," which seems, for O'Connor, to suggest that followers of Jesus are to imitate the self-sacrifice of Jesus (K. Martin 2012, 159).

O'Connor uses the parable of the sower extensively in the novel, so much so that some interpreters have argued that it is the story's guiding metaphor.

The novel begins with the main character, young Francis Marion Tarwater, becoming too drunk to dig his great-uncle's (Mason Tarwater) grave. Fourteen years earlier his great-uncle, "old Tarwater," had "rescued" Francis from George Rayber, a schoolteacher who was Francis's uncle (his mother—Rayber's unmarried sister—had died). Old Tarwater considered himself a prophet, and he raised "the boy to expect the Lord's call himself" (O'Connor 2007, 5).

In an early flashback that initiates the book's incorporation of the parable of the sower, readers learn that old Tarwater had kidnapped Rayber years before, when Rayber was seven, brought him to the farm called Powderhead, baptized him, and "instructed him in the facts of his Redemption." Like some of the seeds in the sower parable, however, the old man's instruction of Rayber did not produce fruit (O'Connor 2007, 7): "What it bore was a dry and seedless fruit, incapable even of rotting. Dead from the beginning" (19; cf. the "thorn bed of that thought," 20; and "he had good sense but later it dried up," 40).

Rayber's father soon came to reclaim him, and the next time Rayber saw old Tarwater he gave his uncle a lot of "sass," which, old Tarwater claims to Francis, Rayber received from his parents:

> "It was sass he had got from them," the old man said. "Just parrot-mouthing all they had ever said about how I was a crazy man. The truth was even if they told him not to believe what I had taught him, he couldn't forget it. He could never forget that there was a chance that that simpleton was not his only father. I planted the seed in him and it was there for good. Whether anybody liked it or not."
>
> "It fell amongst cockles," [Francis] Tarwater said. "Say the sass."
>
> "It fell in deep," the old man said, "or else after that crash he wouldn't have come out here hunting me."
>
> "He only wanted to see if you were still crazy," the boy offered. (66–67)

Old Tarwater still believes that the seed was implanted deep in Rayber, and that, deep down, the grown-up schoolteacher still loved him: "He loved me like a daddy and he was ashamed of it!" (71). Years later, when old Tarwater moved in with Rayber, he secretly had also tried to baptize Francis when he was an infant. Rayber caught him and became incensed. The old man claimed that the infant was therefore "born again" and that Rayber was powerless to do anything about it. Rayber stated that the old man had ruined his (Rayber's) life because of what he had done to him as a young child: "You infected me with your idiot hopes, your foolish violence. I'm not always myself." In those very words, the old man claimed, Rayber "admitted himself the seed was still in him" (73). Nevertheless, the old man realized that his previous efforts for Rayber had failed (cf. 134–35; although the "seed" was implanted in him fruitfully for a while, at least; 170), so he set his sights on raising Francis as the one who would replace him as a prophet of God (72–74).

Francis Tarwater struggles mightily with his destiny as a prophet; will the seed planted in him bear fruit (e.g., 91–92)? His first and primary prophetic task is to baptize his cousin, Bishop, the son of Rayber, whom, ironically, Rayber tried to drown but repented of the action just in time (141–43). On a family trip to a park with Francis and Bishop, Rayber prevents Francis from baptizing Bishop in a shallow pool around a fountain. Rayber realizes that old Tarwater had indeed "transmitted his fixation to the boy, *had* left him with the notion that he must baptize Bishop or suffer some terrible consequence" (146).

It appears, then, that the seed that old Tarwater sowed is continuing to grow and will likely bear some (in this case, terrible) fruit, although Rayber still hopes to cure young Francis of the "morbid impulse to baptize" Bishop (151, 169). We later find out, from Francis's point of view, that this morbid impulse included the possibility that he would drown Bishop (165, 168). Bishop is a focal point of both Rayber's and Francis's desire to "weed out" the seed that old Tarwater had implanted in them, not only because of the theme of baptizing/drowning him but also because of some of Bishop's physical characteristics (e.g., Bishop and old Tarwater both have gray/silver, "fish-colored eyes"; 32, 113–14, 170).

By chapter 9, Rayber begins to despair of helping Francis, telling him: "The old man still has you in his grip. Don't think he hasn't" (192). The boy replies: "'It's you the seed fell in. . . . It ain't a thing you can do about it. It fell on bad ground but it fell in deep. With me,' he said proudly, 'it fell on rock and the wind carried it away'" (191–92). No form of the parable of the sower in Matthew, Mark, or Luke (or the gnostic Gospel of Thomas) has the seed on the rocky soil blown away by the wind. Instead, the seed on the rock started to grow but soon "withered away." This mutated form of the parable perhaps indicates that Francis Tarwater is not an adequate herald of the gospel message.

But then neither, obviously, is Rayber, not only in his explicit denial of belief but also in his confusing of the message: in his response to Francis, he ironically mixes metaphors (parables) by combining the parable of the sower with an element of the parable of the wheat and weeds (which directly follows the sower parable in Matthew 13:18–30): "'Goddam you!' he said in a breathless harsh voice. 'It fell in us both alike. The difference is that I know it's in me and I keep it under control. I weed it out but you're too blind to know it's in you'" (192). Rayber then advises Francis that the wisest thing would be to be like him: "Face it, and fight it, to cut down the weed every time you see it appear" (195). He argues that in this respect he and Francis are similar: the "way they have to fight it is the same" (196). Both are attempting to weed out the deeply implanted "seed" that the elder Tarwater sowed in them. The boy adamantly rejects Rayber's view, though: "It ain't the same. . . . I can pull it up by its roots, once and for all. I can do something. I ain't like you. All you can do is think what you would have done if you had done it. Not me. I can do it. I can act" (196). Ironically, both Rayber and young Francis are speaking of pulling out the "good seed" of the kingdom of heaven (Matt. 13:24), the opposite of the parable, which even rejects pulling out the evil weeds that the "enemy" had sown (Matt. 13:30).

And Francis soon does act. He takes Bishop alone to the lake and decides to drown him to prove that he is not a prophet (210). In doing so, however, he also (by "accident") baptizes Bishop (216). From his hotel room, Rayber hears Bishop "bellow," and he intuitively knows what has happened: that Francis has "baptized the child even as he drowned him." Yet Rayber, this time, "continued to feel nothing . . . there would be no pain" (203). It appears, then, that Rayber has successfully eradicated the seed that was implanted in him, since even his love and concern for Bishop have withered completely away (cf. his "horrifying love" of Bishop, who he believed was "formed in the image and likeness of God," 113). This seed will never bear fruit: "This love, O'Connor implies, may have been his salvation—his entry into the kingdom of heaven whose coming he had vainly awaited as a child" (McFarland 1976, 101).

Eventually, however, Francis realizes that he cannot escape his mission. The implanted seed will continue to grow: like Daniel, Elijah, and Moses, Francis knows that the "fire" will speak to him, and it soon does; it happens when he throws himself on old Tarwater's grave: "He heard the command. GO WARN THE CHILDREN OF GOD OF THE TERRIBLE SPEED OF MERCY. The words were as silent as seeds opening one at a time in his blood" (O'Connor 2007, 242). Finally, then, the seeds that young Francis earlier said were planted on a rock (191–92) are now in his own blood.

An element of the Gospel's interpretation of the parable—after the sower sows the "word of the kingdom," Satan "comes and snatches away what is sown in the heart" (Matt. 13:19)—is also drawn on in the novel. Satan appears initially in the voice of "the stranger" as Francis attempts to carry out old Tarwater's request to be buried ten feet deep (13; the voice also reflects Francis's dark, rebellious inner self; cf. the voice's insistence that there is no devil, 39), and Satan's influence grows over the course of the novel. By the time Francis decides to drown Bishop, the "stranger" is now called his "friend" and his "mentor" (215). Yet, even though Satan helps to persuade Tarwater to drown Bishop, Satan ultimately is unsuccessful, because in that act, "suddenly in a high raw voice the defeated boy [Francis] cried out the words of baptism, shuddered, and opened his eyes. He heard the sibilant oaths of his friend fading away on the darkness" (216). Satan is active in this novel, but in the end—and after a horrifying amount of violence and difficulties, some committed by Francis and some committed on him—Francis accepts his prophetic task. As O'Connor wrote elsewhere, "the devil accomplishes a good deal of groundwork that seems to be necessary before grace is effective" (1969, 125). Or, as O'Connor commented before a reading of "A Good Man Is Hard to Find" at Hollins College in 1963: "I have found that violence is strangely capable of returning my characters to reality and preparing them to accept their moment of grace. Their heads are so hard that almost nothing else will do the work" (112).

In this novel O'Connor writes, in part, as a prophet who criticizes aspects of the prevailing consciousness of modernity in the dominant culture and who seeks to energize those within the community of faith (Kilcourse 2001, 210–12). Although O'Connor was correctly concerned that modern readers would tend to identify with Rayber, Rayber stands as a primary example of the faults of such modernity; he does not have the "ears to hear" (i.e., he cannot hear without his hearing aid; O'Connor 2007, 87) or "eyes to see" (i.e., his eyesight is limited without his glasses, his "twin glass caverns," 88). For O'Connor, in contrast, "it is the old man who speaks for me" (1979, 350). As she writes in a 1957 letter to "A": "I'm still not sure about that title [*The Violent Bear It Away*] but it's something for me to lean on in my conception of the book. And more than ever now it seems that the kingdom of heaven has to be taken by violence, or not at all. You have to push as hard as the age that pushes against you" (O'Connor 1979, 261). Evil, O'Connor believes, is not a problem to be solved; instead, it is "a mystery to be endured" (1969, 209). It is not by chance that three of the four types of seeds in the sower parable do not bear fruit (e.g., Matt. 13:19, where Satan "comes and snatches away what is sown in the heart"; cf. Mark 4:15).

O'Connor's novels and short stories cannot be fully understood without an understanding of how her faith forms the foundation for her writings. Even characters that seem grotesque are on a quest for God and God's grace in a secular and often disturbing world (see Simpson 2005, 27). For O'Connor, the central aspect of human existence is that humanity "has for all its horror, been found by God to be worth dying for" (O'Connor 1987, 45). Human beings must choose constantly between good and evil, because they inhabit a world in which evil and the devil have real existence and engage human beings in a "constant spiritual battle." Humans are depraved; they stumble and fall into sin, are filled with pride, and therefore are in desperate need of God's grace. Many of her characters, therefore, reach a point where they either accept or reject God's grace (Simpson 2005, 52). In O'Connor's stories, joyful resolutions, like a "good man," are hard to find. The world her stories create is often brutal, grotesque, and shocking, but, for O'Connor, the essence of Christian love is to engage directly with those who suffer, and the good news in the midst of suffering is that there are moments in which God's grace is available, sometimes in unlikely ways and surprising places: "O'Connor clearly has hope for the spiritual state of humanity and keeps a door into grace perpetually open for characters in her story who most desperately need it" (Simpson 2005, 68–69).

Martin Luther King Jr. (1929–1968)

Martin Luther King Jr. was the son and grandson of prominent pastors of Ebenezer Baptist Church in Atlanta, Georgia. King graduated from Morehouse College in 1948; Crozer Seminary in 1951, where he was first in his class; and Boston University in 1955, where he earned a PhD in systematic theology. In 1954 King became pastor of Dexter Avenue Baptist Church in Montgomery, Alabama. He also became the leader of the Montgomery Improvement Association and thus the primary leader of the Montgomery Bus Boycott, which began after Rosa Parks's arrest. In 1957, the Southern Christian Leadership Conference was formed with King elected as president, and in 1959 King returned to Atlanta, where he served as copastor, along with his father, of Ebenezer Baptist Church.

During his years as a leader in the civil rights movement, King published many important works, including *Letter from the Birmingham Jail* (1963), *Strength to Love* (1963), *Why We Can't Wait* (1964), and *Where Do We Go from Here?* (1967). King also was awarded the 1964 Nobel Peace Prize when he was only thirty-five. His emphases also included basic human rights and economic justice for all people. King created, for example, the "Poor People's Campaign" in November 1967, which focused on jobs (full employment), unemployment insurance, low-income housing, and raising the minimum wage. As part of those efforts, he went to Memphis, Tennessee, to support striking sanitation workers. He was assassinated on April 4, 1968, as he stood on the second-story balcony at the Lorraine Hotel.

In 1966 King began working for economic equality in Chicago, with the Chicago Freedom Movement, an organization that advocated for fair housing, community development, quality education, fair wages and employment, and a number of other issues. King's sermon on the rich fool parable, "Why Jesus Called a Man a Fool," delivered at Chicago's Mount Pisgah Missionary

Baptist Church in 1967, should be seen in the context of his efforts to promote socioeconomic equality in Chicago.

During the summer when King preached this sermon in the heart of the Chicago slums, where he had lived and worked just a year earlier, race riots had occurred in Newark, Cleveland, Detroit, and other cities. Although King opposed this violence, he argued that white society bore ultimate responsibility for the racism and oppression that led to this rage, and he urged President Lyndon Johnson to focus on the underlying problem: unemployment. King's sermon focused on the evils of materialism and stressed human dependence upon God and interdependence with other human beings (Burns 2004, 352).

Although the rich man in the parable, King said, was successful "by all modern standards" and "would abound with social prestige and community respectability," Jesus, a Galilean peasant, had the audacity to call him a fool (M. King 2012, 69). The man was foolish, King argued, because his economic well-being absorbed all of his thoughts, and he ignored what was most important: "The richer this man became materially the poorer he became intellectually and spiritually" (71). As the man's self-centered soliloquy demonstrates by its use of the first-person singular pronoun twelve times, the rich man was foolish also because he failed to realize his dependence upon others. He did not realize that other human beings contributed to his material wealth. King then applied the parable to the wealthy United States, used the sheep and goats parable as a prescription for how such a wealthy nation should use its resources in an interdependent world, and echoed the words of Theophylact (chap. 2 above) about the best "storehouses" for the excess food:

> When an individual or a nation overlooks this interdependence, we find a tragic foolishness. We can clearly see the meaning of this parable for the present world crisis. Our nation's productive machinery constantly brings forth such an abundance of food that we must build larger barns and spend more than a million dollars daily to store our surplus. Year after year we ask, "What shall I do, because I have no room where to bestow my fruits?" I have seen an answer in the faces of millions of poverty-stricken men and women in Asia, Africa, and South America. I have seen an answer in the appalling poverty on the Mississippi Delta and the tragic insecurity of the unemployed in large industrial cities of the North. What can we do? The answer is simple: feed the poor, clothe the naked, and heal the sick. Where can we store our goods? Again the answer is simple: we can store our surplus food free of charge in the shriveled stomachs of the millions of God's children who go to bed hungry at night. We can use our vast resources of wealth to wipe poverty from the earth. (72)

The rich man was foolish also because "he failed to realize his dependence on God" (73). Such foolishness in modern times, King observed, results in materialism or replacing faith in God with faith in science. The foolishness of expecting science to usher in a better world disappeared, however, in "the explosion of this myth" in the horrors of Nagasaki and Hiroshima (75). Physical power, unless it is controlled by spiritual power, will lead to our doom, as the rich fool's lack of spiritual power led to his: "Without dependence on God our efforts turn to ashes and our sunrises into darkest night" (76). Unfortunately, King noted, the rich man was foolishly unaware of this dependence on God and on others, and

> may it not be that the "certain rich man" is Western civilization? Rich in goods and material resources, our standards of success are almost inextricably bound to the lust for acquisition. The means by which we live are marvelous indeed. And yet something is missing. We have learned to fly the air like birds and swim the sea like fish, but we have not learned the simple art of living together as brothers. Our abundance has brought us neither peace of mind nor serenity of spirit. (76–77)

King closed the sermon by paraphrasing a question asked by Jesus: "What shall it profit a man, if he gain the whole world of externals—airplanes, electric lights, automobiles, and color television—and lose the internal—his own soul?" (78).

An interesting similar use of the sheep and goats parable is found in a sermon that also denounced militarism, "The Drum Major Instinct," the last sermon King preached at Ebenezer Baptist Church. Instead of wanting to be first in such trivial matters as wealth or fame, King said, one should strive to be first in love, first in moral excellence, and first in generosity. But, he said, nations can also suffer from this impulse, when they struggle for supremacy. King did not spare the United States from indictment for the instinct to want to "rule the world":

> I am sad to say that the nation in which we live is the supreme culprit. And I'm going to continue to say it to America, because I love this country too much to see the drift that it has taken.
>
> God didn't call America to do what she is doing in the world now. God didn't call America to engage in a senseless, unjust war. We have committed more war crimes almost than any nation in the world, and I'm going to continue to say it. And we won't stop it because of our pride, and our arrogance as a nation.

King sorrowfully said that God has a way of putting prideful nations such as ancient Babylon, Israel, and Rome, "in their place," and he saw frightening parallels between the United States and those ancient civilizations (M. King 2015, 188–89).

As Jesus said, however, true greatness means being the servant of all, and Jesus lived his own life in that way (189–90). Then, using the parable of the sheep and goats, King turned the spotlight on himself to illustrate the importance of serving others:

> If any of you are around when I have to meet my day, I don't want a long funeral. And if you get somebody to deliver the eulogy, tell them not to talk too long. Every now and then I wonder what I want them to say. . . .
>
> I'd like somebody to mention that day, that Martin Luther King, Jr., tried to give his life serving others. I'd like for somebody to say that day that Martin Luther King, Jr., tried to love somebody. I want you to say that day, that I tried to be right on the war question. I want you to be able to say that day, that I did try, in my life, to feed the hungry. And I want you to be able to say that day, that I did try, in my life, to clothe those who were naked. I want you to say, on that day, that I did try, in my life, to visit those who were in prison. I want you to say that I tried to love and serve humanity.
>
> Yes, if you want to say that I was a drum major, say that I was a drum major for justice; say that I was a drum major for peace; I was a drum major for righteousness. And all of the other shallow things won't matter. . . . I just want to leave a committed life behind. (191)

On April 9, 1968, about two months later, excerpts of the sermon were played at Dr. Martin Luther King Jr.'s funeral at Ebenezer Baptist Church.

King preached on the parable of the good Samaritan numerous times in his career (the most famous sermon being "I See the Promised Land," which King preached on April 3, 1968, the last night of his life). The parable plays a major role in one of King's most significant sermons, "A Time to Break Silence," an address at Riverside Church in New York City, on April 4, 1967. In this sermon, King very publicly opposed the Vietnam War and linked his opposition directly to the civil rights movement. Opposing the war meant opposing President Johnson (who was escalating the war), with whom King had worked to pass the civil rights and voting rights bills, and who had announced the War on Poverty. King thought, however, that the War on Poverty had shown great promise for helping to reduce poverty but then profligate spending on the Vietnam War eviscerated those poverty programs. The war against the people of Vietnam had also become a war against the poor in the United States. In addition, the Vietnam War was being fought by an extraordinarily disproportional number of black young men "to guarantee liberties in Southeast Asia which they had not found in Southwest Georgia and East Harlem" (2015, 203–4).

King could not keep silent in the face of "such cruel manipulation of the poor," but there was one other concern that led him to speak out passionately against the war. For years he had preached that social change should be achieved through nonviolent social action, but now the United States government was using massive violence to bring about change in Vietnam. King realized: "I knew that I could never again raise my voice against the violence of the oppressed in the ghettos without having first spoken clearly to the greatest purveyor of violence in the world today—my own government" (204).

That line—that the United States was "the greatest purveyor of violence in the world today"—was a shocking pronouncement for the majority of Americans, who saw themselves as the preeminent force for good in the world.

King lamented the atrocities that the United States had committed against the Vietnamese people and spoke as a civil rights leader "to save the soul of America" (207–8). He called for an end to the war and also for reparations for the damage the United States had done in Vietnam. Yet he also called for a much deeper change of heart: a radical revolution of values through which the United States would shift from a "thing-oriented" society to a "person-oriented" society, one that would conquer the "giant triplets" of racism, materialism, and militarism (214). Here King cited the parable of the good Samaritan to illustrate true compassion upon one's "enemies":

> A true revolution of values will soon cause us to question the fairness and justice of many of our past and present policies. On the one hand, we are called to play the Good Samaritan on life's roadside, but that will be only an initial act. One day we must come to see that the whole Jericho Road must be transformed so that men and women will not be constantly beaten and robbed as they make their journey on life's highway. True compassion is more than flinging a coin to a beggar. It comes to see that an edifice which produces beggars needs restructuring. A true revolution of values will soon look uneasily on the glaring contrast of poverty and wealth. . . . A true revolution of values will lay hand on the world order and say of war, "This way of settling differences is not just." This business of burning human beings with napalm, of filling our nation's homes with orphans and widows, of injecting poisonous drugs of hate into the veins of peoples normally humane, of sending men home from dark and bloody battlefields physically handicapped and psychologically deranged, cannot be reconciled with wisdom, justice, and love. A nation that continues year after year to spend more money on military defense than on programs of social uplift is approaching spiritual death. (214–15)

King's opposition to the war in Vietnam not only provoked the wrath of President Johnson; it also brought vehement denunciations in the media, including the *New York Times* and the *Washington Post*, and in 1967 King's antiwar position was extremely unpopular among U.S. citizens overall (Dyson 2000, 61).

King is most often memorialized by images and videos of his famous "I Have a Dream" speech, which contributes to the process of "sanitizing" essential elements of his radical Christian message about social justice (Yanco 2014, xi). King, however, not only helped lead a nonviolent movement against racism and for equality, but he also actively fought against materialism, militarism, and economic exploitation and for social and economic justice. Few remember, for example, that King called for such things as a guaranteed annual income, which meant that the United States would guarantee a minimum amount of money be paid to every citizen of the United States so that all people could afford decent housing, food, health care, and education (a form of this idea was later proposed by President Richard Nixon in 1969 in his "Family Assistance Plan"; cf. Yanco 2014, 37).

As his sermons about the parables illustrate, King believed that racial and economic injustices would never be solved without a radical redistribution of political and economic power, and he prophetically denounced the evils of capitalism and militarism just as he denounced the evils of racism.

Godspell (Film, 1973)

Godspell, in many ways an artifact of the early 1970s, is distinctive because it incorporates the parables of Jesus more extensively than any other film about Jesus. The film is based on a play written by John-Michael Tebelak while he was a graduate student at Carnegie Mellon. After attending a disappointing Easter service, Tebelak attempted to write a play that treated the Gospels in a simple and joyful way: "I wanted to make it the simple, joyful message that I felt the first time that I read [the Gospels] and recreate the sense of community, which I did not share when I went to that service" (Giere 2008, 45). Part of the simplicity and joy of the play, *The Godspell*, as it was originally titled, was created by characters dressed as clowns acting out the parables of Jesus, an aspect inspired by Harvey Cox's *The Feast of Fools*, which includes the concept of "Christ the clown" who brings joy (Laird 2014, 15).

The Godspell was a great success at Carnegie Mellon, and in early 1971 was performed in New York City at the La MaMa Experimental Theatre club. It then reopened as *Godspell* at Cherry Lane Theater in May 1971, with a new musical score and lyrics by Stephen Schwartz. The off-Broadway play became a great success, especially after cast members sang the song "Day by

Day" (which reached number 11 on the top-40 charts in 1972) on *The Today Show* on NBC. After that appearance, the play was sold out for virtually every performance (Giere 2008, 67). It became the third-longest-running off-Broadway play in history.

The 1973 film adaption of the play begins with John the Baptist gathering a diverse group of eight disciples out of the crowds of New York City—a student (Lynne), actress (Gilmer), waitress (Katie), professional woman (Robin), taxi driver (Jeffrey), parking lot attendant (Jerry), ballet dancer (Joanne), and clothes delivery man (Merrell)—while blowing a shofar and then singing the song "Prepare Ye the Way of the Lord."

After John baptizes these eight new followers in Bethesda Fountain in Central Park, Jesus appears clad only in underwear and with clown-like makeup, including a red heart on his forehead. John the Baptist also baptizes him, and Jesus is suddenly dressed in a Superman shirt, with striped pants and suspenders, a carnation, and clown shoes. Jesus begins to sing, "Save the People," and the nine other people begin to follow him. The disciples are also clothed in mismatched, clown-like clothes, and they sing along as they make their way through a now eerily deserted New York City.

Jesus and his new followers end up in a junkyard that becomes a playground for speaking and visually representing Jesus's teachings. Jesus paints the faces of his new followers and then begins to teach them, beginning with selections from the Sermon on the Mount. The group's antics, like Jesus's teachings, present an alternative reality—what life should be like in the kingdom of heaven. A whimsical and playful Jesus and his whimsical and playful followers speak of and perform that kingdom for us—and they build a community of believers in doing so (Walsh 2003, 84).

Jesus's parables dominate the nonmusical sections of the first hour of the film, and they include (in order) the parables of the Pharisee and the tax collector, the unforgiving slave, the sheep and goats, the good Samaritan, the rich man and Lazarus, the sower, and the prodigal son, all of which are spoken and acted out in creative ways (cf. Tatum 1997, 121). Jesus, for example, does not narrate the first parable. Instead, Lynne begins: "Two men went up to the Temple to pray. One, a Pharisee. And the other, a tax gatherer" (*Godspell* 1973). Katie acts the part of the Pharisee, and when she is introduced, she gets cheers and applause. Jeffrey performs the tax gatherer's role, and, when he is announced, he receives boos and a cry of "shame."

Lynne continues: "And the Pharisee, he just stood around and prayed," and Katie speaks her part: "I thank thee O God that I am not like other men: greedy, dishonest, adulterous. Or for that matter like that tax gatherer. I pray twice a week; get that? Twice a week. And pay taxes on all that I get." The crowd responds with cheers of approval, echoing the standard understanding of the Pharisee as a respected member of society.

Lynne turns to Jeffrey: "But the other kept his distance and would not even raise his eyes to the good Lord in heaven. I said the Good Lord in heaven, child. And he beat upon his breast, saying . . . ," and Jeffrey chimes in to speak his part: "O God, have mercy on me, sinner that I am." The crowd of followers moans their disapproval, once again echoing society's condemnation of such reprobates. At this critical juncture, Jesus finally interrupts to give an authoritative interpretation: "And it was this man, I tell you"—here his followers already are in disbelief, even before Jesus states the case: "What? You've got to be kidding!"— "and not the other,' who went off acquitted of his sins. For every man who exalts himself [as Katie the "Pharisee" falls through a card table] shall be humbled. But every man who humbles himself . . ."—the film here depicts the disciples being convinced by Jesus's arguments: they celebrate by throwing Jeffrey up in the air in a blanket and join with Jesus to finish the saying: "shall be exalted!"

By opening with this parable, the film immediately establishes that God is a forgiving God and that sometimes God's forgiveness defies human expectations and cultural conventions. The implications of this forgiveness also become immediately clear, because Jesus resumes the Sermon on the Mount material to proclaim that human beings who are angry or in disputes should reconcile and forgive one another. This theme is clearly advanced in the parable that immediately follows, that of the unforgiving slave.

Merrell, not Jesus, narrates the parable. As he describes the king to whom the debt of "millions" is owed (ten thousand talents in Matt. 18:23–35), Robin starts playing the role of the king, climbs up on a truck, and places a mock crown on her head. The other disciples sing "yeah, yeah" after each line of the narration. As Merrell continues his narration of the story, the other disciples actively participate, either in singing numerous responses or acting out the roles of the two debtors—Jeffrey plays the role of the first servant, and Jerry plays the role of the second. Other disciples join in to narrate—John the Baptist, Gilmer, and Lynne each take turns—but once again Jesus supplies the moral of the story at the end: "And that is how my Heavenly Father will deal with you unless you forgive your brothers and sisters from your hearts."

This parable causes an epiphany for Robin, and she sings "Day by Day" in response, thus becoming the first disciple to declare that she follows Jesus. This is a major step toward the various characters pledging their loyalty to Jesus, stating their belief, and having the faith to become a member of the community forming around Jesus and his teachings. To a large extent the majority of the first part of the film consists of the "clown" Jesus inspiring his disciples, mostly through parables, to listen, understand, and believe in very profound insights about love, caring for one another, integrity, humility, and service (Giere 2008, 57).

The next parable, that of the sheep and goats, reinforces that this universal kingdom includes everyone. This time Jesus narrates the parable, while the disciples act out the various roles, separating themselves into "sheep" and "goats." Jeffrey, a "goat," tries to sneak into the group of sheep, but Jesus prevents him and says, "Sorry! No goats!" Two sheep, Robin and Jerry, ask Jesus when they saw him hungry and gave him food, thirsty and gave him drink, or in prison and helped him. Jesus responds, "Anything you did for one of your brothers, however humble, you did for me."

Jesus then turns to the goats and says: "A curse is upon you! Anything you did not do for one of my brothers, however humble, you did not do for me!" Jesus adds that the goats "will take their place in eternal punishment, but the righteous shall have eternal life!" He then says, "Come on!" to the sheep, and they all run up the steps, to the great disappointment of the goats at the bottom of the steps. Here, however, an interesting twist in the parable occurs. Jesus returns to the top of the stairs, smiles, gestures at the goats, and says again, "Come on!" The four goats delightedly scamper up the steps, and then Judas does as well (at some indeterminate point in the film the John the Baptist character becomes Judas). They all receive hugs as they rejoin the group, designating that all can be saved in *Godspell*'s kingdom of heaven.

After the next two parables, the good Samaritan and the rich man and Lazarus, which emphasize the responsibilities that human beings have to take care of one another, the film portrays a dialogue between Jesus and Judas. This dialogue—done, as often is the case, in a vaudeville-like way—perhaps illustrates the whimsical nature of the *Godspell* Jesus and the dialogic nature of parables themselves:

Jesus: Now, how can you take a speck of sawdust out of your brother's eye when all the time there's this great plank in your own?

Judas: I don't know. How can you take the speck of sawdust in your brother's eye when all the time there's this great plank in your own?

Jesus: You hypocrite! First you take the plank out of your own eye so you can see clearly to take the speck of sawdust out of your brother's.

Judas: Wait a moment! That's no answer to the question.

Jesus: Did I promise you an answer to the question?

Judas: No.

After an interpretation of the sower parable and the song "All Good Gifts," which demonstrates that God is behind the growth of the seeds (e.g., the parable of the seed growing secretly; Mark 4:26–29) and that all good things come from God, the group ends up at Cherry Lane Theater, the off-Broadway location where the play became a success. It is there that the group narrates and acts out the parable of the prodigal son. Jesus plays the piano in the theater, as was done during the era of silent films, and the interpretation of the parable includes a drama acted out by the disciples and clips of silent films to illustrate various scenes.

Jesus begins the narration, in comic voice, and others in the group, often in comic voices, take turns narrating the story. Various scenes from silent films are interspersed throughout the narration and enactment of the parable; these clips are often humorous (e.g., when the prodigal returns home, the film clip shows a man riding a camel down a flight of steps and a man apparently running on top of water) and include famous silent-film-era actors, such as Buster Keaton and Charlie Chaplin. These clips are shown after almost every key line, and sometimes the characters act out the parable in concert with scenes from these silent films.

Unlike the parable, but similar to other interpretations of the parable over the centuries, *Godspell* provides a happy reconciliation of the siblings. Initially, the older brother refuses to come inside the house and join the celebration. The father, however—who wears a huge cowboy hat and speaks with an exaggerated "Western" accent—walks across the stage to speak with his older son: "My boy . . . you have always been with me, and everything I have is yours. Now could we help but celebrate on this happy day, for your brother here was dead and has come back to life—metaphorically speaking. Was lost and he's found." As he is speaking, the father brings the older brother across the stage to meet the prodigal. The brothers initially refuse even to look at each other and turn away. After looking at Jesus, who nods at him, the father comically knocks the brothers' heads together; they fall to their knees and hug as their father says, "Them's my boys." The scene ends with the whole group cheering and applauding enthusiastically the complete restoration of community within the family.

Godspell is distinctive among Jesus films because it incorporates parables so deeply into its narrative of Jesus's life and teachings. Jesus proclaims the kingdom of God, and the kingdom is created within the community formed around him. This community, however, grows and develops outside any interactions with other people, except for the robot that symbolizes the opposition to Jesus and the police cars that drive up near the end of the film right before Jesus's death. At the end of the film, the community apparently vanishes as New York City comes back to life; crowds once again fill the streets, and the film leaves unanswered the question of the harvest in the parable of the sower: Will these followers of Jesus become the seed "sown on the good soil" that would "bear fruit, thirty and sixty and a hundred-fold" (Mark 4:20)?

Two Latin American Receptions

The Peasants of Solentiname

In 1966, a Nicaraguan priest named Ernesto Cardenal and a Colombian poet named William Agudelo founded a small contemplative community on the largest island of Solentiname, an archipelago of thirty-eight islands on Lake Nicaragua. The approximately one thousand people of Solentiname (ca. 1970–1982) formed a fishing and farming cooperative, a clinic, a center for artists, a museum of pre-Colombian art found in Solentiname, and a school of primitive painting that became internationally famous.

As part of his mission, Cardenal decided that instead of preaching on the Gospel readings during Sunday mass and other services, he and his congregation would have conversations about those texts. Cardenal later published a collection of these dialogues among those nonspecialist voices within "grassroots" Christianity. Cardenal declares: "The commentaries of the *campesinos* [peasant farmers] are usually of greater profundity than that of many theologians, but of a simplicity like that of the Gospel itself. This is not surprising: The *Gospel* or 'Good News' (to the poor) was written for them, and by people like them" (Cardenal 1976, vii).

The process for these dialogues followed a similar pattern from one week to the next. The Gospel reading was distributed to all in the congregation who could read, and the passage was read aloud so all could participate. The *campesinos* discussed the passage verse by verse, and Cardenal used a tape recorder during the discussions, so that he could preserve the insights of his congregation in written commentaries (Cardenal 1976, viii–x).

Although these commentaries contain common themes about God's love and liberation, the people involved in these dialogues have distinctive and often different reactions to the Gospel text they discuss. The peasants' interpretations of the parable of the rich man and Lazarus (Cardenal 1979, 251–56), for example, quickly lead them into the topics of the rich and poor, salvation and damnation. Felipe begins the discussion by stating that the rich man symbolizes all who are rich and Lazarus denotes all who are poor. He concludes that the story is simple: Jesus condemns the rich, and the poor are saved. Cardenal notes that the rich man is never called evil; he is only called rich. Others respond to this observation bluntly:

> Little Adan: "Because he was happy."
> Elvis: "While the other was screwed."

Cardenal notes that Abraham has the same response in Luke 16:25. Felipe then interprets the parable to mean that there should be no rich or poor; all should live equally both in this world and the next. Alejo agrees: the rich man should not have thrown parties every day—just every once in a while—and he should have invited Lazarus to those parties.

As the congregation interprets the parable in their Nicaraguan contexts, their earthy and apparently simple responses often contain profound expressions of their conviction that Jesus and his parables are alive, present with them, and actively working with and through them:

> Gloria: The rich man's sin was that he had no compassion. Poverty was at his door and that didn't disturb him at his parties.
> Julio: Now there are lots of Lazaruses that the rich have at their doors of their parties.
> Cardenal: And the poor man is badly off because the rich man is well off, or the rich man is well off because the poor man is badly off. There are poor people because there are rich people, and there are rich people because there are poor people. And rich people's parties are at the cost of the poor people. (Cardenal 1979, 252; cf. Gowler 2005)

William takes the interpretation even further. He notes that the parable is commonly used to exploit the poor by persuading them to endure their poverty patiently in the expectation that they will receive their reward in heaven. Felipe agrees:

> Felipe: As I see it, this passage was rather to threaten the rich so they wouldn't go on exploiting; but it seems it turned out the opposite: it served to pacify the people. . . .
> Julio: There is no point in this story being for [the rich] if they don't read it, and if they do read it they pay no heed. The rich man of this parable cares nothing for God; and that's the way the rich still are nowadays.

Cardenal: I believe the parable was not to console the poor but rather to threaten the rich; but, as you said, William, it has had the opposite effect, because the rich weren't going to heed it. But Christ himself is saying that in this parable: that the rich pay no attention to the Bible.

Laureano: In the churches in the big cities you see exactly the same picture that's painted here. . . .

Felipe: Because for [the rich] it's like reading a bunch of nonsense. . . .

Oscar: It seems like it doesn't do any good to be reading the Bible, then, because if you don't want to change the social order, you might as well be reading any damned thing, you might as well be reading any stupid book.

Cardenal: It seems to me that Jesus' principal message is that the rich aren't going to be convinced even with the Bible, not even with a dead man coming to life (and not even with Jesus' resurrection . . .). (Cardenal 1979, 253–55)

Elvis argues that the parable teaches that humanity should not continue with these two classes of rich and poor; the goal should be to eliminate such economic disparities. William responds that the wealthy are ultimately responsible: "Abraham has told the rich man who is being damned that there is an 'abyss' between him and the other man. There is an impassable, total separation. And it's the rich man who has placed that abyss of separation between the two of them" (255–56).

Such readings of Gospel texts proved dangerous. In October 1977, the Somoza regime destroyed the Solentiname community, and Cardenal and others joined the Sandinistas fighting against the Somoza government. In his "Letter to the People of Nicaragua," Cardenal argues that it was the reading and discussing of these Gospel texts that persuaded him to join the Sandinistas:

> The Gospel is what most radicalized us politically. Every Sunday in Mass we discussed the Gospel in a dialogue with the peasants. With admirable simplicity and profound theology, they began to understand the core of the Gospel message: the announcement of the kingdom of God. That is, the establishment on this earth of a just society, without exploiters or exploited, with all goods in common, just like the society in which the first Christians lived. But above all else the Gospel taught us that the word of God is not only to be heard, but also to be put into practice. (Cardenal 1982, 272)

After Somoza was overthrown, some of the surviving peasants returned to Solentiname to rebuild the community and the artists' colony. José Arana, for example, painted his own interpretation of this parable (*The Rich Epicure and Poor Lazarus*; see figure 5.2). In his painting, the rich man sits at his table, which is covered by a white tablecloth and abundant food and drink. There is more than enough to share, but the man sits alone. He is dressed in nice jeans, with a shirt and vest, and his hair is neatly trimmed. The room is brightly painted in purple, orange, and yellow, but the interior does not contain much furniture: his table and chair, a stand with a vase of flowers on it, and a pew-like bench with a small rug in front of it. Tellingly, a book appears on the bench, most likely the unopened Bible, which this rich man ignores in practice. Two windows and one door are open, revealing lush surroundings and a beautiful day. Through the window on the left, a bird is visible in the distance, perhaps a reminder of how Jesus urged his listeners to "look at the birds of the air" and not worry about what they would eat and drink (Matt. 6:25–26).

Lazarus stands, not lies, just inside the door, not outside the gate. The rich man looks straight at him; he can definitely see him and observe his misery. Lazarus is dressed in cutoff jeans and a ripped T-shirt. His hair is long and unkempt; bleeding sores are visible in numerous places—they cover his face, arms, legs, and feet—and he wears rag bandages on his left arm and ankle. A dog stands before him, starting to lick his sores, thereby giving him the attention the rich man does not. By painting the two men in this fashion, the artist makes eminently clear that the rich man, who completely ignores

Figure 5.2 José Arana, *The Rich Epicure and Poor Lazarus*

Lazarus standing just a few feet directly in front of him, indeed created his own chasm and thus deserves his ultimate fate, as the Solentiname peasants many years before had decided.

Elsa Tamez (1951–)

The peasants of Solentiname responded to the parables in the contexts of political and economic oppression, but parables can also be interpreted in light of other aspects of oppression. Elsa Tamez, for example, is a leading proponent of Latin American liberation theology from a feminist perspective. An emerita professor of biblical studies at the Latin American Biblical University in San Jose, Costa Rica, Tamez has analyzed biblical texts in ways that illuminate elements of oppression often overlooked by interpreters. Her first book, *Bible of the Oppressed* (1982), for example, argues that God's self-revelation clearly indicates that "God is on the side of the subjugated" (1–2), God seeks to liberate the oppressed, and God desires that a new and just social order be created (60–61). The principal motive for oppression is the desire to pile up wealth, Tamez says, and the reason the Bible opposes the rich and seeks the liberation of the poor is not that riches themselves are evil, but that the oppressors acquired their riches "at the expense of their neighbors" (71–73).

In Latin America, Tamez notes, many people now interpret the Bible as a "simple text that speaks of a loving, just, liberating God who accompanies the poor in their suffering and their struggle through human history" (1994, 190). In the context of oppression, hunger, unemployment, war, and other suffering, grassroots readings of the Bible give it new meaning and provide ways in which the Bible can be rediscovered when read from the perspective of the poor. Even in this context, however, women find cases in Scripture that clearly marginalize or segregate them. Such texts are used in modern patriarchal sexist societies to claim that women's marginalization is a biblical principle. The inferiority of women is enshrined and reinforced in modern society because it is viewed as being "written [in] the word of God" (192–93).

The parables offer a distinctive interpretive problem because they are dominated by male characters, such as kings, farmers, builders, judges, stewards, bridegrooms, sons, fathers, priests, and rich and poor men. The few women featured are ten bridesmaids, a woman asking a judge for mercy, a woman looking for a lost coin, and "a handful of unspecified wives, mothers, and daughters" (Slee 1990, 41; cf. Gowler 2000, 78–84). Women are not only anonymous in the parables; they are also almost invisible. A feminist reading can look beyond this surface invisibility to find numerous images and scenes in the parables that are "uniquely evocative of women's lives" and therefore speak deeply to them in ways that are sometimes difficult to see, such as in domestic scenes and parables of celebration and feasting (Slee 1990, 41).

The first step is to distance oneself from established interpretations and to come to the text almost as a first-time visitor with few or no presuppositions about what a text means. The second step is to read the text with the understanding that God is on the side of the oppressed—the "hermeneutic key" found in Scripture itself (Tamez 1994, 198). The third step is to read the entire Bible (i.e., not just texts that include or involve women) from a woman's perspective, a step that involves including other oppressed "sectors" besides the poor. In this way, interpreters come "closer" to the Bible, being able to apply these texts to their daily lives. This new way of reading the Bible should result, Tamez declares, not only in experiencing God but also in a practice of justice and caring for other human beings (Tamez 1989, 4, 150).

Tamez demonstrates this approach in an innovative book, *Jesus and Courageous Women* (2001), in which she uses a fictionalized version of Lydia (Acts 16:11–15, 40) to narrate stories of courageous women who follow Jesus. Tamez hopes that such stories will motivate readers "to rethink our lives in relation to the church and to society" (vii). These testimonies of women are part of the "counter-movement" to the dominant Roman Empire that was an essential element of the Jesus movement within Palestine and the Christian movement beyond Palestine. The narration of these women's stories and the courage reflected in them highlight the liberating force of the early Christian movement, because it also includes liberation from the oppression of patriarchy.

The story narrated by "Lydia" includes stories about Mary the mother of Jesus (Tamez 2001, 13–22); Mary and Martha, the friends of Jesus (23–31); and the woman caught in adultery in John 8 (33–42). Then Lydia turns to the parable of the unjust judge. The "stubborn widow" in the parable gives Lydia encouragement to persist in her own resistance to the oppression and injustice she faces:

> The judge represented someone who was the complete opposite of the widow. She was poor, a woman, and a widow; in other words, she was vulnerable and defenseless. She had a legal case pending against someone who had wronged her. She reminds me of thousands of women today in our Greek and Roman cities, and also of our ancestors. The widow, the orphan and the foreigner are the most unprotected persons in our culture; they are frequently overlooked and their rights are denied. That is why we find that the statutes in their favor are repeated frequently in the Scriptures. (43–45)

Corrupt people, like the unjust judge, are found everywhere, which is one reason why the Hebrew Bible repeatedly demands justice for the marginalized, such as the protections for resident aliens, widows, and orphans (e.g., Exod. 22:21–22).

The woman's stubbornness and perseverance were necessary, Lydia notes, because usually those with wealth and power get their way, and the poor and powerless do not. The widow simply stood up for her rights and demanded that the judge do what was right under the law, but he continued to refuse. In this case, the widow's perseverance was her only recourse for seeking justice (45–46).

Lydia guesses that eventually the judge became afraid of the widow, or at least the situation became so scandalous that it became a public embarrassment. The unjust judge did not suddenly become just; the stubborn widow finally wore him down: "Finally she achieved her goal; her insistence and her constant demand that justice be done paid off. The judge didn't concede out of his own good will; the rights of widows did not interest him. The judge gave in because he was overcome by the widow's perseverance. The judge, an arrogant man, had to give in to the request of this poor and very stubborn widow" (46). Lydia concludes that this parable provides a paradigm for how to respond in an unjust patriarchal society. Passivity is not an option; women simply cannot allow themselves to be imprisoned in the roles a patriarchal society assigns them. Women must resist and struggle and persevere, because "Jesus provides the guarantee that justice will triumph" (47).

Another central message of this parable—and of Jesus himself—is that God is in solidarity with the poor and marginalized. God sees them as persons of worth and calls on the followers of Jesus to do likewise (50), and reading parables from the perspective of women opens one's eyes to the often-unchallenged marginalization of women. Tamez offers a reading that instead stresses their liberation from such oppression.

In her works, Tamez argues that even grassroots interpretations usually ignore difficult biblical texts, soften their oppressive content, or say that the marginalization of women in the ancient world reflected in these texts is simply not relevant for the modern world (1994, 193). Tamez counters that the central message of the Bible—and of the parables of Jesus—is profoundly liberating. Interpreters must not ascribe too much importance to the patriarchal ideology that is found in some "peripheral texts," such as Genesis 3: "The gospel's spirit of justice and freedom . . . neutralizes antifemale texts" (194). Therefore, biblical texts that reflect patriarchy, including the inferiority of women and their submission to men, are not normative, just as texts that legitimate slavery are not normative (195). The parables of Jesus, with their dearth of female characters, are an important case in point. Tamez argues that Christians are to use "militant patience" while experiencing oppression, marginalization, or even persecution—steadfastness, resistance, and heroic resistance—while continually practicing justice in their own lives (Gowler 2014, 18), just as the woman acts in the parable of the unjust judge.

David Flusser (1917–2000)

David Flusser, who was professor of early Christianity and Second Temple Judaism at the Hebrew University in Jerusalem, played a significant role in modern scholarship's recognition that Jesus and his parables should be interpreted in the context of first-century Judaism (see Gowler 2000, 42).

Flusser was born in Vienna, Austria, but his family moved to Prague, Czechoslovakia, when he was a child. He studied classic philology at Prague University, and in 1939 British Mandate authorities permitted him to immigrate to Palestine to teach Greek at the Hebrew University in Jerusalem. This emigration from Czechoslovakia, as he noted later, most likely saved his life, since the Nazis invaded that country in March 1939. Flusser received his doctorate in 1955 and then started teaching in the university's Comparative Religion Department (*Telegraph* [London], February 17, 2001, 1).

While a student in Prague, Flusser began a lifelong study of the historical Jesus and Christian origins. He discovered that, as an observant Jew, he could identify with the teachings and worldview of this first-century Jewish sage, which still have "the potential to change our world and prevent the greatest part of evil and suffering" (Flusser 2007, xviii).

Flusser's 1981 book, *Die rabbinischen Gleichnisse und der Gleichniser-zähler Jesus*, emphasizes the similarities between Jesus's parables and certain rabbinic *meshalim* (plural of *mashal*, the Hebrew term usually translated as "parable"). Flusser argues that New Testament parables and rabbinic parables share compositional similarities. These similarities include formulaic elements of diction, conventional themes, and stereotyped motifs, all of which indicate that both rabbinic parables and the parables of Jesus stem from a common narrative tradition. This common tradition has affinities with the fables of Aesop, so Flusser suggests that the antecedents of the Jewish parables can be found in Greek philosophy (Flusser 1989; Gowler 2000, 52).

The parables themselves, however, were a development within Palestine. The differences between Jesus's parables and rabbinic parables, Flusser argues, can be explained by the fact that the parables of Jesus belong to an older type of rabbinic parable, a nonexegetical, "ethical" type (Flusser also postulates an intermediate form, a parabolic proverb, which he sees reflected in Matt. 9:37–38). The differences between Jesus's parables and rabbinic parables are primarily due to a changing focus: in the rabbinic era, after the time of Jesus, the explanation of biblical passages became increasingly important.

As a test case, Flusser analyzes the parable of the pounds in Luke 19:12–27—since Flusser believes it is closer to the version told by Jesus than Matthew's parable of the talents is (25:14–30)—and finds a "process of advancement" from (a) a fable of Aesop that was developed into (b) a new form in Greek philosophy by the Greek sophist Antiphon (fifth century BCE), and finally to (c) a similar motif in the parable of the talents/pounds (1989, 9–25).

This parable follows the pattern of some Jewish parables in which property is entrusted to others and returned either intact or augmented, if circumstances permit. The owner of the property symbolizes God, who "loans" the property to human beings and expects them to develop it fully. Flusser believes that the basic meaning of the parable of the talents is that God bestows on every human being certain abilities and that all human beings therefore are obligated to be productive and to develop fully their God-given talents. In addition, the modern use of the word *talent* (ability) thus stems from the parable itself—the man entrusted the talents to the servants each according to his "ability" (Matt. 25:15; Flusser 1989, 10).

Although the parable has a tripartite structure—with three servants being entrusted with talents—the contrast is between two types of behavior: the first two servants are faithful, obedient, and productive, whereas the third servant is wicked, disobedient, and slothful. This contrast is paralleled to an unusual degree, Flusser argues, in a rabbinic parable about a king with two servants, one clever and the other foolish. The king gave both of them a measure of wheat and a bundle of flax. One servant wove the flax into a tablecloth and used the wheat to make a loaf of bread. The other did nothing (12). Although the rabbinic parable does not directly depend on Jesus's parable, Flusser concludes: "The skeleton of the two parables is identical" (13).

The third servant in Jesus's parable, because of his inordinate fear of his master, had an exaggerated sense of caution, and his caution caused him to be punished severely. This "untimely precaution," Flusser notes, is also found in Aesop's fable "The Miser," which teaches that property has value only if one enjoys it: A miser used all of his money to buy a huge amount of gold and buried it in a hidden place. He went to inspect it every day, but one day someone saw him. After the miser left, the other man dug up the gold and stole it. When the miser returned the next day, he found the gold gone and began to wail with despair. After learning what had happened, someone told him, "Do not grieve like this, my friend, because when you possessed the gold you did not possess it. So put a stone instead of the gold and deem that it is your gold, and the stone will surely fulfill the same task. For as I see, when the gold was yours, you did make no use of it" (15). Similar advice could be given to the third servant in the parable of Jesus, Flusser says, because the fable also teaches that if a treasure is hidden in a field, it is unproductive. The miser hid the gold because he was inordinately in love with it; the third servant hid the talent because he was inordinately afraid of his master (16).

Flusser then finds an ingenious adaptation of Aesop's fable by the Greek sophist Antiphon. In Antiphon's version, a wealthy man is asked for a loan but is too greedy to lend his money, even with interest being added to the debt. He is so distrustful that he decides to hide his money. Unfortunately, a third man discovers the hiding place and steals the money. When the rich man returns to find it gone, he regrets hiding his money and not lending it to the man who had asked for a loan. The money not only would have been safe, but it also would have earned interest. When he sees the man to whom he refused the loan, he laments the decision to him, but the man replies that he should hide a stone in the same place and consider that to be his money: "For even when you had it, you completely failed to use it; so that now too you can think you have lost nothing" (17). Flusser concludes: "When a person does not use a possession and will not use it in the future, what difference does it make whether he actually owns it or not?" (18).

Flusser then investigates how he thinks the theme of the parable was developed into the parable of the talents that Jesus told. Both Aesop's fable and Antiphon's version include an unwise caution that leads a man to bury property. Antiphon, however, stresses that such an action is unwise because thieves could steal the property and because the property becomes idle and unable to earn a profit. This switch of focus also changes the character of the man who hides the property from a miser with an unhealthy fascination with his property to an untrusting man who does not wish to help others. That is why Antiphon introduces a new character into the story: someone who asks the miser for a loan to be repaid with interest. Antiphon's revised fable is "a decisive element in the New Testament parable," Flusser argues, since the story "became richer and more interesting" (19) and closer to the more metaphorical parable of the talents (20–21).

Flusser concludes that Jesus's first hearers would easily understand that the parable equates God with the master and that the master's return symbolizes the reward and punishment of final judgment (20). Likewise, many of Jesus's parables focus on the kingdom of heaven, both its current presence and its future arrival. Although the rabbis also believed in the present and future kingdom of heaven, Jesus is "the only Jew of ancient times known to us who preached not only that people were on the threshold of the end of time, but that the new age of salvation had already begun." Other parables (e.g., that of the leaven; Matt. 13:33) also give evidence that Jesus believed that the kingdom of God was "erupting" in his ministry (Flusser 2007, 80–81).

Although some of Flusser's conclusions about Jesus and his parables are idiosyncratic, modern scholarship has taken to heart that the historical Jesus and his teachings must be interpreted in light of their first-century Jewish contexts. The parables, a central element of Jesus's message about the kingdom of God, were also a central element in his teachings. Therefore, to understand more fully the use and function of parables, as well as the creative understanding involved in their construction, parables must be explored in the first-century contexts in which they were spoken and heard (Gowler 2000, 66–67).

Octavia Butler (1947–2006)

At age twelve, Octavia Butler saw the science fiction film *Devil Girl from Mars*, thought it to be a "silly movie," and was convinced that she could write a better story (Francis 2010, 82). The film inspired her to embark on what would become a prolific writing career before her untimely death in 2006: her books and short stories won numerous awards, including a James Tiptree award, two Hugo awards, and two Nebula awards—science fiction's most prestigious prizes—as well as a MacArthur "genius grant" in 1995.

Butler's father died when she was an infant, and Butler and her mother survived on what her mother earned as a maid. Painfully shy, Butler coped with her difficult childhood by daydreaming, reading, and writing. She read her way through the children's section of the Pasadena (California) Public Library and, since she could not be admitted to the adult section of the library before the age of fourteen, started reading science fiction magazines. It was love at first sight. She started sending stories to publishers at age thirteen. In 1969 Butler was admitted to the Screen Writers Guild Open Door program and then enrolled in the Clarion Science Fiction Writers' Workshop, a six-week "science fiction boot camp" for aspiring writers. Butler sold two stories while attending the workshop, but she did not have another piece accepted for publication for the next five years. Finally, her novel *Patternmaster* was published in 1976, the first of her ten novels and the first of five novels in her Patternmaster series (Francis 2010, 40).

A case of writer's block hampered progress on what was to become the 1993 *Parable of the Sower* novel. For four years, Butler wrote and rewrote the first seventy-five pages of the novel, but, she says, "everything I wrote seemed

like garbage." Finally, poetry broke the logjam: poetry appears in the novel as
excerpts from *Earthseed: The Books of the Living*, a holy text written by the
main character in the novel, Lauren Oya Olamina, poetry that also echoes,
Butler notes, her own developing religious beliefs (Francis 2010, 41).

A quotation from *Earthseed* begins every chapter of the novel. The first
chapter, for example, introduces the concept of God as change, and it is written on Lauren's fifteenth birthday, July 20, 2024:

> All that you touch
> You Change
>
> All that you Change
> Changes you.
>
> The only lasting truth
> Is Change
>
> God
> Is Change (Butler 1993, 3)

Complicating the fact that Lauren is a teenager creating a new religion is that
her father is a Baptist minister, and she does not want to hurt him by telling
him that his God has stopped being her God (Butler 1993, 7). Lauren's father
is a good, pious, and educated man, but he and his religion cannot adequately
respond to the devastating changes around him, Lauren believes. Climate
change has drastically affected much of the planet, and California, where
Lauren lives, is suffering from a devastating drought. Lauren lives with her
family and a few neighbors in an enclave twenty miles from Los Angeles that
is surrounded by walls to protect them from the numerous dangers outside
that are always threatening to attack.

Butler's novel combines the story of a young woman "coming of age"
with a quest story—people searching for a place to survive and lead fulfilling
lives. But, as Mike McGonigal observes, many of Butler's works could better
be categorized as *science fact*, not science fiction: "It is imaginative writing
but it is firmly grounded in the world in which we live, where we come from,
and in the bodies and minds we inhabit, not only physically, but morally and
spiritually" (cited in Francis 2010, 134). Butler herself notes:

> I have written books about making the world a better place and how to make
> humanity more survivable. . . . The Parable series serve as fairy tales. I wrote the
> Parable books because of the direction of the country. You can call it save the
> world fiction, but it clearly doesn't save anything. It just calls people's attention

to the fact that so much needs to be done and obviously [there] are people who are running this country who don't care. I mean look at what the Congress is doing in terms of taking money away from every cause that is helping people who aren't very rich. (Francis 2010, 227)

I want to talk about what's going to happen if we keep doing what we're doing, if we keep recklessly endangering the environment, if we keep paying no attention to economic realities, if we keep paying no attention to educational needs, if we keep doing a lot of the things that are hurting us now, and that's what I wound up writing about. (Francis 2010, 220)

Lauren realizes that life within the walled enclave is unsustainable; sooner or later, their neighborhood will be attacked, looted, and destroyed (Butler 1993, 48). Most of the others in Lauren's community are deluded into thinking that if they survive long enough, the "good old days" will return. One by one, however, people in the community begin to be killed. Thieves regularly break in to steal food or other valuables, so the small community sets up patrols to guard the neighborhood at night. The attacks worsen, and for Lauren, the writing is on the wall. Lauren's long-term plan for the God-is-change Earthseed religion is to bear fruit like the seed of the sower parable that fell on the good soil. Lauren's good soil, however, is ultimately to be found on other planets: "We are all Godseed, but no more or less so than any other aspect of the universe. Godseed is all there is—all that Changes. Earthseed is all that spreads Earthlife to new earths. The universe is Godseed. Only we are Earthseed. And the Destiny of Earthseed is to take root among the stars" (71). Plants "seed themselves" both near and far to survive; they don't "sit in one place and wait to be wiped out." Thus human beings have to move both near and far to ensure their ultimate survival (71–72). Religion is the tool that Lauren (Olamina) uses to create the long-term goal of what Butler calls the "human insurance," of Earthseed taking "root among the stars," where people "go to heaven" while still alive and "save themselves." This emigration is the best way to prevent human extinction (Francis 2010, 113, 175).

It becomes clear that the community's time of relative safety is coming to an end when there are seven intrusions—three successful—by thieves into the community in less than two months. Lauren's brother Keith is killed, and then her father goes missing and is presumed dead. Even though she is no longer a Christian, Lauren takes her father's place at church the next Sunday and preaches a sermon about perseverance to the dwindling congregation of frightened people. Lauren chooses the parable of the importunate widow (unjust judge) as her text, because it tells the story of a woman who is so persistent in her demands for justice that she "wears down" the unjust judge. The moral of the parable is that the "weak can overcome the strong if the weak persist. Persisting isn't always safe, but it's often necessary" (Butler 1993, 124). Lauren's point is that the community must persist, now without her father's leadership, in order to survive: "We have God and we have each other. We have our island community, fragile, and yet a fortress. Sometimes it seems too small and too weak to survive. And like the widow in Christ's parable, its enemies fear neither God nor man. But also like the widow, it persists. *We persist.* This is our place, no matter what" (125). Lauren does not believe these words; she has been preparing to leave the little walled community for over two years, but she preaches this sermon for her father: "As much as I want all that I said to be true, it isn't. We'll be moved, all right. It's just a matter of when, by whom, and in how many pieces" (125).

The end of Lauren's walled community comes on July 31, 2027. Attackers drive a truck through the gate, loot and burn the houses, and kill many people in the community. Lauren escapes and later finds two other survivors from the community, Zahra Moss and Harry Balter, who decide to join Lauren on her trek north to find a safer place to live and where she wants to build her new community.

As Lauren, Zahra, and Harry travel north toward Oregon, they are attacked and threatened numerous times. They also very slowly and carefully begin to trust some of their fellow travelers, and a community begins to build around them. Lauren acts several times as a "good Samaritan" to help people in trouble (e.g., 186–87), and some of the recipients of her altruism join her growing community. Lauren also begins sharing some of her *Earthseed* verses with Zahra, Harry, and others who join them. She evangelically plants the seeds of "Earthseed" within her fellow travelers (note the parallels with the sower parable). As she says about one early member of the group, Travis Douglas: "I'd like to draw him into Earthseed. I'd like to draw them all in. They could be the beginnings of an Earthseed community" (203). Even then, Lauren has the "Destiny" (planting Earthseed on other planets) in mind, and Travis becomes her first convert; Zahra is her second (205). The seeds of Earthseed had finally reached fertile soil and are beginning to grow.

During the journey, Lauren also becomes friends with an older man named Taylor Bankole, who joins their group as they travel north. After Bankole's own altruistic act in which he saves a child, Lauren and Bankole become lovers (although he is fifty-seven and she is eighteen) and, eventually, full partners. Bankole agrees to let Lauren's group settle on his family land, an isolated place in the hills in northern California. It is there that Lauren begins to build her first Earthseed community.

Lauren and the others in her group build shelters and start gardens on the land, and the book ends with a status transformation ritual that symbolizes a more cohesive and determined community with a sense of place:

> So today we remembered the friends and family members we've lost. We spoke our individual memories and quoted Bible passages, Earthseed verses, and bits of songs and poems that were favorites of the living or the dead.
> Then we buried our dead and we planted oak trees.
> Afterward, we sat together and talked and ate a meal and decided to call this place Acorn. (298–99)

To make clear what this transition—and the symbolic name "Acorn"—means, the narrative ends with the parable of the sower as found in Luke 8:5–8 (Butler uses the Authorized King James Version): Lauren's quest and the quest of the community gathering around her are to be seeds sown upon the good soil that bring forth fruit. As with all of her novels, *Parable of the Sower*'s ending is a hopeful one, and it follows, more or less, the biblical parable for which it is named. Lauren, Zahra, Harry, Bankole, and the others who join them have lost almost everything, but they find a way to be the fruitful seeds who are planted in good soil.

In 2000, Butler reflected on her use of the biblical parable in her novel. Butler was raised Baptist but left the faith and came to despise religion. Later in her life, however, even though she never became religious, she began to understand and appreciate religion, and she especially regretted that people without religiously inspired consciences had so much power in society. So she decided that it would be better for there to be *more* religion, not less, in the sense that people should have consciences and struggle every day, like Butler's mother, to live according to the religion in which they believe:

> Religion really is a part of human nature. We never grow out of that need to call "Mama!" and have somebody come running to make it OK. And once we're old, "God help me!" serves the same function. The sower in the biblical parable of the sower is despairing. The sower goes out to sow his seed, and the birds eat some of it, some falls on rocks and doesn't germinate, some falls in very shallow soil and dies soon after germination. But a little bit of it falls on good ground, and it reproduces a hundredfold. That's why I used it as the title—I *did* see some significance to it! (Francis 2010, 187)

Whereas Butler's *Parable of the Sower* functions as a cautionary tale of where society might be heading if current trends continue, the second novel in the series, *Parable of the Talents*, offers some ideas about how to solve those problems. But Butler argues that she wasn't *proposing* solutions; instead she looked "at some of the solutions that human beings come up with when they're feeling uncertain and frightened, as they are right now" (Francis 2010, 132).

Both *Parable of the Sower* and *Parable of the Talents* end with a complete text of the parable after which each is named. *Parable of the Talents*, however, also includes the parable explicitly early in the narrative, where Olamina (what Lauren is usually called in the second novel) relates a dream about her father preaching a sermon on the parable of the sower. Olamina observes:

> My father loved parables—stories that taught, stories that presented ideas and morals in ways that made pictures in people's minds. He used the ones he found in the Bible, the ones he plucked from history, or from folk tales, and, of course, he used those he saw in his life and the lives of the people he knew. He wove stories into his Sunday sermons, his Bible classes, and his computer-delivered history lectures. Because he believed stories were so important as teaching tools. . . .
>
> My father was a great believer in education, hard work, and personal responsibility. "Those are our talents," he would say as my brothers' eyes glazed over and even I tried not to sigh. "God has given them to us, and he'll judge us according to how we use them." (Butler 1998, 19)

Olamina believes that her "talent" is Earthseed, and the book ends with Olamina at age eighty-one witnessing her dream coming true. Members of Earthseed depart in shuttles for the stars, and Earthseed begins to fulfill its essential purpose, according to Olamina: "*It will force us to become more than we might ever become without it. And when it's successful, it will offer us a kind of species life insurance*" (Butler 1998, 352; emphasis original). Olamina has used her talents; she has been a good and faithful servant; the rewards are sure to come as Earthseed fulfills its destiny.

Butler explains what this hopeful ending symbolizes for her. Although some of the Earthseed people who travel into space will die, she hopes that the difficulties of surviving on another planet will enable others to grow into something better. People will have to work together—and avoid the "worst behaviors"—in order to survive. So, Butler says, this novel about the dangers of global warming and abuses of power ultimately reflects her hopefulness for the human race (Francis 2010, 185). The conclusion, like those of many of Jesus's parables, is open ended; it is up to the readers/hearers to respond.

Butler did not consider her works as prophecy, preferring instead to consider them as "cautionary tales" (Francis 2010, 60, 168, 172). In a biblical sense, however, they could be viewed as prophetic, since biblical prophets proclaim a present critique of society and announce consequences that will occur in the relatively near future if society does not change its patterns of behavior. Likewise, Butler extrapolated from what she saw as current trends in society—the increasing divide between rich and poor, the changes in the earth's climate, the fear of crime, and all of the centrifugal forces that were "tearing . . . society apart"—and she examined the resulting issues of social power and its effects (69). In 1994, Butler noted that she was greatly concerned about what she saw going on around her: "There are so many terrible things that are going on that no one is paying attention to because they aren't quite that bad yet" (54). These problems included climate change, modern examples of slavery, and other dire economic circumstances, especially of the poor, examples of which she "pulled out of the newspapers" (55). Butler's novels, like the parables themselves, thus challenge readers to respond actively and responsibly.

Thich Nhat Hanh (1926–)

Thich Nhat Hanh is a Buddhist monk who was born in 1926 in Quang Tri province in central Vietnam. He was ordained in 1949 and moved to Saigon to help reform Buddhism so that it would become more socially engaged. In between trips to the United States, where he studied at Princeton University and taught at Columbia University, Nhat Hanh worked for justice, reconciliation, and peace in his home country, as well as for social change—what he calls "Engaged Buddhism," which includes active, nonviolent civil action.

During his trips to the United States, Nhat Hanh became friends with the American Trappist monk Thomas Merton and with Dr. Martin Luther King Jr., who, partly due to Nhat Hanh's influence, started speaking out against the war in Vietnam. In 1969, Nhat Hanh led the Buddhist delegation that participated in the Paris Peace talks that aimed to end the war in Vietnam. Because of his criticisms of the South Vietnamese government, however, Nhat Hanh was exiled from his country and was not permitted to visit Vietnam again until 2005. He moved to southwestern France, where he established a retreat center, Plum Village.

Nhat Hanh, as a young Buddhist living under the oppressive South Vietnamese government, initially saw Christianity as a colonial instrument of injustice against non-Christians. Through dialogues with Christian friends like King, Merton, and Daniel Berrigan, however, he began to discover the beauty of Jesus's teachings and "to touch the depths of Christianity." He now has images of Jesus and Buddha, his "spiritual ancestors," on his altar (Nhat Hanh 1995, 5–6, 100).

Nhat Hanh's book *Living Buddha, Living Christ* includes discussions of what he sees as positive elements in the Christian tradition, as well as elements that he considers to foster intolerance and religious hatred. He argues that no one should presume to possess changeless, absolute truth and that all should be open to the viewpoints of others (Nhat Hanh 1995, 2). One can enter into the reality of God both through the "living Buddha" (not the historical person but the Buddha of ultimate reality, who "is available to us at any time") and through the living Christ (not the historical Jesus but the living Son of God). But since Jesus is both the Son of Man and the Son of God, we can also investigate the historical Jesus's words and actions and use them "as a model for our own practice" (35–36).

For example, Buddha became enlightened under a Bodhi tree; Jesus became enlightened at his baptism. That same enlightenment is possible for all human beings, as the parable of the mustard seed demonstrates; the parable, Nhat Hanh says,

> means that the seed of the Kingdom of God is within us. If we know how to plant that seed in the moist soil of our daily lives, it will grow and become a large bush on which many birds can take refuge. We do not have to die to arrive at the gates of Heaven. In fact, we have to be truly alive. The practice is to touch life deeply so that the Kingdom of God becomes a reality. This is not a matter of devotion. It is a matter of practice. The Kingdom of God is available here and now. (38)

The living Jesus, like the living Buddha, is a door to the kingdom of God, because he is made of the energy of the Holy Spirit. Buddhism, however, speaks of 84,000 *Dharma doors*—ways of entering into the way of understanding and love taught by the Buddha (202)—so Jesus's path is not unique. Each person must find her or his own path to enlightenment.

Actions are also crucial. Nhat Hanh notes that Buddhism personifies traits to which Buddhists aspire, such as understanding, love, and mindfulness—the "energy" to experience deeply everything that happens in the present moment. In this way, students of the Buddha are themselves continuations of the Buddha. In a similar way, the living Christ is the Christ of love, and "Christians have to help Jesus Christ be manifested by their way of life, show those around them that love, understanding, and tolerance are possible. This will not be accomplished just by books and sermons. It has to be realized by the way we live" (57).

The "energy" of the Buddha and the "energy" of Jesus are present through those who follow the teachings of Buddha and Jesus in their actions: "We can touch the living Buddha and we can touch the living Christ" (58). Nhat Hanh thus concludes that the "living teaching" evident in the lives of the Buddha and Jesus "should always be the models for our practice." For the teachings to be "true" and effective, we must emulate the life and work of the Buddha and Jesus; we have to water those seeds of the "awakened qualities that are already in us," by practicing the teachings of Jesus or the Buddha—that is the highest form of prayer (126).

Nhat Hanh argues that enlightenment, entering nirvana, is available now. "Nirvana" denotes the release from suffering, being liberated from karma, rebirth, and the dangers that assault us, and experiencing inner peace (138). What Jesus calls the kingdom of God, Nhat Hanh argues, is that same reality of no-birth and no-death of nirvana (143). Nirvana is simply the kingdom of God within our hearts, so the kingdom is available here and now (167).

The parable of the mustard seed, for example, speaks about God being within our consciousness:

What is the seed? Where is the soil? What is it if not our own consciousness? We hear repeatedly that God is within us. To me, it means that God is within our consciousness. Buddha nature, the seed of mindfulness, is in the soil of our consciousness. It may be small, but if we know how to care for it, how to touch it, how to water it moment after moment, it becomes an important refuge for all the birds of the air. It has the power of transforming everything. (155)

The kingdom of God—nirvana, in other words—is within our hearts; "Buddha nature" is sometimes called the seed of enlightenment that is within the consciousness of every human being, just as the parable of the mustard seed speaks of the kingdom of God as being planted in the consciousness of every human being. Once again, for Nhat Hanh, action and practice are key elements:

The practices of prayer and meditation help us touch the most valuable seeds that are within us, and they put us in contact with the ground of our being. Buddhists consider nirvana, or the ultimate dimension of reality, as the ground of our being. The original mind, according to Buddhism, is always shining. Afflictions such as craving, anger, doubt, fear, and forgetfulness are what block the light, so the practice is to remove these five hindrances. When the energy of mindfulness is present, transformation takes place. When the energy of the Holy Spirit is within you, understanding, love, peace, and stability are possible. God is within. You are, yet you are not, but God is in you. This is interbeing. This is non-self. (167–68)

Likewise, in the parable of the leaven/yeast, the flour is one's consciousness. Even though that consciousness contains negative "seeds" of fear, hatred, and confusion, if one has the "seed" of the kingdom of God inside and knows how to nurture it, "it will have the power to leaven, to transform everything" (156). The parable of the treasure in the field, then, illustrates that nothing can be compared to the treasure of enlightenment, the source of true joy, peace, and happiness. Nothing else matters; nothing else is of any consequence (157).

Although Nhat Hanh does not explicitly mention the parable of the sheep and goats, the similarities and differences between that parable and Nhat Hanh's discussions about the necessity of actions, including love and compassion, are noteworthy. For example, it is up to the individual to be able to "see" Jesus or the Buddha: "Many who looked directly into the eyes of the Buddha or Jesus were not capable of seeing them. One man who wanted to see the Buddha was in such a hurry that he neglected a woman in dire need whom he met along the way. When he arrived at the Buddha's monastery, he was incapable of seeing him. Whether you see the Buddha or not depends on you, on the state of your being" (52).

In Matthew's parable of the sheep and goats, human beings are supposed to help others in need, and Jesus is found in those people in need (Matt. 25:40). Compassion or kindness (*karuna*) is an essential virtue in Mahayana Buddhism and is the most important expression of the first goal: wisdom. In Mahayana Buddhism, however, the rationale for such love and compassion in action (*dana*; "generosity" or "giving") is that all are one: "We do whatever we can to benefit others without seeing ourselves as helpers and the others as the helped. This is the spirit of non-self" (66). One must no longer envision the world in a selfish way but in a selfless way; one is to "let go" not only of one's possessions but also to the attachment one feels to any possible reward for such altruism or even to the act of giving itself.

Nhat Hanh often minimizes the differences between the Buddha and Jesus, as well as between Buddhism and Christianity. Some biblical scholars question how similar the Buddha could be to a Jewish prophet like Jesus who proclaimed not only the presence of the kingdom of God but also an imminent eschatological arrival of God's kingdom (including a final judgment; cf. Luz and Michaels 2006, 35–48). Nhat Hanh, however, calls the boundaries between the two traditions "artificial" and argues that the differences between them "may be mostly differences in emphasis" (Nhat Hanh 1995, 154). In addition, Nhat Hanh discovers that Jesus and Buddha are brothers (Nhat Hanh 1999), and he connects them through a common call to action and practice from their followers, actions that link Christians to the living Christ through the Holy Spirit and link Buddhists to the living Buddha through mindfulness, which functions very much like the Holy Spirit in Christianity (Nhat Hanh 1995, 14): "When we understand and practice deeply the life and teachings of Buddha or the life and teachings of Jesus, we penetrate the door and enter the abode of the living Buddha and the living Christ, and life eternal presents itself to us" (56).

In addition, Jesus becomes a bodhisattva, a person of deep compassion who in a self-sacrificing way assists others to be enlightened. Since wisdom and compassion are inseparable, the insights gained, especially once one recognizes that all people and things are interrelated, inevitably result in acts of compassion that work for the well-being of others, including justice and peace. The transformation of the individual necessarily means that one must work to transform the world, including unjust political and economic structures (Lefebure 1993, 162–63; Gross and Muck 2000, 147). Both Christians and Buddhists must practice nonviolence and social justice against violence, hatred, and discrimination (Nhat Hanh 1995, 72). What we also learn from the "gospel of non-violence" that Jesus taught is: "*Nonviolence does not mean non-action. Nonviolence means we act with love and compassion*" (81; cf. Nhat Hanh 2001, 156; emphasis original).

Conclusion

What Do Parables Want?

"For action is the life of all, and if thou dost not act, thou dost nothing."
—Gerrard Winstanley, "A Watch-Word to the City
of London and the Armie" (1649)

This book explores the "afterlives" of the parables of Jesus from fifty-seven interpreters, receptions that engage and apply thirty-three parables. These responses demonstrate very clearly that many of Jesus's parables are open ended; they resist characterization, and their inherent ambiguity means, as noted in the preface's quotations from William Blake and C. H. Dodd, that they "[rouze] the faculties to act" and "tease [the mind] into active thought."

Over the centuries, some interpreters have attempted to explain what parables *mean*. Other interpreters endeavored to articulate what parables *do*—how they "work" rhetorically or poetically. With the parables of Jesus, however, more is required because they always have demanded and always will demand that their readers or hearers *respond*. Interpreters, therefore, should also seek to ascertain what parables *want*, because the parables of Jesus not only stake claims and demand responses; they also challenge their hearers to act (cf. Mitchell 2005, xv; Gowler 2007, 103).

Parables are literary works of art that, in some ways, can function similarly to works of visual art. I have elsewhere, for example, compared parables especially to paintings that use chiaroscuro (dramatic variations of light and shade), because parables can illuminate some things as clear as day, whereas other elements—because of the nature of the parabolic word—remain (deliberately?) in the shadows, provoking divergent responses as interpreters endeavor to understand them (see Gowler 2012, 199–217). Thus responses to the parables can diverge significantly, and the chiaroscuro-like, ambiguous nature of parables increases the significant role that interpreters play in responding to them. Each interpreter has her or his unique context, point of view, and conceptual system, and each one responds to Jesus's parables differently. In addition, no interpreter is an island. All interpreters must realize that their interpretations depend in some way on the interpretations of those who preceded them. Later works of visual art, music, literature, and other responses to parables of Jesus can fundamentally change, develop, or extend one's interpretations of the parables.

Like every person discussed in this book, I am not a disinterested observer or interpreter of the parables told by Jesus of Nazareth. My own perspective is that understanding should lead to action—"if thou dost not act, thou dost nothing"—that there should be both a responsive and responsible ethical moment in the act of reading, one that leads to action in a number of realms (see J. H. Miller 1987, 4–5). The parables of Jesus in particular often challenge their hearers/readers to reimagine themselves, the world, other human beings, and God in radically different ways—and to put Jesus's radical vision into action in concrete ways.

Mikhail Bakhtin puts it this way: "I have to answer with my own life for what I have experienced and understood in art, so that everything I have experienced and understood would not remain ineffectual in my life" (1990, 1). This responsibility to "answer"—part of what Bakhtin appropriately calls *answerability*—means that individuals have not only a responsibility but also an obligation that leads to action, including actions for the benefit of others. We owe a profound moral obligation to other human beings; we are "responsible, answerable, and obligated" to individuals and communities in specific, concrete ways (Haynes 1995, 173–74).

I agree with Bakhtin that art, like life, often involves a moral obligation to "answer" concretely, to respond, and to interact with others and with the world. Such responsiveness can be a key element of artistic creativity and the ethical responses of interpreters. These aspects are also critical for the literary works of art called parables—and for many of the responses to the parables found in this book—which challenge readers/viewers to respond in ways that include ethical actions in our daily lives.

To readers of the parables of Jesus, however, this *answerability* should not come as a surprise (see Gowler 2007, 103). From the Gospel of Luke, for example, we learn that Jesus told the parable of the good Samaritan after a lawyer "tested" Jesus by asking what the lawyer had to do to inherit eternal life. The lawyer already knew the answer when Jesus asked him what the law had to say: "You shall love the Lord your God with all your heart, and with all your soul, and with all your strength, and with all your mind; and your neighbor as yourself." After the lawyer gave that answer, Jesus responded by saying: "You have given the right answer; do this, and you will live" (10:25–28).

The lawyer then asked Jesus: "And who is my neighbor?" (10:29), and Jesus replied with a parable that describes the extraordinary actions of a man, a hated Samaritan, who assisted another human being in need, a man half dead by the side of the road who had already been ignored by two religious people who had "passed by on the other side." The Samaritan, in contrast, had compassion for the man, demonstrated that compassion in concrete ways, and "took care of him" (10:34).

As always, Jesus expects a response from his audience concerning his parables, a response that involves both understanding and action, because Luke tells us this is what happened after Jesus finished the parable:

[Jesus asked,] "Which of these three, do you think, was a neighbor to the man who fell into the hands of the robbers?" [The expert in the law] said, "The one who showed him mercy." Jesus said to him, "Go and do likewise." (10:36–37)

Appendix

Descriptions of the Parables
Cited in the Interpretations

I encourage those readers who are unfamiliar with the parables cited in this book to explore the parables themselves in their literary contexts in the Gospels. Below is an addendum of the parables discussed in this book and brief summaries of those parables. In addition, I have listed the interpreters included in the book who discuss each parable (some references are extended; some are in passing).

Barren Fig Tree (Luke 13:6–9)

A man had a fig tree planted in his vineyard. When it was still barren after three years, he told his gardener to cut it down. The gardener recommended, however, to fertilize the tree and to give the tree one more year to bear fruit.

Interpretations found in: Irenaeus, John Calvin, John Bunyan.

Building a Tower (Luke 14:28–30)

Anyone who seeks to build a tower first estimates whether he has the resources to complete the project. Otherwise he might lay the foundation, discover that he cannot finish the tower, and become an object of ridicule.

Interpretation found in: Theophylact.

Dishonest Manager [*Unjust Steward*] (Luke 16:1–8)

This parable involves a rich man with a manager who was accused of squandering the rich man's property. The man summoned his manager, demanded an accounting of his management, and fired him. The manager debated about what to do to earn money, since he was not strong enough to dig and was ashamed to beg, so he decided to win friends among those who owed his master so that they might welcome him into their homes out of gratitude. He summoned the master's debtors, and one by one reduced their debts. A man who owed a hundred jugs of olive oil was told that he owed only fifty. Another who owed a hundred containers of wheat was told that the debt was reduced to eighty. Jesus concludes the parable by saying: "And his master commended the dishonest manager because he had acted shrewdly; for the children of this age are more shrewd in dealing with their own generation than are the children of light" (Luke 16:8).

Interpretations found in: Ephrem the Syrian, Theophylact, Hildegard of Bingen, Bonaventure, Martin Luther, John Calvin, William Shakespeare, Leo Tolstoy, Adolf Jülicher.

Good Samaritan (Luke 10:25–37)

A man traveling from Jerusalem to Jericho was stripped, beaten, and left half dead by robbers. A priest and then a Levite saw the man and passed by on the other side of the road. A Samaritan, however, saw the man and had compassion on him. He treated the man's wounds, brought him to an inn, took care of him, and then paid the innkeeper to take care of the man in his absence, promising to pay any additional costs when he returned.

Interpretations found in: Irenaeus, The Gospel of Philip, Clement, Origen, Augustine, Ephrem the Syrian, Rossano Gospels, Chartres Cathedral, Bonaventure, Rembrandt, Frederick Douglass, Adolf Jülicher, Martin Luther King Jr., *Godspell*.

Good Shepherd (John 10:11–16; cf. Luke 15:4–7)

Jesus says that he is the Good Shepherd who lays down his life for his sheep (John 10:11–16; cf. Ezek. 34:1–4). Although that figurative language is not a parable, the image of the Good Shepherd also came to represent the parable of the lost sheep in Luke 15:4–7 (see below), where the shepherd goes out to find and bring back one lost sheep out of the hundred in his flock.

Interpretations found in: Tertullian, The Good Shepherd in Early Christian Art, Byzantine Mosaics, Fanny Crosby.

Great Dinner/Banquet (Luke 14:16–24 // Thomas 64[1])

Jesus tells this parable while dining at the house of a leader of the Pharisees. The parable portrays three people giving excuses for not attending a dinner that they have already agreed to attend. The angry host then tells his slave to bring in the poor, crippled, blind, and lame to the dinner and to "compel" others to attend until the house is filled with guests. A different version, the parable of the wedding feast, is found in Matthew 22:1–14.

Interpretations found in: Clement, Tertullian, Gregory the Great, Golden Gospels of Echternach, Hildegard of Bingen, Bonaventure, George Herbert, Frederick Douglass.

Laborers/Workers in the Vineyard (Matt. 20:1–16)

Matthew compares the kingdom of heaven to a landowner who went out early to hire laborers for his vineyard. The workers he found agreed upon the usual daily wage (a denarius) for their labors, and the man sent them to the vineyard to work. At nine in the morning, however, he saw other men in the marketplace, and he sent them also to work in his vineyard, telling them that he would pay them "whatever is right." He did the same thing at noon. Finally, about five o'clock, he found others standing around and asked them why they were not working. After hearing that no one had hired them, he sent them as well into his vineyard to work.

That evening, the owner of the vineyard told his manager to call the workers and pay them, specifically instructing him to pay them in reverse order, beginning with those who started working at five o'clock and ending with those who started early in the morning. The workers who started work at five all received the usual daily wage, which raised the expectations of those workers who had started earlier: they believed they would receive more, so they were disappointed when all the workers, including them, received the same usual daily wage.

When they finally got paid, those first workers grumbled against the landowner, complaining that the workers who labored only one hour got paid the

---

1. The Gospel of Thomas is a collection of 114 sayings of Jesus—about half of which resemble sayings of Jesus in the Synoptic Gospels (Matthew, Mark, and Luke)—that was found, along with The Gospel of Philip and other texts, at Nag Hammadi, Egypt, in 1945 (see chap. 1).

same as they, who worked all day, even in the scorching heat, did. The land-owner picked out one of the grumbling workers and replied to him. Calling him "friend," he told the man that he did not treat him unfairly, since the man had agreed to work for the usual daily wage: "Take what belongs to you and go; I choose to give to this last the same as I give to you. Am I not allowed to do what I choose with what belongs to me? Or are you envious because I am generous?" (Matt. 20:14–15). Jesus then supplies his own conclusion: "So the last will be first, and the first will be last" (Matt. 20:16).

Interpretations found in: Irenaeus, Origen, John Chrysostom, Augustine, Ephrem the Syrian, Gregory the Great, *Sahih al-Bukhari*, Golden Gospels of Echternach, Hildegard of Bingen, Martin Luther, John Maldonatus, William Shakespeare, Rembrandt, John Everett Millais, Adolf Jülicher.

Leaven/Yeast (Matt. 13:33 // Luke 13:20–21 // Thomas 96)

This parable/similitude contrasts the humble beginnings of Jesus's proclamation of the kingdom of God with the future glory of that kingdom by comparing it with a small amount of yeast that leavens a large amount of flour.

Interpretations found in: Wazo of Liège, Thich Nhat Hanh.

Lost Coin/Drachma (Luke 15:8–10)

A woman has ten silver coins. If she lost one, she would light a lamp, sweep the house, and search diligently until she found the lost coin. When she found it, she would call together her friends and neighbors to celebrate with her.

Interpretations found in: Tertullian, Ephrem the Syrian, Domenico Fetti, John Everett Millais, Adolf Jülicher, Elsa Tamez.

Lost Sheep (Matt. 18:12–14 // Luke 15:4–7 // Thomas 107 // Gospel of Truth 31–32[2])

In all four versions of the parable Jesus starts with how a man has a hundred sheep and that, if he lost one, he would leave the ninety-nine other sheep in the wilderness and search for the lost one until he found it. Matthew's and Luke's versions include the shepherd rejoicing when the sheep is found, and Luke adds the detail that, when the man arrived home with the sheep, he would call his

---

2. The Gospel of Truth is a Valentinian Gnostic Gospel that was found, along with The Gospel of Philip and other texts, at Nag Hammadi, Egypt, in 1945 (see chap. 1).

friends and neighbors to ask them to celebrate with him. In The Gospel of Thomas the shepherd tells the lost sheep, "I love you more than the ninety-nine."

Interpretations found in: Tertullian, The Good Shepherd in Early Christian Art, Antonia Pulci, William Shakespeare, Domenico Fetti, Fanny Crosby, Adolf Jülicher.

Mote and Beam (Luke 6:41–42)

Luke calls this similitude a parable. Jesus asks how people can see a speck (mote) in someone else's eye but not notice the log (beam) in their own eye. Jesus advises people to take the log out of their own eye so that they will see clearly enough to remove the speck from the eyes of others.

Interpretation found in: Domenico Fetti, *Godspell*.

Mustard Seed (Matt. 13:31–32 // Mark 4:30–32 // Luke 13:18–19 // Thomas 20)

This parable depicts the kingdom of God as a small mustard seed that, after it is sown, grows into "the greatest of [all] shrubs" (Mark; Matthew) and even into a tree (Matthew; Luke). Birds then come to make nests in the tree's branches (Matthew; Luke) or shade (Mark). In The Gospel of Thomas, the mustard seed grows into a large plant that becomes "a shelter for birds of the sky."

Interpretations found in: John Chrysostom, Thich Nhat Hanh.

Net [Dragnet] (Matt. 13:47–50)

The kingdom of heaven is compared to a net that catches fish of every kind from the sea. When the net becomes full, it is pulled to shore. The good fish are placed in baskets, but the bad fish are thrown away. Likewise, the angels will separate the evil ones from the righteous at the last judgment and throw the evil ones into the "furnace of fire."

Interpretations found in: Origen, Gregory the Great, John Calvin, John Maldonatus.

Pearl of Great Value (Matt. 13:45–46 // Thomas 76)

The kingdom of heaven is like a pearl merchant, who, when he found a pearl of great value, sold everything he owned to buy it.

Interpretations found in: Origen, Ephrem the Syrian, Gregory the Great, John Calvin, George Herbert, John Bunyan, John Everett Millais.

Pharisee and the Tax Collector/Publican (Luke 18:10–14)

Jesus tells this parable against some people who "trusted in themselves that they were righteous and regarded others with contempt" (Luke 18:9). A Pharisee and a tax collector were praying in the temple. The Pharisee stood off by himself and thanked God that he was not like other people, such as the sinful tax collector, and stressed that he both fasted and tithed. The tax collector, however, stood far off and did not dare to look up to heaven. Instead, he beat his breast in mourning and said, "God, be merciful to me, a sinner!" Jesus declares that the tax collector and not the Pharisee was justified by God.

Interpretations found in: Irenaeus, Ephrem the Syrian, Romanos the Melodist, Theophylact, Hildegard of Bingen, John Calvin, William Shakespeare, John Bunyan, Søren Kierkegaard, John Everett Millais, Adolf Jülicher, *Godspell*.

Prodigal Son (Luke 15:11–32)

Jesus tells this parable—the third and final of the "lost" parables in Luke 15—immediately after the parables of the lost sheep and the lost coin. All three parables are directed to those who are complaining that Jesus "welcomes sinners and eats with them" (Luke 15:2).

A man had two sons, and the younger son asked for his inheritance. The father acquiesced and divided his property between his two sons. The younger son then left home, traveled to a distant country, and spent his entire inheritance in "dissolute living." Soon a famine came, and the son hired himself out as a keeper of pigs. He was so hungry that he desired to eat the pigs' food, but no one gave him anything. The son then "came to himself" and devised a plan to return to his father and ask to be treated as one of his father's hired hands. His father, however, joyfully welcomed him home as a son, even having the prized fatted calf slain for the celebratory dinner.

When the older son learned about the celebration for his younger brother's return, he became angry and refused to enter the house. When his father pleaded with him to join the celebration, the older son complained that his father had never rewarded him for his faithfulness with such a celebration. The father assured him, "All that is mine is yours," but declared that the family had to celebrate because the older son's brother "was lost and has been found." The parable ends without revealing the older son's response.

Interpretations found in: Irenaeus, Clement, Tertullian, Romanos the Melodist, Hildegard of Bingen, Antonia Pulci, Albrecht Dürer, William Shakespeare, George Herbert, Rembrandt, John Everett Millais, Adolf Jülicher, Thomas Hart Benton, Robert Wilkins, *Godspell*.

Rich Fool (Luke 12:16–21 // Thomas 63)

Jesus tells this parable in Luke after warning people to be on guard against greed, because "one's life does not consist in the abundance of possessions." A rich man's land produced a large amount of crops. The man decided to pull down his barns and build larger ones so that he would have enough room to store the abundant harvest. Then, he thought, he would have enough to last for many years so that he could relax, eat, drink, and be merry. God had other ideas, however. God called the man a fool, declared that the man would die that very night, and asked (rhetorically) who would be the owner of the possessions the man had prepared.

Interpretations found in: Theophylact, Bonaventure, Rembrandt, Adolf Jülicher, Martin Luther King Jr.

Rich Man and Lazarus (Luke 16:19–31)

A rich man dressed opulently and feasted extravagantly every day. At his gate lay a poor man, Lazarus, who was starving, disabled, and suffering but never received assistance from the rich man. When they both died, Lazarus was carried by angels to be with Abraham, but the rich man was tormented in Hades. The rich man, upon looking up and seeing Abraham and Lazarus, called out to "Father Abraham" to send Lazarus to help relieve the rich man's agony by dipping his finger in water and cooling the rich man's tongue. But Abraham reminded his "child" that he had received good things during his life and Lazarus had received evil things; therefore Lazarus was being comforted and the rich man was being (justly) tormented. After being rebuffed by Abraham, the rich man then asked Abraham to send Lazarus to warn the rich man's five brothers about what fate awaited them. Again Abraham refused, saying that "Moses and the prophets" (Scripture) were enough of a warning. The rich man objected one last time, saying that his brothers would repent if someone "from the dead" went to them. Abraham, in a sentence that in the Gospel of Luke also alludes to the forthcoming death and resurrection of Jesus, responded: "If they do not listen to Moses and the prophets, neither will they be convinced even if someone rises from the dead" (16:31).

Interpretations found in: Clement, Macrina the Younger, Ephrem the Syrian, Gregory the Great, Golden Gospels of Echternach, Hildegard of Bingen, Bonaventure, John Gower, Martin Luther, William Shakespeare, John Bunyan, Frederick Douglass, Adolf Jülicher, *Godspell*, Peasants of Solentiname, José Arana.

Seed Growing Secretly (Mark 4:26–29 // Thomas 57)

Jesus compares the kingdom of God to someone who scatters seed on the ground. The seed then sprouts and grows, and the sower does not know how, because the earth produces "of itself," first the stalk, then the head, then the full grain. When the grain is ripe, however, the man goes in with his sickle, "because the harvest has come."

Interpretations found in: Adolf Jülicher, *Godspell*.

Sheep and Goats [*Final Judgment*] (Matt. 25:31–46)

This parable explains the criteria by which the "Son of Man" will judge human beings at the final judgment. The Son of Man, who sits on his throne of glory as all the nations are gathered before him, separates people into "sheep" and "goats." The "king" (the Son of Man) welcomes the sheep into his kingdom, since they fed the king when he was hungry, provided drink for him when he was thirsty, welcomed him when he was a stranger, clothed him when he was naked, took care of him when he was sick, and visited him when he was in prison. These righteous sheep respond by asking the Lord when they did all these things for him, and he responds by saying: "Truly I tell you, just as you did it to one of the least of these who are members of my family, you did it to me" (Matt. 25:40). In contrast, the king condemns the goats to an eternal fire, because they did not do any of those things for him (feed him, give him a drink, welcome him, clothe him, tend him while he was sick, or visit him in prison). The unrighteous goats respond by asking the Lord when they failed to do all these things for him, and he answers, "Truly I tell you, just as you did not do it to one of the least of these, you did not do it to me" (25:45). The righteous sheep inherit eternal life, but the unrighteous goats depart into eternal punishment.

Interpretations found in: Irenaeus, John Chrysostom, Augustine, Byzantine mosaics, Martin Luther, Anna Jansz, John Maldonatus, Roger Williams, Rembrandt, William Blake, Frederick Douglass, Fanny Crosby, Leo Tolstoy, Emily Dickinson, Martin Luther King Jr., *Godspell*, Thich Nhat Hanh.

Sower (Matt. 13:3–8, 18–23 // Mark 4:3–8, 13–20 // Luke 8:5–8, 11–15 // Thomas 9)

As a sower sowed, some seeds fell on a path, and birds came and ate them. Others fell on rocky soil, where they germinated quickly because there was no depth of soil. These plants, because they had no roots, were scorched by the hot sun and withered away. A third group of seeds fell among thorns, and the plants were choked by the thorns and yielded no grain. The fourth group of seeds, however, fell into good soil and produced great amounts of grain, as much as thirtyfold, sixtyfold, and even a hundredfold.

Interpretations found in: Clement, Tertullian, John Chrysostom, Ephrem the Syrian, John Maldonatus, George Herbert, Roger Williams, Charles Spurgeon, Adolf Jülicher, Flannery O'Connor, *Godspell*, Octavia Butler, Thich Nhat Hanh.

Talents (Matt. 25:14–30) / *Pounds* (Luke 19:12–27)

In Matthew's version, Jesus tells this parable to demonstrate that people should work actively to be ready for the arrival of the kingdom of God and the final judgment. A man leaving on a journey entrusted five talents (one talent equals about fifteen to twenty years of a laborer's wages) to one slave, two talents to a second slave, and one talent to a third. When the man returned, the slaves with five and two talents had both traded with the funds and had thereby doubled the money entrusted to them. The man rewarded both "good and trustworthy" slaves and gave them more things to oversee. The third slave, however, had dug a hole in the ground and hidden the talent entrusted to him, because he was afraid of his "harsh" master. The master rebuked this "wicked and lazy slave," telling him that he should have at least invested the money with bankers to earn some interest. The master took the one talent away from that slave and gave it to the first slave, the one who had earned an additional five. The parable concludes that those who have will be given more and that from those who have nothing even what they have will be taken away. The master then commanded that the "worthless slave" be thrown "into the outer darkness, where there will be weeping and gnashing of teeth" (Matt. 25:30).

In Luke, Jesus tells the parable to those who think that the arrival of God's kingdom is imminent. Some details in the parable in Luke are not consistent (e.g., the number of slaves: ten in 19:13, but three in 19:16–25). In Luke's version, a nobleman traveled to a distant country and, before he left, entrusted ten of his slaves with ten pounds (one pound equals about three months of a laborer's wages) and instructed them to "do business" with the funds until he returned. Luke includes an aside that the citizens of the nobleman's country despised him and sent a delegation stating their opposition to his rule. The nobleman received "royal power," however, and returned home. He then summoned his slaves so they could give an account of what they earned by trading. The first slave earned ten more pounds, so the nobleman congratulated him on his trustworthiness and gave him charge over ten cities. The second slave made five pounds, so he was given rule over five cities. The third slave, however, since he was afraid of his harsh master, simply wrapped the pound in a piece of cloth. The nobleman condemned this "wicked slave," asking him why he did not at least deposit the money into a bank, where it would have earned interest. He then commanded that that slave's pound be given to the slave who had earned ten pounds more, explaining to those around him that more will be given to those who have, but from those who have nothing, "even what they have will be taken away." The nobleman finally ordered that his "enemies," those who did not want him as king, be brought to him and slaughtered (Luke 19:27).

Interpretations found in: John Chrysostom, Gregory the Great, William Shakespeare (mention), George Herbert, Fanny Crosby, Octavia Butler, David Flusser.

Treasure in the Field (Matt. 13:44 // Thomas 109)

Jesus compares the kingdom of heaven to someone who discovered a treasure in a field: he joyfully hid the treasure again, sold everything he owned, and bought that field. The version in Thomas states that the field was sold and that the treasure was discovered by the new owner when he plowed the field. The new owner then started lending money (and charging interest) to others.

Interpretations found in: Origen, Gregory the Great, John Calvin, John Everett Millais, David Flusser, Thich Nhat Hanh.

Two Debtors (Luke 7:41–43)

When Jesus dined at Simon the Pharisee's house, a sinful woman wet Jesus's feet with her tears, dried them with her hair, and anointed his feet with ointment. After perceiving the unspoken opposition by his host, Jesus responded with this parable that compared the amount Simon was forgiven by God with the amount the sinful woman had been forgiven: A creditor had a debtor who owed five hundred denarii and one who owed him fifty denarii. When neither could pay, the creditor canceled both of their debts. Jesus then asked Simon which person would "love" the creditor more. Simon replied, "I suppose the one for whom he canceled the greater debt." Jesus then used that answer to demonstrate to Simon that the sinful woman had been forgiven many sins; therefore, she showed "great love."

Interpretations found in: Theophylact, Søren Kierkegaard, Leo Tolstoy, Charles Spurgeon, *Godspell*.

Two Sons (Matt. 21:28–32)

Jesus tells this parable after his authority has been challenged as he taught in the temple in Jerusalem. A man with two sons told his first son to go work in the vineyard. The son refused but later changed his mind and went to work. When the father told his second son to go, he told his father that he would go, but he did not. Jesus then asks his opponents which one "did the will of the father." When they respond that it was the first son, Jesus tells them that tax collectors and prostitutes will enter the kingdom of God before his opponents do, because the tax collectors and prostitutes believed the teachings of John the Baptist while Jesus's opponents did not.

Interpretation found in: Irenaeus.

Unforgiving Slave [*Unmerciful Servant*] (Matt. 18:23–35)

Jesus tells this parable in Matthew in the context of stressing the importance of forgiveness. After Jesus told Peter to forgive someone who sinned against him "seventy-seven times" (or "seventy times seven"), he compared the kingdom of heaven to a king who decided to settle his accounts with his slaves. One slave owed the king ten thousand talents (since one talent equals about fifteen to twenty years of a laborer's wages, this debt is the equivalent of 150,000 to 200,000 years of labor). The slave could not repay this astronomical debt, so the king ordered him, his wife, his children, and all his possessions to be sold to repay the debt. The slave knelt before the king, begged the king to have patience, and promised to repay what he owed. The king had pity on him, released him, and forgave him the debt.

Immediately after leaving the king, the slave came upon a fellow slave who owed him one hundred denarii (a denarius is the usual daily wage for a laborer, so this debt is the equivalent of a hundred days' wages), a tiny fraction of what he had owed the king; but he grabbed that other slave by the throat and demanded payment of the hundred denarii. His fellow slave fell down before him, begged him to have patience, and promised to repay the debt. The first slave, however, refused and threw his fellow slave into prison until the debt was paid.

Other slaves, having witnessed what happened, reported it to the king. The king summoned the first slave back and said that, since the king had mercifully forgiven the slave's great debt, the slave should likewise have had mercy upon his fellow slave. The angry king then had the first slave tortured until he would pay the entire amount he owed the king. Jesus concludes that God will give the same treatment to those who do not forgive their brothers and sisters.

Interpretations found in: Augustine, William Shakespeare, Domenico Fetti, John Everett Millais, Charles Spurgeon, *Godspell*.

Unjust Judge [*Importunate Widow*] (Luke 18:2–8)

This parable illustrates why constant and faithful prayer is necessary. A woman kept coming to a judge asking for justice against her "opponent," but since the judge did not fear God or respect other human beings, he refused. Eventually, however, the judge grew tired of the widow "bothering" him and granted her justice so that she would not "wear him out" by her continual pleas. Jesus concludes by saying: "And will not God grant justice to his chosen ones who cry to him day and night? Will he delay long in helping them? I tell you, he will quickly grant justice to them. And yet, when the Son of Man comes, will he find faith on earth?" (Luke 18:7–8).

Interpretations found in: Ephrem the Syrian, John Everett Millais, Elsa Tamez, Octavia Butler.

Waiting/Watchful Slaves (Mark 13:34–37 // Luke 12:35–38)

Jesus compares the arrival of the Son of Man (in Luke) or "that day or hour" / "the time" (in Mark) to the arrival of a man who has gone on a journey and put his slaves in charge during his absence, each with a particular task. Jesus concludes by advising his hearers to "keep awake," to be watchful for the unexpected arrival.

Interpretation found in: Fanny Crosby.

Wedding Feast (Matt. 22:1–14)

This parable is Matthew's more allegorized version of Luke's parable of the great dinner (see above). A king gave a wedding banquet for his son. He sent his slaves to announce to those who had been invited that they should come right away, but they refused. So he sent other slaves to explain that they should come to the wedding banquet right away because the oxen and "fat calves" had been slaughtered and everything was ready. The invitees, however, made "light of it" and went about their business, and some seized, maltreated, and killed his slaves. The enraged king then sent troops to destroy those who murdered his slaves and to burn their city. Then, since those who were invited in the first place were unworthy to be guests, the king sent his slaves into the main streets to invite everyone to the wedding banquet. The slaves followed the king's orders and gathered everyone, both good and bad, with the result that the wedding hall was filled with guests.

When the king arrived, however, he noticed a man without a wedding robe and asked him how he entered without one. The man could not reply, and the king told his attendants to bind the man hand and foot and to cast him into outer darkness, "where there will be weeping and gnashing of teeth" (Matt. 22:13).

Interpretations found in: Irenaeus, Clement, Origen, John Chrysostom, Augustine, Gregory the Great, John Bunyan, Fanny Crosby.

Wheat and Weeds / Tares / Cockle (Matt. 13:24–30 // Thomas 57)

In this parable Jesus compares the kingdom of heaven to someone who sowed good seed in a field. When everyone was asleep, an "enemy" came and sowed weeds among the wheat. When both the wheat and weeds appeared in the field, the slaves asked their master, the householder, from where the weeds had come. After he told them that "an enemy" had sowed them in the field, the slaves asked whether they should go gather the weeds from the field. The householder replied that they should not because gathering the weeds would also uproot the wheat. It was better to let the wheat and weeds grow together, he said, until the harvest. The Gospel of Thomas adds that the weeds will be "conspicuous" at the harvest. Only then would the master tell the reapers to gather the weeds in bundles to be burned and then to gather the wheat for storage in the barn.

Interpretations found in: Irenaeus, Tertullian, Origen, John Chrysostom, Macrina the Younger, Ephrem the Syrian, Wazo of Liège, Thomas Aquinas, John Maldonatus, Roger Williams, Flannery O'Connor.

Wicked Tenants / Husbandmen (Matt. 21:33–46 // Mark 12:1–12 // Luke 20:9–19 // Thomas 65–66)

The version of this parable in The Gospel of Thomas is less allegorized, but the versions in Matthew, Mark, and Luke all allegorically interpret the man as God, the vineyard as Israel, the slaves as the prophets, and the son as Jesus. The parable begins with a man leasing his vineyard to tenants. After the harvest, he sent slaves to collect his share of the produce, but the slaves were beaten and sent away empty-handed. Some were even killed (in Matthew and Mark). After sending various slaves who were treated this way, the man decided to send his son, since he thought the tenants would at least respect his son. When the tenants saw the son, however, they decided to kill him so that they (and not the son) would receive the vineyard as their "inheritance." So they grabbed him, murdered him, and threw him out of the vineyard. Jesus concludes by saying that the owner of the vineyard would then come and destroy the tenants and give the vineyard to others.

Interpretations found in: Irenaeus, Augustine, Golden Gospels of Echternach, John Everett Millais.

Wise and Foolish Bridesmaids/Virgins (Matt. 25:1–13)

This parable functions as an allegory that speaks of being ready for the final judgment at the return of the "Son of Man." Jesus compares the kingdom of heaven to ten bridesmaids—five wise and five foolish—who took their lamps to meet the bridegroom. The five foolish bridesmaids did not bring along oil for their lamps, but the five wise bridesmaids brought along flasks of oil. When the bridegroom was delayed, the ten bridesmaids fell asleep, but they were awakened at midnight by the announcement of the bridegroom's arrival. All ten of the bridesmaids trimmed their lamps, but the lamps of the five foolish ones were running out of oil. When they asked to borrow some oil from the wise bridesmaids, the wise bridesmaids said no because there was not enough oil for all to share. Instead, they told the foolish bridesmaids to go buy some oil from oil dealers. While the five foolish bridesmaids were buying more oil, the bridegroom arrived, went into the wedding banquet with the bridesmaids who were ready, and shut the door. When the foolish bridesmaids came back and found the door shut, they asked the "lord" to open the door. The parable ends with his response, "Truly I tell you, I do not know you," and Jesus's resulting admonition, "Keep awake therefore, for you know neither the day nor the hour" (Matt. 25:13).

Interpretations found in: Tertullian, Ephrem the Syrian, Rossano Gospels, John Calvin, John Bunyan, William Blake, Fanny Crosby.

Wise and Foolish Builders [Two Builders; House Built on the Rock] (Matt. 7:24–27 // Luke 6:47–49)

Jesus compares people who hear and act on his teachings to a wise man who built his house with the foundation upon a rock. When rain fell and floods rose and wind beat upon the house, it stood securely. Jesus then compares people who hear his teachings but do not follow them to a foolish man who built his house with the foundation upon sand. When rain fell and floods rose and wind beat upon that house, it fell. Luke's version speaks instead of a flooding river bursting against the houses, with one house having a foundation upon rock and the other being built on the ground without a foundation.

Interpretations found in: Irenaeus, Theophylact, Leo Tolstoy.

Works Cited

Askew, Pamela. 1961. "The Parable Paintings of Domenico Fetti." *The Art Bulletin* 43 (1): 21–45.

Aufdemberge, C. T. 1997. *Christian Worship*. Milwaukee, WI: Northwestern.

Augustine. 1994. *Sermons (273–305A) on the Saints*. Translated by Edmund Hill. Part 3, vol. 8 of *The Works of Saint Augustine*. Edited by John E. Rotelle. Hyde Park, NY: New City.

———. 2003. *Expositions of the Psalms, Psalms 99–120*. Translated by Maria Boulding. Part 3, vol. 19 of *The Works of Saint Augustine*. Edited by John E. Rotelle. Hyde Park, NY: New City.

———. 2014. *The New Testament I and II*. Translated by Kim Paffenroth, Roland Teske, and Michael Campbell. Part 1, vols. 15 and 16 of *The Works of Saint Augustine*. Edited by Boniface Ramsey. Hyde Park, NY: New City.

Awmiller, Craig. 1996. *This House on Fire*. London: Franklin Watts.

Aymer, Margaret P. 2008. *First Pure, Then Peaceable: Frederick Douglass, Darkness and the Epistle of James*. London: T&T Clark.

Baigell, Matthew. 1984. "Recovering America for American Art: Benton in the Early Twenties." In *Thomas Hart Benton: Chronicler of America's Folk Heritage*, edited by Linda Weintraub, 13–31. Annandale-on-Hudson, NY: Edith C. Blum Art Institute.

Bakhtin, Mikhail. 1984. *The Problem of Dostoevsky's Poetics*. Translated by Caryl Emerson. Minneapolis: University of Minnesota Press.

———. 1990. *Art and Answerability*. Austin: University of Texas Press.

Barnstone, Aliki. 2006. *Changing Rapture: Emily Dickinson's Poetic Development*. Hanover, NH: University Press of New England.

Barrett, Lee C., and Jon Stewart. 2010. *Kierkegaard and the Bible*. Tome 2, *The New Testament*. Burlington, VT: Ashgate.

Bartlett, Rosamund. 2010. *Tolstoy: A Russian Life*. London: Profile.

Beavis, Mary Ann. 2002. *The Lost Coin: Parables of Women, Work, and Wisdom*. London: Bloomsbury.

Bede the Venerable. 1985. *The Commentary on the Seven Catholic Epistles*. Kalamazoo, MI: Cistercian.

Bennett, Fordyce R. 1997. *A Reference Guide to the Bible in Emily Dickinson's Poetry*. Lanham, MD: Scarecrow.

Bentley, G. E. 2001. *The Stranger from Paradise: A Biography of William Blake*. New Haven: Yale University Press.

Benton, Thomas Hart. 1979. *The Lithographs of Thomas Hart Benton*. Edited and compiled by Creekmore Fath. Austin: University of Texas Press.

———. 1983. *An Artist in America*. Columbia: University of Missouri Press.

Besserman, Lawrence L. 1988. *Chaucer and the Bible*. New York: Garland.

Bindman, David. 1970. *William Blake: Catalogue of the Collection in the Fitzwilliam Museum*. Cambridge: Heffer.

———. 1977. *Blake as an Artist*. Oxford: Phaidon.

Blake, William. 1969. *Blake: Complete Writings*. Oxford: Oxford University Press.

———. 2008. *The Complete Poetry and Prose of William Blake*. Berkeley: University of California Press.

Blumhofer, Edith. 2005. *Her Heart Can See: The Life and Hymns of Fanny J. Crosby*. Grand Rapids: Eerdmans.

Bonaventure. 2001. *St. Bonaventure's Commentary on the Gospel of Luke, Chapters 1–8*. St. Bonaventure, NY: Franciscan Institute, St. Bonaventure University.

———. 2003. *St. Bonaventure's Commentary on the Gospel of Luke, Chapters 9–16*. St. Bonaventure, NY: Franciscan Institute, St. Bonaventure University.

Booty, John E., ed. 1976. *The Book of Common Prayer, 1559*. Charlottesville: University Press of Virginia.

Bradstock, Andrew. 2009. "John Bunyan." In *The Blackwell Companion to the Bible in English Literature*. Edited by Rebecca Lemon, Emma Mason, Jonathan Roberts, and Christopher Rowland, 286–96. Oxford: Wiley-Blackwell.

Bradstock, Andrew, and Christopher Rowland. 2002. *Radical Christian Writings*. Oxford: Blackwell.

Brettschneider, Werner. 1978. *Die Parabel vom verlorenen Sohn*. Berlin: Schmidt.

Brock, Sebastian. 1987. *The Syriac Fathers on Prayer and the Spiritual Life*. Kalamazoo, MI: Cistercian.

———. 1992. *The Luminous Eye: The Spiritual World Vision of Saint Ephrem*. Kalamazoo, MI: Cistercian.

Brubaker, Leslie. 1999. *Vision and Meaning in Ninth-Century Byzantium*. Cambridge: Cambridge University Press.

Bruyn, J., et al. 1982. *A Corpus of Rembrandt Paintings*. Vol. 3. The Hague: M. Nijhoff.

Bukhārī, Muḥammad ibn Ismā'īl. 1971. *Sahih al-Bukhari*. 9 vols. Medina: Dar al-Fikr.

Bunyan, John. n.d. *The Pilgrim's Progress*. New York: American Tract Society.

———. 1976. *Some Gospel-truths Opened; A Vindication of Some Gospel-truths Opened; A Few Sighs from Hell*. Edited by T. L. Underwood and Roger Sharrock. Miscellaneous Works of John Bunyan 1. Oxford: Clarendon.

———. 1986. *The Barren Fig-tree; The Strait Gate; The Heavenly Foot-man*. Edited by Graham Midgley. Miscellaneous Works of John Bunyan 5. Oxford: Clarendon.

———. 1988. *Seasonable Counsel; A Discourse upon the Pharisee and the Publicane*. Edited by Owen C. Watkins. Miscellaneous Works of John Bunyan 10. Oxford: Clarendon.

———. 1998. *Grace Abounding*. Oxford: Oxford University Press.

Burns, Stewart. 2004. *To the Mountaintop: Martin Luther King Jr.'s Sacred Mission to Save America, 1955–1968*. San Francisco: HarperSanFrancisco.

Burroughs, Polly. 1981. *Thomas Hart Benton: A Portrait*. Garden City, NY: Doubleday.

Butler, Octavia E. 1993. *Parable of the Sower*. New York: Four Walls Eight Windows.

———. 1998. *Parable of the Talents: A Novel*. New York: Seven Stories Press.

Byrd, James P. 2002. *The Challenges of Roger Williams*. Macon, GA: Mercer University Press.

Calvin, John. n.d. *Commentary on the Psalms*. Vol. 1. Translated by James Anderson. Grand Rapids: Christian Classics Ethereal Library. Available at http://www.ccel .org/ccel/calvin/calcom08.html.

———. 1972. *A Harmony of the Gospels Matthew, Mark, and Luke*. 3 volumes. Translated by A. W. Morrison and T. H. L. Parker. Calvin's New Testament Commentaries: A New Translation. Grand Rapids: Eerdmans.

———. 1973. *The Epistles of Paul the Apostle to the Romans and to the Thessalonians*. Translated by Ross Mackenzie. Calvin's New Testament Commentaries: A New Translation. Grand Rapids: Eerdmans.

Capps, Jack L. 1966. *Emily Dickinson's Reading*. Cambridge, MA: Harvard University Press.

Cardenal, Ernesto. 1976. *The Gospel in Solentiname*. Vol. 1. Maryknoll, NY: Orbis.

———. 1979. *The Gospel in Solentiname*. Vol. 3. Maryknoll, NY: Orbis.

———. 1982. *The Gospel in Solentiname*. Vol. 4. Maryknoll, NY: Orbis.

Cars, Laurence des. 2000. *The Pre-Raphaelites: Romance and Realism*. New York: Abrams.

Casteras, Susan P. 1990. *English Pre-Raphaelitism and Its Reception in America in the Nineteenth Century*. Rutherford, NJ: Fairleigh Dickinson University Press.

Chilvers, Ian, ed. 2004. *The Oxford Dictionary of Art*. Oxford: Oxford University Press.

Clark, Kenneth. 1966. *Rembrandt and the Italian Renaissance*. London: Murray.

Collins, James. 1983. *The Mind of Kierkegaard*. Princeton: Princeton University Press.

Cone, James H. 1972. *The Spirituals and the Blues*. New York: Seabury.

Cosaert, Carl P. 2008. *The Text of the Gospels in Clement of Alexandria*. Atlanta: Society of Biblical Literature.

Crouzel, Henri. 1996. "The School of Alexandria and Its Fortunes." In *History of Theology: The Patristic Period*, edited by Angelo Di Berardino and Basil Studer, 145–84. Collegeville, MN: Liturgical Press.

Cunningham, Mary. 1999. "The Orthodox Church in Byzantium." In *A World History of Christianity*, edited by Adrian Hastings, 66–109. Grand Rapids: Eerdmans.

Dallimore, Arnold A. 1984. *Spurgeon*. Chicago: Moody Press.

Daniélou, Jean. 1955. *Origen*. New York: Sheed and Ward.

Davies, Michael. 2002. *Graceful Reading: Theology and Narrative in the Works of John Bunyan*. Oxford: Oxford University Press.

Davis, Francis. 1995. *The History of the Blues*. New York: Hyperion.

Davis, James. 2004. *The Moral Theology of Roger Williams*. Louisville: Westminster John Knox.

Dickinson, Emily. 1986. *The Master Letters of Emily Dickinson*. Edited by R. W. Franklin. Cambridge, MA: Belknap.

———. 1999. *The Poems of Emily Dickinson*. Edited by R. W. Franklin. Cambridge, MA: Belknap.

Dodd, C. H. 1961. *Parables of the Kingdom*. Rev. ed. Glasgow: Collins.

Dodwell, C. R. 1993. *Pictorial Arts of the West, 800–1200*. New Haven: Yale University Press.

D'Oench, Ellen. 1995. *Prodigal Son Narratives, 1480–1980*. New Haven: Yale University Art Gallery.

Doriani, Beth. 1996. *Emily Dickinson: Daughter of Prophecy*. Amherst: University of Massachusetts Press.

Doss, Erika. 1991. *Benton, Pollock, and the Politics of Modernism*. Chicago: University of Chicago Press.

Dostoevsky, Fyodor. 1993. *Crime and Punishment*. Translated by Richard Pevear and Larissa Volokhonsky. New York: Vintage.

Douglass, Frederick. 1845. *Narrative of the Life of Frederick Douglass, an American Slave*. Boston: Anti-slavery Office.

———. 1979. *The Frederick Douglass Papers*. Series 1, *Speeches, Debates, and Interviews*. Vol. 1. New Haven: Yale University Press.

———. 1982. *The Frederick Douglass Papers*. Series 1, *Speeches, Debates, and Interviews*. Vol. 2. New Haven: Yale University Press.

———. 1985. *The Frederick Douglass Papers*. Series 1, *Speeches, Debates, and Interviews*. Vol. 3. New Haven: Yale University Press.

———. 1991. *The Frederick Douglass Papers*. Series 1, *Speeches, Debates, and Interviews*. Vol. 4. New Haven: Yale University Press.

———. 1992. *The Frederick Douglass Papers*. Series 1, *Speeches, Debates, and Interviews*. Vol. 5. New Haven: Yale University Press.

Dowley, Tim, ed. 2011. *Christian Music: A Global History*. Minneapolis: Fortress.

Dronke, Peter. 1984. *Women Writers of the Middle Ages*. Cambridge: Cambridge University Press.

Drury, John. 2013. *Music at Midnight: The Life and Poetry of George Herbert*. London: Allen Lane.

Dunn, Geoffrey D. 2010. "Roman and North African Christianity." In *The Routledge Companion to Early Christian Thought*, edited by D. Jeffrey Bingham, 154–71. New York: Routledge.

Durham, John I. 2004. *The Biblical Rembrandt*. Macon, GA: Mercer University Press.

Dyson, Michael Eric. 2000. *I May Not Get There with You: The True Martin Luther King Jr*. New York: Free Press.

Elmostafa, Rema. 2015. "On Hadiths of *Sahih al-Bukhari*." Honors seminar project, Oxford College of Emory University. Available at https://scholarblogs.emory.edu/parables/workers-in-the-vineyard/on-the-hadiths-of-sahih-al-bukhari/on-the-hadiths-of-sahih-al-bukhari-draft-4-95.

Ephrem. 1989. *Ephrem the Syrian: Hymns*. Translated by Kathleen E. McVey. New York: Paulist.

———. 1990. *Hymns on Paradise*. Translated by Sebastian P. Brock. Crestwood, NY: St. Vladimir's Seminary Press.

———. 1994. *Selected Prose Works*. Translated by Edward G. Mathews Jr. and Joseph P. Amar. Washington, DC: Catholic University Press of America.

Evans, C. Stephen. 2009. *Kierkegaard: An Introduction*. Cambridge: Cambridge University Press.

Fenske, Wolfgang. 2003. *Ein Mensch hatte zwei Sohne: Das Gleichnis vom verlorenen Sohn in Schule und Gemeinde*. Göttingen: Vandenhoeck & Ruprecht.

Fichtenau, Heinrich. 1998. *Heretics and Scholars in the High Middle Ages, 1000–1200*. Philadelphia: Pennsylvania State University Press.

Flaming, Darlene. 2006. "Calvin as Commentator on the Synoptic Gospels." In *Calvin and the Bible*, edited by Donald McKim, 131–63. Cambridge: Cambridge University Press.

Flusser, David. 1981. *Die rabbinischen Gleichnisse und der Gleichniserzähler Jesus*. Bern: Peter Lang.

———. 1989. "Aesop's Miser and the Parable of the Talents." In *Parable and Story in Judaism and Christianity*, edited by Clemens Thoma and Michael Wyschogrod, 9–25. New York: Paulist.

———. 2007. *The Sage from Galilee: Rediscovering Jesus' Genius*. Grand Rapids: Eerdmans.

Francis, Conseula. 2010. *Conversations with Octavia Butler*. Jackson: University Press of Mississippi.

Gallup, George, Jr., and Robert Bezilla. 1990. *The Role of the Bible in American Society*. Princeton: Princeton Religion Research Center.

Gambone, Robert L. 1989. "Religious Motifs in the Work of Thomas Hart Benton." In *Thomas Hart Benton: Artist, Writer, and Intellectual*, edited by R. Douglas Hurt and Mary K. Dains, 65–93. Columbia, MO: State Historical Society of Missouri.

Gaustad, Edwin S. 2005. *Roger Williams*. Oxford: Oxford University Press.

Giere, Carol de. 2008. *Defying Gravity: The Creative Career of Stephen Schwartz, from "Godspell" to "Wicked."* New York: Applause Theatre & Cinema Books.

Godspell. 1973. Film directed by David Greene. Culver City, CA: Columbia TriStar, 2000. DVD.

Goethe, Johann Wolfgang von. 1986. *Essays on Art and Literature*. Vol. 3. New York: Suhrkamp.

Gordis, Lisa M. 2003. *Opening Scripture*. Chicago: University of Chicago Press.

Gottfried of Disibodenberg and Theodoric of Echternach. 1996. *The Life of the Saintly Hildegard*. Toronto: Peregrina.

Gower, John. 2006. *Confessio Amantis*. Kalamazoo, MI: Medieval Institute Publications.

Gowler, David B. 2000. *What Are They Saying about the Parables?* New York: Paulist.

———. 2005. "'At His Gate Lay a Poor Man': A Dialogic Reading of Luke 16:19–31." *Perspectives in Religious Studies* 32 (3): 249–65.

———. 2007. *What Are They Saying about the Historical Jesus?* Mahwah, NJ: Paulist Press.

———. 2012. "The Enthymematic Nature of Parables: A Dialogic Reading of the Parable of the Rich Fool (Luke 12:16–20)." *Review and Expositor* 109 (2): 199–217.

———. 2014. *James through the Centuries*. Blackwell Bible Commentary Series. Chichester, UK: Blackwell Press.

———. 2016. "The Characterization of the Two Brothers in the Parable of the Prodigal Son (Luke 15.11–32): Their Function and Afterlives." In *Characters and Characterization in Luke-Acts*, edited by Frank Dicken and Julia Snyder, 55–72. London: Bloomsbury.

Grant, Robert M. 1963. *A Short History of the Interpretation of the Bible*. New York: Macmillan.

———. 1997. *Irenaeus of Lyons*. London: Routledge.

Greaves, Richard L. 2002. *Glimpses of Glory: John Bunyan and English Dissent*. Stanford, CA: Stanford University Press.

Gregory of Nyssa. 1989. *The Life of Saint Macrina*. Translated by Kevin Corrigan. Toronto: Peregrina.

Gregory the Great. 1960. *Parables of the Gospel*. Translated by Nora Burke. Chicago: Scepter.

Griffith, Sidney H. 2004. "Ephraem the Exegete." In *Handbook of Patristic Exegesis: The Bible in Ancient Christianity*, vol. 2, edited by Charles Kannengiesser, 1379–1446. Leiden: Brill.

Gross, Rita M., and Terry C. Muck. 2000. *Buddhists Talk about Jesus, Christians Talk about the Buddha*. New York: Continuum.

Gruber, J. Richard. 1998. *Thomas Hart Benton and the American South*. Augusta, GA: Morris Museum of Art.

Guralnick, Peter, et al. 2003. *Martin Scorsese Presents the Blues*. New York: Amistad.

Hägg, Henny Fiskå. 2010. "Clement and Alexandrian Christianity." In *The Routledge Companion to Early Christian Thought*, edited by D. Jeffrey Bingham, 172–87. New York: Routledge.

Hamlin, Hannibal. 2013. *The Bible in Shakespeare*. Oxford: Oxford University Press.

Hanson, R. P. C. 1959. *Allegory and Event*. London: Bloomsbury.

Hastings, Adrian. 1999. *A World History of Christianity*. Grand Rapids: Eerdmans.

Hauser, Allan J., and Duane F. Watson, eds. 2009. *A History of Biblical Interpretation*. Vol. 2. Grand Rapids: Eerdmans.

Haynes, Deborah J. 1995. *Bakhtin and the Visual Arts*. Cambridge: Cambridge University Press.

Heine, Ronald E. 2010. *Origen*. Oxford: Oxford University Press.

Helgerson, Richard. 1976. *The Elizabethan Prodigals*. Berkeley: University of California Press.

Herbert, George. 2007. *The English Poems of George Herbert*. Edited by Helen Wilcox. Cambridge: Cambridge University Press.

Hildegard of Bingen. 1986. *Scivias*. Santa Fe, NM: Bear.

———. 2011. *Homilies on the Gospels*. Collegeville, MN: Liturgical Press.

Honan, Park. 1998. *Shakespeare: A Life*. Oxford: Oxford University Press.

Hornik, Heidi J., and Mikeal C. Parsons. 2013. "*The Parable of the Lost Coin*, by Domenico Fetti (1589–1624)." *Christian Century* 130 (17): 47.

Hults, Linda C. 1996. *The Print in the Western World*. Madison: University of Wisconsin Press.

Iglauer, Bruce. 2012. Foreword to *Blues, Philosophy for Everyone*, edited by Jesse R. Steinberg and Abrol Fairweather, x–xv. Chichester, UK: Wiley-Blackwell.

Jaeger, C. Stephen. 1994. *The Envy of Angels*. Philadelphia: University of Pennsylvania Press.

Jeffrey, David L. 1992. *A Dictionary of Biblical Tradition in English Literature*. Grand Rapids: Eerdmans.

Jensen, Robin Margaret. 2000. *Understanding Early Christian Art*. London: Routledge.

Jeremias, Joachim. 1972. *The Parables of Jesus*. New York: Scribner.

Johnson, James Weldon. 1990. *God's Trombones*. New York: Penguin.

Jones, Geraint V. 1964. *The Art and Truth of the Parables*. London: SPCK.

Jülicher, Adolf. 1963. *Die Gleichnisreden Jesu*. Darmstadt: Wissenschaftliche Buch-gesellschaft.

Kelly, J. N. D. 1995. *Golden Mouth: The Story of John Chrysostom*. London: A&C Black.

Kerby-Fulton, Kathryn. 2010. "Hildegard of Bingen." In *Medieval Holy Women*, edited by Rosalynn Voaden and Alastair Minnis, 343–68. Turnhout: Brepols.

Kermode, Frank. 1979. *The Genesis of Secrecy*. Cambridge, MA: Harvard University Press.

Kerr, Fergus. 2009. *Thomas Aquinas: A Very Short Introduction*. Oxford: Oxford University Press.

Khalidi, Tarif. 2001. *The Muslim Jesus*. Cambridge, MA: Harvard University Press.

Kienzle, Beverly. 2009. *Hildegard of Bingen and Her Gospel Homilies*. Turnhout: Brepols.

Kierkegaard, Søren. 1971. *Christian Discourses*. Princeton: Princeton University Press.

———. 1978. *Parables of Kierkegaard*. Princeton: Princeton University Press.

———. 1995. *Works of Love*. Princeton: Princeton University Press.

———. 2004. *Training in Christianity*. New York: Vintage Books.

Kilcourse, George. 2001. *Flannery O'Connor's Religious Imagination*. New York: Paulist.

King, James. 1991. *William Blake: His Life*. New York: St. Martin's.

King, Martin Luther, Jr. 2012. "The Man Who Was a Fool." In *A Gift of Love: Sermons from* Strength to Love *and Other Preaching*, 69–78. Boston: Beacon.

———. 2015. *The Radical King*. Edited by Cornel West. Boston: Beacon.

Kissinger, Warren S. 1979. *The Parables of Jesus*. Metuchen, NJ: American Theological Library Association.

Klonsky, Milton. 1977. *William Blake: The Seer and His Visions*. New York: Harmony.

Kümmel, Werner Georg. 1972. *The New Testament: The History of the Investigation of Its Problems*. Nashville: Abingdon.

Kuretsky, Susan Donahue. 1995. "Rembrandt's 'Good Samaritan' Etching: Reflections on a Disreputable Dog." In *Shop Talk: Studies in Honor of Seymour Slive*, edited by William Robinson, 150–53. Cambridge, MA: Harvard University Art Museum.

Ladin, Jay. 2008. "Meeting Her Maker: Emily Dickinson's God." In *Emily Dickinson*, edited by Harold Bloom, 197–204. New York: Bloom's Literary Criticism.

Laird, Paul R. 2014. *The Musical Theater of Stephen Schwartz: From "Godspell" to "Wicked" and Beyond*. Lanham, MD: Rowman & Littlefield.

Lefebure, Leo D. 1993. *The Buddha and the Christ: Explorations in Buddhist and Christian Dialogue*. Maryknoll, NY: Orbis.

Leirvik, Oddbjørn. 2010. *Images of Jesus Christ in Islam.* 2nd ed. London: Continuum.

Leiter, Sharon. 2007. *Critical Companion to Emily Dickinson.* New York: Facts on File.

Lienhard, Joseph T., trans. 1996. *Homilies on Luke.* By Origen. Fathers of the Church 94. Washington, DC: Catholic University of America Press.

Luther, Martin. 1955–1986. *Luther's Works.* Vols. 1–30. Edited by Jaroslav Pelikan. Saint Louis: Concordia. Vols. 31–55. Edited by Helmut T. Lehman. Philadelphia: Muhlenberg.

———. 1995. *Sermons of Martin Luther.* 8 Volumes. Charlottesville, VA: InteLex Corporation.

Luz, Ulrich, and Axel Michaels. 2006. *Encountering Jesus & Buddha: Their Lives and Teachings.* Minneapolis: Fortress.

MacCulloch, Diarmaid. 2009. *Christianity.* New York: Penguin.

Maldonatus, John. 1888. *A Commentary on the Holy Gospels: St. Matthew's Gospel.* Translated by George J. Davie. 2 vols. London: John Hodges.

Marling, Karal Ann. 1985. *Tom Benton and His Drawings.* Columbia: University of Missouri Press.

Martin, Karl E. 2012. "Suffering Violence in the Kingdom of Heaven: *The Violent Bear It Away.*" In *Dark Faith: New Essays on Flannery O'Connor's "The Violent Bear It Away,"* edited by Susan Srigley, 157–84. Notre Dame, IN: University of Notre Dame Press.

Martin, Wendy. 2007. *The Cambridge Introduction to Emily Dickinson.* Cambridge: Cambridge University Press.

McCarthy, Carmel, trans. 1993. *Saint Ephrem's Commentary on Tatian's Diatessaron.* Oxford: Oxford University Press.

McFarland, Dorothy Tuck. 1976. *Flannery O'Connor.* New York: F. Ungar.

McKim, Donald K., ed. 2007. *Dictionary of Major Biblical Interpreters.* Downers Grove, IL: IVP Academic.

Metz, Peter. 1957. *The Golden Gospels of Echternach.* London: Thames and Hudson.

Meyer, Marvin, ed. 2007. *The Nag Hammadi Scriptures.* New York: HarperOne.

Milburn, Robert. 1988. *Early Christian Art & Architecture.* Berkeley: University of California Press.

Millais, John Everett. 1975. *The Parables of Our Lord and Saviour Jesus Christ.* New York: Dover.

Miller, J. Hillis. 1987. *The Ethics of Reading.* New York: Columbia University Press.

Miller, Malcolm. 1996. *Chartres Cathedral.* New York: Riverside Book Company.

Minns, Denis. 2012. "The Parable of the Two Sons (Matt. 21:28–32) in Irenaeus and Codex Bezae." In *Irenaeus,* edited by Sara Parvis and Paul Foster, 55–64. Minneapolis: Fortress Press.

Mitchell, W. J. T. 2005. *What Do Pictures Want?* Chicago: University of Chicago Press.

Moucarry, Chawkat. 2002. *The Prophet and the Messiah*. Downers Grove, IL: InterVarsity.

Mullett, Margaret. 1997. *Theophylact of Ochrid*. Brookfield, VT: Variorum.

Murray, Peter, and Linda Murray, eds. 1996. *The Oxford Companion to Christian Art and Architecture*. Oxford: Oxford University Press.

Nhat Hanh, Thich. 1995. *Living Buddha, Living Christ*. New York: Riverhead Books.

———. 1999. *Going Home: Jesus and Buddha as Brothers*. New York: Riverhead Books.

———. 2001. *Thich Nhat Hanh: Essential Writings*. Maryknoll, NY: Orbis.

Nicholson, Peter. 2005. *Love and Ethics in Gower's "Confessio Amantis."* Ann Arbor: University of Michigan Press.

Nicolai, Vincenzo, Fabrizio Bisconti, and Danilo Mazzoleni. 2009. *The Christian Catacombs of Rome*. Regensburg: Schnell & Steiner.

Norris, Richard A. 1965. *God and World in Early Christian Theology: A Study in Justin Martyr, Irenaeus, Tertullian and Origen*. London: Adam & Charles Black.

Nouwen, Henri. 1994. *The Return of the Prodigal Son*. New York: Doubleday.

Oberhaus, Dorothy Huff. 1995. *Emily Dickinson's Fascicles*. University Park: Pennsylvania State University Press.

O'Connor, Flannery. 1952. *Wise Blood*. New York: Harcourt, Brace.

———. 1969. *Mystery and Manners: Occasional Prose*. New York: Macmillan.

———. 1979. *The Habit of Being: Letters*. Edited by Sally Fitzgerald. New York: Farrar, Straus and Giroux.

———. 1987. *Conversations with Flannery O'Connor*. Jackson: University Press of Mississippi.

———. 2007. *The Violent Bear It Away*. New York: Farrar, Straus and Giroux.

Outcalt, Todd. 2014. *The Other Jesus*. London: Rowman & Littlefield.

Owens, W. R. 2010. "John Bunyan and the Bible." In *The Cambridge Companion to Bunyan*, edited by Anne Dunan-Page, 39–50. Cambridge: Cambridge University Press.

Papandrea, James. 2012. *Reading the Early Church Fathers*. New York: Paulist.

Parsons, Mikeal C. 1996. "The Prodigal's Elder Brother: The History and Ethics of Reading Luke 15:25–32." *Perspectives in Religious Studies* 23:147–74.

Peterson, Eugene H. 2008. *Tell It Slant: A Conversation on the Language of Jesus in His Stories and Prayers*. Grand Rapids: Eerdmans.

Poeschke, Joachim. 2010. *Italian Mosaics, 300–1300*. New York: Abbeville.

Pooley, Roger. 2010. "*The Pilgrim's Progress* and the Line of Allegory." In *The Cambridge Companion to Bunyan*, edited by Anne Dunan-Page, 80–94. Cambridge: Cambridge University Press.

Prothero, Stephen R. 2007. *Religious Literacy: What Every American Needs to Know—and Doesn't*. San Francisco: HarperSanFrancisco.

Pulci, Antonia. 1996. *Florentine Drama for Convent and Festival: Seven Sacred Plays.* Edited by James Wyatt Cook and Barbara Collier Cook. Translated by James Wyatt Cook. Chicago: University of Chicago Press.

———. 2010. *Saints' Lives and Bible Stories for the Stage.* Toronto: Centre for Reformation and Renaissance Studies.

Ray, Robert H. 1995. *A George Herbert Companion.* New York: Garland.

Reventlow, Henning Graf. 2009. *History of Biblical Interpretation.* 4 vols. Atlanta: Society of Biblical Literature.

Rohrbaugh, Richard L. 1997. "A Dysfunctional Family and Its Neighbors (Luke 15:11b–32): The Parable of the Prodigal Son." In *Jesus and His Parables: Interpreting the Parables of Jesus Today*, edited by V. George Shillington, 141–64. Edinburgh: T&T Clark.

Rolf, Julia, ed. 2007. *Blues: The Complete Story.* London: Flame Tree.

Romanos the Melodist. 1995. *On the Life of Christ: Kontakia.* Translated and introduced by Ephrem Lash. San Francisco: HarperCollins.

Rosenfeld, Jason, and Allison Smith. 2007. *Millais.* London: Tate.

Roukema, Riemer. 1999. *Gnosis and Faith in Early Christianity.* Harrisburg, PA: Trinity Press.

Rowland, Christopher. 2010. *Blake and the Bible.* New Haven: Yale University Press.

———. 2014. "Blake: Text and Image." In *The Edinburgh Companion to the Bible and the Arts*, edited by Stephen Prickett, 307–26. Edinburgh: Edinburgh University Press.

Ruffin, Bernard. 1976. *Fanny Crosby.* Philadelphia: United Church Press.

Rutgers, Leonard V. 2000. *Subterranean Rome.* Leuven: Peeters.

Safarik, E. A. 2007–2015. "Domenico Fetti." In *Oxford Art Online.* Oxford: Oxford University Press.

Schwartz, Gary. 2006. *Rembrandt's Universe.* London: Thames & Hudson.

Shaheen, Naseeb. 1999. *Biblical References in Shakespeare's Plays.* London: Associated University Presses.

Shakespeare, William. 2011. *The Arden Shakespeare Complete Works.* Edited by Richard Proudfoot, Ann Thompson, and David Scott Kastan. London: Arden Shakespeare.

Siebald, Manfred, and Leland Ryken. 1992. "Prodigal Son." In *A Dictionary of Biblical Tradition in English Literature*, edited by David L. Jeffrey, 640–44. Grand Rapids: Eerdmans.

Simpson, Melissa. 2005. *Flannery O'Connor: A Biography.* Westport, CT: Greenwood.

Slee, Nicola. 1990. "Parables and Women's Experiences." *Religious Education* 80:232–45.

Smalley, Beryl. 1984. *The Study of the Bible in the Middle Ages.* Oxford: Basil Blackwell.

Snyder, C. Arnold, and Linda Hecht, eds. 1996. *Profiles of Anabaptist Women.* Waterloo, ON: Wilfrid Laurier University Press.

Snyder, Susan. 1979. *The Comic Matrix of Shakespeare's Tragedies*. Princeton: Princeton University Press.

Spencer, Jon Michael. 1993. *Blues and Evil*. Knoxville: University of Tennessee Press.

Spier, Jeffrey, ed. 2007. *Picturing the Bible*. New Haven: Yale University Press.

Spivey, Nigel. 2001. *Enduring Creation*. Berkeley: University of California Press.

Spurgeon, Charles Haddon. 1883. *Spurgeon's Sermons*. Vol. 29. Grand Rapids: Christian Classics Ethereal Library. Available at http://www.ccel.org/ccel/spurgeon/sermons29.html.

Steinbeck, John. 1996. *The Grapes of Wrath, and Other Writings, 1936–1941*. New York: Literary Classics of the United States.

Stokstad, Marilyn, and Michael Cothren. 2010. *Art History*. 4th ed. 2 vols. Boston: Prentice Hall.

Studer, Basil. 1996. "The Bible as Read in the Church." In *History of Theology: The Patristic Period*, edited by Angelo Di Berardino and Basil Studer, 353–73. Collegeville, MN: Liturgical Press.

Tamez, Elsa. 1982. *Bible of the Oppressed*. Maryknoll, NY: Orbis.

———. 1989. *Through Her Eyes: Women's Theology from Latin America*. Maryknoll, NY: Orbis.

———. 1994. "Women's Rereading of the Bible." In *Feminist Theology from the Third World: A Reader*, edited by Ursula Kin, 190–201. Maryknoll, NY: Orbis.

———. 2001. *Jesus and Courageous Women*. New York: Women's Division, General Board of Global Ministries, United Methodist Church.

Tatum, W. Barnes. 1997. *Jesus at the Movies*. Santa Rosa, CA: Polebridge.

Teske, Roland. 2001. "St. Augustine on the Good Samaritan." In *Augustine the Exegete*, edited by Frederick Van Fleteren and Joseph Schaubelt, 347–367. New York: Peter Lang.

Theophylact. 1997. *The Explanation by Blessed Theophylact of the Holy Gospel according to St. Luke*. House Springs, MO: Chrysostom.

Thomas Aquinas. 1947. *Summa Theologica*. Translated by Fathers of the English Dominican Province. New York: Benziger. Available at http://www.ccel.org/ccel/aquinas/summa.i.html.

———. 2002. *The Essential Aquinas*. Edited by John Y. B. Hood. Westport, CT: Praeger.

Thoreau, Henry David. 2004. *Walden and Civil Disobedience*. New York: Signet Classics.

Tippens, Darryl. 1988. "Shakespeare and the Prodigal Son Tradition." *Explorations in Renaissance Culture* 14:57–77.

Tissot, Yves. 1978. "Patristic Allegories of the Lukan Parable of the Two Sons, Luke 15.11–32." In *Exegetical Problems of Method and Exercises in Reading (Genesis 22 and Luke 15)*, edited by François Bovon and Grégoire Rouiller, 362–409. Pittsburgh: Pickwick.

Tolstoy, Leo. 1894. *The Kingdom of God Is within You.* New York: Cassell.

———. 1907. *Twenty-Three Tales.* New York: Funk & Wagnalls. Available at http:// www.ccel.org/ccel/tolstoy/23_tales.html.

———. 2006. *Leo Tolstoy: Spiritual Writings.* Maryknoll, NY: Orbis.

Trypanis, Constantine. 1971. *The Penguin Book of Greek Verse.* Harmondsworth, UK: Penguin.

Turner, Martha Lee. 1996. *The Gospel according to Philip.* Leiden: Brill.

Van Braght, Thieleman J. 1987. *The Bloody Theater, or, Martyrs' Mirror.* Translated by Joseph F. Sohm. Scottdale, PA: Herald. Available at http://www.homecomers .org/mirror/contents.htm.

Vendler, Helen. 1975. *The Poetry of George Herbert.* Cambridge, MA: Harvard University Press.

Wailes, Stephen L. 1987. *Medieval Allegories of Jesus' Parables.* Berkeley: University of California Press.

Wakefield, Walter L., and Austin P. Evans, eds. 1991. *Heresies of the High Middle Ages.* New York: Columbia University Press.

Walker Art Gallery. 1967. *Millais: An Exhibition Organized by the Walker Art Gallery.* Liverpool: Walker Art Gallery.

Walsh, Richard G. 2003. *Reading the Gospels in the Dark: Portrayals of Jesus in Film.* Harrisburg, PA: Trinity Press International.

Ward, Benedicta. 2002. *The Venerable Bede.* London: Continuum.

Weitzmann, Kurt. 1970. *Illustrations in Roll and Codex.* Princeton: Princeton University Press.

———. 1977. *Late Antique and Early Christian Book Illumination.* New York: G. Braziller.

Westermann, Mariët. 2000. *Rembrandt.* London: Phaidon.

Wetering, Ernst van de. 2008. *Rembrandt: A Life in 180 Paintings.* Amsterdam: Local World BV.

Wilkins, Robert. 1964. "The Prodigal Son." On *Rev. Robert Wilkins: Memphis Gospel Singer.* Memphis: Memphis Records. MP3.

———. 1994. "That's No Way to Get Along." On *Memphis Blues Vol. 1, 1928–1935.* Document Records. Originally recorded 1929. CD.

Williams, Roger. 1963. *The Complete Writings of Roger Williams.* Vol. 4. New York: Russell & Russell.

———. 2001. *The Bloudy Tenent of Persecution for Cause of Conscience.* Macon, GA: Mercer University Press.

———. 2008. *On Religious Liberty.* Cambridge, MA: Belknap.

Williamson, Scott C. 2002. *The Narrative Life: The Moral and Religious Thought of Frederick Douglass.* Macon, GA: Mercer University Press.

Witcombe, Christopher. 1998. "Albrecht Dürer's *Prodigal Son*." *Notes in the History of Art* 17:7–13.

Wolff, Cynthia Griffin. 1988. *Emily Dickinson*. Reading, MA: Addison-Wesley.

Wolff, Justin P. 2012. *Thomas Hart Benton: A Life*. New York: Farrar, Straus and Giroux.

Wordsworth, Charles. 1892. *Shakspeare's Knowledge and Use of the Bible*. London: Eden, Remington.

Yanco, Jennifer J. 2014. *Misremembering Dr. King: Revisiting the Legacy of Martin Luther King Jr*. Bloomington: Indiana University Press.

Young, Abigail. 2012. "Hildegard of Bingen." In *Handbook of Women Biblical Interpreters*, edited by Marion Ann Taylor, 259–64. Grand Rapids: Baker Academic.

Young, Alan R. 1979. *The English Prodigal Son Plays*. Salzburg: University of Salzburg.

Young, Frances. 1997. *Biblical Exegesis and the Formation of Character*. Cambridge: Cambridge University Press.

Zuffi, Stefano. 2003. *Gospel Figures in Art*. Los Angeles: Getty Museum.

Scripture Index

Hebrew Bible

Genesis

1 31, 87–88
1–3 62, 90
1:6–8 88
1:26 62
2:1–15 62
2:15 92
2:15–17 93
2:21–22 92
3 86, 92–93, 239
3:1–7 93
3:3 33
3:7 62
3:11 86
3:15 94
3:22–24 93
8:6–12 51
8:21 33
18:8 33

Exodus

22:18 101
22:21–22 239

Numbers

23:22 23

Deuteronomy

32:21–22 27

Job

20:20–22 96

Psalms

in toto: 71
18:25 127
23 54
32:1 63
37:27 118
44:5 23
45:14–15 57
53:5 57
68:23 69
118 42
121:5 34, 43

Proverbs

3:34 84
27:1 96

Ecclesiastes

2:14 96
5:12 96

Isaiah

5:4 36
53:7 23
58:7 27

Jeremiah

7:23–24 27

Ezekiel

34:1–4 51, 260

Hosea

7:13 58

Joel

3:18 26

Amos

6:1–6 96

Jonah

1–2 51
4 51

New Testament

Matthew

3:7–10 156
5:3 96
5:34 120
6:19–20 96
6:25–26 236
7:12 118
7:21 25

7:24–27 18, 184, 272–73
8:2–4 63
8:16–17 25
9:37–38 241
10:16 95
11:12 218
11:16–19 203
12:31–32 75
12:40 51
13 37, 128
13:1–9 204
13:3 36
13:3–8 128, 267
13:10–17 6
13:11 32
13:12–15 36
13:13–15 23
13:16 33
13:18–23 36, 204
13:18–30 220
13:19 221, 222
13:24 221
13:24–30 18, 271
13:30 221
13:31–32 263
13:33 75, 243, 262
13:34 6, 23
13:36 37
13:38 149
13:42 33
13:44 31, 268
13:45–46 263
13:47 129
13:47–50 32, 263
18:12–14 203, 262–63
18:22 142
18:23–35 199, 230, 269–70
18:28 131
18:33 142
19:30 38, 77
20:1–16 18, 204, 261–62
20:9 33
20:12 77
20:14–15 262
20:15 133
20:16 38, 77, 262
21:28–32 18, 269
21:33 38
21:33–41 41
21:33–45 18
21:33–46 271–72
22:1–14 18, 31, 261, 270–71
22:4 179

22:11–13 19, 180
22:13 271
22:37–39 184
24–25 168
24:29–44 168
24:30 168
25 70
25:1–13 17–18, 180, 272
25:6 168
25:9 167
25:13 272
25:14–30 118, 180, 241, 267
25:15 241
25:30 267
25:31–46 18, 60, 266
25:34 41
25:34–36 vi
25:34–40 25
25:35 187, 194
25:36 182
25:40 187, 195, 252, 266
25:45 266
26:11 124

Mark

1:3–4 102
4:1–9 204
4:3–8 267
4:10–12 23
4:11–12 196, 202
4:13–20 15, 204
4:15 222
4:20 233
4:26–29 204, 232, 266
4:30–32 263
4:33–34 23
10:17–31 24
12:1–12 271
13 168
13:33–37 180
13:34–37 270
16:14 54

Luke

4:18 123, 208
6:35–36 97
6:37–38 42
6:39–42 8, 137
6:41–42 263
6:44 170
6:46 25, 60

6:47–49 18, 84, 272
7:31–34 203
7:36–50 171, 185
7:41–43 268
8:4–8 204
8:5–8 247, 267
8:10 160
8:11–15 204
10:25–28 257
10:25–37 xi, 260
10:27 97
10:29 257
10:30 42
10:33 35
10:34 257
10:36 25
10:36–37 257
12:16–21 265
12:32 124
12:35 125
12:35–38 180, 270
12:37 145
12:41 180
13:6–9 18, 259
13:18–19 263
13:20–21 75, 262
14:16–24 27, 176, 261
14:23 144
14:28–30 84, 259
15 12, 27, 91, 108, 134, 140, 264
15:1–2 29
15:1–3 90
15:1–10 27
15:2 264
15:3–7 51
15:4–7 203, 260, 262
15:8 139
15:8–10 204, 262
15:11–32 xiii, 18, 204, 264
15:12 136
15:13 113
15:17 113
15:21 144
15:30 150
16:1–8 xi, 260
16:8 260
16:9 119
16:19–31 265
16:25 234
16:31 82, 265
18:2–8 270
18:6–8 192

18:7–8 270
18:9 264
18:9–14 18
18:10–14 264
18:13 133
18:18–25 48
19:12–27 241, 267
19:13 267
19:16–25 267
19:27 268
20:9–19 271
21 168

John

1:1–18 22
1:29 23
3:33 23
4 157
4:4–42 63
5:46 69
6:51 42
8 238
8:11 108
8:32 20
10:11–16 51, 260
13:13 23

Acts (of the Apostles)

8:32 23
16:11–15 238
16:40 238

Romans

1:21 29
13:13 40

1 Corinthians

1:5–7 96
5:5 100
5:6 75, 101

2 Corinthians

6:10 96
8:9 96
9:6 129
9:10 129

Galatians

5:9 75
6:7 129
6:8 129

Ephesians

4:25 42

Philippians

2:10 45
3:8 32
4:18 96

Colossians

2:3 32

1 Thessalonians

4:16 168

1 Timothy

2:4 62
6:7 96

Hebrews

11:6 119

James

3:18 129
4:6 84
4:14 96
5:5 96

1 Peter

in toto: 17
1:3–4 96
4:8 21
5:5 84

1 John

in toto: 17

Revelation

in toto: 17
6:9–11 122
20:2 82

Subject Index

Bold page ranges indicate the location of the main discussion of that subject.

Aaron, 41
Abraham, 33, 41, 46, 48–49, 67, 71, 73, 81–82, 96, 104, 176–77, 234–35, 265
Adam, 29, 33–34, 41, 43, 48, 54, 61–62, 67, 71, 73, 86–87, 88–90, 92–94, 98, 204
Aesop (Esop), xii, 8, 204, 240, 241–42
Agudelo, William, 233
Albert the Great, 114
Alexandria, 21, 22, 30, 40
Alexandrian school, 2, 22, 40
allegory, 19, 20–21, 23, 24, 25–26, 31, 40, 43, 65–66, 70–71, 85, 95, 99, 115, 116–17, 124–25, 159, 165, 202–5, 272. *See also* metaphor
  and John Gower, 102
  and the parables
    good Samaritan, 19, 20–21, 24–25, 34–35, 42, 57, 89–94, 97–98
    great dinner/banquet, 80, 95
    laborers/workers in the vineyard, 38, 67–68, 77–78, 118, 131
    net (dragnet), 67
    pearl of great value, 125
    prodigal son, 23, 28, 154
    rich man and Lazarus, 45–46, 69–70, 96
    talents/pounds, 39
    treasure in the field, 67, 125
    wedding feast/banquet, 38, 68, 179, 270
    wheat and weeds/tares/cockles, 26, 45
    wicked tenants/husbandmen, 271
    wise and foolish bridesmaids/virgins, 27, 39, 181, 272
  and Plato, 45

ambiguity, 4, 5, 17, 125, 255–56
Ambrose, 42
Anselm of Liège, 75–76
answerability, 256
Antiochene school, 2, 40
Antiphon, 241–42
Arana, José, 208, 235–37, 266
  Rich Epicure and Poor Lazarus, The, 236–37
Arians, 40, 66
Aristotle, 98, 203, 205
Askew, Pamela, 137, 139, 141, 142
Athanasius, 130
Aufdemberge, C. T., 179
Augustine, 2, 10, 16, 21, 34, 38, **40–44**, 67–68, 73, 94, 96, 98, 99, 101, 129–130, 131, 132, 260, 262, 266, 270, 271, 272
  City of God, 44
  Confessions, 40
  Expositions on the Psalms, 42
  On Christian Doctrine, 41–42
  On the Trinity, 40
  Questions on the Gospels, 43
  Tractate on John, 43
Ausbund, 121
Awmiller, Craig, 213–14
Aymer, Margaret P., 174, 176

Baigell, Matthew, 213
Bakhtin, Mikhail, 3, 5, 256
baptism, 10, 29, 49, 53–54, 60–62, 68, 120, 132, 197, 219, 220–22, 229, 250
Barnstone, Aliki, 196

Barrett, Lee C., 171, 172
Bartlett, Rosamund, 184, 187
Basil the Great, 16, 44
Beavis, Mary Ann, 10
Bede the Venerable, 66, 96, 130
Behrs, Sofya, 184
Bennett, Fordyce R., 194
Bentley, G. E., 165
Benton, Thomas Hart, xiii, 3, 11, 12, **209-13**,
    265
    Artist in America, An, 209
    Departure of the Joads, The, 212
    Flanders' House, The, 210
    Lord Is My Shepherd, The, 210
    Meeting, The, 210
    Prayer Meeting (Wednesday Evening), 210
    Prodigal Son, 12, 208-9, 210-13
    Social History of Missouri, A, 209
    Sunday Morning, 210
Bernard of Clairvaux, 86
Berrigan, Daniel, 249
Besserman, Lawrence L., 65
Bezilla, Robert, 208
Bindman, David, 165, 168
Blake, William, xi-xii, 3, 7-8, 158, **164-68**, 255,
    266, 272
    All Religions Are One, 165
    Malevolence, 7
    Marriage of Heaven and Hell, The, 7
    Parable of the Wise and Foolish Virgins, The,
    165-68
    There Is No Natural Religion, 165
blues music, xiv, 12-13, 209, 213-18
Blumhofer, Edith, 179, 181, 183
Boethius, 96
Bonaventure, 66, **95-98**, 260, 261, 265, 266
Book of Common Prayer, 144, 161
Booty, John E., 144
Bradbury, William, 179
Bradstock, Andrew, 120, 159, 198
Breckerveld, Herman, 156
Brettschneider, Werner, 10
Brock, Sebastian, 50
Brubaker, Leslie, 57
Bruyn, J., 156
Buddha/Buddhism/Buddhist, 209, 249-53
Bultmann, Rudolf, 201
Bunyan, John, 1, 116, **158-62**, 259, 264, 266,
    271, 272
    Barren Fig Tree, The, 160-61
    *Discourse upon the Pharisee and the Publi-
    cane, A*, 162

Few Sighs from Hell, A, 159-60
Grace Abounding to the Chief of Sinners, 158
Pilgrim's Progress, The, 1, 158-59
Burns, Stewart, 224
Burroughs, Polly, 210
Butler, Octavia E., xi, 208, **243-49**, 267, 268, 270
    Parable of the Sower, 208, 243-47, 248
    Parable of the Talents, xi, 247-48
    Patternmaster, 243
Butts, Thomas, 165
Byrd, James P., 148, 149, 151
Byzantine mosaics, 2, **58-60**, 261, 266

Calvin, John, 6, 115, **124-28**, 129-30, 132, 202,
    259, 260, 263, 264, 268, 272
    Commentary on Matthew, Mark, and Luke,
    124-27
    Commentary on the Psalms, 124
    Institutes of the Christian Religion, 124
Calvinist, 194, 201
Capps, Jack L., 194
Caravaggio, Michelangelo, 137, 157
Cardenal, Ernesto, 233-36
Cars, Laurence des, 188
Cassian, John, 65
Castellani, Castellano, 106
Casteras, Susan P., 192
Catholic (church), 76, 111, 116, 119, 120, 128,
    158, 218. *See also* Reformation: Catholic
    Counter-
Chabris, Christopher, 3
Chaplin, Charlie, 232
Charles II (king), 148, 158, 161, 162
Chartres Cathedral (Cathedral of Notre
    Dame), 12, **89-94**, 111, 260
Chaucer, Geoffrey, 102, 105, 110
Chilvers, Ian, 111, 152, 165, 188
Chorus of Voices, A, xii
Chrysostom, John, 2, 3, 6, 10, 16, 34, **35-40**,
    85, 96, 100, 130, 132, 262, 263, 266, 267,
    268, 271
    Homilies on Matthew, 36-39, 100
Cicero, 40
Clark, Kenneth, 154, 156-57
Clement of Alexandria, 5-6, 10, 16, 20, **21-25**,
    26, 34, 94, 260, 261, 265, 266, 267, 271
    Fragments, 23
    Miscellanies, 5-6, 22-25
    Who Is the Rich Man That Shall Be Saved?,
    24-25
Cleveland, Grover, 179
Coke, Edward, 147

Collins, James, 169
Cone, James H., 214
Cosaert, Carl P., 22
Cothren, Michael, 90
Council of Trent, 128, 137
Counter-Reformation, 115, 137, 140, 142
Cox, Harvey, 228
Crosby, Fanny, 2, 164, **178–83**, 261, 263, 266,
    268, 270, 271, 272
  "All Is Ready," 179–80
  "Blessed Assurance," 183
  "Dark Is the Night," 183
  "Have You Sought?," 181–83
  "I Am Thine, O Lord," 183
  "Will Jesus Find Us Watching?," 180–81
Crouzel, Henri, 15
Cunningham, Mary, 60
Curry, John Steuart, 210
Cyril of Alexandria, 10, 140

Dallimore, Arnold A., 197
Dalziel brothers, 188–89, 190
Daniel, 33, 221
Daniélou, Jean, 34
David (king), 47, 54, 56, 57, 71, 106
Davies, Michael, 160
Davis, Francis, 214
Davis, James, 147
Defoe, Daniel, 158
devil, 13, 19, 26, 37, 43, 75–76, 94, 130, 217–18,
    221–22. *See also* satan
dialogue, xii, xiii, 1–2, 3, 4–8, 60, 108, 143, 192,
    194, 209, 231, 233, 235, 249
Diatessaron, 47–49, 53
Dicken, Frank, xiii
Dickens, Charles, 136, 188
Dickinson, Emily, 2, 6, 164, **193–97**, 266
Doane, William, 179
Dodd, C. H., xii, 255
Dodwell, C. R., 77
D'Oench, Ellen, 111, 113, 152, 212
Donatists, 40, 66, 130
Doriani, Beth, 196, 197
Doss, Erika, 213
Dostoevsky, Fyodor, xii, 184
Douglass, Frederick, 9, 164, **173–78**, 260, 261,
    266
Dowley, Tim, 213
Dronke, Peter, 86
Drury, John, 143, 147
Dunn, Geoffrey D., 25
Dura-Europos, **53–54**

Dürer, Albrecht, 11, 12, **110–13**, 213, 265
  Prodigal Son amongst the Pigs, The, 12,
    111–13
  Sudarium Held by Two Angels, The, 113
Durham, John I., 156, 157
Dyson, Michael Eric, 228

Elijah, 221
Elmostafa, Rema, xiii, 72
Ephrem the Syrian, 2, 7, 16, **47–50**, 260, 262,
    264, 266, 267, 270, 271, 272
  Commentary on Tatian's Diatessaron, 47–49
  Hymns on Paradise, 48–49
  Hymns on the Pearl, 7, 49–50
Epiphanius, 20
Eucharist/Holy Communion, 23, 29, 49, 54,
    60–62, 144, 170–72, 195
Euripides, 22
Eusebius, *Church History*, 16, 25, 30
Evans, Austin P., 75–76
Evans, C. Stephen, 169

Fenske, Wolfgang, 10
Fetti, Domenico, 116, **137–42**, 262, 263, 270
  Mote and the Beam, The, 137–39
  Parable of the Lost Coin, The, 139–41
  Unmerciful Servant, The, 141–42
Fichtenau, Heinrich, 9
Finn, Huckleberry, 209
Flaming, Darlene, 125
Flusser, David, 3, 205, 208, **240–43**, 268
Francis, Conseula, 243–45, 247–48

Gallup, George, Jr., 208
Gambone, Robert L., 210, 212
Garrison, William Lloyd, 173
Gaustad, Edwin S., 148, 151
Giere, Carol de, 228–29, 230–31
gluttony, 37, 96, 102–3, 105, 107, 136
gnostic(s), 5, 10, 16–18, 19, 20–21, 23, 25–27,
    220, 262. *See also* Marcion; Valentinus/
    Valentinian gnostics
Godspell, 3, 8, 11, 12, 209, **228–33**, 260, 263,
    264, 265, 266, 267, 269, 270
Goethe, Johann Wolfgang von, 154, 155–56
Golden Gospels of Echternach, **76–82**, 261,
    262, 266, 272
  Great Dinner, 79–80
  Laborers in the Vineyard, 77–78
  Rich Man and Lazarus, 81–82
  Wicked Tenants, 78–79
Golden Rule, 118, 176, 184

Goliath, 54

Good Shepherd, 28, **50–54**, 59, 182–83, 260–61, 263

Gordis, Lisa M., 148

Gospel of Philip, 16, **20–21**, 260, 261, 262

Gospel of Thomas, 220, 261, 263, 271

Gospel of Truth, 262

Gottfried of Disibodenberg, 86

Gower, John, 66, **102–5**, 266
  Confessio Amantis, 102–5
  Mirroir de l'Omme (renamed *Speculum Meditantis*), 102
  Vox Clamantis, 102

Gowler, David B., 2, 5, 11, 40, 66, 152, 154, 164, 168, 173, 202, 234, 237, 240, 243, 255–56

Grant, Robert M., 20, 66, 102

Grant, Ulysses S., 176, 177

Greaves, Richard L., 161, 162

Gregory IX (pope), 9

Gregory of Nyssa, 16, 44–46
  Life of Saint Macrina, 44
  On the Soul and the Resurrection, 44–46

Gregory the Great, **66–71**, 73, 94, 96, 98–99, 130, 261, 262, 263, 264, 266, 268, 271

Griffith, Sidney H., 47–48

Gross, Rita M., 253

Gruber, J. Richard, 209

Guralnick, Peter, 213

Hägg, Henny Fisk, 23

Haines, William, 166

Hamlin, Hannibal, 133, 136

Hanson, R. P. C., 34

Hastings, Adrian, 128

Hathaway, Anne, 132

Hauser, Allan J., 71

Haynes, Deborah J., 256

Hebrew Bible, 6, 16, 17–20, 22, 27–28, 30, 32, 47, 48, 51, 53, 54–55, 57, 71, 99, 148, 215, 239

Hecht, Linda, 120–21

Heine, Ronald E., 33, 34

Helgerson, Richard, 134

Herbert, George, 2, 11, 116, **142–47**, 261, 264, 265, 267, 268
  "Church-Porch, The," 143
  "Love (III)," 143–45
  "Pearl, The," 145–47

heresy/heretics, 5, 9, 16, 26, 28, 30, 49–50, 66, 75–76, 99–100, 129–30, 148–49, 193

Hesketh, Thomas, 132

Het Offer des Heeren (The Sacrifice of the Lord), 121

Hildegard of Bingen, 11, 66, **85–89**, 260, 261, 262, 264, 265, 266
  Book of Divine Works, 85
  Book of Life's Merits, 85
  Homilies on the Gospels, 86–89
  Know the Ways (Scivias), 85, 86

Holy Spirit, 15, 19, 25, 29, 30–31, 34, 43, 50, 66, 75, 84, 86, 95, 146, 159, 161, 162, 250–51, 252–253

Homer, xii, 8, 22, 54

Honan, Park, 132

Hornik, Heidi J., 140

Hosea, 57, 58

Hults, Linda C., 165

Hunt, William Holman, 187–88, 192

Iglauer, Bruce, 214

Ignatius of Loyola, 128

invisible gorilla, 3–4, 13

Irenaeus, 5, **16–20**, 21, 22, 25, 26, 27, 33, 34, 42, 73, 94, 130, 131, 259, 260, 262, 264, 265, 266, 269, 271, 272, 273
  Against Heresies, 5, 16–19

Isaac, 41

Jacob, 41

Jaeger, C. Stephen, 75

James, Frank, 209

James, Jesse, 209

James, LeBron, 208

Jansz, Anna, 116, **120–24**, 266

Jay, William, 175

Jefferson, Thomas, 151

Jeffrey, David L., 136

Jensen, Robin Margaret, 54

Jeremias, Joachim, 202

Jerome, 10, 22, 30, 39, 47, 117, 130
  Lives of Illustrious Men, 22, 30, 47

Jerusalem, 26, 34, 42–43, 49, 57, 91–94, 98, 161, 175, 204, 240, 260, 269

Jim the slave (*Huckleberry Finn*), 209

Johnson, James Weldon, 11

Johnson, Lyndon B., 224, 226, 227

Jonah, 51, 215

Jones, Geraint V., 205

Joseph (Hebrew Bible), 106

Joseph (New Testament), 20, 188

Josephus, 22

Jülicher, Adolf, 164, **201–5**, 260, 262, 263, 264, 265, 266, 267

Keaton, Buster, 232
Kelly, J. N. D., 35
Kerby-Fulton, Kathryn, 86
Kermode, Frank, 1, 15
Kerr, Fergus, 98
Khalidi, Tarif, 71, 72
Kienzle, Beverly, 86
Kierkegaard, Søren, 2, 6, 164, **168–73**, 264, 269
Kilcourse, George, 222
king, 122, 146, 237, 266, 268, 269–71
  and the parables
    Good Shepherd, 183
    laborers/workers in the vineyard, 131
    Pharisee and the tax collector/publican, 63
    sheep and goats (final judgment), vi
    talents/pounds, 241
    unforgiving slave (unmerciful servant), 142, 230
    wedding feast/banquet, 38, 68, 161, 179
    wise and foolish bridesmaids/virgins, 57
King, James, 165
King, Martin Luther, Jr., 3, 208, **223–28**, 249, 260, 265, 266
  "Drum Major Instinct, The," 225–26
  "I See the Promised Land," 226
  Letter from the Birmingham Jail, 223
  Strength to Love, 223
  "Time to Break Silence, A," 226–27
  Where Do We Go from Here?, 223
  "Why Jesus Called a Man a Fool," 223–25
  Why We Can't Wait, 223
kingdom of God/heaven, 123, 129, 160, 183, 187, 209, 218, 222, 229, 232, 235, 242–43, 261, 262, 263, 266, 267, 268, 269, 271, 272
  and the parables
    good Samaritan, 157
    laborers/workers in the vineyard, 33–34, 261
    mustard seed, 250–52
    net (dragnet), 129, 169
    pearl of great value, 7, 49–50, 126, 146
    rich man and Lazarus, 96
    sheep and goats (final judgment), vi, 157, 231
    sower, 37, 129, 150, 221
    treasure in the field, 31–32, 125
    wheat and weeds/tares/cockles, 149–50, 221
    wise and foolish bridesmaids/virgins, 39
Kissinger, Warren S., 66, 102, 117
Klonsky, Milton, 167
kontakion, 12–13, 47, 60–63
Kümmel, Werner Georg, 203, 205
Kuretsky, Susan Donahue, 156, 157–58

Ladin, Jay, 194
Laird, Paul R., 228
Langland, William, 105
Lee, Robert E., 176
Lefebure, Leo D., 253
Leirvik, Oddbjørn, 72
Leiter, Sharon, 193, 196
liberation, 9, 123, 177, 178, 213, 233, 237, 238, 239
liberation theology, 208, 237
Lienhard, Joseph T., 34, 35
Lincoln, Abraham, 9, 177
Linnell, John, 165
Logos (Word), 20, 22, 23
London Prodigal, The, 134
Luther, Martin, 115, **116–20**, 125, 128, 129–30, 132, 260, 262, 266
Luz, Ulrich, 252

MacCulloch, Diarmaid, 30, 47
Macrina the Younger, 16, **44–47**, 97, 266, 271
Maldonatus, John, 115, **128–32**, 202, 262, 263, 266, 267, 271
  Commentary on the Gospels, 128–32
Manichaean(s), 40, 75
Marcion, 16–17, 19, 26, 27, 47. *See also* gnostic(s); Valentinus/Valentinian gnostics
marginalized, the, 2, 11, 237, 239–40
Marling, Karal Ann, 213
Martin, Karl E., 218
Martin, Wendy, 193
Martyrs' Mirror, 121
McCarthy, Carmel, 49
McFarland, Dorothy Tuck, 221
McKim, Donald K., 26, 36, 66, 95, 124, 169, 203
Merton, Thomas, 249
metaphor, 6, 15, 23, 25, 26, 30, 124, 139, 159–160, 165, 169, 197, 203, 205, 208, 218, 232, 242. *See also* allegory
Metz, Peter, 77
Meyer, Marvin, 20–21
Micah, 56
Michaels, Axel, 252
Milburn, Robert, 51, 56
Millais, John Everett, xiii, 11, 139, 164, **187–92**, 262, 264, 265, 268, 270, 272
  Christ in the House of His Parents, 188
  Importunate Widow / The Unjust Judge, The, 190–92
  Lost Piece of Silver, The, 192
  Pearl of Great Price, The, 192
  Pharisee and the Publican, The, 189–90, 192

Pizarro Seizing the Inca of Peru, 187
Unmerciful Servant, The, 192
Wicked Husbandmen, The, 192
Miller, J. Hillis, 256
Miller, Malcolm, 89, 90
Minns, Denis, 18
Mitchell, W. J. T., 255
Moody, Dwight L., 181
Moses, xii, 8, 19, 33, 41, 67, 69, 71, 73, 178, 221, 265
Moucarry, Chawkat, 71
Muck, Terry C., 253
Muhammad, 71, 72, 73
Mullett, Margaret, 82
Murray, Linda, 111
Murray, Peter, 111

Nhat Hanh, Thich, 3, 209, **249–53**, 262, 263, 266, 267, 268
Nicholson, Peter, 105
Nicolai, Vincenzo, 52
Nixon, Richard M., 228
Noah, 33, 41, 51, 67, 73
Norris, Richard A., 16
Nouwen, Henri, 10, 12, 153

Oberhaus, Dorothy Huff, 195–96
O'Connor, Flannery, 208, **218–23**, 267, 271
    "Good Man Is Hard to Find, A," 222–23
    Violent Bear It Away, The, 208, 218–23
    Wise Blood, 218
Origen, 2, 16, **30–35**, 40, 42, 43, 45, 67, 68, 73, 77, 88, 94, 98, 117, 130–31, 204, 260, 262, 263, 264, 268, 271
    Commentary on John, 34
    Commentary on Matthew, 31–34, 124
    Homilies on Luke, 34–35
    Homily on Jeremiah, 34
    On First Principles, 30–31
Outcalt, Todd, 71, 72
Owens, W. R., 159

Papandrea, James, 16
parables
    barren fig tree, 18, 86, 126, 160–61, 259
    building a tower, 84, 259
    dishonest manager (unjust steward), xi, 48, 82–83, 86–87, 95, 119, 127, 134, 205, 260
    good Samaritan, xi, 19, 20–21, 24, 34, 42–43, 49, 55–57, 65, 89, 90–94, 97, 152, 154–57, 174–75, 189, 204, 207, 226–27, 229, 231, 246, 256–57, 260

Good Shepherd, 28, 50–54, 59, 182–83, 260–61, 263
great dinner/banquet, 24, 27, 79–81, 86, 95, 143–45, 176, 261, 270
laborers/workers in the vineyard, 16, 18, 19, 33, 38, 40–41, 47, 66, 67–68, 72–74, 77–78, 86, 87–89, 118, 130–32, 133, 152, 204, 261–62
leaven/yeast, 75, 243, 252, 262
lost coin/Drachma, 12, 27, 48, 109, 139–41, 203–4, 237, 262, 264
lost sheep, 27–28, 51, 109, 136, 140, 181–83, 203, 260–61, 262–63, 264
mote and beam, 137–39, 263
mustard seed, 37, 209, 250, 251, 263
net (dragnet), 31, 32–33, 67, 129, 160, 263
pearl of great value, 7, 31, 32, 49–50, 67, 125–26, 145–46, 159, 192, 263–64
Pharisee and the tax collector/publican, 18, 47, 63, 83–84, 86, 127, 133, 162, 170–71, 171–72, 189, 192, 204, 229–30, 264
prodigal son, xiii, 9–13, 18, 23, 27, 28–29, 38, 60–63, 65, 86, 106–10, 111–13, 134–37, 144–45, 152–54, 189–90, 204, 207–8, 210–13, 214–18, 229, 232, 264–65
rich fool, 83, 96, 152, 204, 223–25, 265
rich man and Lazarus, 9, 24, 45–46, 48, 65, 69–70, 81–82, 86, 96–97, 102–5, 118–19, 135–36, 159, 176–78, 204, 205, 208, 229, 231, 233–37, 265
seed growing secretly, 204, 232, 266
sheep and goats (final judgment), 18, 39–40, 41, 58–60, 118, 122, 123, 132, 150, 157, 168, 174, 176, 182, 184, 187, 194, 224, 225–26, 229, 231, 252, 266
sower, 6, 15, 25, 26, 36–38, 48, 75, 128–29, 143, 150, 198, 204, 208, 218–22, 229, 232, 233, 245–48, 267
talents/pounds, xi, 38–39, 68–69, 118, 133, 143, 180–81, 199, 241–42, 247–48, 267–68
treasure in the field, 31–32, 67, 125–26, 188–89, 242, 252, 268
two debtors, 85, 172–73, 185, 198–201, 230, 268–69
two sons, 18, 269
unforgiving slave (unmerciful servant), 41–42, 133, 141–42, 186, 192, 199–200, 229, 230, 269–70
unjust judge (importunate widow), 47–48, 190–92, 238–39, 240, 245–46, 270
waiting/watchful slaves, 180, 270

wedding feast/banquet, 18, 19, 31, 38, 41, 68, 161, 179–80, 261, 270–71
wheat and weeds/tares/cockles, 9, 18, 26, 33, 37, 45, 49–50, 66, 75–76, 99–101, 130, 148–51, 208, 220–21, 271
wicked tenants/husbandmen, 18, 19, 41, 78–79, 192, 271–72
wise and foolish bridesmaids/virgins, 17–18, 27, 38–39, 41, 49, 55–56, 57–58, 65, 125, 161, 165–68, 180–81, 272
wise and foolish builders (two builders; house built on the rock), 18, 84, 184, 185, 272–73
Parsons, Mikeal C., 11, 140
Paul III (pope), 128
peasants of Solentiname, 208, **233–37**, 266
Pelagians, 40, 66
Pendergast, Tom, 209
Peter (apostle), 39, 54, 269
Peter of Ravenna, 96
Peter of Sebaste, 16, 44
Pevear, Richard, xii
Peterson, Eugene H., 197
Pharisee(s), 28–29, 36, 85, 90, 156, 171–72, 175, 185, 261, 268. *See also* parable: Pharisee and the tax collector/publican
Philo of Alexandria, 22
Plato, xii, 8, 20, 22, 27, 44–45
Pliny the Elder, *Natural History*, 54, 58
Poeschke, Joachim, 58, 59
Pollock, Jackson, 209
Polycarp, 16
polyvalency, 7, 50, 178, 197. *See also* dialogue
Pooley, Roger, 159
poor, the, 24, 35, 47, 123–24, 208, 237, 249
  and the parables
    dishonest manager (unjust steward), 83
    good Samaritan, 156, 226–27
    great dinner/banquet, 27, 80, 95, 144–45, 176, 261
    prodigal son, 108, 214–16
    rich fool, 83, 223–24
    rich man and Lazarus, 48, 70, 96, 104–5, 119, 176, 233–36, 265
    sower, 36, 48
    talents/pounds, 39
    unjust judge (importunate widow), 191, 238–39
    wise and foolish bridesmaids/virgins, 39
poverty, 30, 47, 70, 72, 103, 105, 107, 214, 224, 226–27, 234
Pre-Raphaelite Brotherhood (PRB), 187–88, 192

pride, 37, 69, 83–84, 85, 95, 96, 107, 145–46, 148, 170–71, 222, 225
prophet(s), 6, 19, 27, 32–34, 36, 41, 49, 59, 71, 73, 79, 86, 121, 159, 165, 178, 196, 219–22, 248, 252, 265, 271
Protestant, 111, 120, 124, 129, 132, 134, 217. *See also* Reformation: Protestant
Prothero, Stephen R., 207
Pulci, Antonia, 3, 11, 66, **105–10**, 215, 263, 265

Ray, Robert H., 143, 145, 146
Reformation
  Catholic Counter-, 115, 137, 140, 142
  Protestant, 115, 116, 128
Rembrandt (Rembrandt Harmenszoon van Rijn), xiii, 3, 10, 11, 12, 111, 116, **151–58**, 213, 260, 262, 265, 266
  Christ and the Woman of Samaria, among Ruins, 157
  Departure of the Prodigal Son, The, 152
  Good Samaritan Bringing the Wounded Man to the Inn, The, 154–58
  John the Baptist Preaching, 156
  Night Watch, The, 152
  Return of the Prodigal Son, The (etching; 1636), 152–54
  Return of the Prodigal Son, The (painting; 1667–1669), 12, 153–54
  Self-Portrait with Saskia in the Guise of the Prodigal Son, 12, 152
Reventlow, Henning Graf, 128, 132
rich, the, 24–25, 237, 242, 245, 249. *See also* parables: rich fool; parables: rich man and Lazarus; wealth
  and the parables
    dishonest manager (unjust steward), 86–87
    prodigal son, 107–8
    sower, 36–37, 48
    treasure in the field, 126
riddle, 4, 6, 15, 196, 205
Robert of Brunne, 105
Rohrbaugh, Richard L., 10
Rolf, Julia, 214
Rolling Stones, The, 217
Romanos the Melodist, 2, 11, 12, 16, **60–63**, 264, 265
Roosevelt, Franklin Delano, 213
Root, Abiah, 193
Root, George, 179
Rosenfeld, Jason, 188–89, 192
Rossano Gospels, **54–58**, 260, 272
Rossetti, Dante Gabriel, 187

Rothko, Mark, 196
Roukema, Riemer, 21, 25
Rowland, Christopher, xiii, 120, 165, 168, 198
Ruffin, Bernard, 179
rule of faith/truth, 17, 25, 28
Rutgers, Leonard V., 51
Ryken, Leland, 10

Safarik, E. A., 137, 142
Sahih al-Bukhari, 66, **71–74**, 132, 262
Sankey, Ira, 179, 181
satan, 49, 50, 62, 82, 89, 104, 149–50, 221–22.
     See also devil
Saul, 106
Schwartz, Gary, 154
Schwartz, Stephen, 228
Septuagint, 30, 55, 56, 57, 58, 63
Sermon on the Mount, 8, 36, 72, 184, 187, 229,
     230
Shaheen, Naseeb, 133, 134, 135
Shakespeare, Hamnet, 132
Shakespeare, Judith, 132
Shakespeare, Susanna, 132
Shakespeare, William, 3, 10, 11, 102, 116,
     132–37, 143, 208, 260, 262, 263, 264, 265,
     266, 268, 270
   As You Like It, 134–35
   Comedy of Errors, The, 133, 136
   Cymbeline, 134
   Hamlet, 133
   Henry IV, Part 1, 134, 135, 136
   Henry IV, Part 2, 135, 136
   Henry VIII, 133
   King Lear, 135, 136
   King Richard II, 133
   Love's Labour's Lost, 133, 136
   Merchant of Venice, The, 133, 134
   Merry Wives of Windsor, The, 136
   Pericles, 102
   Timon of Athens, 133–34, 136
   Twelfth Night, 136
   Two Gentlemen of Verona, 136
Siebald, Manfred, 10
similitude, 31–33, 124, 159, 203–4, 262, 263
Simons, Daniel, 3
Simpson, Melissa, 218, 222–23
Sirach (person), 56
Sirach (text), 96
slave/slavery, 198, 209, 213–14, 239, 249, 269–72
   and the parables
      good Samaritan, 174–75
      great dinner/banquet, 176, 261

prodigal son, 62
rich man and Lazarus, 9, 136, 176–78
sheep and goats (final judgment), 174
talents/pounds, 267–68
unforgiving slave (unmerciful servant), 133,
     141–42, 186, 199, 229–30, 269–70
waiting/watchful slaves, 180, 270
wedding feast/banquet, 270–71
wheat and weeds/tares/cockles, 271
wicked tenants/husbandmen, 78–79, 271–72
Slee, Nicola, 237–38
Smalley, Beryl, 65
Smith, Allison, 188–89, 192
Snyder, C. Arnold, 120, 121
Snyder, Julia, xiii
Snyder, Susan, 135
Socrates, 44
Solomon, xii, 8
Spencer, Jon Michael, 217, 218
Spier, Jeffrey, 51
Spivey, Nigel, 157
Spurgeon, Charles Haddon, 164, **197–201**, 267,
     269, 270
Steinbeck, John, 212
Stewart, Jon, 171, 172
Stokstad, Marilyn, 90
Studer, Basil, 15
symbol/symbolism, 5–6, 15, 20, 22–23, 25, 28,
     45. See also allegory
   and the parables
      barren fig tree, 161
      dishonest manager (unjust steward), 86–87
      good Samaritan, 19, 21, 34–35, 42–43, 89,
         94, 98, 157, 204
      great dinner/banquet, 27
      laborers/workers in the vineyard, 16, 34,
         40–41, 131
      lost coin/Drachma, 27–28, 48, 140–41
      lost sheep, 27–28, 140, 182
      net (dragnet), 32–33, 67
      pearl of great value, 7, 32, 49–50
      prodigal son, 10–11, 13, 23, 29, 61–62, 154
      rich man and Lazarus, 46, 69, 82, 96,
         233–34
      talents/pounds, 68, 180–81, 241–42
      treasure in the field, 31
      waiting/watchful slaves, 180
      wedding feast/banquet, 38, 41, 68
      wheat and weeds/tares/cockles, 148–50
      wise and foolish bridesmaids/virgins, 27, 39,
         49, 180–81

Tamez, Elsa, 208, **237–40**, 262, 270
  Bible of the Oppressed, 237
  Jesus and Courageous Women, 238–39
Tatian, 47, 49, 53
Tatum, W. Barnes, 229
Tertullian, 10, 16, **25–30**, 140, 261, 262, 263,
  265, 267, 271, 272
  Against Marcion, 26, 27
  On Modesty, 28–29
  On the Resurrection of the Flesh, 26
  Prescription against Heretics, The, 26–27
  Treatise on the Soul, A, 27
Theodoric of Echternach, 86
Theodoric the Great, 59
Theophylact, 66, **82–85**, 130, 132, 224, 259,
  260, 264, 265, 269, 273
Thomas Aquinas, 2, 9, 66, **98–102**, 271
  Summa Theologiae, 98–102
Thoreau, Henry David, 163–64, 208
Tintoretto, 137
Tippens, Darryl, 10, 134, 136
Tissot, Yves, 10
Titian, 137
Tolstoy, Leo, 164, **183–87**, 260, 266, 269, 273
  Anna Karenina, 183, 184
  Childhood, 184
  Confession, A, 184
  Kingdom of God Is within You, The, 184
  Resurrection, 184
  War and Peace, 183, 184
  What I Believe, 187
  "Where Love Is, God Is," 184–87
True Chronicle History of King Leir, The, 135
Trusler, Rev. Dr. (John), xi–xii, 7–8
Trypanis, Constantine, 60
Turgenev, Ivan, 184
Turner, Martha Lee, 21

Valentinus/Valentinian gnostics, 16–17, 20–21,
  27, 262. *See also* gnostic(s); Marcion
van Braght, Thieleman J., 121, 124
Vendler, Helen, 143, 145
Veronese, 137
Virgil, *Aeneid*, 54

Wailes, Stephen L., 39, 68, 70, 96
Wakefield, Walter L., 75, 76
Walsh, Richard G., 229
Ward, Benedicta, 66
Watson, Duane F., 71

Watts, Isaac, 179
Wazo of Liège, 2, 9, 66, **74–76**, 99, 101, 262, 271
wealth, 35, 237, 242. *See also* rich, the
  and the parables
    dishonest manager (unjust steward), 83, 119
    good Samaritan, 227
    prodigal son, 107
    rich fool, 83, 224
    rich man and Lazarus, 96, 105, 119, 205, 235
    sheep and goats (final judgment), 225
    sower, 48
    talents/pounds, 39, 69
    unforgiving slave (unmerciful servant),
      199–200
    unjust judge (importunate widow), 239
Weitzmann, Kurt, 54, 55, 57
Westermann, Mariët, 157
Wetering, Ernst van de, 152
Wilkins, Robert, xiv, 2, 11, 12, 13, 209, **213–18**,
  265
Williams, Roger, 2, 9, 101, 116, **147–51**, 266,
  267, 271
Williamson, Scott C., 174
Winstanley, Gerrard, 255
Witcombe, Christopher, 111
Witte, Emanuel de, 156
Wolff, Cynthia Griffin, 195
Wolff, Justin P., 209, 212
woman/women, 9, 53, 63, 65, 86, 120, 158, 173,
  185–87, 237–38, 244, 270. *See also* para-
  bles: wise and foolish bridesmaids/virgins
  and the parables
    good Samaritan, 156–57, 227
    lost coin/Drachma, 139–41, 192, 237, 262
    prodigal son, 13, 108, 153, 214
    rich man and Lazarus, 177–78
    sheep and goats (final judgment), 224
    two debtors, 95, 171–73, 185, 268–69
    unjust judge (importunate widow), 190–92,
      237–40, 245–46, 270
Wood, Grant, 210
Wordsworth, Charles, 133
Wouwerman, Philips, 156

Yanco, Jennifer J., 228
Young, Abigail, 86, 89
Young, Alan R., 134
Young, Frances, 40

Zuffi, Stefano, 140